Studies in German Literature, Linguistics, and Culture

Edited by James Hardin
(*South Carolina*)

German Literature of the 1990s and Beyond

Normalization and the Berlin Republic

Stuart Taberner

CAMDEN HOUSE

First published 2005
by Camden House

Camden House is an imprint of Boydell & Brewer Inc.
668 Mt. Hope Avenue, Rochester, NY 14620, USA
www.camden-house.com
and of Boydell & Brewer Limited
PO Box 9, Woodbridge, Suffolk IP12 3DF, UK
www.boydellandbrewer.com

ISBN: 1–57113–289–9

Library of Congress Cataloging-in-Publication Data

Taberner, Stuart.
    German literature of the 1990s and beyond: normalization and the
Berlin Republic / Stuart Taberner.
        p. cm. — (Studies in German literature, linguistics, and culture)
Includes bibliographical references and index.
ISBN 1–57113–289–9 (hardcover : alk. paper)
        1. German literature—20th century—History and criticism. 2. Ger-
man literature—21st century—History and criticism.   3. Germany—
Intellectual life—20th century.   4. Germany—Intellectual life—21st
century.   I. Title.   II. Series: Studies in German literature, linguistics,
and culture (Unnumbered)

PT405.T33 2004
833'.9209—dc22

                                                                            2004022546

A catalogue record for this title is available from the British Library.

This publication is printed on acid-free paper.
Printed in the United States of America.

Contents

Illustrations

All photographs by the author.

Acknowledgments

WITHOUT THE SUPPORT of a number of institutions this book would not have been possible. I would like to thank the Alexander von Humboldt-Stiftung for its award of a fellowship to spend a year at the University of Konstanz in 1999 and for its subsequent assistance, the British Academy for a number of grants which enabled me to travel to Germany for research purposes, the Arts and Humanities Research Board for making it possible for me to take a sabbatical to complete this volume, and to the School of Modern Languages and Cultures at the University of Leeds, in particular the German Department, for time away from teaching and various travel grants. I am also indebted to the staff of the Literary Archive in Marbach for their help during my many visits there.

I am especially grateful to Professor Frank Finlay and Dr. Paul Cooke, both of the University of Leeds, and Professor Bill Niven, of Nottingham Trent University. Friends as well as colleagues, Frank, Paul, and Bill have all engaged in tireless discussion, offered advice, and provided great inspiration.

S. T.
Leeds, December 2004

Abbreviations

THE FOLLOWING ABBREVIATIONS for the titles of primary works are used throughout. Full bibliographical details can be found in the Bibliography.

A   W. G. Sebald, *Austerlitz*

AB   Botho Strauß, "Anschwellender Bocksgesang"

ABM   Uwe Timm, *Am Beispiel meines Bruders*

AG   Falko Hennig, *Alles nur geklaut*

AK   Hanns-Josef Ortheil, *Abschied von den Kriegsteilnehmern*

AKE   Thomas Brussig, *Am kürzeren Ende der Sonnenallee*

AT   F. C. Delius, *Amerikahaus und der Tanz um die Frauen*

DA   W. G. Sebald, *Die Ausgewanderten*

DB   Bernhard Schlink, "Die Beschneidung"

DBR   F. C. Delius, *Die Birnen von Ribbeck*

DDG   Ulrich Greiner, "Die deutsche Gesinnungsästhetik"

DEC   Uwe Timm, *Die Entdeckung der Currywurst*

DHQ   Iris Radisch, "Der Herbst des Quatschocento. Immer noch, jetzt erst recht, gibt es zwei deutsche Literaturen: selbstverliebter Realismus im Westen, tragischer Expressionismus im Osten"

DIA   Hans-Ulrich Treichel, *Der irdische Amor*

DK   F. C. Delius, *Der Königsmacher*

DKL   Karen Duve, *Dies ist kein Liebeslied*

DM   Rafael Seligmann, *Der Milchmann*

DS   F. C. Delius, *Der Spaziergang von Rostock nach Syrakuse*

DSA   F. C. Delius, *Der Sonntag, an dem ich Weltmeister wurde*

DT	Maxim Biller, *Die Tochter*
DTI	Arnold Stadler, *Der Tod und ich, wir zwei*
DV	Bernhard Schlink, *Der Vorleser*
DW	Martin Walser, *Dorle und Wolf*
EES	Martin Walser, *Erfahrungen beim Erfassen einer Sonntagsrede*
EZE	Jens Sparschuh, *Eins zu Eins*
F	Christian Kracht, *Faserland*
FB	Ingo Schramm, *Fitchers Blau*
FH	Marcel Beyer, *Flughunde*
FK	Botho Strauß, *Die Fehler des Kopisten*
FM	Jakob Hein, *Formen menschlichen Zusammenlebens*
FZ	F. C. Delius, *Die Flatterzunge*
GL	Andreas Neumeister, *Gut laut*
GS	Peter Handke, *Eine winterliche Reise zu den Flüssen Donau, Save, Morawa und Drina oder Gerechtigkeit für Serbien*
GV	Zafer Şenocak, *Gefährliche Verwandtschaft*
GW	Hans Magnus Enzensberger, *Die große Wanderung*
HS	Arnold Stadler, *Ein hinreissender Schrotthändler*
HWW	Thomas Brussig, *Helden wie wir*
I	Frank Schirrmacher, "Idyllen in der Wüste oder Das Versagen vor der Metropole"
IK	Günter Grass, *Im Krebsgang*
L	Georg Klein, *Libidissi*
LD	Martin Hielscher, "Literatur in Deutschland"
LE	Uwe Wittstock, *Leselust. Wie unterhaltsam ist die neue deutsche Literatur? Ein Essay*
LG	Elke Naters, *Lügen*
LH	Christa Wolf, *Leibhaftig*

LK   W. G. Sebald, *Luftkrieg und Literatur*

LL   Martin Walser, *Der Lebenslauf der Liebe*

LM   Thomas Brussig, *Leben bis Männer*

M   Jakob Hein, *Mein erstes T-Shirt*

MH   Arnold Stadler, *Mein Hund, meine Sau, mein Leben*

PB   Monika Maron, *Pawels Briefe*

PG   Martin Walser, *Das Prinzip Genauigkeit*

R   Judith Hermann, "Ruth (Freundinnen)"

RA   Rainald Goetz, *Rave*

RK   Judith Hermann, "Rote Korallen"

RM   Peter Sloterdijk, *Regeln für den Menschenpark*

RO   Uwe Timm, *Rot*

RR   Karen Duve, *Regenroman*

S   Arnold Stadler, *Sehnsucht*

SB   Martin Walser, *Ein springender Brunnen*

SIM   Ingo Schulze, *Simple Storys*

SML   Rafael Seligmann, *Schalom meine Liebe*

SV   Maxim Biller, "Soviel Sinnlichkeit wie der Stadtplan von Kiel"

SZ   Tanja Dückers, *Spielzone*

T   Hans-Ulrich Treichel, *Tristanakkord*

TB   Thomas Meinecke, *Tomboy*

UW   Peter Schneider, *"Und wenn wir nur eine Stunde gewinnen . . ."*

V   Hans-Ulrich Treichel, *Der Verlorene*

VK   Martin Walser, *Die Verteidigung der Kindheit*

W   Andreas Maier, *Wäldchestag*

WF   Günter Grass, *Ein weites Feld*

ZG   Iris Radisch, "Zwei getrennte Literaturgebiete. Deutsche Literatur der neunziger Jahre in Ost und West"

ZV   Botho Strauß, "Zeit ohne Vorboten"

The Reichstag

Preface

ON 19 APRIL 1999 THE PARLIAMENT of the Federal Republic of Germany (FRG) was convened as an all-German body for the first time in fifty eight years at the *Reichstag* in central Berlin during a ceremony marking the transfer of the newly reunited country's capital from the west German city of Bonn. The ceremony also commemorated the completion of renovations to an edifice which, in 1894, had been inaugurated as the parliamentary seat of the first unified German state created in 1870–71, and which had witnessed key moments in the drama of German history as it had unfolded during the Wilhelmine period, the First World War, the Weimar Republic, and the twelve years of the Nazi dictatorship. In June and July 1995 the "wrapping of the *Reichstag*" by Bulgarian artist Christo had attracted millions of spectators even as no one was entirely sure whether this signaled the assembly's reincarnation or was intended as ironic comment on its ambivalent history.[1] In 1999, nine years after unification, however, it was apparent that in this building the Berlin Republic — the term that many commentators had already begun applying to united Germany from the mid-1990s onwards — had finally come into existence.

Sir Norman Foster's innovative redesign for the *Reichstag* proclaims the values that are to be associated with the "new" Germany. The glass cupola set upon the building's nineteenth-century skeleton containing galleries from which the public is able to peer down into the debating chamber thus symbolizes a very contemporary commitment to the definitive realization of the ideal of democratic transparency. Indeed, this would represent a vast improvement on the imperfect parliamentarianism of Bismarck's day. At the same time, the preservation of physical traces of the fighting which had raged around the building during the final days of the Second World War formalizes an undertaking to integrate the past, and especially the Nazi past, into the country's historical consciousness. In this reading, then, the "new" *Reichstag* embodies a vision of progressive liberal democracy dedicated to openness and tolerance in the present and to its particular obligation to remember the catastrophe of German militarism.

This projection of Germany as a country at ease with itself yet still able to incorporate the lessons of the Nazi period into its commitment to "western" values may be seen as a step along the road to the "normalization" of post-1990 Germany. Or, more accurately, it may be seen as *one* particular conception of what a "normal" Germany would look like. Politicians, intellectuals, and media voices from across the spectrum agreed that a reunited Germany should emerge from the shadow of its Nazi past, overcome the legacy of forty years of division, and become more self-confident, even assertive. Yet this consensus was in itself quite new. Until the early 1990s, the discourse of "normality" had been almost exclusively associated with conservative thinkers, politicians, and especially historians; for that reason it had been regarded with suspicion by the left who viewed it as a means of "relativizing" Nazi crimes and promoting an "unburdened" national identity.[2] And despite the seeming convergence around the desirability of "normalization" later in the decade, the various parties had conflicting ideas about how this should come about and about the specific set of criteria of "normality" against which the country should, implicitly or explicitly, measure itself. "Normalization" became *the* uncontested buzzword of the 1990s, and, unsurprisingly, means different things to different people.[3]

The renovation and redesign of the *Reichstag*, accordingly, might be taken to imply a view of a post-unification German "normality" best described as "latitudinal normality." The Federal Republic should seek to be as "normal" as France, Great Britain, and the United States by showing itself to be a progressive state devoted to the rule of law and demonstrating that it has learned from history. A democratic self-confidence, therefore, would be combined with what Karl Wilds has termed the "culture of contrition."[4] This concept of "normalization" began emerging in the early 1990s under Helmut Kohl's CDU government but was more explicitly formulated following the election of the SPD-Green coalition in late 1998. In early 1999, Foreign Minister Joschka Fischer's plea for NATO military intervention in the Serbian province of Kosovo to inhibit the mistreatment of ethnic Albanians — to prevent a new "Auschwitz" — hence reflected the formalization of the new regime's wish to project an impression of a humane and enlightened Germany capable of fulfilling its obligations in the international arena.[5] Of especial significance was the way in which leftist politicians, notably Chancellor Schröder, and intellectuals for the first time began to feel comfortable with the notion that it might be — or rather *should* be — possible to be proud to be German. Of course, the notion of a "latitudinal normality," rooted in multilateralism and shared western values, as defined by Schröder in a statement to the lower house of parliament on 10 November 1998,[6] for example, or in his interview with *Die Zeit* of 4 February 1999, "Eine offene Republik,"[7] may break down when the gap between rhetoric and *Realpolitik* pushes countries which profess to be pursuing the same aims into outright opposition. This was the case during the months of disagreement between Schröder's coalition (following its re-election in late 2002) and the United States in advance of the Second Gulf War in March 2003.

Contrasting with the concept of "latitudinal normality," it is possible to speak of an aspiration towards a kind of "longitudinal normality." Conservatives in particular argued that post-unification Germany should do more than simply "imitate" like-minded nations in the present. Instead, it should look to "German norms" located in its own past — this notion of "normalization" was frequently advanced by former Chancellor Helmut Kohl from the mid-1980s until his defeat in 1998. Indeed, it should not be forgotten that the redesign of the *Reichstag* was instigated by Kohl, who most likely saw the addition of the cupola to the late nineteenth-century structure not so much as a break with the past as an *integration* of the present into a form of continuity with Germany's first "successful" constitution as a European nation state. A similar aspiration towards "continuity" is to be found on the eastern side of the Brandenburg Gate, in the "new" Hotel Adlon, completed in 1997 at the site of the original structure on the Pariser Platz. In this building a late nineteenth-century and pre-1914 monumentalism and imperial grandeur is painstakingly reconstructed, invoking, Janet Stewart argues, an "idealised golden age," an era of stylish sophistication and unproblematic national

The Hotel Adlon

pride.[8] As such, the subsequent history of the Pariser Platz is elided with the return to the architectural glories of the late Wilhelmine period. The torchlight procession of 30 January 1933 celebrating Hitler's accession to power fades from view as does the fact that the entire area was part of the no-man's-land on the eastern side of the Berlin Wall. As a consequence, the "new" Pariser Platz may appear to align the first German unification with the second, erase the travails of the Weimar Republic, the horrors of Nazism, and the "historical error" of the communist German Democratic Republic (East Germany or the GDR), and proclaim the metropolitan self-confidence of the Berlin Republic.

So-called "critical reconstruction" would return the Berlin Republic to the "normality" of a period in which Germany was a premier European power combining self-confident diplomacy with scientific endeavor and excellence in literature, music, and the arts. Yet the attempt to revive this "normality" may feel forced. The buildings on the Pariser Platz, with their uncannily pristine exteriors, hence resemble, in the words of Catherine Slessor, a "collection of rather bland, expensively dressed guests mingling politely at an upmarket cocktail party."[9] This sense of artificiality in the attempt to exclude less comforting aspects of the past from the reconstruction of such an important urban space is further reinforced by the

Pariser Platz and the Brandenburg Gate

fact that the back of the DG Bank, which stands next to the Hotel Adlon, looks out over the site reserved for the Berlin Holocaust memorial. "That memory," Elke Heckner points out, "may not be intelligible in the context of the square's new, polished look."[10] Certainly, the years of controversy provoked by the plan to construct such a memorial as well as the radically disruptive nature of American architect Peter Eisenmann's design, with its disorientating, undulating fields of concrete slabs, suggest that a backward-looking "normality" may be impossible to achieve.[11]

A version of German "normality" which emphasizes the country's present-day embeddedness in the western community of values and which views national history and national traditions through the prism of the Nazi past is thus set against a notion of "normality" that seeks to "contextualize" the Hitler period and to reclaim other, more positive aspects of German heritage for the purposes of shaping a more self-confident German identity. Each of these concepts of "normality" alludes to history, but in different ways and with different aims. In the first reading, "normality" is understood in terms of the "universal" values of liberal democracy with the Nazi past — and, to a lesser extent, the GDR past — posited as the embodiment of everything that the new Germany should

The Holocaust memorial under construction,
with the new Potsdamer Platz in the background

strive *not* to be. In the second reading, a vision of a set of uniquely "German" values is legitimated by insisting that the twelve years of National Socialism do not invalidate a thousand years and more of German culture. This recalls the *Historikerstreit* of the mid-1980s when conservative historians such as Ernst Nolte, Michael Stürmer, and Andreas Hillgruber argued for a "historicization" of the Nazi period which would approach it like any other episode in the past rather than see it as the inevitable culmination of the German experience.[12]

A third model of German "normality" may be glimpsed in the architecture of the Potsdamer Platz, only a fifteen-minute walk from the Pariser Platz. Here, we may contrast the historical referentiality of notions of "latitudinal normality" and "longitudinal normality" with the promotion of an "ahistorical normality." If the reconstruction of the Pariser Platz points to a desire to freeze German history in the Wilhelmine period, then the Potsdamer Platz and, in particular, the "arcades" of the Sony Center allude to the urban modernity of the 1920s. The monumental entrance to the *S-Bahn* station, movie theaters, and cafés occupying the external and internal space defined by the postmodern extravagance of the Sony Center's polygonal glass canopy are clearly intended to invoke the heady excitement of the golden years of the Weimar Republic. Yet the Sony Center differs from both the *Reichstag* and the Pariser Platz. It neither duplicates a more glorious, nineteenth-century elegance *in toto* nor attempts to integrate a shameful history into a present-day emphasis on western values. Instead, its allusions to the past, in this case to the 1920s, are decontextualized, arbitrary, and entirely decorative. The *Kaisersaal* belonging to the Hotel Esplanade — a meeting place for musicians and movie stars in the 1920s — now graces the entrance to the Sony Center but seems out of place amongst the glass structures that surround it. There is little reference, moreover, to the fact that the hotel was destroyed by bombing during the Second World War, after which its ruins had remained concealed in the no-man's-land between East and West Berlin.

The Sony Center seeks to legitimate its celebration of a highly contemporary consumer culture by referring back to the emphasis on consumption and leisure associated with the 1920s, but in the process it turns that history into a product, into a curiosity, an ornamental feature or an advertisement. The real economic driver for this collapse of the past into consumerism, moreover, can be inferred from the glass skyscrapers towering just across from the Sony Center. Conglomerates such as Daimler-Chrysler — a fusion of Daimler-Benz and the Chrysler corporation dating back to 1998 — dominate the square and thereby attest to the true power of the multi-nationals and proclaim the inevitability of economic globalization.[13] This may imply the *standardization* of the German experience. A "latitudinal normality" in which the western consumerist ethic is pow-

Potsdamer Platz

Potsdamer Platz — Entrance to the Sony Center

erfully emphasized is transformed into a bland replication of a triumphalist and global "ahistorical normality."

This book is first and foremost a survey of German fiction since unification, with particular reference to novels written from the mid-1990s onwards. As such, it attempts to pick up where Stephen Brockmann's excellent 1999 book *Literature and German Unification* leaves off[14] by taking the impact of unification on contemporary German literature as a given and exploring the efforts of German writers in the 1990s to interrogate the emerging identity of their new state. It starts out from the premise that a negotiation of competing versions of a new German "normality," including the three models outlined above but also variations on these, is at least implicit in many of the texts under consideration. At all times, it is taken for granted that current deliberations on "normality" are best viewed as a contemporary manifestation of the enduring debate on the feasibility, desirability, and structure of a German identity after Auschwitz. Rival notions of where a German "normality" — and German identity — might be located are mediated via a variety of forms ranging from an evocation of literary Modernism to an Anglo-American "new readability," to "pop" literature. The same can be said regarding content. In their choice of what to write about, authors define different kinds of "normality."

Even before unification a number of critics had begun to probe and question the conventional centrality of ethical issues in postwar German writing, and especially the engagement with the Nazi period. In chapter one, accordingly, we review literary debates of the late 1980s and early 1990s and the way the search for a new "normality" in the cultural sphere led some critics and authors to call for a return to *German* aesthetic traditions. In the same chapter, we look at responses which take issue with this demand and reject it. In particular, we focus on the plea for a *Neue Lesbarkeit* and greater *Unterhaltsamkeit*, that is, for a "normalization" of German narratives within *international* literary trends. The discussions that followed this appeal raised the question of the extent to which German literature would be able to project a distinctive profile and identity within the standardization of form and content driven by Anglo-American "norms."

The remainder of chapter one is dedicated to an examination of the conditions of the literary market in the late 1990s based on a consideration of fictional works. This is followed by a chapter on novels by authors from the former GDR and one on fiction by west German writers. These are concerned with the tension between local or biographically rooted identity and the "ahistorical normality" associated, in the early 1990s, with the erasure of both east and west German pasts within the triumph of the capitalist order and then, later in the decade, with globalization. If there has been a convergence between fiction by east and west German writers, it may reside precisely in the way in which, towards the end of the 1990s, both began to "inflect" a dominant Anglo-American culture with depictions of a supposedly "local" distinctiveness. East German writers' focus on "justifying" their experiences of the GDR — responding to the presumption in post-1990 Germany that these were experiences that *needed* to be legitimated[15] — thus gave way to a more assertive appraisal of the east German past, just as west German writers' ambivalence with regard to the "old" west Germany was often succeeded by a more celebratory portrayal of the achievements of the pre-1990 Federal Republic. This inflection of globalized consumer culture may be an example of the phenomenon of "glocalization" described in a different context by economist Roland Robertson, poised here between ultimate incorporation into the hegemonic discourse of contemporary capitalism and a desire to subvert the same.[16]

The three subsequent chapters focus on modern-day literature dealing with the Nazi past. In chapter four, we look at the way debates in the social and political spheres on the subject of "political correctness" pit those who claim that German identity in the present should no longer be read through the prism of the Nazi past against those who see in this an attempt to relativize German crimes and undermine Germany's commitment to western values. In chapter five, we turn to the implications of recent discussions about the suffering Germans endured in the final phases of the Second World War for the debate on a new German "normality." This leads into chapter six, which starts from the premise that Germany can never be truly "normal" until Jewish and non-Jewish Germans are able to address each other and their shared past in a manner that promotes understanding, avoids stereotypes — on both sides — and does not elide historical injustices. The way the Holocaust inevitably disrupts any attempt to achieve a German "normality" which expunges German crimes is again aptly demonstrated by a recent architectural project: Daniel Libeskind's Jewish Museum in Berlin.[17] The uncannily fragmented form of the building's external walls — representing a splintered Star of David — and its internal voids undermines the contemporary commercialization and appropriation of traces of Jewish history in districts such as the *Scheunenviertel* and the *Hackesche Höfe* where, Elke Heckner argues, "the staging of Jewish life [. . .] risks turning into a Disneyworld media spectacle."[18]

Chapter seven returns to some of the themes raised in the first three chapters and examines the particular resonance of the *Provinz* in contemporary German fiction. Once again, a vision of "longitudinal normality" is pitted, implicitly, against the notion of "latitudinal normality." Both, moreover, are set against the "ahistorical normality" associated with economic globalization and cultural homogenization. At the close of this chapter, an alternative vision of "normality" is explored via Georg Klein's novel *Libidissi* (1998). This is a mode of hybridity which would render the very concept of "normality" redundant.

Many of the issues examined in this volume are to be found in equal measure in any number of related and seemingly unrelated domains, as demonstrated, for example, in our allusions above to architectural debates.[19] Other areas pertinent to the discussion of the emergence of a new German "normality" range from the establishment of museums and memorials focusing on the Nazi, GDR, and "old" West German pasts, to immigration, the end of the "German economic model," the benefits or otherwise of globalization, Germany's relations with the European Union and the United States, and the Federal Republic's support for military interventions in places such as Kosovo in 1999, to name but a few.[20] In writing this book, however, I have for the most part limited my consideration of the "normalization" debate to the way it has been played out, and continues to be played out, in literature. Even here some readers will miss references to any number of key novels and authors or will feel

The Jewish Museum

The Jewish Museum, vertical detail

that certain texts might have warranted a more detailed examination, while others might have been dealt with more swiftly. For my own part, I would have liked to have given over additional space to a more detailed consideration of older east German authors, ethnic-minority writers other than Emine Sevgi Özdamar, Zafer Şenocak, and Feridun Zaimoğlu (who receive less attention than they deserve), and artists such as Herta Müller, Richard Wagner (originally from Romania), Terézia Mora, and Libuše Monikova (from the German-speaking areas of Hungary and the Czech Republic, respectively). In spite of these limitations — which are more than compensated for by other colleagues working in the field of contemporary German literature — I hope readers will be able to glimpse something of the richness, variety and interest of modern Germany, and in particular of recent German writing.

Entrance to the Hackesche Höfe

Notes

[1] See Brian Ladd, *The Ghosts of Berlin* (Chicago: U of Chicago P, 1997), 84–96.

[2] See Stefan Berger, *The Search for Normality* (Oxford: Berghahn, 1997).

[3] See Peter Pulzer, "Unified Germany: A Normal State?," *German Politics* 3:1 (1994): 1–17.

[4] See Karl Wilds, "Identity Creation and the Culture of Contrition: Recasting 'Normality' in the Berlin Republic," *German Politics* 9:1 (2000): 83–102.

[5] Adrian Hyde-Price, "Germany and the Kosovo War: Still a Civilian Power?," *German Politics* 10:1 (2001): 19–34, here 32–33. See also Rainer Baumann and Gunther Hellmann, "Germany and the Use of Military Force: 'Total War,' the 'Culture of Restraint,' and the Quest for Normality," *German Politics* 10:1 (2001): 61–82.

"Jiddische Musik am historischen Ort" in the
Hackesches Theater, Hackesche Höfe

[6] Gerhard Schröder, "'Weil wir Deutschlands Kraft vertrauen . . . ,' Regierungserklärung des Bundeskanzlers vor dem Deutschen Bundestag vom 10. November 1998," *Bulletin der Bundesregierung,* No. 74, 11 November 1998, 902.

[7] "'Eine offene Republik': Gespräch mit Bundeskanzler Gerhard Schröder," *Die Zeit,* 4 February 1999, 33–34.

[8] Janet Stewart, "*Das Kunsthaus Tacheles:* The Berlin Architecture Debate of the 1990s in Micro-Historical Context," in Stuart Taberner and Frank Finlay, eds., *Recasting German Identity* (Rochester: Camden House, 2002), 53–68, here 55.

[9] Catherine Slessor, "Gehry's Geode," *Architectural Review,* 210.1254 (2001): 48–54, here 48.

[10] Elke Heckner, "Berlin Remake: Building Memory and the Politics of Capital Identity,'" *Germanic Review* 77:4 (2002): 304–25, here 307.

[11] See Michael S. Cullen, ed., *Das Holocaust-Mahnmal: Dokumentation einer Debatte* (Zurich: Pendo Verlag, 1999); Michael Jeismann, ed., *Mahnmal Mitte: Eine Kontroverse* (Cologne: Dumont, 1999); and Ute Heimrod, Günter Schlusche, and Horst Seferens, eds., *Denkmalstreit — das Denkmal? Die Debatte um das "Denkmal für die ermordeten Juden Europas"* (Berlin: Philo, 1999). See also James E. Young, "Berlin's Holocaust Memorial: A Report to the Bundestag Committee on Media and Culture," *German Politics and Society* 17:3 (1999): 54–70.

[12] See Charles Maier, *The Unmasterable Past* (Cambridge, MA: Harvard UP, 1988) and Richard J. Evans, *In Hitler's Shadow: West German Historians and the Attempt to Escape from the Nazi Past* (New York: Pantheon, 1989).

[13] See Werner Sewing, "Herz, Kunstherz oder Themenpark? Deutungsversuche des Phänomens Potsdamer Platz," in Yamin von Rauch und Jochen Visscher, eds., *Der Potsdamer Platz* (Berlin: Jovis, 2000), 47–58.

[14] Stephen Brockmann, *Literature and German Unification* (Cambridge: Cambridge UP, 1999).

[15] See Felix Philipp Lutz, "Historical Consciousness and the Changing of German Political Culture," *German Politics* 11:3 (2002): 19–34, here 22.

[16] Roland Robertson, "Globalisation or Glocalisation?," *Journal of International Communication,* 1:1 (1994): 33–52. See also Roland Robertson, *Globalization: Social Theory and Global Culture* (London: Sage, 1992).

[17] See Michael Blumenthal, *Daniel Libeskind and the Jewish Museum of Berlin. Leo-Baeck Memorial Lecture 44* (New York: Leo Baeck Institute, 2000). See also James Young, *At Memory's Edge* (New Haven: Yale UP, 2000), 152–83.

[18] Elke Heckner, "Berlin Remake," 323.

[19] For a more extensive examination of the Berlin architecture debates of the 1990s, see Kathleen James-Chakraborty, "Memory and the Cityscape: The German Architectural Debate about Postmodernism," *German Politics and Society* 17:3 (1999): 71–83.

[20] See the special edition of *German Politics* (11:3 [2002]) for articles on the "normality" debate in relation to these and other areas.

1: Literary Debates since Unification: "European" Modernism or "American" Pop?

soviel Sinnlichkeit wie der Stadtplan von Kiel
— Maxim Biller

WHAT IS MOST IMMEDIATELY STRIKING about the German literary market since unification, and in particular since the mid-1990s, is its sheer diversity. This variety was reflected in, though not necessarily a direct result of, a series of heated discussions that took place from the end of the 1980s amongst newspaper critics and professional readers working for publishing houses — authors, with some exceptions, continued to write novels. As a by-product of these disputes, literary scholars have been furnished with a lexicon for their readings of post-1990 German fiction, including, as we shall see, "Gesinnungsästhetik," "Unterhaltsamkeit," "Realismus," and "Neue Lesbarkeit."

The most dramatic but by no means the first of these debates concerned the person and literary achievements of East German writer Christa Wolf, following the belated publication of her *Was bleibt* (1990). Had this short narrative appeared, in West Germany, at the time of its composition more than ten years previously, argued Ulrich Greiner, literary critic at *Die Zeit,* in a commentary of 1 June 1990, its portrayal of the way the East German security apparatus had spied on the author during the protests following the expulsion of songwriter Wolf Biermann in 1976 would have been an explosive exposure of the true nature of the GDR.[1] Instead, her failure to release the manuscript at this point testified, Greiner claimed, to the fatal alliance of intellectuals and the state; the decision to issue such a text just after the fall of the communist regime, he insisted, smacked of opportunism. The very next day, Frank Schirrmacher of the *Frankfurter Allgemeine Zeitung* (*FAZ*) intervened with further criticism. He argued that Wolf was representative of a generation of writers whose experience of Nazism had caused them to be unduly idealistic, and excessively forgiving, in their support for the supposedly anti-fascist GDR.[2] Predictably, legions of colleagues from east and west weighed in against these calumnies, notably Walter Jens, Stefan Heym, Heiner Müller, and Günter Grass, as well as Wolf herself.

The arguments about Christa Wolf soon expanded into a discussion of politics and literature in both East *and* West Germany. Schirrmacher followed his criticisms of Wolf with an article announcing a "leave-taking" from the literature not only of the GDR but also the "old" West Germany, and this on the eve of unification, on 2 October 1990.[3] On 9 November 1990, a year after the fall of the Wall, Ulrich Greiner then decried the "Gesinnungsästhetik," the "aesthetics of morality," that had purportedly dominated German fiction for decades.[4] This assertion was political as well as aesthetic. Greiner deplored the manner in which authors in both parts of Germany had occupied themselves with "extra-literary" themes, that is, with "dem Kampf gegen Restauration, Faschismus, Klerikalismus, Stalinismus etcetera" (*DDG*, 215). What was needed, according to the two critics, was a return to aesthetic criteria.

"Wer bestimmt, was gewesen ist, der bestimmt auch, was sein wird. Der Streit um die Vergangenheit ist ein Streit um die Zukunft," insisted Greiner (*DDG*, 208). The echo here of the statement made by conservative historian Michael Stürmer at the height of the so-called *Historikerstreit* of the mid-1980s: "In einem geschichtslosem Land [gewinnt derjenige] die Zukunft, wer die Erinnerung füllt, die Begriffe prägt und die Vergangenheit deutet,"[5] is almost certainly conscious. Like Stürmer and his colleagues Andreas Hillgruber and Ernst Nolte five years earlier, Stephen Brockmann notes, Schirrmacher and Greiner were arguing "that Federal Republican history had been frozen, and that it was time for a new 'normality,' this time aesthetic rather than historical."[6] If the *Historikerstreit* had pitted revisionist historians, with their pleas that the Nazi past should cease to dominate debates about German identity, against left-leaning intellectuals, and in particular philosopher Jürgen Habermas,[7] then the *Literaturstreit* was about wresting control of the cultural sphere from a left-liberal elite that had allegedly imposed its agenda of contrition and moral self-improvement upon German letters since the late 1950s. On this occasion, however, it seemed that the challenge might be more successful. The "demise of the GDR," Andreas Huyssen remarks, marked "the end of the unquestioned role in West German intellectual life of the left-liberal consensus."[8] Shaken by revelations of the extent of corruption, abuse of state power, and the *Stasi* surveillance of the population via a network of informal contacts, and all too conscious of their own previous sympathies for the GDR as a "better" alternative to capitalism, many on the West German left focused on what writer Peter Schneider, caustically, but perhaps accurately, described as efforts at "Schadensbegrenzung."[9] Indeed, the end of the GDR would provoke a more general questioning of those on the *west* German left who had emerged from the student movement of the late 1960s with a worldview that was perhaps overly critical of the 'old' Federal Republic and too indulgent of East German socialism.

Shortly before the fall of the Berlin Wall, on 10 October 1989, Schirrmacher had published an essay entitled "Idyllen in der Wüste oder das Versagen vor der Metropole." This piece listed more specifically what it was that the critic found so uninspiring about West German literature and, more significantly, linked the aesthetic limitations of contemporary German writing with "political correctness" and German "provinciality." Thus Schirrmacher attacked the system of prizes and subsidies for literature which, he claimed, produced only a mass of inferior writing. The bulk of recent German fiction, he professed, was "staubig, unsouverän, nachgeahmt, kurz: epigonal."[10] Yet, above all, it was the absence of a genuinely metropolitan culture in the Federal Republic that meant that present-day writers, in contrast to the "Dichter der literarischen Moderne" (*I*, 18), remained provincial, both in their themes and their use of form: German literature failed to portray the thrills, excess, and dangers of modern urban existence. In the words of Wolfram Schütte, "es ist solche literarische Urbanität im weitesten Sinne, welche der deutschen Nachwuchsliteratur fehlt."[11]

"Die literarischen Standards sind auf dem tiefsten Niveau der Nachkriegszeit angelangt," insisted Karl Heinz Bohrer in a 1995 essay.[12] Bohrer, onetime *FAZ* journalist, professor of literature in Bielefeld and co-editor of the literary periodical *Merkur*, is described by Jan-Werner Müller as "one of the most influential intellectuals in postunification Germany and as "the most important thinker of the aesthetic" in the German-speaking world."[13] His recent thinking is set out in a number of books including *Das absolute Präsens* (1994) and *Die Grenzen des Ästhetischen* (1998), as well as in articles in *Merkur*. Andreas Huyssen notes Bohrer's powerful influence on Greiner and Schirrmacher,[14] as does, somewhat facetiously, critic Jochen Vogt: "Das muß gewiß noch keine Kampagne sein, aber es zeigt doch ein verdammt hohes Maß an Intertextualität."[15] Indeed, Bohrer brings together the charges leveled against German literature around 1990: first, that culture in the FRG was dominated by a left-liberal consensus driven by moral rather than aesthetic concerns, second, that present-day writing is provincial, and, third, that it lacks quality.

The 1987 treatise "Die permanente Theodizee" examines a literary tradition that has eliminated "das Böse" and replaced it by "das Gute." The history of German writing since Romanticism, Bohrer asserts, is the tale of philosophy's triumph over aesthetics. German idealism, he argues, confronted the problem of evil in the world by rationalizing it out of existence: "Das Gute hatte Konjunktur."[16] Once the authentic work of art is subjected to a universalist ethics, it is reduced to an instrument of moral instruction. After 1945, this was all the more the case. The experience of Nazism meant that postwar literature was fatally limited in its aesthetic possibilities. Similar claims are made in "Die Ästhetik am Ausgang ihrer Unmündigkeit" (1990). In a further essay of 1990 "Warum wir keine Nation sind. Warum wir eine werden wollen," published in the *FAZ*, Bohrer attacks those intellectuals in both East and West Germany protesting unification and denigrates a German tradition of provinciality. This was best exemplified by Heinrich von Kleist, a "romantischer Kleinstädter," who, Bohrer intimates, was unable to adjust to the pace of life in the "europäischen Glanzmetropole" of Paris and longed for the "Enge einer machtgeschützten Innerlichkeit" back in Prussia.[17] In the modern period too, he contends, many Germans had preferred the comforting irrelevance of East and West Germany: two states mercifully spared by their semi-colonial dependency — after the catastrophe of 1933–45 — the responsibility of developing a sovereign culture. Too deferential to create a modern, metropolitan culture of their own, West Germans in particular had contributed to the annihilation of national identity. Jürgen Habermas' promulgation of *Verfassungspatriotismus*, Bohrer argues, was the only permissible form of identification — a rational, unemotional affirmation of the constitutional order — with a state whose intellectual elites considered that German identity had come to an end with the Holocaust.

During the discussions of the early 1990s on moving the capital to Berlin, Bohrer noted the way many politicians appeared to prefer the "Fortführung Deutschlands als Provinz," to retain Bonn as the political center of united Germany.[18] These remarks appear in an article entitled "Seit '45 ohne Metropole," collated with pieces expressing regret over Germany's eagerness to stand aside from global conflicts and the loss of historical memory.[19] In each case, the message is similar to that published in essays on "Provinzialismus" in *Merkur* between 1990 and 1992.[20] Germany, Bohrer contends, is provincial: it is diffident, inhibited and — in both senses of the word — artless.

Bohrer's thought betrays, as Jan-Werner Müller points out, "a nostalgia for a 'classical modernity' associated with the culture of High Modernism, sovereign political decision-making honed through imperial rule, and the *großbürgerliche* metropolitan culture of Paris and London."[21] Indeed, as Stephen Brockmann suggests, Bohrer is an "intellectual Westerner," desiring to reconnect Germany with the modernist traditions of France and Britain, with the self-assured, urban sophistication of Flaubert, Wilde, and Baudelaire.[22] His vision of the new, post-unification Germany is one in which a "normal" Germany would become a "real" country, a properly *European* nation-state, with a culture to match. This would be an ingenious combination of a "longitudinal normality," that is, a confident projection of national identity drawing on an allegedly heretofore repressed German heritage, and a "latitudinal normality" that would integrate this tradition into a supposedly European preference for "high culture."

Maxim Biller's 1991 essay "Soviel Sinnlichkeit wie der Stadtplan von Kiel" is equally dismissive of contemporary fiction. Biller too is unimpressed by those of his colleagues who compensate for their inability to tell a story with postmodern self-reflexion, "mit einer ästhetisch-verschlüsselten Reportage von seinem strukturalistischen Hermetik-olymp."[23] Here, Biller is most likely referring to the wave of intensely self-reflexive, demonstratively "theoretical" fiction by members of his own generation which began in the mid-1980s and would continue into the late 1990s with texts such as Mattis Manzel's *Peinlich* (1995) — a novel in which the narrator pleads with himself to introduce more "action" into his story.[24] A similar attack is insinuated by Matthias Altenburg who, in his essay "Kampf den Flaneuren," decries the subsidies which encourage stylized and self-indulgent fiction. Writing has become a pose: "flanieren."[25] Yet the solution offered by Biller and Altenburg is quite different from that proposed by Schirrmacher, Greiner or Bohrer. Biller rejects the notion of the work of art as a "geheiligtes Produkt" as reminiscent of a German tradition emphasizing introspection rather than engagement with the wider world (*SV*, 69). What is needed is a new realism which, in Altenburg's words, would explore "jene dirty places [. . .] wo Bisse und Küsse so schwer zu unterscheiden sind."[26]

Biller, born in 1960, and Altenburg (1958), are both associated with what Altenburg, along with Matthias Politycki (1955), has termed the "generation of '78." Born between the mid-1950s and early 1960s, this cohort had been defined by Reinhard Mohr in *Zaungäste: Die Generation, die nach der Revolte kam* (1992) as an "inbetween-generation." Its members were born too late to have been involved in the upheavals of '68, yet are too rooted in the "old" FRG to feel much affinity with those younger Germans for whom the fall of the Berlin Wall implied a complete break with the past. "Wer sind wir?," asks Altenburg: "Eine Generation von durchsichtigen Nullen, von farblosen Flaschen."[27] In Altenburg's *Landschaft mit Wölfen* (1997), the protagonist speaks for his generation: "Heute glaube ich, daß das Eigentliche immer gerade jetzt passiert oder daß man es womöglich schon hinter sich hat, was ja das Schlimmste wäre."[28] Wedged, as it were, between "den guten alten 68ern" and "den Neonkids der 89er-Generation," Matthias Politycki complains, this is a generation condemned to a hurtful irrelevance, "als gäbe's so einen wie mich gar nicht? Und auch keine(n) Burkhard Spinnen, Hans Pleschinski, Dagmar Leupold, Thomas Kling, Matthias Altenburg, Reinhard Jirgl, Robert Schneider, Thomas Meinecke, Jens Sparschuh, Andreas Man, Ralf

Rothmann . . . und wie sie alle heißen."[29] Many of these names are familiar, some even well-known — none, however, a major success.

Yet this generation had an substantial impact on the literary debates of the 1990s. From Biller's and Altenburg's contributions at the beginning of the decade to Politycki's essays of the late 1990s: "Das Gequake von satten Fröschen" (1997) and "Kalbfleisch mit Reis!" (1997), a major effort was underway to delineate the aesthetic program of the "sogenannten 'jüngeren Kulturträger,'"[30] the generation of '78 now rising to positions of influence in the arts and media. But it was not only a question of overcoming the deference of a once marginalized generation. It was also a matter of rescuing German culture. "Kein Hahn mehr kräht in Frankreich, England, USA nach unsrer Literatur, und selbst in deutschen Buchhandlungen gilt der Wunsch danach bereits vielfach als unsittlicher Antrag," Politycki claimed, adding that an awful irrelevance had taken hold of the country.[31] The struggle for self-definition by the thirty to forty-year-olds now coming into their own would also define Germany.

"Heute ist die deutsche Gegenwartsliteratur nicht nur in Europa, sondern auch in Amerika eine schwindende Größe, und die amerikanische Literatur gilt zugespitzt als Synonym für das, was man an der deutschen vermißt," declared Martin Hielscher, then commissioning editor at the Cologne publishing house Kiepenheuer & Witsch, in an 1995 article.[32] The same complaint was at the core of Uwe Wittstock's piece in the *Neue Rundschau* in late 1993, "Ab in die Nische," and a subsequent article in the *Süddeutsche Zeitung* of February 1994; both were later published in a collected edition of Wittstock's works with the programmatic title *Leselust: Wie unterhaltsam ist die neue deutsche Literatur?* (1995). The state of German literature, Wittstock claimed, was anything but pleasant, as it has a tiny audience domestically and is seen abroad as "unsinnlich und weltfern."[33] Deploying a phrase that recalls descriptions of the country pre-1945 as lagging behind western norms, he declared Germany a "verspätete Nation" (*LE*, 25) that has yet to catch up with the USA, Britain, or France. "Wir leben hierzulande inzwischen in einer pluralistischen und erstaunlich gefestigten Demokratie," he noted, and yet the Republic's intellectual elites appeared to view the population only with moralizing condescension, and this "mit den alten Mitteln der Moderne" (*LE*, 158–59).

Wittstock, born in 1955, tenders an entirely different solution to the seeming crisis of German literature than does his near contemporary Frank Schirrmacher (born 1959). Both critics agree that German writing is provincial, lacking in urban sophistication; each of them suggests that German culture, shaped since 1945 by the obligation to confront the Holocaust, has been "abnormal" — Wittstock uses the term "Sonderweg" (*LE*, 24) often used to describe the country's rejection of the West on its path to fascism. Yet, whereas Schirrmacher wishes for German culture to return to the traditions of European Modernism, Wittstock looks to an "American" postmodernism with admiring allusions to Leslie Fiedler's 1968 lecture in Freiburg, "cross the border, close the gap,"[34] and the novels of Philip Roth, Don DeLillo, and Thomas Pynchon.

Wittstock's praise was reserved, therefore, for those German authors who began emerging in the 1980s, such as Patrick Süskind, Sten Nadolny, Klaus Modick, Michael Krüger, or Christoph Ransmayr, whose work combines popular pastiche, allusion, and intertextual quotation with a disregard for distinctions between "high" and "low" art (*LE*, 56–61). As Wittstock observes, postmodernism had long been suspect in the Federal Republic; Jürgen Habermas, in his 1980 treatise "Die Moderne — ein unvollendetes Projekt,"[35] had pointed to what he saw as the reactionary spirit of French postmodern thought. Yet what was now flourishing was a creative chaos, an individualism with a "moral" aspect: the breaking down of barriers between elite and popular discourses promoted "Toleranz und Demokratie." In a newly united Germany, he claimed, the advantages of diversity and a more profound pluralism (*LE*, 44) should be obvious to all. Growing heterogeneity, Wittstock stated, would have a positive impact on public discourse "und zwar sowohl im politischen wie im ästhetischen Bereich" (*LE*, 46). This would be a "latitudinal normality" in which Germany would share the values of diversity and respect for the individual preached throughout the western world.

"Welche Postmoderne?," asked Martin Hielscher in his 1995 essay "Literatur in Deutschland — Avantgarde und pädagogischer Purismus."[36] For Hielscher, as for Wittstock, the answer was the "American" form of postmodernism, as elaborated by Leslie Fiedler, "nämlich die Vermittlung von U und E, oben und unten, autonomem Kunstwerk und Massenkunst" (*LD*, 159), not the dismissal in the name of the French postmodernism of Foucault, Lacan, and Derrida of everything "was Identifikation erlaubt, Lust bereitet, Vergnügen gewährt" (*LD*, 156). For Hielscher, the models were Pynchon, William Gaddis, Nicolson Baker, and Gilbert Sorrentino, whose novels, he insisted, possessed "Humor *und* Charme, Unterhaltungswert *und* Intelligenz, Brillanz, Welterfahrung *und* Menschenkenntnis" (*LD*, 162). German culture, it seemed, needed to abandon its provinciality and complete its opening up to the west. This would not be achieved, however, by mimicking French postmodern theory (which, some argued, was a route back to Heidegger and Nietzsche, two thinkers discredited in the FRG by their association with fascism), or the resuscitation of European Modernism. The "German" tradition of literature as "priestlich-elitäre Erbauung" was to give way to *Lust am Lesen*, a delight in plot and narrative: *Neue Lesbarkeit*. A volume edited by Hielscher, *Wenn der Kater kommt: Neues Erzählen – 38 deutschsprachige*

Autorinnen und Autoren (1996), was subsequently produced to give substance to this demand.

Discussions of German literature — and of its viability — since unification revolve around a number of key themes. The first of these is the relationship between politics and aesthetics, with conservatives such as Greiner, Schirrmacher, and Bohrer dismissing the politically-engaged literature so beloved of those they denounce as the left-liberal intellectual elite of the "old" FRG. The debate then mutates into a contest between "European" Modernism and "American" postmodernism as the generation of '78 battles to make its mark. This discussion sets opposing visions of a new German "normality" against one another. In our next section, we look at the way these topics re-emerge in reflections by critics and writers on the literary market post-1990. Subsequently, we return to our concern with "normalization" and identify a series of trends that will be of vital importance in later chapters.

The Literary Market

"Mit einundvierzig bin ich auch als junger Autor nicht mehr zu verkaufen," complains Albert Rusch, the woeful narrator of F. C. Delius's *Der Königsmacher* (2001), a once moderately successful author now ignored by the reading public and his literary agent in equal measure.[37] Not only is Rusch too old to be marketed with the series of youthful first-time "stars" so heavily promoted in the 1990s — Judith Hermann was 28 when her *Sommerhaus, später* (1998) appeared, Benjamin Lebert only 17 on the publication of *Crazy* (1999) — he also lacks the aristocratic "von" (*DK*, 186) in his name which might make him a star of the new pop scene: he cannot compete with the likes of Alexander von Schönburg, Benjamin von Stuckrad-Barre, or Alexa Hennig von Lange, whose compositions combine patrician disdain with hedonistic wallowing in modern-day trash culture. His disadvantages are compounded by the fact that he is quite manifestly not an attractive young woman writer. "Ja, Frauen, die schreiben, haben es leichter, besonders wenn sie jung sind und mit raffinierten Fotos in die unschlagbare Aura der Attraktivität aufsteigen" (*DK*, 79), he moans, alluding to the marketing of a new generation of female writers at the end of the 1990s with stylish photographs and melancholic poses. Moreover, the topic reserved for writers of his generation has been usurped by younger authors employing a contemporary idiom. In his scribblings on German identity in east and west he fails to tap into a modish "Ost-Nostalgie" — "der brüllend komische B" mentioned is surely Thomas Brussig, who captured this market with his *Helden wie wir* (1995; *DK*, 142) — yet is equally unable to reproduce a hip "westliche Selbstverliebtheit" (*DK*, 80).

Rusch's observations on his lack of success point to the fragmentation of the literary market into a series of discrete categories within which writers are packaged for groups of consumers targeted by agents and the sales departments of publishing houses. In the process, the author's person becomes the product as much as does the work: "es geht gar nicht um diese Texte, sondern der Autor ist das Ereignis, der um den Text herum sein Marketing betreibt oder betreiben läßt," suggests his friend Schoppe (*DK*, 188). What is being sold is not literature as such, but lifestyle. And middle-aged men, whether Rusch or Delius himself — despite the fact that the latter claims not to be the novel's author but a fellow writer who has simply agreed publish the text under his name — have few advantages in the struggle to establish brand name recognition.

Delius draws together in a witty and self-evidently ironic manner much of the discussion of developments in the literary market in the 1990s. This discussion began with a general acknowledgment of the manner in which the consolidation of specialist publishing houses into a small number of large concerns had imposed homogeneity upon the literary market even as the segmentation of the wider reading public by gender, age, sexual orientation, and opportunities for the cross-marketing of fashion, CDs, and clubs fostered the illusion of market differentiation. A dwindling number of multinational publishing houses compete for the few authors able to establish themselves as durable brand names. "Die Manager der Großkonzerne," comments critic Thomas Kraft, "wedeln mit Blankoschecks und kaufen alles, was nicht niet- und nagelfest ist."[38] Massive advances are paid to first-time authors who are able to offer up an exposé, a lifestyle and, importantly, good looks that are suitably original yet also immediately subsumable, that is, *con*sumable, within contemporary fashions. Matthias Politycki argues in an allusively and ironically titled essay of 2000, "Das Medium ist die Massage," literature has become a marketing event. And nobody has grasped this better than the new wave of pop authors. Rainald Goetz, Christian Kracht, and Benjamin von Stuckrad-Barre — fêted for their musings on the internet, pop music, and adolescent anxiety — realize "dass der Autor — genau genommen: der in der Talkshow auftretende Autorendarsteller — heute wichtiger ist als sein Werk."[39] Likewise, Kathrin Röggla, who achieved some success with her melancholic vision of the ephemerality of modern life in *Abrauschen* (1997) and *irres wetter* (2000), and her report on New York on 11 September 2001, *really ground zero* (2001), declares that a book is only noticed when it makes money, and that commercially successful authors are the most important, "aber wahrgenommen werden ohnehin nicht so sehr deren bücher, sondern ihr auftreten in der öffentlichkeit."[40] What matters is that the face fits. In Joachim Zelter's *Das Gesicht* (2003), a writer travels throughout Germany and is received with rapturous applause despite the fact that he reads from an empty book.

Unease about the effects on literary production of publishing houses' ever narrower focus on profit is not restricted to any particular political position. In a short essay of 1998, for example, Ulrich Greiner, more properly situated in the *conservative* anti-capitalist camp, regrets the dissolution of an elite culture in the age of mass consumerism and anticipates Politycki's comments on developments in the book market: "Der sogenannte *event* ist an die Stelle der Literatur getreten."[41] For those on both left and right who bemoan the permeation of the aesthetic sphere by a profit-driven free-market economy, literary culture has come to mimic the ideology of instant gratification propagated by a media industry in which entertainment equates to advertisement. This is the nightmare scenario of talk shows, music videos, and reality TV, as glimpsed by Jochen Hörisch, the "unübersehbaren Schar von MTV-, 'Der-Preis-ist-heiß'-, 'Zur-Sache-Kanzler'-, Sportchannel-, 'Grüße-aus-der-Lederhose'-, 'Literarisches-Quartett'-, 'Wetten-daß'-, und-und-und-Fans."[42] In an epoch in which speed is everything and novelty an absolute value, it seemed that literature, even reading, might not survive. Alluding to the title of Sten Nadolny's novel *Die Entdeckung der Langsamkeit* (1983), Günter Grass spoke in 1999 of the need for an "Erlernung der Langsamkeit," a "Gegengift zur allgemein vorherrschenden Beschleunigung."[43]

Literature did survive, of course. Indeed, in the late 1990s even début novels could record astounding sales figures — helped along by media hype. Lebert's *Crazy* (1999), for example, a rather insipid novel of adolescent anxiety regarding sexuality, the tribulations and rewards of friendship, and dysfunctional families, sold 30, 000 copies in the first ten days after its publication, went on to sell many more tens of thousands in the following months, and was subsequently released in CD form and as a movie. Lebert himself, who began his career writing on teenage culture for *Jetzt,* the youth magazine of the *Süddeutsche Zeitung,* set off on a whirlwind of book tours and talk shows. In the course of his travels, he was happy to pander to his audiences' desire to believe that the novel — in which the mildly disabled protagonist, Benjamin, is packed off to boarding school by his parents so they can fight out their marital differences in peace — was autobiographical. The reality of his family circumstances, and in particular the fact that his father and uncle worked in the media and were well placed to advise the young author, did not detract from his readers' enjoyment.

The promotion of Benjamin Lebert as a "boy wonder," as a painfully honest spokesperson for a generation of teenagers, exemplifies the manner in which the media shape the expectations of the public and the market within which authors operate. In particular, it points to the way critics, more than ever before, are able to manufacture a demand for a genre, theme, or an attitude, as well as to create and destroy careers on the basis of but a single review of a first book or, more often, of a second, less "successful" novel. Author Helmut Krausser, reacting to this excessive influence, dismissed Marcel Reich-Ranicki, Germany's most famous critic and the convener of the television show *Das literarische Quartett,* as a "Trivialkritiker" and a "leibgewordene Machtphantasie."[44] Yet this was relatively benign compared to Martin Walser's assault on Reich-Ranicki. Walser had long been disparaging of critics in essays from the 1960s onwards and in novels such as *ohne einander* (1993). In his *Tod eines Kritikers* (2002), however, a work in which the merging of popular and elite fiction is held to have produced what one character calls "*E-O-Kultur,*" a culture of "*Ejakulation und Orgasmus*" in which reviewers have become far "*wichtiger als die Schreibenden,*"[45] controversy was all but assured. Its unflattering depiction of André Ehrl-König, a Jewish critic resembling Reich-Ranicki, whose murder is faked as a publicity stunt, was widely condemned.

The careers of three writers who rose to prominence from the middle of the 1990s, Thomas Brussig, Michael Kumpfmüller, and Judith Hermann, exemplify the way critics may influence a novel's reception by declaring it to satisfy a demand that they in fact have manufactured. Thus Brussig's *Helden wie wir* was the first in a series of texts heralded as *the* novel of unification: the impossibly-named Uhltzscht's claim to have felled the Berlin wall with a penis vastly inflated following a blood transfusion he had given to Erich Honecker indicts East German passivity — Uhltzscht had worked for the *Stasi* and the present story may simply be another of his masturbatory fantasies — *and* the propensity of the western readers of his interview with *The New York Times* to believe the most fantastical of conspiracy theories regarding the former communist state. Michael Kumpfmüller's *Hampels Fluchten* (2000) was similarly acclaimed as the long-awaited depiction of German division. Heinrich Hampel, whose family endured Russian retribution during a period of forced labor after 1945, quits East Germany for the FRG, becomes a bed salesman before living up to his name as a "jumping Jack" who flees back to the east to avoid creditors and the women featured in his *Bettgeschichten*. There he ends up in prison for bad debts and is recruited by the *Stasi*. The implication is that, in the west, postwar deprivation mutates into the confidence trick of the economic miracle, and, in the east, into renewed conformity. Judith Hermann's *Sommerhaus, später,* on the other hand, was seized upon as the "sound" of a generation of disaffected thirty-somethings at the end of the 1990s. More than a decade after unification, moreover, reviewers were still eagerly awaiting the great "Berlin novel" of the present.

This is what the protagonist of Matthias Zschokke's *Der dicke Dichter* (1995), a writer, aims to deliver: "Es ist gleichsam Stadtgespräch, daß Berlin neu geschrieben werden will, muß, wird,"[46] but, tellingly, he repeatedly falls asleep while going about the task.

Hermann's first collection was edited by Uwe Wittstock and assisted by grants from the *Literarisches Colloquium* in Berlin — lampooned in Joachim Lottmann's 1999 novel *Deutsche Einheit*, as a "geistiges Zentrum" of the post-unification German "Subventionsliteratur"[47] — the *Stiftung Kulturfonds,* the *Akademie der Künste,* and other literary foundations. Indeed, a glance inside the cover of almost any début novel reveals a dedication to the institutions just named, the *Deutscher Literaturfonds,* one of the many *Literaturhäuser* scattered throughout the Federal Republic, the *Deutsches Literaturinstitut* run by Hans-Ulrich Treichel at the University of Leipzig, or a similar body. Yet this support is not uncontroversial. Matthias Biskupek's *Schloß Zockendorf* (1998), with its tales of in-fighting between writers in receipt of a grant from this aptly-named institution in the east German province, of bizarre conceptual art, poetry slams, and murder is pure satire. The same is true of Jens Sparschuh's *Lavaters Maske* (1999), which ridicules the media circus, afternoon talk shows, and book readings, as well as the phenomenon of the *Stipendium als Stadtschreiber,* and — contrary to Lavater's theory of the identity of countenance and character — exposes the gap between appearance and reality. Both, however, hint at the more concrete criticisms made by Frank Schirrmacher and left-wing commentators alike. Thomas Kraft, for example, suggests: "Wer heute in Deutschland einen halbwegs vernünftigen Text abliefert, kann kaum einem der zahlreichen Literaturpreise entgehen."[48]

It is possible that such a generous network of subsidies may be responsible for a surfeit of badly-written texts. Yet a system that is seemingly independent of the laws of supply and demand, and which appears strangely archaic, in fact provides the market with a supply of new entrants. The difficulty for these hopeful individuals, of course, is to make the transition from being cosseted by prizes, subsidies, and grants to surviving the harsh economic reality of commercial publishing. Here, the role of the *Lektor* within the publishing house to both read and develop the market is crucial; thus Rose Bartmer: "Der Lektor ist zusehends zum Produktmanager geworden, der sich mehr mit Fragen der Marktpositionierung beschäftigen muß als mit den Texten selber."[49] For those who can capture the imagination of such influential readers as Martin Hielscher or Uwe Wittstock, triumph is almost guaranteed. Others are left to wonder at the apparent arbitrariness of what is published. For Matthias Politycki, it is the undiscerning promotion of pop literature that once again attracts his ire: "Was ist los mit unseren Profi-Lesern, dass sie ein Get-up mit Literatur verwechseln."[50]

Delius's Albert Rusch finds himself in exactly this position: "verletzt von den wechselnden Winden der Moden" (*DK*, 18). Too old to benefit from the subsidy system — "diese Phase war lange vorbei" (*DK*, 18) — he is at the mercy of his *Lektorin* Karla Peschken. His first book a success, his second a flop; it is imperative that he write a bestseller at his third attempt. Consequently, he plans a novel about an affair between the man who would later become Willem I of Holland and a "commoner," Marie Hoffmann, and the fate of their child, Minna. In the course of this historical romance, he will also depict the tribulations of Willem's wife and cousin, Wilhelmine (Mimi), the court of Frederick the Great, Willem's brother-in-law, and the steadfastness of Frederick's wife, Luise, who stood up to Napoleon and became a symbol of the pride of the German nation, and whose memorial stands in the *Tiergarten*. The link to this history, for Rusch, is the discovery that he is a descendent of Minna and is related to the royal dynasties of Prussia and the House of Orange.

Rusch's efforts to write a novel that will satisfy Karla Peschken's insistence on a marketable book leads him into extensive ruminations on the present-day fad for collapsing the barriers between *U- und E-Literatur*, between trivial fiction written to entertain and more serious literature. Hence he attaches the advice his *Lektorin* gives him as an accompaniment to the draft version of the novel and thereby appears to accomplish precisely the opposite of what she suggests. The inclusion of his reflections on how to adapt his literary style to the demands of the market might appear to undermine her demand that he write "*so konventionell wie möglich*," and without "*Experimente*," whilst maximizing the potential for audience identification with the central figure: "*Im Mittelpunkt immer das arme Kind-Mädchen-Frauenzimmer*" (*DK*, 67). In truth, however, this self-reflexivity is itself part of the marketing conceit of contemporary fiction. It hints at the dissolution of barriers between elite and popular writing by introducing a modernist self-consciousness into an entirely predictable story of love and deceit. The author subsequently becomes the focus of attention, the plot merely a means by which he might profile himself. He tours the country, appearing on talk shows to defend Frederick the Great from charges of adventurism and to extol the virtues of Queen Luise. Eventually, of course, his popularity wanes as he is replaced in the public's affection, perhaps inevitably, by an attractive young woman.

So much for Rusch's motives — Delius's gain is that his instrumentalization of a protagonist who is simultaneously a writer allows him to reflect precisely on the way authorial self-reflection has become a constituent part of the marketing of modern-day fiction. It also allows for reflection on contemporary society in the Berlin Republic, that is, in the more "normal" Germany which many predicted would emerge from the 1990s as a European power with its own self-confident metropolitan culture. Rusch, then, claims to have been the inspiration of the "Preußenjahr" (*DK*, 314), a major retrospective in 2001, the tercentennial of the crowning of Frederick I. Here, the novel alludes to debates on Prussian heritage throughout the 1990s ranging from the controversy over rebuilding the *Berliner Stadtschloß* (destroyed by the GDR authorities in 1950)[51] to suggestions at the beginning of the new millenium that the state of Prussia (abolished by the Allies as too closely associated with German nationalism) might be revived. The entire discussion, of course, was also an inquiry into the identity of the incipient Berlin Republic itself. Would the new Germany take its cue from the hyper-modern skyscrapers on the Potsdamer Platz, or would it succumb to the nostalgia of a "critical reconstruction" which aims, as Janet Stewart suggests, to situate Berlin as the "capital of a newly reunited Wilhelmine Germany"?[52]

Delius's novel implies that such questions, and the debates that provoke them, are, to a degree, non-questions. Nostalgia for Prussia, viewed by many as a dangerous indication of an incipient, chauvinistic German nationalism, by no means represents a rejection of the west, or of a globalized, hegemonic American culture in the name of local patriotism, or, indeed, of the modern aesthetic of mass consumerism for the sake of authentically "German" traditions. On the contrary, it embodies the victory of the superficial sensibility of cultural globalization with its ceaseless recycling of fads and fashions, the sentimental retrospective and the apolitical. This is not the embrace of an untainted German past desired by many neo-conservatives, nor even the deluge of nationalistic revanchism feared by the left. Hence the politically incorrect comments the narrator makes regarding Frederick I, decried by many as the *Soldatenkönig* who preferred soldiers to prosperity, as a proponent of the Enlightenment are not meant seriously but are designed to feed the media spectacle "der deutschen Selbstfindung" (*DK*, 258). This is a "cultural normalization" of another kind, and one to be regretted at both ends of the political spectrum — a depoliticization of all historical consciousness within a consumer society obsessed with celebrity. "Die Wilhelminengeschichte," Rusch notes, "ist auch eine Art Dianageschichte" (*DK*, 78–79). Mimi, whose cause he promotes until he is confined to an asylum after claiming to have slept with Queen Luise — as much an icon, for Rusch, of the new Germany as she was after the first unification of 1870 — is, he implies, simply a nineteenth-century version of Diana Princess of Wales.

The dissolution of the barriers between elite and popular culture demanded by some critics and professional readers equates, as presented by Delius, at least, to a systematic depoliticization within the consumer aesthetic. Rusch, indeed, writes in the middle of the Kosovo conflict of early 1999, but is left cold by the "verbalen Gefechte zwischen Befür- wortern und Gegner des Krieges," preferring instead to withdraw into history: "Die Konflikte der Herrscher im 18. Jahrhundert, die Bündnisfragen zwischen 1806 und 1813 erschienen mir spannender als die Konflikte über Menschenrechte, Moral und Milošević" (*DK*, 99– 100). Politics either have no place in contemporary writing or they must be reworked as entertainment. The same proposition is com- municated to the narrator of Birgit Vanderbeke's *Abgehängt* (2001), an author who receives the following advice from her editor: "Man sollte gelegentlich auch mal ein E zu einem U und ein U zu einem E hindurchschlüpfen lassen," she is told, "weil sie sich möglicherweise auf diese Weise befruchten und etwas wie ein Ü erzeugen könnten, zum Beispiel eine RevÜ."[53]

The depoliticization of the writer and of literature itself has been re- ported by any number of observers of contemporary fiction. Volker Hage, for example, notes that literature has given up "ihre öffentliche Rolle,"[54] whereas author Bodo Kirchhoff declares: "Es gab bei uns eine Zeit, in der Schriftsteller Einfluß auf die öffentliche Meinung hatten. Diese Zeit ist vorüber."[55] The harmful consolidation of the literary market, the rise of the "lifestyle aesthetic," the obsession with celebrity, and the emergence of a vacuous pop culture — for many reviewers these were the striking features of the literary market a decade after unification. To be sure, some authors had embraced the call for a return to aesthetic criteria as elabo- rated by Greiner and Schirrmacher on the eve of unification. Martin Walser and Botho Strauß are two names that will feature in later chapters. Others had followed Biller, Politycki, and Altenburg in exploring the new social reality. Here, author Helmut Krausser comes to mind. His *Hagen- Trinker-Trilogie*, and a string of novels from the 1990s, depict life on the streets of modern-day Germany for alcoholics, drug addicts, the homeless, and runaways. Yet these two trends, united in rejecting the moralizing tone associated with the generation of '68 even as they propounded quite different aesthetic programs, were, at the end of the 1990s, relatively marginal. Instead, the dominant *new readability* appeared to many to be superficial, apolitical, and commercial in attitude. Volker Hage suggested in 1999 in the *Spiegel* magazine that "Die neuen deutschen Dichter" might well write "saftig, unterhaltsam, und unbekümmert,"[56] but what was it that they were writing *about*?

Two authors who had been vocal at the beginning of the decade re- emerged at its close to express their criticism of later developments in German writing which they had once seemed keen to set in motion. In April 2000 at the *Evangelische Akademie* in Tutzing, Maxim Biller con- vened a meeting of a hundred authors and critics at which he delivered a condemnation of the "moralischen Gleichgültigkeit einer ganzen Gesellschaft," and in particular "ihrer intellektuellen Elite,"[57] and took issue with its "Schlappschwanz-Literatur." This attack echoed Politycki's plea for a break with the "etikettenhaften Fixierung auf 'Lesebarkeit,' 'Vergnüglichkeit' und dergleichen" in his 1997 essay "Kalbfleisch mit Reis."[58] In his influential contribution "Der amerikanische Holzweg" (2000), Politycki subsequently evaluated the "Rekolonisalisierung Europas (und eigentlich der Gesamtwelt außer vielleicht Bhutans oder Burundis) durch die Amerikaner" and concluded that the reference to American models was damaging to the viability of *German* writing.[59]

Politycki's comments in "Kalbfleisch mit Reis" and "Der amerikanische Holzweg" were directed against the stars of the new pop literature, and yet also indicted the continued failure of his own generation, the "78ers" now in positions of influence in publishing and the media, to define its own aesthetic program. What was *still* required was a self-confident German culture, open to American influences, as to other global trends, and yet more than purely imitative. What Politycki longed for, in fact, was the belated completion of his generation's historical mission: the accomplishment of the "postmodernen europäischen Romans."[60] Not modernism but postmodernism — delight in the charmingly superficial ("Ohne Oberfläche ist auch der schönste Tiefsinn nur, Pardon, 'typisch deutsch'") combined with a "Bedürfnis nach Schönheit." This would be a striving to rework surface reality with "Anspielungen, Leitmotiven, gewagten Metaphern"[61] in order to reveal something of the alternative perspectives masked by the optical illusion of modern consumerism.

The debate on German writing a decade after unification had moved some way from the *Literaturstreit* instigated by Greiner and Schirrmacher. In what follows, we turn to the work of a number of young women writers associated with the label *das literarische Fräuleinwunder*. Celebrated by some critics as a positive symptom of the rebirth of German literature and decried by others as marketing hype, their novels and short stories offer insight into the broader conditions of literary production and developments in theme and form in post-unification fiction as a whole.

"Ein literarisches Fräuleinwunder"?

It was, Volker Hage averred in the *Spiegel* magazine in early 1999, "vor allem die jungen Frauen, die in diesem Frühjahr dafür sorgen, daß die deutsche Literatur wieder ins Gespräch kommt."[62] Indeed, this *literarische Fräuleinwunder*, as Hage termed it, seemed to exemplify the revival of German fiction as a record of the dissolution of the self within the shopping and fashion culture. To Jan Koneffke, alluding to the image on the

22 March 1999 cover of the *Spiegel* depicting young women "in Bademantel und rosa Hausschuhen, mit verruchtem Blick und zwischen verstreuten Kleidern auf der Chaiselongue," they were the very embodiment of the marketing of lifestyle even as they posed "vor einer Bücherwand, damit nicht ganz in Vergessenheit gerät, daß es sich hier um Schriftstellerinnen handelt."[63] And for Michael Landolf, the protagonist in Walser's *Tod eines Kritikers*, the craze for "schicksallose, ihres Aufblühens noch nicht ganz sichere Mädels oder Mädelchen" provided further evidence of the perverse standards of a literary market dictated by critics such as André Ehrl-König (a.k.a Reich-Ranicki): "Und er fragte nie: Schreibt sie gut, sondern: Ist sie hübsch."[64]

The proposition that women writers can be bundled together and packaged as a product, a brand or a "concept," is itself most likely indicative of the dominance of marketing over literary criteria. It perhaps also says something about the way women are conventionally associated with consumerism, both as "objects of desire" of varying "value" and as consumers. Yet, as Peter Graves contends with reference to Hermann, Karen Duve and Kathrin Schmidt — author of the *Gunnar-Lennefsen-Expedition* (1998), which projects the journey undertaken by Josepha Schlupfburg and her great-grandmother through twentieth-century German history on to the wall of their living room — what is truly striking about the epithet *ein literarisches Fräuleinwunder* is "the artificiality of the grouping."[65] One of the many collections of short stories unabashedly intended to capitalize on women's market success provides further evidence of this, albeit unwittingly. Jörg Bong and Oliver Vogel thus bring together in their oddly-titled *Verwünschungen* (2001) a selection of female authors as dissimilar as Birgit Vanderbeke, born in 1956 and the author of a series of short texts presenting the social constructedness of female roles within the family unit, and Silvia Szymanski and Sibylle Berg. Szymanski and Berg are of a similar age to Vanderbeke, but their work, notably Szymanski's *Chemische Reinigung* (1998) and Berg's *SEX II* (1998), is part of the new pop literature, replicating its delight in surface, underground, and sex, and, in Berg's case, self-stylization. The anthology also includes Dagmar Leupold, a "78er" whose fiction could not be more remote from the sparse, lowercase snapshots of the solitude of the internet age typical of Kathrin Röggla (born 1971).

Women writers are, of course, as diverse as their male contemporaries. In Sarah Khan's *Gogo Girl* (1999) and in Malin Schwerdtfeger's volume of short stories *Leichte Mädchen* (2001), for example, the damage done to young women as they begin to confront the deceptions of adult relationships figures prominently, yet Schwerdtfeger's cautious, self-effacing narratives are a world away from Khan's brash, confessional tone and pop allusions. Their subsequent writing, too, testifies to the very different trajectories of their careers. Khan's second novel, *Dein Film* (2001), accordingly, abandons the disaffected, love-sick twenty-something featured in so many pop literature débuts and attempts to present the more complex social reality of the world of media and movies. Robert Altman's filmic reworking of Raymond Carver's *Short Cuts* (1993) may — as in the work of authors as disparate as Ingo Schulze and Judith Hermann — be the inspiration for this series of episodic insights into the way individuals avoid confronting their true selves by constantly referring to the clichés of Hollywood movie and pop culture. Schwerdtfeger, on the other hand, in her *Café Saratoga* (2001), continues to develop a bent for the surreal reminiscent of her older colleague, Felicitas Hoppe. A novel of great poetic intensity, *Café Saratoga* relates the sexual awakening of Sonia, its narrator, along with her sister Maika and their friend Jane, and of Sonja's endeavors to adapt to western consumer culture when, just before unification, her father extracts the family from Poland in order to settle in the Federal Republic.

Other writers, in contrast, employ a distinctly unpoetic, perhaps even harsh, realism. In Karen Duve's short story "Keine Ahnung," from the 1999 collection of the same name, for example, the teenage protagonist feels abandoned by her parents, is hated by her sister, and is incapable of ambition: "Mir war das Sein schon zuviel, ich wollte nicht auch noch etwas werden."[66] In the course of the narrative she is raped, experiments with prostitution, and takes drugs at a local disco. At its close, she has no idea what is to become of her, and so registers for the entry test for the *Finanzamt*. Duve's *Dies ist kein Liebeslied* (2002) likewise dwells on its protagonist's morbid revulsion with her own body, her bulimia, and suicidal fantasies, and, in revisiting her disastrous relationships with men via the pop music of the 1980s, creates a dark impression of the provinciality of the "old" FRG. In similar fashion, Elke Naters's *Königinnen* (1998) begins an unremittingly depressing investigation into the "reality" of female friendships and the seductions of fashion — "Da stehen diese wirklich wunderschönen Schuhe von Patrick Cox"[67] — which she continues in her 1999 novel *Lügen*. Like Duve, Naters combines a fascination with "products" with a brutal vision of her characters' psychological disintegration. This paralleling of fashion with the distortion of the protagonist's psyche raises vital questions about the fate of the feminist politics of the 1970s and 1980s and about the way they were repackaged in the 1990s and adopted into the consumerist idyll as "postfeminism."

Augusta, the narrator of *Lügen*, is obsessed with her friend Be, with her limitless autonomy, her hold over men — including Karl whom Augusta also loves — and her ability endlessly to reinvent herself with a new "look" or a lesbian affair. In fact, Be propounds the new ideology of emancipation — emancipation, that is, from "first wave feminism" and the dreary politics of oppression: "Sie [. . .] spricht vom *Postfeminismus* und daß es nicht mehr darum geht, gegen die Weiblichkeit und die Unterdrückung der Frauen anzukämpfen." In the place of the manifestly worthy, yet patently "unsexy," struggle for equality with men, this new, style-conscious feminism promotes a selective, supposedly sovereign, appropriation of femininity. In the battle between the sexes, women are to avail themselves of their "natural" advantages, even if this means playing the "Hilfslose"[68] as Augusta does when she flatters Karl's male ego or when she tries to maneuver Peter, the brother of Be's girlfriend, into desiring her.

Helen Fielding's international bestseller *Bridget Jones's Diary* (1996) is an obvious point of reference for both Duve's *Dies ist kein Liebeslied* and Naters's *Lügen*. In each of the two German texts, however, a brutal realism interrupts the superficial harmonies of the globalized consumer culture and subverts the marketing deception of postfeminism, that is, its false promise that the self can be continually re-invented with the help of fashion. Naters's Augusta longs for a more genuine love than that advertised by the "have-it-all" consumer ideology of postfeminism — "Ich mag es nicht, weil ich immer noch an die Liebe glaube" (*LG*, 126) — but is finally compelled to recognize that she has become as empty of meaning as the products she consumes: "Das Leben ist banal. Mein Leben ist banal. Ich bin banal" (*LG*, 180). Unlike Fielding's *Bridget Jones,* therefore, there is no happy ending, no man to give meaning to a life that would otherwise consist solely of a surfeit of consumption and self-purging.

In his reading of Duve's *Dies ist kein Liebeslied,* Andrew Plowman speaks of its "(re)inscription of signifiers of 'Germanness,'" its tendency to color the consumerist facade of globalized pop culture with shades of local specificity.[69] For example, the protagonist Strelau "consumes" Goethe's *Werther* yet discovers in it the prospect of a more authentic form of subjectivity: "Und dennoch — als er anfing von seiner Liebe und seinem Unglück zu sprechen, da war mir als sähe ich in mein eigenes Herz."[70] Likewise, her propensity for wider rumination on the more profound existential significance of her circumstances, Plowman claims, infiltrates the form of the narrative with a tendency towards "distortion, dissonance" and signals "an abstract self-absorption with 'mind' and *Weltschmerz.*"[71] This is a more "German" sensibility, he argues, which subverts the novel's outward imitation of the rhetoric of surface.

Judith Hermann similarly localizes an apparently hegemonic global consumer culture and thereby perhaps challenges it. With her allusions to specific Berlin locales in "Sommerhaus später," her re-writing of Hemingway in "Hurrikan (Something farewell)," transposing conflicts begun in Berlin into the American short-story form — in *Sommerhaus später* (1998) — or her evocation of the provincial "Kleinstadt," with its

"Fußgängerzone," "Tchibo," "Kaufhaus," and "Marktplatzhotel," in "Ruth (Freundinnen)" in the volume *Nichts als Gespenster* (2003),[72] Hermann adapts Anglo-American models to her German context.[73] Perhaps more convincingly than Naters and Duve, however, she develops a central concern with memory and the longing for an authentic subjectivity which ensures that her texts avoid the danger of being misappropriated as part of the very culture that they mimic. In effect, her fiction projects a thematic unity across a number of short stories set in diverse locations and at different times which militates against the temptation to become too engrossed with the surface reality they describe. If Naters and Duve reproduce the rhetoric of globalized consumerism in the hope that its own overabundance will cause it to collapse in upon itself, Hermann asks how, in the post-ideological, "ahistorical normality" of the Berlin Republic, the sensitive individual can survive the absence of meaning.

In the title narrative of Hermann's second collection, *Nichts als Gespenster,* Ellen and Felix travel across the vistas of the American west, much as their fathers' generation did before them, hoping to find release from the ambivalence of modern German identity and the claustrophobic narrow-mindedness of the FRG. In truth, however, just as in the work of Peter Handke (*Der kurze Brief zum langen Abschied,* 1972) or Wim Wenders's *Alice in den Städten* (1974), their America is nothing more than a projection. The land of movies, serial killers, and Stephen King novels, "existierte nicht, nicht wirklich," Ellen admits.[74] In fact, she barely remembers having been there at all, even as she tells the story of her time in Austin, with Felix, of the *Hotel International* in the middle of the desert, of Buddy and the *Geisterjägerin.*

America is a canvas onto which Hermann projects the anxieties of her German characters.[75] Buddy, the man they meet in the hotel bar, merely acts as the catalyst for Ellen's ruminations on her life in Berlin: "Sie erzählte von Berlin und von dem Leben in Berlin, sie versuchte, es zu beschreiben, die Tage und die Nächte, ihr kam alles etwas verwirrend vor, durcheinander und ziellos" (*NG,* 225). Even those living at the very heart of the Berlin Republic, in the "new-old" capital with its bold claim to be the hub of the nation's cultural and political renaissance, appear confused by its lack of integrity or direction. Yet the two Germans refuse to be seduced by a constant invitation to think positively all too reminiscent of the trite advertising rhetoric of an internationalized American consumer mentality: "Jegliches 'Wie wär's' und 'Du könntest' ließ Felix schlagartig erlahmen und depressiv werden" (*NG,* 222). Indeed, for Ellen, even the ghosts who haunt the hotel — spirits uprooted from their original abodes and relocated in the featureless wastelands of the west — embody a peculiarly German sense of physical, emotional, and intellectual displacement.

"'Diese Geister da oben können sich nicht abfinden mit dem Leben'" (*NG*, 229), or so we are told.

An overinvestment in the supposed moment of happiness, or in the moment of anticipation before the happiness that never arrives — "Glück ist immer der Moment davor,"[76] was perhaps the most-cited sentence from *Sommerhaus, später* — as well as in individual words or objects is typical of Hermann's figures. Initially, this might suggest the thing-fetishism of consumerism. This is certainly the case in the fiction of Elke Naters and Karen Duve, or in the writing of other pop authors such Christian Kracht or Benjamin von Stuckrad-Barre, where fashion accessories and advertising slogans are endowed with the promise of gratification. Hermann's texts, on the other hand, constantly reiterate the historical dimension repressed within modern culture. In attempting to recover those unique moments, words or objects that have specific, non-integrable meaning to them, her characters struggle to tell their own stories. These, paradoxically, speak of the anguish of having no story to relate. Indeed, when all the decisions facing an individual approximate to the choice between seemingly different, but in fact identical, products — a partiality for one lifestyle over another — then nothing is of any consequence and nothing of significance can ever be narrated.

Hermann's narratives mimic the thing-fetishism of the global consumer culture in order to point up the ill-fit between its ideology of surface and the longing for depth harbored by her German protagonists, caught as they are between their internalization of the rhetoric of limitless choice and the desire for authenticity. In the story "Hurrikan (Something farewell)," in *Sommerhaus, später*, the characters play a game on their paradise Caribbean island: "'Sich-so-ein-Leben-vorstellen.'" Yet their imagining what it would be like to remain on the island, to marry an inhabitant and live there forever, cannot disguise the fact that Kaspar and Nora had an unhappy and as yet unresolved relationship in Berlin or that Christine must return to Germany. In fact, the illusion of boundless choice makes any decision they come to seem arbitrary. Cat kisses Christine, an event of some importance to his wife, no doubt, who, like her husband, is part of the black population that will remain long after the tourists have left. For the German woman, on the other hand, their flirtation is merely a facet of her fantasy projection of her life on the island. When, at the end of the story, Nora stays with Kaspar, her decision possesses a similar air of fantasy. "'Ach Christine,'" sagt Nora. 'Das hier nennt man Urlaub. Eine Reise, verstehst du? Nichts mehr.'"[77]

In spite of their inability to invest decisions with anything more than the provisional status of an almost capricious choice between a phony overabundance of possibilities, each of the four characters appears to be aware, albeit dimly, that the real story they had hoped to have been a part of has failed to materialize. The storm that threatens the island passes by and, again, nothing of consequence has happened in their lives. The indistinct longing for an authentic experience that seemed to inhere in their frequent references to the dramatic, and perhaps devastating, impact the storm might have on the island dissipates with the hurricane itself. Yet at no point do they grasp that their intense anticipation of the storm's arrival had once more pre-positioned them as mere consumers of an event they apprehend as pure distraction.

It is in "Rote Korallen" from *Sommerhaus, später* that the tension between the craving for genuine experience and the bogus freedom and asphyxiating airlessness of contemporary consumer culture is most poignantly depicted. In this piece, the narrator speaks of her German great-grandmother in St. Petersburg just before the first Russian revolution of 1905, of her husband's frequent, lengthy absences and her many admirers, and of the necklace of red corals given her by Nikolai Sergewitsch. It is a story of great passions, vivid colors, homesickness, and melancholia, telling of her great-grandmother's fragile beauty and of the love that she inspired — challenged to a duel, the Russian shoots her husband in the chest, fatally wounding him. Pregnant with the child of Nikolai Sergewitsch — the narrator's grandmother — the German woman returns home, accompanied by Isaak Baruw, a friend of her husband, who, though he marries a Pomeranian maid, remains devoted to her until the very end of his life.

"Ist das die Geschichte, die ich erzählen will?," asks the narrator.[78] Certainly, it is a tale that seems to resonate in the present, alluding to uprooting, displacement, and the gulf between those who adapt easily to the dynamic change that often comes with economic modernization and those, like her great-grandmother, who cannot "aus dem Fenster hinaussehen in eine Fremde" (*RK*, 12). The narrator's great-grandfather adopts the Russian language as his own and spreads the benefits of progress throughout Russia in the form of the latest oven-technology. His wife, however, although she mingles with Russian artists and intellectuals, longs for the idyllic landscapes of her *Heimat:* "aber sie konnte sich an die Blomesche Wildnis erinnern, an die Weide und an das flache Land, an die Heuballen auf den Feldern und den Geschmack von süßem, kaltem Apfelmost im Sommer" (*RK*, 13). And it is with her great-grandmother that the young woman identifies. *Her* story, the narrator seems to believe, may be able to mediate her sense of dislocation in the present.

Yet the narrator is not her great-grandmother. Her own fragility points to a quite different form of subjectivity and to a very contemporary disorder. "Ich fühlte mich wirklich so dünn und mager" (*RK*, 25), she says, and we think of the anorexia or bulimia that invariably affects characters in the fiction of Duve or Naters. Later, she speaks "von meinem dünnen und mageren Handgelenk" (*RK*, 26). Hermann's narrator, however, does not seek to compensate for the feelings of inconsequentiality at the root of such self-negating disorders by *con*suming the commodities of modern-day fashion and design in order to be *sub*sumed by them. Rather, her sense of her own redundancy is exposed by her conviction that there is no story she might tell for herself. All she is left with is introspection, that most modern of diseases of which her anorexia may be a symptom: "Ich interessierte mich ausschließlich für mich selbst" (*RK*, 20). Endless reflection on one's own superfluity leads to feelings of guilt and the craving to purge the excess. And the only recourse for those who long to articulate a non-integrated subjectivity is a visit to the therapist. Indeed, her boyfriend, the great-grandson of Isaak Baruw, with his fish-gray eyes and fish-gray skin and lethargic acceptance of his life's emptiness, desires no story of his own: "Aber er ging zweimal in der Woche zu einem Arzt, einem Therapeuten" (*RK*, 21). If she is to achieve the same state of self-negation, she must be cured of a craving for authenticity that the modern, incorporated society can only see as pathological.

At the close of the text, however, the narrator throws the necklace she inherited from her great-grandmother at the therapist. Its red corals overpower him with their allusions to Petersburg, her great-grandmother, Russia, the Volga, the Black Sea and the Caspian. She reports: "Das Wasser der Weltmeere wogte in einer großen, grünen Welle über den Schreibtisch des Therapeuten und riß ihn vom Stuhl" (*RK*, 28). Consequently, she begins shaping a narrative that says something about her. Like her great-grandmother, she resists the proscriptions of her time and sets about writing her own life. This is a story that is individual and unique, that is, a story that is *hers*.

New Modernism — or "New Readability"?

Responding to Dorothea Dieckmann's dismissal of the "triviality" in most recent fiction by younger writers in her article in *Die Zeit* (22 November 2001), Uwe Wittstock took issue with what he saw as a continued hankering for a renewed Literary Modernism. "Kann es sein," he asked, pointing to Dieckmann's savaging of present-day "pop" tendencies and her praise for the "difficult" prose style of ex-GDR writers Reinhard Jirgl and Wolfgang Hilbig, Austrian authors Elfriede Jelinek and Peter Handke, and W. G. Sebald — an "exile" in England until his death — with his nineteenth-century cadences, "dass hinter diesem Kriterium die Grundüberzeugung der literarischen Moderne steht?" Can it really be true that the German language has been so degraded by journalism and the modern vernacular of everyday life, "dass sich mit ihr das Wahre, Schöne, Gute überhaupt nicht mehr formulieren läßt?"[79]

Wittstock's criticism hints at the perceived split between those writers who, in the face of the accelerating commercialization of the German book market after 1990, are felt to have remained true to "aesthetic" principles and those who are seen to have conformed to the industry's demand for "products" designed to promote "lifestyle." On the one side, we have the non-incorporated, multivalent fiction of typically older writers from German-speaking territories considered to be less "infected" by an American-style popular culture than the FRG, or removed by virtue of "exile." On the other side, we are presented with the self-styled cultural DJs of the *Generation Golf,* as described in Florian Illies' programmatic bestseller of that title from the year 2000, whose "pop" prose, as Horst Spittler notes, reflects the fact that almost all were at one time employed in the "Moedienbranche."[80] Subsumed under the pop label, moreover, are the "78ers," the likes of Altenburg, Politycki, Meinecke, and Andreas Neumeister, who, along with Rainald Goetz, are charged with having begun the dumbing-down of German literature. The same accusation is made in relation to marketing phenomena such as Dietrich Schwanitz, otherwise credited with single-handedly bringing the American campus novel to Germany with his 1995 *Der Campus.* In addition, younger, female writers such as Duve, Naters, Hermann, Tanja Dückers or Julia Franck may also be arraigned.

Yet contemporary German fiction, as Thomas Ernst has argued, cannot be reduced to a single "pop" tendency or uniformly dismissed as wholly market driven, a mere reflection of the demand for novelty.[81] Indeed, evidence of this was provided by our deconstruction of the marketing epithet *das literarische Fräuleinwunder.* And it is here too that we may find proof of Modernist techniques cohabitating with a purportedly more contemporary emphasis on readability. Julia Franck, for example, combines an existential concern with the self with a bent for the surreal within plots that are compelling and up-to-date. Her depiction of the pitfalls of intimacy in *Liebediener* (1999) thus recalls Judith Kuckart's enigmatic novel *Der Bibliothekar* (1998), in which the middle-aged Kolbe longs to be loved by Jelena, an exotic dancer he meets for sex. Yet Franck's tales are typically more uncompromising. Short stories from *Bauchlandung* (2000), therefore, tell of how a sister pictures her muchenvied sibling being roughly penetrated,[82] of a woman's emotional disengagement and her recourse to arbitrary sexual fantasies,[83] and of the successful seduction of a friend's boyfriend merely for the sake of the new "experience": "Natürlich habe ich Paul nicht gemocht, und im Grunde hasse ich ihn noch immer, das macht den Sex so gut."[84]

The realistic, matter-of-fact, even brutal depiction of sex, betrayal, and mutual cruelty clearly bears a resemblance to the "pop" narratives of Naters or Duve. Yet the more intense focus on character psychology and the domestication of the "abnormal" within the "normal," including incest, sexually-charged sibling rivalry, and forbidden fantasies, offer up a pathology of social deviance, of the profound sickness within the individual psyche, reminiscent of Modernism. In Franck's *Der neue Koch* (1997), moreover, a stream-of-consciousness effect is created by the narrator's unremittingly introspective interior monologue. Isolation, disconnection, misperception — these are incorporated into a fragmented narrative process which mirrors the split between perception and reality and the destructive effects of interminable self-reflection and self-doubt. Hence the narrator persists in relating the minor victories she achieves in her battle to assert herself against more dominant personalities. The truth, however, is that the new cook, as much as the guests in her hotel, or her dead mother, will do with her as he desires: "Er öffnet seine Hose und greift nach meiner Hand. Das habe ich nicht erwartet."[85]

Jenny Erpenbeck's novel *Geschichte vom alten Kind* (1999) or her collection of short narratives *Tand* (2001) might also be adduced as examples of the simultaneity of techniques and themes associated with Literary Modernism and an emphasis on readability. In the short story "Im Halbschatten meines Schädels," then, a girl is kept locked away in her room, attended only by the wife of her lover, the man who visits her in order to abuse her. His insistence that she remember the humiliations he inflicts on her can be resisted only by means of the surreal fantasies playing in her head. Here, the debris of her subjectivity feature as "Meeresstaub und Fetzen von Algen, Holz und abgestorbene Schalen" swirling around her head eventually to be flushed out in an act of self-purification: "dann kommt die Flut und trägt es wieder hinaus, an den Tag."[86] A predilection for such bizarre, yet highly allusive imagery, suggesting the flight of female subjectivity into fantasy as a means of self-conservation, recalls the work of fellow east German writer Monika Maron, in particular her *Die Überläuferin* (1986), in which Rosalind revisualizes the world in accordance with her own idiosyncratic perspective, or her *Animal Triste* (1996). This novel tells of its self-confined narrator's dreamlike rearrangement of time and place as she rewrites the memory of her (possible) desertion by her lover "vor vierzig oder fünfzig Jahren."[87] There may also be echoes of the *west* German writer Felicitas Hoppe. Erpenbeck's "Tand," in which a girl relates how her grandmother, a *Sprechmeisterin*, performs her texts until she is too old to ventriloquize the woman's role expected of her,[88] hence brings to mind Hoppe's story "Die Handlanger" (1996). In this text, a woman wanders around a local park allowing various men to seduce her, but finds that each of them soon tires of her stories. This, in fact, was the difficulty her lover had had with her propensity, as a writer, to speak of the imperfect intimacy existing between men and women: "Natürlich neigt der

Schriebende zur Rechthaberei, weshalb mein Geliebter nicht mehr Hand an mich legen will und mich zwingt, ohne Gartenschere unter einem Busch zu liegen." Determined not to become lost in the undergrowth, she finally finds a man to direct her — literally: "Ich will von nun an mein Leben an der Seite des Dirigenten unseres Kurparkorchesters verbringen."[89]

German Literature and "Normalization"

These references to the work of Duve, Naters, Hermann, Franck, Erpenbeck, Maron, and Hoppe have brought us a long way from our initial discussions. Yet an analysis of these figures alongside our assessment of the work of older colleagues such as Delius illuminates some of the key features of German fiction into the new millennium. First, by the mid-1990s, writers were engaging not only with impact of unification but also with the accelerating globalization of an American-style consumer culture. In chapters two and three, then, we look at the manner in which authors from the ex-GDR and the "old" FRG, respectively, deal with the social, political, and economic transformation initially of the newly united Germany and then of the Berlin Republic. This relates, above all, to the way they look back to their experiences of the two former German states in order to challenge the "ahistorical normality" of the present.

Second, the attenuation in the importance of Nazism in the work of young writers in particular is noteworthy. The narrator of Franck's *Der Liebediener,* for example, feels "Entsetzen" when she travels to Ravensbrück concentration camp, but this is relativized by her insight that she has exploited the visit for her own purposes: "ich hatte Ravensbrück mißbraucht (gebraucht?), um mir die Lächerlichkeit meines Verdachts gegen Albert deutlich zu machen."[90] Likewise, Vera, the narrator of Tanja Dücker's story "Lakritz (Warzawa)" (2001), is unsure how to respond when she visits the place from which members of her family were deported: "Ich versuchte, an meine Tante zu denken und traurig zu sein."[91] In Erpenbeck's *Geschichte vom alten Kind,* an account of the British Airforce's February 1945 fire-bombing of Dresden is relevant only insofar as it prompts the novel's withdrawn young protagonist to work through the abuse she has suffered at the hands of her mother.[92] Indeed, this apparent inability to perceive the Nazi past other than in relation to oneself points to a key shift in the ideological, moral, and political context of the 1990s, and in particular to a new skepticism regarding the moral fervor of the generation of '68, the former student radicals now at the head of the Berlin Republic. In chapter four, this challenge to the "politically correct" reiteration of German guilt is examined in more detail with special reference to older writers such as Bernhard Schink and Martin Walser and to concepts of "latitudinal normality" and "longitudinal normality." Chapter five, on the other hand, focuses on the interest in the late 1990s in "German wartime suffering."

In Elke Naters's *Lügen,* the narrator listens to a cassette tape "mit jüdischen Gesängen oder so was ähnlichem." The reference to "Ethnozeug" (*LG,* 78) that follows is clearly provocative — a challenge to "political correctness" as much as an allusion to the new "fashionability" of ethnic minorities — and yet it also serves to illustrate a third characteristic of contemporary German literature: that the relationship between Germans and Jews is vital to any understanding of the "normality" of the modern-day Germany. As such, our discussions in chapters four and five of the way the Nazi past has been reevaluated by figures ranging from Martin Walser and Günter Grass to Bernhard Schlink, a newcomer who has questioned the certainties of his own "68er" cohort, to the younger author Marcel Beyer, lead directly into a chapter on recent literary representations of German attitudes to Jews and of Jewish fates.

A fourth characteristic of recent German writing is its concern with the notion of provinciality: Julia Franck, Elke Naters, Judith Hermann, and others of this generation portray lives lived on the periphery — even when the location is Berlin — and infused with a sense of their own mediocrity. Frank Schirrmacher, of course, as discussed at the beginning of this chapter, had already insinuated in his essay of 1989, "Idyllen in der Wüste oder Das Versagen vor der Metropole," that West Germany, as it was then, was itself also balefully provincial: complacent, unambitious, imitative, and unwilling to assert itself. In the course of the 1990s, this provinciality would be regarded by some authors with a degree of nostalgia — these writers are examined in our chapter on literature in the west. More substantively, our final chapter looks at the way the ongoing search for a definable national identity within the global consumer culture led authors such as Botho Strauß and Arnold Stadler (the latter with a good deal more irony) to look to the province — as in the nineteenth century — as a place in which "authentic" German traditions might be found. Their search for a "longitudinal normality" is contrasted with Hans-Ulrich Treichel's investigation of the possibility of a "latitudinal normality" in which Germany would become part of a global metropolitan culture. Towards the close of this chapter, we return to younger writers such as Hermann and Tanja Dückers and focus on their responses to the campaign to reinvent Berlin as a "global" city. An analysis of Georg Klein's *Libidissi* (1998) and its relevance to the notion of "normality" itself rounds off the volume.

In the discussions that follow, we look at literary developments from the early 1990s until the end of the decade and beyond. Throughout, four themes dominate: the consequences of unification on both east *and* west Germany, the impact of economic globalization, the continued importance of the Nazi past, and, finally, the attempt to define an identity which is characterized neither by a smothering provinciality nor by the hegemonic "sameness" of the global consumer culture. These are the issues currently informing debates on the new German "normality."

Notes

[1] See Ulrich Greiner, "Mangel an Feingefühl," *Die Zeit*, 1 June 1990. This essay and other contributions to what came to be known as the *Literaturstreit* are collated in Thomas Anz, ed., *"Es geht nicht nur um Christa Wolf." Der Literaturstreit im vereinten Deutschland* (Munich: Spangenberg, 1991).

[2] Frank Schirrmacher, "Dem Druck des härteren, strengeren Lebens standhalten," *Frankfurter Allgemeine Zeitung*, 2 February 1990. Also in Thomas Anz, *"Es geht nicht nur . . . ,"* 77–89.

[3] Frank Schirrmacher, "Abschied von der Literatur der Bundesrepublik," *Frankfurter Allgemeine Zeitung*, 2 October 1990, L1, 2.

[4] Ulrich Greiner, "Die deutsche Gesinnungsästhetik," *Die Zeit*, 9 November 1990. In Thomas Anz, *"Es geht nicht nur . . . ,"* 208–16. Hereafter *DDG*.

[5] Michael Stürmer, "Geschichte in geschichtslosem Land," in *"Historikerstreit": Die Dokumentation der Kontroverse um die Einzigartigkeit der nationalsozialistischen Judenvernichtung* (Munich and Zurich: Piper, 1987), 36–38, here 37.

[6] Stephen Brockmann, "The Politics of German Literature," *Monatshefte* 84:1 (1992): 46–58, here 54.

[7] See Charles Maier, *The Unmasterable Past* (Cambridge, MA: Harvard UP, 1988); Richard Evans, *In Hitler's Shadow* (New York: Pantheon, 1989); and the special issue of *New German Critique* 44 (1998).

[8] Andreas Huyssen, "After the Wall: The Failure of German Intellectuals," *New German Critique* 52 (1991): 109–43, here 117.

[9] Peter Schneider, "Man kann sogar ein Erdbeben verpassen," in Peter Schneider, *Extreme Mittellage: Eine Reise durch das deutsche Nationalgefühl* (Reinbek: Rowohlt, 1990), 54–78, here 64.

[10] Frank Schirrmacher, "Idyllen in der Wüste oder Das Versagen vor der Metropole," *Frankfurter Allgemeine Zeitung*, 10 October 1989, cited in Andrea Köhler and Rainer Moritz, eds., *Maulhelden*, 15–27, here 23. Hereafter *I*.

[11] Wolfram Schütte, "Leservergnügen: Den Sorgen lektorierender Hausväter entsprungen," in *Frankfurter Rundschau*, 29 July 1992; reprinted in Franz Josef Görtz, Volker Hage, Uwe Wittstock, eds., *Deutsche Literatur 1993* (Stuttgart: Reclam, 1994), 325–28, here 328.

[12] Karl Heinz Bohrer, "Erinnerung an Kriterien. Vom Warten auf den deutschen Zeitroman," in *Merkur* 49 (1995); reprinted in Andreas Köhler and Rainer Moritz, eds., *Maulhelden*, 137–50, here 137.

[13] Jan-Werner Müller, "Karl Heinz Bohrer on German National Identity: Recovering Romanticism and Aestheticizing the State," *German Studies Review* 23:2 (2000): 297–316, here 297.

[14] Andreas Huyssen, "After the Wall," 138–42.

[15] Jochen Vogt, "Langer Abschied von der Nachkriegsliteratur," in Karl Deiritz and Hannes Krauss, eds., *Der deutsch-deutsche Literaturstreit oder "Freunde, es spricht sich schlecht mit gebundener Zunge"* (Hamburg: Luchterhand, 1991), 53–68, here 62.

[16] Karl Heinz Bohrer, "Die permanente Theodizee," *Merkur* 41 (1987): 267–86, here 274.

[17] Karl Heinz Bohrer, "Warum wir keine Nation sind. Warum wir eine werden wollen," *Frankfurter Allgemeine Zeitung*, 13 January 1990, *Bilder und Zeiten*, 1–4, here 1.

[18] Karl Heinz Bohrer, "Seit '45 ohne Metropole," in Karl Heinz Bohrer, *Provinzialismus* (Munich: Carl Hanser, 2000), 81–98, 81.

[19] Karl Heinz Bohrer, "Nationale Nachgedanken zur Wehrmachtsausstellung," in *Provinzialismus*, 142–49, here 144. See also "Verlust an historischem Gedächtnis," in *Provinzialismus*, 150–63.

[20] Karl Heinz Bohrer, "Provinzialismus." *Merkur* 44 (1990): 1096–1102; 45 (1991): 255–66, 358–56, 719–27; 46 (1992): 89–90.

[21] Jan-Werner Müller, "Karl Heinz Bohrer," 306.

[22] Stephen Brockmann, *Literature and German Unification* (Cambridge: Cambridge UP, 1999), 120.

[23] Maxim Biller, "Soviel Sinnlichkeit wie der Stadtplan von Kiel," in *Die weltworte* 64, 25 July 1991, reprinted in Andrea Köhler and Rainer Moritz, eds., *Maulhelden und Königskinder: Zur Debatte über die deutschsprachige Gegenwartsliteratur*. Leipzig: Reclam Verlag, 1998), 62–71. Hereafter *SV*.

[24] Mattis Manzel, *Peinlich* (Zurich: Ammann, 1995), 41.

[25] Matthias Altenburg, "Kampf den Flaneuren. Über Deutschlands junge, lahme Dichter," in *Der Spiegel*, 12, October 1992; reprinted in Andreas Köhler and Rainer Moritz, eds., *Maulhelden*, 72–85, 73 and 72.

[26] Matthias Altenburg, "Kampf den Flaneuren," 75.

[27] Matthias Altenburg, "Generation Nix." In Matthias Altenburg, *Irgendwie alles Sex* (Cologne: Kiepenheuer & Witsch, 2001), 122–24, here 123.

[28] Matthias Altenburg, *Landschaft mit Wölfen* (Cologne: Kiepenheuer & Witsch, 1997), 22.

[29] Matthias Politycki, "Endlich aufgetaucht: Die 78er Generation," in Matthias Politycki, *Die Farbe der Vokale* (Munich: Luchterhand, 1998), 19–22, here 19.

[30] Matthias Politycki, "Das Gequake von satten Fröschen. Die Generation der Vierzigjährigen und ihre Angst vor Verantwortung," in *Die Farbe der Vokale*, 13–18, 15–16.

[31] Matthias Politycki, "Das Gequake," 17.

[32] Martin Hielscher, "Literatur in Deutschland — Avantgarde und pädagogischer Purismus," in Andrea Köhler and Rainer Moritz, eds., *Maulhelden*, 151–55, here 151.

[33] Uwe Wittstock, *Leselust. Wie unterhaltsam ist die neue deutsche Literatur? Ein Essay* (Munich: Luchterhand, 1995), 8 and 10. Hereafter *LE*.

[34] Leslie Fiedler, "cross the border, close the gap," *Playboy*, December 1969, 230; in German as "Das Neue Zeitalter der neuen Literatur," *Christ und Welt*, 13 and 20 September 1968.

[35] Jürgen Habermas, "Die Moderne — ein unvollendetes Projekt," in Jürgen Habermas, *Kleine politische Schriften I-IV* (Frankfurt a.M.: Suhrkamp, 1981), 444–64.

[36] Martin Hielscher, "Literatur in Deutschland," 156. Hereafter *LD*.

[37] F. C. Delius, *Der Königsmacher* (Berlin: Rowohlt, 2001), 80. Hereafter *DK*.

[38] Thomas Kraft, "Einleitung," in Thomas Kraft, ed., *aufgerissen: Zur Literatur der 90er* (Munich: Piper, 2000), 11–22, here 13.

[39] Matthias Politycki, "Das Medium ist die Massage," *die tageszeitung*, 25 May 2000, Kultur, 13–14, here 13.

[40] Kathrin Röggla, "unsere gesamtgesundheit," *Akzente* 3 (2001): 59.

[41] Ulrich Greiner, "Der Betrieb tanzt: Über Literatur und Öffentlichkeit," *neue deutsche literatur* 520:4 (1998): 159–69, here 166.

[42] Jochen Hörisch, "Verdienst und Vergehen der Gegenwartsliteratur," in Christian Döring, ed., *Deutsche Gegenwartsliteratur: Wider ihre Verächter* (Frankfurt a.M.: Suhrkamp, 1995), 30–48, here 45.

[43] Günter Grass, "Der lernende Lehrer," in Günter Grass, *Für und Widerworte* (Göttingen: Seidl, 1999), 7–35, here 23 and 22.

[44] Helmut Krausser, *Tagebuch des Oktober 1997. Tagebuch des November 1998. Tagebuch des Dezember 1999* (Reinbek: rororo, 2000), 17.

[45] Martin Walser, *Tod eines Kritikers* (Frankfurt a.M.: Suhrkamp, 2002), 202–3.

[46] Matthias Zschokke, *Der dicke Dichter* (Cologne: Bruckner & Thünker Verlag, 1995), 128.

[47] Joachim Lottmann, *Deutsche Einheit* (Zurich: Haffmans Verlag, 1999), 39.

[48] Thomas Kraft, "Einleitung," 13.

[49] Rose Bartmer, "Die Debütanten und der Markt," *Sprache im technischen Zeitalter* 162 (2002): 193–205, here 198.

[50] Matthias Politycki, "Das Medium ist die Massage," 13.

[51] See Brian Ladd, *The Ghosts of Berlin* (Chicago: U of Chicago P, 1997), 47–70.

[52] Janet Stewart, "*Das Kunsthaus Tacheles:* The Berlin Architecture Debate of the 1990s in Micro-Historical Context," in Stuart Taberner and Frank Finlay, eds., *Recasting German Identity* (Rochester: Camden House, 2002), 53–68, here 55.

[53] Birgit Vanderbeke, *Abgehängt* (Frankfurt a.M.: Fischer Verlag, 2001), 96.

[54] Volker Hage, "Zeitalter der Bruchstücke," in Andrea Köhler and Rainer Moritz, eds., *Maulhelden*, 28–41, here 30.

[55] Bodo Kirchhoff, "Das Schreiben: ein Sturz. In der Wüste des Banalen — zur Lage des Schriftstellers in glücklicher Zeit," in *Die Zeit*, 6 November 1992; reprinted in Franz Josef Görtz, Volker Hage, Uwe Wittstock, eds., *Deutsche Literatur 1992* (Stuttgart: Reclam, 1993), 295–306, here 299.

[56] Volker Hage, "Die neuen deutschen Dichter," *Der Spiegel* 11, October 1999, 244–58, here 245.

[57] Maxim Biller, "Feige das Land, schlapp die Literatur: Über die Schwierigkeiten beim Sagen der Wahrheit," *Die Zeit*, 13 April 2000, 47–49, here 47 and 49.

[58] Matthias Politycki, "Kalbfleisch mit Reis! Die literarische Ästhetik der 78er Generation," in *Die Farbe der Vokale*, 23–44, 30 and 37.

[59] Matthias Politycki, "Der amerikanische Holzweg," *Frankfurter Rundschau*, 18 March 2000, *Zeit und Bild*, 2.

[60] Matthias Politycki, "Kalbfleisch mit Reis!," 39.

[61] Matthias Politycki, "Kalbfleisch mit Reis!," 40.

[62] Volker Hage, "Literarisches Fräuleinwunder," *Der Spiegel*, 22 March 1999, 7.

[63] Jan Koneffke, "Der Traum von der Nationalliteratur," *Wespennest* 115 (1999): 61–65, here 64.

[64] Martin Walser, *Tod eines Kritikers*, 112.

[65] Peter Graves, "Karen Duve, Kathrin Schmidt, Judith Hermann: 'Ein literarisches Fräuleinwunder,'" *German Life and Letters* 55:2 (2002): 196–207, here 198.

[66] Karen Duve, "Keine Ahnung," in Karen Duve, *Keine Ahnung* (Frankfurt a.M.: Suhrkamp, 1999), 7.

[67] Elke Naters, *Königinnen* (Cologne: Kiepenheuer & Witsch, 1998), 8.

[68] Elke Naters, *Lügen* (Cologne: Kiepenheuer & Witsch, 1999), 51. Hereafter *LG*.

[69] Andrew Plowman, "'Was will ich denn als Westdeutscher erzählen?': The 'old' West and Globalisation in Recent German Prose," in Stuart Taberner, ed., *German Literature in the Age of Globalisation* (Birmingham: Birmingham UP, 2004), 47–66, here 49.

[70] Karen Duve, *Dies ist kein Liebeslied* (Frankfurt a.M.: Eichborn, 2002), 163.

[71] Andrew Plowman, "'Was will ich denn als Westdeutscher erzählen?,'" 58.

[72] Judith Hermann, "Ruth (Freundinnen)," in Judith Hermann, *Nichts als Gespenster* (Frankfurt a.M.: Fischer, 2003), 11–59, here 15. Hereafter *R*.

[73] See, for example, Judith Hermann, "On Carver: Ein Versuch," *Transatlantik* 3 (October) 2001: 4–5, and her introduction to the German-language edition of Carver's *Cathedrals* (2001).

[74] Judith Hermann, "Nichts als Gespenster," in *Nichts als Gespenster*, 195–232, here 205. Hereafter *NG*.

[75] Beth Linklater, in her reading of this narrative and short stories by Hermann, Franck, Erpenbeck, Dückers, and Katrin Dorn, argues that Germany functions as "background" rather than as the primary concern of the texts. See Beth Linklater, "Germany and Background: Global Concerns in Recent Women's Writing in German," in Stuart Taberner, ed., *German Literature*, 67–88.

[76] Judith Hermann, "Camera Obscura." in Judith Hermann, *Sommerhaus, später* (Frankfurt a.M.: Fischer, 1999 [1998]), 157–65, here 158.

[77] Judith Hermann, "Hurrikan (Something farewell)," in *Sommerhaus, später*, 31–54, here 44.

[78] Judith Hermann, "Rote Korallen," in *Sommerhaus, später*, 11–29, here 11. Hereafter *RK*.

[79] Uwe Wittstock, "Das Gebot mit dem Freund der Freundin zu schlafen," *Die Welt*, 26 November 2001, 29.

[80] Horst Spittler, "Die Dichter der 'Generation Golf,'" *literatur für leser* 25:3 (2002): 189–96, here 190.

[81] See Thomas Ernst, "German Pop Literature als Moment kultureller and Cultural Globalization," in Stuart Taberner, ed., *German Literature*, 169–88.

[82] Julia Franck, "Bäuchlings," in Julia Franck, *Bauchlandung. Geschichten zum Anfassen* (Cologne: Dumont, 2000), 7–16, here 14.

[83] Julia Franck, "Strandbad," in *Bauchlandung*, 37–49.

[84] Julia Franck, "Mir nichts, dir nichts," in *Bauchlandung*, 95–111, here 99.

[85] Julia Franck, *Der neue Koch* (Zurich: Ammann, 1997), 24.

[86] Jenny Erpenbeck, "Im Halbschatten meines Schädels," in Jenny Erpenbeck, *Tand* (Frankfurt a.M.: Eichborn Verlag, 2001), 7–13, here 11.

[87] Monika Maron, *Animal Triste* (Frankfurt a.M.: Fischer, 1996), 17.

[88] Jenny Erpenbeck, "Tand," in *Tand*, 31–45.

[89] Felicitas Hoppe, *Picknick der Friseure* (Reinbek bei Hamburg: Rowohlt Verlag, 1998 [1996]), 7–9, here 7 and 8.

[90] Julia Franck, *Liebediener* (Cologne: Dumont, 1999), 181.

[91] Tanja Dückers, "Lakritz (Warzawa)," in Christine Eichel, ed., *Es liegt mir auf der Zunge* (Munich: Goldmann, 2002), 227–49, here 244.

[92] Jenny Erpenbeck, *Geschichte vom alten Kind* (Berlin: Eichborn, 1999), 85.

2: Literature in the East

In der DDR war alles merkwürdig,
die Zeitungen, das Fernsehen und
die meisten Bücher.
— Falko Hennig, *Alles nur geklaut*

I N AN INFLUENTIAL ESSAY of October 1997, "Der Herbst des Quatschocento. Immer noch, jetzt erst recht, gibt es zwei deutsche Literaturen: selbstverliebter Realismus im Westen, tragischer Expressionismus im Osten," first published in *Die Zeit,* resident critic Iris Radisch pointed to the difference between fiction from the east of the now united Germany and that from the west: "Der Osten ist tragisch, der Westen lustig." In the east of the Republic, writers were prone to draw on the "metaphysischen Traditionen der deutschen Geistesgeschichte"; in the west, they were more likely to imitate an "amerikanischen Pragmatismus."[1] Radisch describes Matthias Politycki's *Weiberroman* (1997), for instance, as deliberately banal in its focus on the fashions of the 1980s in the "old" West Germany, as "nostalgisch, ein wenig ironisch und minimal gedrechselt" and, she concludes, "von unschlagbarer Diesseitigkeit" (*DHQ,* 183). *Hundsnächte* (1997) by east German writer Reinhard Jirgl, in contrast, is commended as a "gelaufenes, kreischendes, psalmodierendes, blutiges, unerträgliches, aggressives, faszinierendes, wütendes, obsessives und intelligentes Buch" (*DHQ,* 186). Set in the deathstrip along the now defunct inner-German border, this novel tells of the encounter between an engineer sent to convert the former no-man's-land into a bicycle path and an *Untoten,* the zombie lawyer and exile from East Germany — now turned writer — metaphorically trapped in the desolate landscape between the ideals of the GDR and the depressing reality of the post-1990 Federal Republic.

In a subsequent article written in the year 2000, "Zwei getrennte Literaturgebiete," Radisch was more wide-ranging in her criticism of the kind of fiction that appeared to have been encouraged by the appeals in the early 1990s for a greater emphasis on "entertainment," a "new readability," and an "Anglo-American" readiness to mix high and low culture without inhibition. Hence she spoke of a "minimierten Kunstanspruch," "abgeklärten Lifestyle-Realismus" and "Konsumfetischismus"[2] and dismissed a "western" "Literatur der reinen Immanenz," omnipresent in two versions: "Sie hat sich häuslich oder postmodern soundtrackmäßig eingerichtet an der Oberfläche der Erscheinungen und Diskurse" (*ZG*, 25). Summing up the first half of the 1990s, and hinting at what was to follow, Radisch saw "Ironie, Indifferenz und Konsum" in the west and, in the east, "Ideale, Ernst und Seele" (*ZG*, 17).

Radisch's portrayal of German literature in the 1990s, she concedes, is simply "der vergröberte Schattenriss der neuen deutschen Selbstbilder" (*ZG*, 17). Her stock-taking is useful, however, insofar as it acts as a corrective to our focus in the preceding chapter on the debates of the early 1990s — almost exclusively a *west* German discourse — and on the literary market as the key determinants of post-unification fiction. In this chapter, we complicate Radisch's positing of an eastern partiality for more "serious" forms and themes, examine the phenomenon of *Ostalgie* and look at the manner in which, from the late 1990s onwards, younger authors begin to inflect an increasingly homogenized German "normality" with a specifically *east* German sensibility.

East German Writing after Unification

The impact of unification on the older generation of eastern writers and intellectuals has routinely been summed up by reviewers with reference to Volker Braun's "Das Eigentum," the poem seen by Wolfgang Emmerich as "der vielleicht signifikanteste Text der Wendezeit."[3] Nonetheless, it is worth reproducing this again in full:

> Da bin ich noch: mein Land geht in den Westen.
> KRIEG DEN HÜTTEN FRIEDE DEN PALÄSTEN.
> Ich selber habe ihm den Tritt versetzt.
> Es wirft sich weg und seine magre Zierde.
> Dem Winter folgt der Sommer der Begierde.
> Und ich kann *bleiben wo der Pfeffer wächst.*
> Und unverständlich wird mein ganzer Text.
> Was ich niemals besaß, wird mir entrissen.
> Was ich nicht lebte, werd ich ewig missen.
> Die Hoffnung lag im Weg wie eine Falle.
> Mein Eigentum, jetzt habt ihrs auf der Kralle.
> Wann sag ich wieder *mein* und meine alle?[4]

The country Braun's generation had helped build has "gone west," to use an apt English idiom, wealth and power has won out, past achievements — admittedly meager — have been sacrificed, and the hopes of a true socialism in which whatever belongs to one belongs to all have been delivered up to clawing greed. The writer's life work, as a consequence,

now seems incomprehensible. His dissidence, intended to *improve* socialism, contributed to its dissolution. He is condemned to utter irrelevance
and to miss that which he never had: the GDR's *potential* to realize his
dreams.[5]

Braun's poem alludes to the sense of alienation and redundancy that
many east German writers felt in the aftermath of unification, and more
particularly in the wake of their realization that they had been hopelessly
out-of-touch with the aspirations of the broader population in the late
autumn of 1989. Christoph Hein, Christa Wolf, and Stefan Heym, for
example, had spoken out for a reformed socialism at the massive demonstration at Alexanderplatz on 4 November; on 26 November, Heym and
Wolf joined Volker Braun as the initiators of the proclamation "Für unser
Land" urging that the independence and values of the GDR be preserved.
A few months later, however, on 18 March 1990, their fellow citizens, for
the most part heartily disillusioned with GDR socialism, would vote in
their first free elections for political parties to take them into a united
Germany. East German writers had not only witnessed the brutal discrediting of their utopian hopes, they were also forced to ask themselves
whether they had been naïve in their conviction that they had acted on
behalf of their compatriots in their endeavors, by means of literary allusion and judicious censure, to nudge the GDR towards the realization of
its own ideals. Thus Heiner Müller in a poem written in late 1989,
"SELBSTKRITIK":

> Auf dem Bildschirm sehe ich meine Landsleute
> Mit Händen und Füßen abstimmen gegen die Wahrheit
> Die vor vierzig Jahren mein Besitz war
> Welches Grab schützt mich vor meiner Jugend?[6]

Müller would later have to endure criticism directed against him as a result of the revelations that a number of writers had colluded with the
Stasi, the state security services. Indeed, Müller was amongst those
prominent East German intellectuals who had engaged in "dialogue"
with *Stasi* agents, in order, he claimed, to debate conditions in the GDR
with the only institution with effective lines of communication to those in
power.[7] Christa Wolf — who had had a short-lived association with the
Stasi some decades prior to unification — Monika Maron and Fritz Rudolf Fries were also implicated. Most notoriously, Sascha Anderson, a key
figure in the "alternative" East German literary landscape was renamed
"Sascha Arschloch" by Wolf Biermann in his 1991 Büchner Prize speech
for his collaboration with the *Stasi* even after he had relocated to the FRG
in 1986; Anderson's autobiographical text *Sascha Anderson,* published
eleven years later in 2002, responds to such accusations with a postmod-

ern indifference to questions of individual responsibility. Rainer Schedlinski, like Anderson part of the "Prenzlauer Berg scene" (the loose grouping of younger, "alternative" artists and intellectuals, many of whom lived in this area of East Berlin), first ascribed his cooperation to personal weakness then later insisted, like Müller, that this was the only way of engaging with the state.[8]

A sense of despondency can be detected in a range of works by eastern writers in the years immediately following unification. In many cases, despair at the collapse of utopian ideals — if not at the collapse of the GDR itself — is mixed with discontent over the new, enlarged Federal Republic. Thomas Rosenlöcher's diaries entries from the period in early September 1989 to March 1990, collated in *Die verkauften Pflastersteine* (1990), for example, combine self-criticism — "Mitschuld, meine, am So-Sein der derzeitigen Verhältnisse" — and, by implication, criticism of a "passive" GDR population, with uncertainty about what will come next: "Andererseits ist der jetzige Kapitalismus eben auch ein Übel."[9] A second text, *Die Wiederentdeckung des Gehens beim Wandern* (1991), satirizes the alacrity with which some confronted the past in order, "so, mit erneueuertem Selbstwertgefühl," to adapt all the more quickly to the new system: "soviel zur Bewältigungsfrage";[10] his *Ostgezeter* (1997) contains the same mix of melancholia and anger at a population which, before and after 1990, had proved to be "entsetzlich nickensfähig."[11] Helga Königsdorf's *Gleich neben Afrika* (1992), in which the narrator takes refuge on an island off the coast of Africa, similarly speaks of previous loyalty to the communist party, of the arrival of the "free market" in the former GDR, and of its protagonist's sense that she is now "unbehaust" and bewildered.[12] In *Im Schatten des Regenbogens* (1993), Königsdorf continues in much the same manner with a depiction of the dismantling of the East German intelligentsia after 1990. *Die Entsorgung der Großmutter* (1997), on the other hand, portrays with bitter irony the breakdown of a family unable to afford the costs of caring for a grandmother afflicted by Alzheimer's disease in the new Germany.

Indeed, what Wolfgang Emmerich has referred to as a "*Furor melancholicus*" is present in texts as diverse as Jirgl's *Abschied von den Feinden* (1995), in which a train comes to a standstill on the old border between two Germanys whereupon a man steps out to reflect on this no-man's-land, his memories of his mother being dragged off by the uncouth warders of an East German psychiatric institute, and his estranged brother,[13] and Wolfgang Hilbig's *Alte Abdeckerei* (1991), <<*Ich*>> (1993), or *Die Kunde von den Bäumen* (1994). Hilbig's novels attack the pervasiveness of state surveillance, the GDR's environmental record and its humiliation of its citizens, as much as the passivity of those who lived "in der Anpassung"[14] and the intellectuals who imagined that they could lead the masses — this was a writer who had had little faith in the ability of GDR socialism to reform itself. More concretely, <<*Ich*>> is a continuation of the post-unification wave of *Stasi*-novels beginning with Reiner Kunze's *Deckname Lyrik* (1990), Erich Loest's *Der Zorn des Schafes* (1990) and Uwe Saeger's *Die Nacht danach und der Morgen* (1991).[15] In the texts by Kunze and Loest, the writer-figure records his observation by the *Stasi;* in Saeger's novel, the *Stasi*'s fictionalization of the routines of those it monitors is paralleled with the protagonist's activities as an author. This idea is extended in <<*Ich*>>. Here, however, the focus is on the dissolution of the protagonist's sense of self as he becomes increasingly unable to separate what he reports for the security services from his own endeavors to write "real" fiction.[16]

What came after the collapse of the GDR, however, appears to be little better. Hilbig's *Das Provisorium* (2000), for instance, casts back to the Federal Republic just before unification and foreshadows the total commodification of culture in post-1990 Germany in the absence of any socialist alternative: "*shopping macht frei*" (the reference to the slogan *Arbeit macht frei* on the gates of Auschwitz draws a chilling parallel between fascism and capitalism).[17] Volker Braun's *Der Wendehals* (1995) and *Das Nichtgelebte* (1995), on the other hand, expose the alacrity with which many rewrote their biographies after 1990 to insinuate opposition to the communist state; at the same time, they critique capitalism. The same is true of Angela Krauß's *Die Überfliegerin* (1995), described by Emmerich as "melancholiedurchtränkt," which depicts its protagonist's travels to America and Russia without, Emmerich suggests, ever relinquishing its fixation "auf die neue Geldgesellschaft."[18] Christoph Hein's *Willenbrock* (2000), whilst far less nostalgic — the protagonist demonstrates little affection for those who once denounced him to the *Stasi* — likewise sees little improvement in the post-1990 present. Initially enamored of the new capitalist order, in which he can make a steady profit on his sales of second-hand cars to the Russian mafia and thereby impress the women he seeks to seduce, Willenbrock becomes increasingly paranoid after he is assaulted by intruders at his country home. Finally, he comes to believe that the self-evident ills of the GDR have simply been supplemented by violence, racism, and anarchy: "'Ich habe Typen wie dich satt. Die einen denunzieren mich, die anderen bestehlen mich oder wollen mich totschlagen.'"[19] In the new Germany, all that counts is money, connections, and the right kind of "protection." Willenbrock takes the gun that his mafia partner procures for him, becomes increasingly dependent on the sense of security it offers and ultimately shoots a man attempting to burglarize his home. In his *Napoleonspiel* (1993), in which a murderer justifies his crime by situating it as an elaborate game in a world without morality, Hein had already hinted at the dissolution of all values in a society in which people are driven largely by self-interest. In Bernd Wagner's *Paradies* (1998), similarly, Judith Mehlhorn — no admirer of the GDR in which she was pumped full of drugs in order to improve her performance as an athlete — discovers nothing but racial discrimination and social inequality in the west.

The disintegration of the GDR was followed by a number of autobiographies by writers of an older generation that had come to the east after the war in order to build socialism. Most notable were Hermann Kant's 1991 *Abspann,* a justification of his loyalty to the regime, to be followed by the novels *Kormoran* (1994) and *Escape. Ein WORD-Spiel* (1995), and Günter de Bruyn's *Zwischenbilanz: Eine Jugend in Berlin* (1992), which covered his youth in the capital up until just after the war, and *Vierzig Jahre* (1996), dealing with his life in the GDR, and particularly key dates such as the workers' uprising of 1953, the building of the Wall in 1961, the expulsion of Wolf Biermann in 1976 and the fall of the GDR.[20] Younger writers too were keen to depict their experience of the state into which they had been born, in their case in fictional rather than overtly autobiographical form. Christoph Brumme's *Nichts als das* (1994), for example, recounts the narrator's disagreements with his father, a man embittered by the loss of his father in Stalingrad and silently hostile to the communist authorities, his own indoctrination at school, and the consequent split between public and private selves. His is a childhood that takes place in a village near the German-German border called Elend, a word as apt in its now obsolete meaning as in its more modern usage: "das war altes Deutsch und hieß: in der Fremde, im Ausland."[21] Kurt Drawert's *Spiegelland* (1992), which relates in the form of an extended prose essay its protagonist's sense of existing in a biographical no-man's-land, as much as Kerstin Hensel's *Im Schlauch* (1993), draws on an established East German tradition of the *Vaterbuch*. Like Volker Braun's *Unvollendete Geschichte* (1975 in the journal *Sinn und Form,* then 1988 in book form), Hensel's short narrative, accordingly, tells of a daughter's rebellion against her father and, through him, against the state. Yet her adolescent revolt goes almost entirely unnoticed: "Keiner sucht sie."[22] In Hensel's *Tanz am Kanal* (1994), the exploitation continues even after unification. Raped and abused, and recruited by the *Stasi* to spy on a circle of poets, the young Gabriela von Haßlau ends up sleeping under a bridge after the fall of the Wall and begins to write her life's story, shifting as she does so between fantasy and reality. In a hint as to what will pass in the years after 1990, she presents her manuscript to two west German journalists working for a women's magazine only to discover that her biography can be all too quickly commodified for a western audience mesmerized by sensationalist images of the former GDR: "um Gottes willen, schauen Sie, wie Sie immer schauen: gekränkt, geknickt, gefoltert."[23] At the same time, it may be that her entire narrative intentionally colludes in this presentation of the east German woman as victim.[24]

Just how bad *was* the GDR? In the early 1990s, various attempts were made, largely by conservative historians, to revive the "totalitarianism" theories of the 1950s and to compare the GDR with Nazism.[25] The results of the parliamentary commission on the *Aufarbeitung von Geschichte und Folgen der SED-Diktatur in Deutschland,* published in late 1995, similarly deplored the East German state as an historical error. In what follows, we look at novels from the end of the 1990s by two very different writers in order to examine the fascination that both the ideals and the actuality of the GDR exert on those struggling to come to terms with *this* German past. We then look at nostalgia for the "old" East, *Ostalgie,* in fiction from the mid-1990s onwards.

Christa Wolf and Monika Maron

Christa Wolf's *Medea. Stimmen* (1996) sets up an opposition between her reworking of the Medea-figure of Greek legend — now acquitted of all the crimes customarily attributed to her, including the killing of her children — and the rulers of Corinth who have emerged victorious in the battle against the kingdom of Colchis. The inhabitants of Colchis, a state on the eastern shore of the Mediterranean, had been "beseelt von unseren uralten Legenden," charmed by the dream of a population living "in Eintracht miteinander" and amongst whom all goods would be "gleichmäßig verteilt."[26] The new order, imposed by the western city of Corinth, on the other hand, is one in which gold is more important than equality. As Georgina Paul argues, this version of the Medea myth communicates a robust impression of the despair Wolf felt in the wake of the GDR's collapse. Her Medea, Paul proposes, is "ein Wunschbild, ein moralisches Ideal, das jetzt nur noch in einen leeren Raum jenseits der Geschichte hineinprojiziert werden kann."[27] She is a fantasy projection of the realization of the socialist project untainted by compromises that, in the event, accompanied the transformation of ideals into deeds, including its inability to advance beyond patriarchy and dogma. As such, it might be argued that *Medea. Stimmen* has less to do with coming-to-terms with the "real" GDR past than with the desire to confront a clearly imperfect post-unification present with a vision of what socialism in the east *could* have been.

Wolf's *Leibhaftig* (2002), alternatively, seems more directly concerned with tackling the GDR past and, in particular, with the necessity of facing up to the reality of at least partial conformity. It is set entirely in the pre-unification period, in the last full year of the GDR, 1988, and tells the story of a woman confined to an East German hospital for a series of operations to remove her appendix. The success of the procedure is inhibited by the dearth of appropriate drugs on the one hand — the woman's doctors are obliged to send a courier to West Berlin to procure what they lack in the GDR — and, on the other, by the failure of her immune system to function properly, if at all. The text opens with a brief description of her condition which, however, most likely serves as much to summarize her state of mind as her physical ailments: "Verletzt. Etwas klagt, wortlos. Ein Ansturm von Worten gegen die Stummheit, die sich beharrlich ausbreitet, zugleich mit der Bewußtlosigkeit."[28]

This short novel, with its clearly autobiographical elements, verbalizes its narrator's need to engage with the hurt she feels as a result of the discrediting of the ideals for which she had fought and her insistence that the history she belonged to must not be silenced. Her confinement to bed within the hospital may inhibit her freedom of movement but — as was so often the case in GDR literature — physical restrictions merely activate the unconscious and mobilize the transformative potential of fantasy. Subsequently, the patient finds herself transported through layer upon layer of German history into the underworld labyrinth of tunnels, interconnected cellars, and wartime air raid shelters running beneath Friedrichstraße. She is accompanied during her descent by Kora, a woman on the hospital staff who, although supposedly ignorant of Greek mythology, participates in her ruminations on the utility of her existence and brings her back from her personal Hades into the realm of the living.

In this post-GDR novel, the narrator's flights of fantasy connote not so much the displaced realization of an otherwise inhibited subjectivity — a motif familiar in Wolf's work from *Nachdenken über Christa T.* (1968) to *Kassandra* (1983) — as a more recent need to confront the accusation, leveled with particular venom during the *Literaturstreit* and on many occasions since, that precisely by displacing criticism into idealism and literary artifice intellectuals such as Wolf compromised with a repressive state. Her voyages through the subterranean history of the GDR, taking her from the border crossing at Friedrichstraße railway station to the *Palast der Republik* at the top of Unter den Linden, hence lead her back to her relationship with Urban, the former friend, who, over the years of the GDR's existence, had come to embody the resolute inflexibility that set the communist leadership against its critics from the cultural intelligentsia. A functionary of the regime determined to enforce compliance, Urban had often countered the narrator's wish for open debate on the state's inadequacies with arguments as persuasive as they were solipsistic. Discipline had to be preserved, he insisted, "um den geordneten Rückzug zu decken. Oder, fragte er, würde sie den ungeordneten Zusammenbruch vorziehen." Trapped between "falschen Alternativen" (*LH*, 183), that is, faced with the choice of either giving up her ideals or of contributing to the collapse of the only ideology that might ever bring about their realization, the narrator had found herself in an increasingly schizophrenic situation. On the one hand, she had lived "in ihrer realen Stadt," a city in which her telephone is tapped by the *Stasi*. Simultaneously, she claims, she had also lived "in einer anderen Hoffnungs- und Menschheitstadt, die ihre eigentliche Heimat war oder sein würde" (*LH*, 136).

To this extent, Wolf's narrative might be considered to offer a strikingly frank insight into the difficulties of avoiding compromise with a state that oppresses its people and yet still seems to offer a unique opportunity for the achievement of true equality and justice at some point in the future. The narrator, a writer, remembers an encounter with a young man and his sister who are angry at her refusal to lend her weight to his protests against official wrongdoing, and asks herself whether her rebuff was really motivated by concern at the negative consequences they would suffer as a result, or by her conviction that there would be little popular support for such dissent, or whether it was cowardice, "Feigheit" (*LH*, 79). Elsewhere, she speaks of the "Häufung alltäglicher und weniger alltäglicher Anlässe" which caused her to lose her faith and provoked the "Dauerschmerz" (*LH*, 136) that she still endures, but intimates that her insight into the inadequacies of the system brought about a retreat into the self rather than action.

Yet even as it appears to submit a *mea culpa* on behalf of its narrator, and, most probably, on behalf of its author — Wolf too underwent a series of operations on her appendix in 1998 — *Leibhaftig* also endeavors to contextualize the choices made by the writer in her dealings with the state. Indeed, the cranes and diggers she pictures along the Friedrichstraße appeared only *after* 1990 as the area was being redeveloped into a commercial center at the heart of what would come to be known as the Berlin Republic. Metaphorically, however, the excavation of this key site exposes the pre-history of the GDR, and in particular the Nazi past against which the communist state would define itself. In descending into the GDR's history, even before the end of the regime, rather than remain fixated on an analysis of its undoubted imperfections in the course of its forty-year existence, the narrator prefigures post-1990 debates on the validity of East Germany's claim to represent a genuine anti-fascism. At the same time, of course, she also justifies the origins of her own backing for the state.

Specifically, the narrator tells of an aunt, now deceased, whom she encounters on the Weidendammer bridge near the Friedrichstraße station and then again, later, in an old air raid shelter in the system of cellars linking her house with those of her neighbors. Motivated to descend into the depths of both time and space by the report she overhears of an infant found murdered, in the present, in just such a cellar, she is relieved to discover her aunt with a baby in her arms. This is the child conceived with the Jewish doctor whom her aunt had refused to renounce despite the Nazi ban on sexual relations between Jews and non-Jews. What makes this passage especially significant is the fact that the child survives and that the family, followed by the narrator, is able to go forward into a new future: "jetzt gehen sie selbdritt vor mir her" (*LH*, 114). From the ruins of Nazism, the GDR would emerge and offer new hope. All the suffering of the past, including, in the narrator's case, the agonies endured during the expulsions from the east in 1945 (*LH*, 100–101), would be redeemed in the socialist state to come.

The narrator's rendition of her unconscious travels beneath Berlin restates the anti-fascist assertions of the GDR and seeks to justify, to some extent, the way many continued to support the state even after it had become obvious that it had reneged on its own promises. Indeed, she goes farther. The horrors of Nazism, it is intimated, were at least followed by the hope of a better future — what follows the discrediting of the GDR's utopian potential, on the other hand, is the destruction of hope itself. Accordingly, her admission that she may have been naïve in the past is relativized by her repeated ruminations on the seemingly endless stream of bad news that makes its way into her unconscious from the outside world:

> daß wieder ein Flugzeug aus allen Himmeln gestürzt oder ein atomgetriebenes U-Boot vor einer nördlichen Küste auf Grund gelaufen ist, daß eine Geisel in einem entfernten Teil der Welt auf der Flucht erschossen wurde, daß also der Lauf der Welt, den jeder Mensch außer ihr anscheinend aushält, weitergegangen ist. (*LH*, 54)

The end of the GDR will be accompanied by an upsurge in human misery, extreme but entirely predictable dangers and random violence — in the present, of course, the infant mentioned in the news is not rescued but murdered. And, it is implied, although it may have been a mistake to trust in the GDR, it would be an even graver error to give up hope itself, for this would be to misunderstand the message communicated in the expressions of the millions of tortured individuals "die sich durch die Geschichte schleppen und die mich aus meinem Innern heraus anblicken." The pain she suffers as a result of the shattering of her ideals is an essential reminder of the need for such ideals in the first instance: "Ich stehe den Leidenden gegenüber. Das schaffe ich nur in Zeiten, in denen ich selbst leide. Der geheime Sinn des Leidens geht mir auf, ich weiß, daß ich ihn wieder vergessen werde" (*LH*, 128). Her faith in the GDR may have been naïve, but it was a necessary illusion, a means of bringing about *some* change in a world full of suffering. The present, it is suggested, lacks all such idealism.

The presence of autobiographical elements is as evident in Monika Maron's fiction as in that of Christa Wolf. Nor should this be surprising given the degree to which the author's own history intersects with the traumas of the German past. Maron is a quarter Jewish, and part of the "progeny" of the GDR, having been raised as the stepdaughter of the SED member and onetime Minister of the Interior, Karl Maron. She was an uncompromising critic of East German politics and society both before and after her move to Hamburg in 1988. More specifically, the relationship between power, patriarchy, and the oppression of women in a state outwardly committed to full equality between the sexes is central to her pre-1990 novels *Flugasche* (1981) and *Die Überläuferin* (1988). In her first post-unification narrative *Stille Zeile Sechs* (1991), on the other hand, the focus is more generally on the injustices, and indeed hypocrisy, of GDR socialism. Set in the mid-1980s, this novel depicts the relationship between Rosalind and Beerenbaum, a retired party member whose life history she is employed to type up. Unable to endure the excuses and evasions of a man whose life biography, as Brigitte Rossbacher notes, "meshes with that of such political personages as Walter Ulbricht, Wilhelm Pieck and [Maron's] own stepfather, Karl Maron,"[29] and as sickened by the (to her, at least) apparent parallels between Nazi and Soviet crimes — "Sibirien liegt bei Ravensbrück"[30] — as by the efforts of writer Victor Sensmann (otherwise known as Christoph Hein) to downplay the misery of the Berlin Wall, she ultimately loses her temper and attacks her stubbornly unrepentant employer. Maron's 1996 *Animal Triste* likewise launches a frontal assault on the GDR within a novel that combines reflection on the seemingly "absurd" existence of the communist state with a surreal account of the protagonist's failed affair with a married man. The narrator is unable to imagine how it was ever possible for a "Gangsterbande" to hermetically seal off "das gesamte osteuropäische Festland einschließlich der Binnenmeere, einiger vorgelagerter Inseln und der okkupierten Hoheitsgewässer von der übrigen Welt."[31]

In a *New German Critique* essay (published in English in 1991), Maron berated East German intellectuals as a "particularly spoiled group" and went on to lambast their conviction that they had the "right, even the duty, to speak in the name of a majority condemned to silence." In the same piece, she denounced the "craving for action of West German utopian thinkers,"[32] and disparaged their inability to acknowledge the bankruptcy, moral and political, of the state they had seen as a "better" alternative to capitalism. And even today, notwithstanding the revelations in *Der Spiegel* in 1995 of her *own* involvement with the state security services between 1976 and 1978, the author remains a staunch critic of those who stayed in the GDR and continued to support its ideals if not its reality.

Maron's *Pawels Briefe* (1999) sets out to answer the question at the heart of the novel: "ob es sich bei diesem Experiment um eine gescheiterte Utopie oder um ein Verbrechen gehandelt hat."[33] Did the GDR truly offer a utopian alternative to what had gone before — was it an experiment that sadly "failed" — or was it criminal in its very intentions and even, to a certain degree, at least, perhaps comparable with Nazi Germany?[34] These questions are themselves motivated by the author's investigations into her own family history. We are presented with an account of her grandfather, a converted Jew murdered by the Nazis, and with an exploration of her mother's conduct as a communist activist in the immediate postwar years and later in the GDR. Family photographs, Monika's visit to her grandfather's village in Poland, and, first and foremost, Pawel's letters to his wife and children from the ghetto in Belchatow are set alongside an account of the narrator's frequent disagreements with her mother regarding the true nature of East German communism. Thus the history of the GDR, and her mother's role in that history both as a committed party member and as the dedicated wife of Karl Maron, is embedded within the narrator's quest to reconstruct her grandfather's fate as a victim of the Holocaust. These investigations are integrated, moreover, as Andrew Plowman argues, into a text which "mobilises the story of Maron's grandfather" in defense of the author's own "tarnished reputation" following the exposure of her collaboration with the *Stasi*.[35]

Shortly before his death Pawel had written a letter, to be translated from Polish by Hella, that is, Monika's mother, and to be bequeathed later to Monika. Yet Pawel's farewell letter had remained undiscovered until 1994 when it turned up again during a search for photographs and documents instigated by a Dutch television documentary on the subject: "Wann werden die Deutschen endlich normal?" (*PB*, 10). Monika, as might be expected, is baffled by her mother's oversight. And yet, for the narrator, this act of forgetting is symptomatic of her mother's, and indeed the GDR's, betrayal of the past. Monika hence suggests that Hella's negligence is linked to the building of East German socialism: "Und später [. . .] als die Zeitungen 'Neues Leben,' 'Neuer Weg,' 'Neue Zeit' und 'Neues Deutschland' hießen, als die Gegenwart der Zukunft weichen mußte und die Vergangenheit endgültig überwunden wurde, wurde da auch die eigene Vergangenheit unwichtig?" (*PB*, 113–14). Hella's enthusiasm for the GDR, she suggests, could only be sustained at the price of repressing the parallels between it and the regime that murdered her father. This act of betrayal causes a rift between the generation that founded the GDR and their children, "weil die Kinder das Pathos des antifaschistischen Widerstands ernst genommen haben" (*PB*, 170). The only choice open to her, Monika implies, was to reject the state that her mother held dear.

The fate suffered by Monika's grandparents endows them with a significance that extends beyond the purely biographical. Indeed, they offer deliverance from the past — "Sie waren der gute, der geheiligte Teil der furchtbaren Geschichte" (*PB*, 8)⁻ and represent the only hope of messianic redemption: "das nicht getilgte Wort, der nicht gelöschte Name Iglarz, wie eine Erlösung für uns" (*PB*, 104). The murder of the grandfather by the Nazis, and the grandmother's refusal to be disloyal to her husband by divorcing him or giving up hope of seeing him again, for the narrator, at least, serves to underscore the betrayal of their suffering by their daughter in her complicity with the GDR's repression of its citizens. This image of her grandparents is, of course, an "Idylle" (*PB*, 52) of sorts. Monika's attempts to recreate their lives are doomed to failure, and, from time to time, she is forced to confront difficult truths, for example, the fact that her grandfather was briefly a member of the communist party. Yet the fate of her grandparents seems to tender a unique instance of untainted authenticity: "Vor allem aber gab es ihren Tod, der sie immer mehr sein ließ als meine Großeltern" (*PB*, 8). It is precisely this "mehr" — the memory of the Holocaust — that the GDR, for all its claims to be an anti-fascist state, had forgotten and thus betrayed.

It was only after the fall of the Berlin Wall, Monika maintains, that she finally became an adult (*PB*, 131). She continued to disagree with her mother's political stance, including her support for the PDS, the successor party to the communist party, but no longer felt the need to oppose her on every point. After all, history had proved the daughter right, and East Germany was no more. In its efforts to expose what its author perceives to be the myth of GDR anti-fascism, however, *Pawels Briefe* perhaps instrumentalizes the genocidal campaign against European Jews. "Bestimmte Dinge lassen sich auch nicht vergleichen, das heißt, sie lassen sich zwar vergleichen aber nicht gleichsetzen,"[36] so Maron claimed in 1992, and yet, even as it avoids directly equating Nazism and the GDR, her novel implies continuity. For Maron, the answer to the question "wann werden die Deutschen endlich normal" is to be found in the struggle to overcome *both* of Germany's totalitarian pasts. For Wolf, on the other hand, the "normality" of the post-unification present will remain illusory for as long as the utopian potential of the former GDR, its communitarian promise and anti-fascist ideals, is dismissed within the hegemony of the victorious capitalist order.

In our next section, we turn to fiction by younger eastern writers concerned less with grand ideological debates than with the everyday experience of life in the socialist state into which they were born. Memories of an East German *Alltag* shapes both their sense of identity in the present and their attitudes towards post-unification Germany. Their work engages — sometimes critically, sometimes humorously, and frequently both — with the wave of nostalgia for the GDR, or *Ostalgie,* that has attracted so much attention since the mid-1990s. As we shall see, this *Ostalgie* may have as much do with the search for "authenticity" as a form of resistance to the "ahistorical normality" of globalization as with the rejection of west German "colonization."

Ostalgie

Iris Radisch's assertion that fiction by authors from the east of Germany might best be characterized as "tragischer Expressionismus" is certainly borne out by the work of the three writers she discusses in her 1997 essay, Reinhard Jirgl, Wolfgang Hilbig, and Ingo Schramm. Jirgl in particular is known for his manipulation of syntax and for his lexical inventiveness. Ingo Schramm, an author of the younger generation who stands apart from his peers with his bent for complex, philosophical narratives, presents a similarly dark perspective on the annihilation of the hapless individual within western modernity. A post-utopian novel, Schramm's *Fitchers Blau* (1996) relates the story of a brother and sister, he a bookbinder rendered superfluous to requirements by technological progress, she a student attempting to "compute" the parameters of human happiness, and of their father, the totalitarian figure who seeks to expunge difference in the name of a perfect rationality. Along the way, the western tradition and what is presented as a German propensity for the radical elimination of diversity in pursuit of fanatical utopianism are condemned.[37] In a reworking of the Grimm brothers' version of the Bluebeard legend, the father thus tells his son of the scientist Fitze Fitcher who endeavors to predict the behavior of women tempted to venture through the door into a room declared off limits to them by their husbands. His efforts to calculate human nature fail, and this failure incites correspondingly greater brutality. Even worse, it seems impossible to resist this dynamic, whether politically or aesthetically. "(Was glaube ich, wer ich bin, ein Motor der Gegenbewegung, der Sprache verbrennt wie einen Kraftstoff des Lebens; filigrane Sätze ausstößt, deren Bedeutung sich selbst birgt?),"[38] the narrator asks, evidently rhetorically.[39] In the consumerist order of the present, it seems, all art has been commodified and its critical voice neutralized. Wolfgang Hilbig, accordingly, is cited approvingly yet with despair: "denn solch Sprechen zergeht im Sturm einer Weltzeit aus Lärm" (*FB,* 206).

The darkly expressionist tone adopted by Schramm's narrator, however, is not always imitated by the narrators of other novels. Bernd Schirmer's *Schlehweins Giraffe* (1992), for instance, anticipates Matthias Biskupek's *Der Quotensachse* (1996), Martin Kane contends, as a defensive assault against "the western cultural and political juggernaut"[40] with outrageous flights of fantasy and pointed satire. In Biskupek's novel, a "schräges Blinzeln" learnt in the GDR remains best suited to the narrator's depiction of life in post-1990 Germany.[41] Kerstin Hensel's *Auditorium Panoptikum* (1991), Brigitte Burmeister's *Unter dem Namen Norma* (1994),[42] Fritz Rudolf Fries's *Die Nonnen von Bratislava* (1995) and Jens Sparschuh's *Der Zimmerspringbrunnen* (1995) likewise parody responses to unification in both east and west. Fries's book is the most extravagant of these titles. Here, the narrator, Golden Age Spanish novelist Mateo Alemán, is reborn into the present, travels across the world with Retard, an ex-GDR scientist, in the service of an unidentified spy organization, and engages in discussions of patterns of state repression across time and place, and of various literary responses to the same. At the close of the narrative, the appropriately named Retard attempts to resurrect the GDR by threatening to bomb the waterworks in Bonn and by occupying, along with historical figures such as Marx and Lenin, the *Palast der Republik*.

In his analysis of the final section of Fries's *Die Nonnen von Bratislava*, Kane asks, "Are the bizarre effects which propel the tale a variety of 'Ostalgie,' or are they a satirical unmasking of it?"[43] More generally, this novel raises issues concerning the phenomenon of exuberantly satirical images of the GDR. Against whom is the satire primarily directed? Is it aimed at the east Germans whose former passivity and present nostalgia is parodied or against the western reader who sees his or her stereotypes of the east reproduced without realizing that these prejudices are the true target of the satire? Does satire itself all too quickly give way to a more indulgent image of amusing "eastern" idiosyncrasies? Might the latter tend to romanticize a state that was certainly repressive, but ostensibly only mildly so, and which, in retrospect, appears to have been comfortingly inept, even lovable? Or, might it indeed be the case that *Ostalgie*, as Thomas Rosenlöcher argues in *Ostgezeter* (1997), is nothing more than a "Versuch, die eigene Anpassung vor sich selbst zu verbergen"?[44] For west German readers, on the other hand, the "exoticization" of the GDR may represent an escape from the trials of the here and now into a charmingly archaic myth of solidarity.

These questions might be posed with regard to the work of Thomas Brussig, beginning with perhaps the most frequently reviewed of all post-unification texts by an east German writer, *Helden wie wir* (1995). This novel, as briefly noted in chapter one, tells the story of Klaus Uhltzscht, as narrated by him (so he claims) to a reporter from the *New York Times*, of his childhood in the GDR, his first sexual experiences (a tale of unremitting humiliation on account of the diminutive size of his penis), his relationship with his bullying father (an employee of the *Stasi*), and, most importantly, the way he single-handedly — for want of a more precise adverb — brought down the Wall with a sexual organ "inflated" following a blood transfusion he had just given to the ailing GDR leader Erich Honecker, "Die Geschichte des Mauerfalls ist die Geschichte meines Pinsels."[45] Indeed, the entire narrative is permeated by sexual punning, more or less subtle innuendo and phallic allusion speaking of the castration of the gerontocracy of the GDR and the "rise," to employ a wordplay typical of the text itself, of a generation desperate to unleash years of pent-up frustration.

Stephen Brockmann argues that Brussig's *Helden wie wir* tells of the "death of the father and the usurpation of the father's power by his offspring."[46] This claim is persuasive insofar as key passages of the text display hostility to the older generation of intellectuals, and in particular to Christa Wolf, whose 4 November speech is parodied (*HWW*, 283–85), as much as to the ageing leaders of the communist state.[47] Yet at least two other key issues are also at stake in the novel. First, the narrator's whimsically impossible account of his own past encourages the reader to consider the extent to which those born into the GDR may have colluded in their own impotence and seek to rewrite that history in the present. The novel's title is almost certainly meant to be viewed ironically. Uhltzscht's sensationalizing account of his contribution to world history might be regarded as opportunistic, as a continuation of his conformity in the GDR and an attempt to blame others for his own passivity. Second, and equally important, the technique of the frame narrative raises questions about the status of such "stories from the former GDR." Uhltzscht's report, therefore, may exploit western audiences' sudden interest in the "exoticism" of everyday life in the East.[48]

Brussig's *Am kürzeren Ende der Sonnenallee* (1999), which appeared just after the release of the wildly successful movie of the same name on which the author had collaborated with director Leander Haußmann,[49] is the story of a group of young people living in the shorter end of a street truncated by the Berlin Wall. Michael Kuppisch, the inhabitant of a street, and indeed a state, born of historical accident — Winston Churchill, it is reported, gave Stalin 60 meters of the Sonnenallee at the Potsdam conference of 1945 in return for lighting his cigar![50] — is conscious of living in circumstances "die ihm nicht normal vorkamen" (*AKE*, 8) but is resolved, as are his peers, to pursue the customary pleasures of male adolescence: hanging around, music, and girls. In the background, we see typical markers of life in the GDR: East German objects such as the "Ausziehtisch" (*AKE*, 37), the visits of an uncle from West Germany, or the outward conformity of reading *Neues Deutschland* (*AKE*, 40). In the foreground, however, is the story of how Michael falls for Miriam, the girl he thinks he can never have and on whose account he repeatedly makes a fool of himself.

Often hailed — or derided — as a *prima facie* case of *Ostalgie*, Brussig's short novel in fact contains a critique both of the romanticized misconceptions of western readers vis-à-vis the former GDR and of the understandable desire on the part of east Germans in the late 1990s to demonstrate that they were not merely victims of the regime but were relatively autonomous and remarkably "ordinary" people.[51] The West German tourists horrified by the "desperation" of the boys running behind their bus shouting out "Hunger!" (*AKE*, 42) most likely stand in for a *post*-1990 western gullibility and tendency to believe the most dramatic tales regarding the totalitarian GDR. At the same time, if life in the GDR was more "normal" than those gawping from the observation towers in West Berlin across into the exotic landscapes of the east chose to believe, then the non-conformity of Michael and his friends must have been correspondingly conventional. The trivial experimentation with drugs undertaken by Mario and his "existentialist" girlfriend was not dissent but teenage rebellion; later, they get married. Equally, the boys' chicanery of a local border guard was intended not to bring about the collapse of the state but as a means of alleviating boredom.

This is a vision of everyday life in the former East Germany that can only be sustained by judicious editing. Incidents which we might expect to have provoked outrage at the inequity or even brutality of the GDR are presented, in retrospect, as tiresome rather than directly repressive, or even as comic. The pressure to conform to the prescriptions of the state, accordingly, now seems to have had more to do with entirely "normal," even bourgeois, calculations of self-interest — the desire to "get ahead" and gain certain advantages — than with any real fear of persecution. When Michael's friend Wuschel is shot as he ventures into the death strip in an endeavor to retrieve a love letter intended for Miriam, moreover, we are relieved to discover that he has not been killed but rather that the bullet was stopped by the Rolling Stones album he was carrying. Certainly, the desire to remember adolescence in universal terms — as a time of excitement, confusion, and self-discovery — overwhelms the specific experience of everyday life in the GDR throughout. At the same time, this very process is itself overtly thematized. "*Es war von vorn bis hinten zum Kotzen*," Michael recalls, "*aber wir haben uns prächtig amüsiert*" (*AKE*, 153). This appears to justify an "ostaglic" view of the GDR. The italics, however, signaling temporal and intellectual distance, may also point to the construction of the past as narrative and anticipate the closing lines of the text: "Wer wirklich bewahren will, was geschehen ist, der darf sich nicht den Erinnerungen hingeben." Memory, the narrator proposes, wraps the past in a "Schleier der Nostalgie" (*AKE*, 156–57).

Brussig's short text *Leben bis Männer* (2003) warns more explicitly of the dangers inherent in an unreflective *Ostalgie*. The narrator, a soccer coach, complains in an extended rant that everything has become worse since the collapse of the GDR. In a new, post-unification world, in which "alles drunter und drüber geht, mit Börse, Internet, den Genen, doppelter Staatsbürgerschaft, den ganzen Politikern, den Banken, den Multis, den Joint Ventures,"[52] it is only the discipline of his soccer team, such as it was in the GDR, that can provide a sense of order. Yet his star player, Heiko, is prevented from playing on account of "legal difficulties." The fact that he is being held to account for his actions as a border guard in shooting a citizen trying to flee west is seen by the narrator as another form of discrimination against east Germans. "Sind wir jetzt etwa die Neger Deutschlands?" (*LM*, 55), he asks, without irony.

By the end of the 1990s, *Ostalgie*, as much as the "Ossi pride" described by Patricia Hogwood,[53] had become an established component of Germany's consumer culture. Paul Cooke draws attention to the marketing of eastern goods from the early 1990s such as *Juwel* cigarettes, *Rotkäppchen* sparkling wine, and *Club Cola* as goods that might reconnect east Germans with their past. Later in the decade the advertising agency Fritzsch und Mackat would begin to accentuate the "simplicity" and "honesty" of *western* commodities in campaigns aimed at east Germans in the belief that their target audience would be flattered by the implication that these values were more important to them than a product's purely "commercial" properties.[54] In addition, Cooke notes, the internet soon became a key medium for the sale and distribution of *Ostalgie* merchandise. In 2003, the website *Ossi-Versand,* with its slogan "Kost the Ost" (a parody of the cigarette advertisement "Test the West") increased its turnover by sixty percent before going bust following its overly precipitous expansion.

In the course of its commercialization, *Ostalgie* soon began to assume many of the characteristics of the modern tourist industry. Its journey into the past undertook to transport consumers from both east and west Germany into a form of "everyday life" that had been eradicated by "progress" post-unification. Nostalgia for what had been lost — although it had, of course, never existed in the manner it was being presented — was marketed along with the paradoxical amalgamation of the comfort of the (ostensibly) familiar and the thrill of the exotic. The past, literally, was another country. In the new millennium, movies such as Wolfgang Becker's *Good Bye, Lenin* (2003), in which a son recreates the GDR for his sick mother, the upsurge of *Ostalgie* shows on major television stations as much as the planned GDR theme park, *Ossi World*, to be built by the Massine Production Company in Berlin, conjured up the promise of an escape from the anonymity of global consumerism into a fantasy vision of an almost provincial authenticity and jocular sociability.

In reality, of course, such "events" were themselves part of the "disneyfication" of the past.

The marketing of *Ostalgie* had already been satirized by Jens Sparschuh in his *Der Zimmerspringbrunnen* (1995). Hinrich Lobek, a self-described "'ruhiger Bürger'" at the time of GDR's existence,[55] rewrites his biography in the post-1990 period in order to transform himself from a confirmed "Vertreter der sozialistischen Ordnung" into a salesman with "Erfahrung im Vertreterbereich" (*Z*, 19), is unable to desist from recording his wife's every movement in an unconscious imitation of *Stasi* methodology, and achieves a degree of unexpected success with his design for an interior fountain which he calls the "Atlantis." Molded in the form of the GDR, his tribute to a state that has seemingly sunk without a trace spurts water through the funnels of pens bearing the inscription "Berlin — Hauptstadt unserer Republik" (*Z*, 94–95) and quickly becomes a "Kultgegenstand" (*Z*, 104) amongst his east German customers.

In *Eins zu Eins* (2003), Sparschuh updates his critique of *Ostalgie*. The title, referring to the occupation of cartographer practiced by the protagonist Olaf Gruber, alludes to the text's central theme: the attempt to map everyday life in the GDR with an ever greater degree of detail at some point becomes indistinguishable from the desire to reproduce it "one-to-one," that is, to recreate it in its entirety. Of course, this is impossible — the novel is replete with references to the inaccuracy of maps and the way they reflect the social and political expediencies of those who commission them — but the risk remains that the object to be charted either becomes fetishized by those seeking to protect its "integrity" or exploited by those seeking to penetrate its interior for the purposes of colonization, or in more recent times, commercial expansion. Each group hopes to take possession of this exotic "other" for itself, either as a form of subversive identity construction or as a marketing tool.

Gruber's name brings to mind the noun "Grube" and the verb "grübeln" and indicates his penchant for both excavating the past and brooding on it. Superficially, the particular past that fascinates him most is the story of the *Wenden*, the Slav race that inhabited the Mark Mecklenburg before German knights arrived in the early middle ages to (re)colonize what — five hundred years prior — had been German lands and to impose militant Christianity onto a reluctant population. Lengthy anthropological passages punctuate the narrative, along with quotations from Theodor Fontane's *Wanderungen durch die Mark Brandenburg* and speculation on the location of the pagan temple of Rethra. In the course of his pursuit of Wenzel, the colleague who has abandoned his desk at *andersWandern*, the former GDR enterprise for which he and Gruber work, however, the narrator rediscovers the east German province. The fate of the *Wenden* comes to be mapped onto the fate of the current in-

habitants of the now defunct GDR. The *Wenden* and the *Ossis* were two
peoples committed to the ideal of community — "Die Wenden kannten
kein Eigentum am Boden [und] lebten in großen Gemeinschaften"[56] —
and forced to endure colonization by more "advanced" tribes from the
west as well as the erasure of their culture.

Sparschuh's novel lampoons both the idealization of the past in which
its east German narrator occasionally indulges and the exoticization of the
former GDR by his west German boss, Cora Trottenburg. For Trottenburg, the east is simplicity itself, a refreshing contrast to the weary cynicism of the west: "'Die Leute hier im Osten, ich weiß nicht, die sind noch
so urwüchsig, so unverbraucht'" (*EZE*, 203). For Gruber, the eastern
landscapes outside Berlin represent a journey back "in meine Vergangenheit, zu den schlichten Barbaren des Ostens" (*EZE*, 298). Both
the east German and the woman from the west, therefore, stylize the
ex-GDR hinterland. Gruber's account of his encounters with the shop assistant at the bratwurst stand with her cheap sun tan, the "New Age" pot-
terer, the priest whose communicants have been "appropriated" by the
Mormon Church, or the hobby builder still struggling to complete the
home that he began with great difficulty during the GDR, and many
others, reinforce stereotypes of a population overwhelmed by progress
and in need of the special protection afforded to an exotic and endan-
gered species. At the same time, these characters are also offered up as
representative of an east German population which has all too quickly
adopted the cheap fadism of the west. Trottenburg's obvious enthusiasm
for the "'Wir — und das Andere'" (*EZE*, 220) program offered by the
west German psychologist they meet in a castle once used by the East
German leadership and now converted into a seminar center for busi-
nessmen from the "old" Federal Republic likewise reveals much about her
attitude, as a west German, towards the "new lands" in the east. A mixture of condescension, patronizing curiosity, and forced humility thus
marks her efforts to deal with her new fellow citizens.

What distinguishes Sparschuh's *Ein zu Eins* from *Der Zimmerspringbrunnen,* however, is its contextualization of the fascination of both
east and west Germans with the "exoticness" of the ex-GDR as a consequence of an ever deepening cultural uniformity across the globe. On
leaving the depths of the province, therefore, the narrator looks around
him and observes with caustic wit: "Ich war zurück in Brandenburg, alles
sah wieder aus wie in Amerika" (*EZE*, 356). His nostalgia for the GDR
now has less to do with west German colonization than with the near total hegemony of America. And in the cut-throat business climate of the
late 1990s, Cora Trottenburg too seems to find it more comforting to
identify with the slower pace of life associated with the "old" east than
with the "new" west. Following the apparently complete victory of neo-

liberal capitalism, the west German has become the *Ossi*. Her managerial style is quaintly humane and clearly not what is required if the company is to survive in the face of competition from the downmarket *Chaos* with its palate of themed tours presenting the ex-GDR as a kind of Disneyworld. At the end of the text, she is forced to watch on as *andersWandern* is eventually devoured by its more commercially-minded rival.

In a final act of resistance, Olaf refuses to sacrifice the temple at Rethra to the indignities of "Event-Marketing" (*EZE,* 307) and to disclose the site where he believes it to have been located. In fact, he is mistaken. The figures that he saw digging up the ground were Russian construction workers and not resurrected *Wenden*! Yet this merely underlines the message elaborated in the course of the previous four hundred or so pages. Just when we think we have mapped the past, it is exposed as a product of our fantasy. At the same time, Olaf's hankering for his past ceases to be dangerous once he understands that it is simply a mirage. Even as he continues to dream of a one-to-one mapping of the GDR, he moves forward, gets over the failed affair that previously dominated his memories, falls in love, and retains his job in the firm whilst maintaining both a critical distance from his new bosses and a sense of autonomy.

Sparschuh's *Eins zu Eins* alludes to the manner in which the former GDR, and the east German province in particular, came to be idealized in the course of the 1990s by east *and* west Germans. For the inhabitants of the new states, as Wolfgang Hilbig has suggested, it may initially have been the case "daß erst jener Beitritt zur Bundesrepublik uns zu den DDR-Bürgern hat werden lassen, die wir nie gewesen sind, jedenfalls nicht solange wir dazu gezwungen waren."[57] For citizens from the "old" Federal Republic, on the other hand, and, from the mid-1990s, an increasing number of east Germans as well, fascination with the ex-GDR was as likely to derive from the belief that "German" values of intellectual depth and aesthetic receptivity had been "protected" from Americanization as it was from any attachment to the ideals of the communist state. In this, they were following the lead of established left-wing writers and the new Germany's increasingly vocal cultural conservatives alike. Although skeptical about the romanticization of East Germany, Karl Heinz Bohrer, for example, concluded that it had preserved a sensibility that was "altfränkisch, verstaubt und scholastisch" but also capable of "Widerstand gegenüber den Fast-Food-Allüren."[58] More generally, the GDR's slower pace and the supposed authenticity of its human relationships were emhasized. In this context, Stephen Brockmann cites Irene Dische's 1993 novel *Ein fremdes Gefühl,* in which a western psychologist encourages a patient to travel to the untouched landscapes of the ex-GDR, in addition to Peter von Becker's *Die andere Zeit* (1994) and Martin Walser's 1988 essay "Über Deutschland reden." Here, Walser praised the East German poet Wulf Kirsten for his "purer, more original language."[59] Günter Grass's *Ein weites Feld* (1995), might also be mentioned, as might the author's praise just before unification for a "langsameres Lebenstempo" in the now defunct GDR.[60]

By the end of the 1990s, the GDR began to appear in a number of novels as a more or less "normal" background for narratives with universal themes. Examples of this include Brigitte Burmeister's *Pollock und die Attentäterin* (1999), Angela Krauß's *Milliarden neuer Sterne* (1999) or Kerstin Hensel's *Im Spinnhaus* (2003). In Christoph Hein's *Von allem Anfang an* (1997), the protagonist's sexual awakening in the 1950s seems more significant than allusions to the discrimination suffered by the boy's grandfather on account of his refusal to enlist in the Party, the workers' uprising of 1953 and the suppression of the 1956 Hungarian insurrection. Or, insofar as it denotes anything at all, the ex-GDR often functions more generally to connote the barrenness of a protagonist's life. In the short story "Die Autorenwitwe" (2003), by the west German writer Judith Kuckart, for instance, the east German backwater in which Olga Stosskopf finds herself serves as an atmospheric backdrop to the sense of despair she experiences after having been deserted by her husband.

At the same time, however, the "old" East Germany also features in a number of important texts from the late 1990s by writers from both east and west as a place in which stories might be discovered, or fabricated, which *disrupt* the standardization of experience within the globalized consumer culture. This has less to do with *Ostalgie* than with a determination to create a perspective from which the "ahistorical normality" of the economic neo-liberalism which many felt was being established in Germany as a whole might be critiqued. In our next section, we look at texts by Karen Duve, from the west, and Ingo Schulze, from the east, in order to illustrate this phenomenon. Following this, we explore the way a number of younger east German writers began, in the late 1990s, to inflect their narratives with "eastern difference" in order to mark out a specific identity within an increasingly homogenized world.

"Simple Storys" from the East German Province

In *Endmoränen* (2002), Monika Maron describes how her protagonist moves for the autumn from Berlin to her vacation home in Basekow in the northeast of the former GDR, leaving behind a husband who, it is implied, has already deserted her and a daughter who has moved to the United States and become "American." The text also hints at the fractured life story of a woman who, having inserted subversive passages into the biographies of literary figures she wrote in the GDR, realizes that her talents are not required in the present and that she is redundant, economically and personally. Yet Maron's novel, as Julia Schröder contends, is not "durchzogen von ostalgischem Gejammer."[61] Instead, it reflects back on the situation in *both* parts of the recently united Germany and raises questions about the profit-driven ethos of the dominant neo-liberal capitalist order. Johanna's friend Christian, for example, experiences a very similar sense of alienation in his job as a *Lektor* in a Munich-based publishing house. *Endmoränen,* in short, starts out from the east German province but then proceeds to paint a picture of modern-day German society in east *and* west.

The novel *Regenroman* (1999) by the younger west German writer Karen Duve employs gloomy and outlandish eastern backdrops for its depiction of conflicts quite literally imported from the west. A by-now conventional image of the "western colonization" of the GDR as a form of sexual conquest, or even rape,[62] is linked with a broader representation of the crisis of gender relations in the west of the country where, even after three decades of feminism, a woman might still be regarded as chattel and may, indeed, internalize this subordinate role. All the men and women in this novel appear damaged or abnormal in some respect. Kay, one of the two east German sisters inhabiting the house on the moor nearest the property bought by Martina and her writer husband Leon, cannot express her lesbian cravings; the other sister, Isadora, is implausibly overweight and sexually rapacious. The owner of the local shop, moreover, delights in wearing women's underwear. Yet the west Germans who venture into the east, expecting to be shocked by its "deviance," merely superimpose their own psychological deformations onto its apparently uninscribed landscapes. In Leon, then, the impenetrability of the heath inspires anxiety and the need to dominate: an aggressive masculinity is coupled with an unforgiving rationality that cannot tolerate any indeterminacy. Indeed, the moor is treacherously ambiguous. It is like Isadora, whose layers of fat provide perverse comfort to Leon — when she seduces him, it is "als würde er mit dem ganzen Moor schlafen"[63] — but whose disconcertingly "irrational" genitalia revolt him: "Haare, Schrumpeliges und ein tiefes rotes Loch — und hinterher fühlte es sich an wie zerkochte Nudeln" (*RR,* 155).

Peter Graves associates Duve's *Regenroman* with writer Matthias Altenburg's injunction to rediscover all those "dirty places . . ., wo Bisse und Küsse so schwer zu unterscheiden sind,"[64] pointing to the graphic nature of the story and the "direct mode of narration."[65] Beth Linklater, on the other hand, focuses on the fate of Martina, who is raped by Leon's friend, Harry, on the orders of Pfitzner, the Hamburg gangster who comes to express his disappointment with Leon's failing efforts to concoct a flattering biography for him. The explicit depiction of Martina's brutali-

zation, Linklater argues, challenges "rape and the silencing which it produces."[66] At the close of the narrative, Martina, Kay, and Isadora, accordingly, establish an alliance that erases both the stereotype of the eastern
woman as unfeminine and the cliché of the western woman as shallow
(Martina had changed her name to please Leon and is bulimic and obsessive about her looks). It also destroys the men who abuse them: the
women incinerate Harry and Pfitzner with a flamethrower. Martina later
returns to Hamburg and sets fire to the car in which, as a teenager, she
had first sacrificed her self-respect to a man's lusts.

Linklater's reading is certainly convincing. Yet throughout the novel
sexual violence is linked not only with the export of west German gender
inequalities to the east after unification but also with a colonizing, neo-
liberal capitalism. Pfitzner buys and sells women without regard for their
fates; his determination to present himself as the poor boy made good in
his biography testifies to his awareness of the need for a distinct corporate
image and his grasp of the sentimentalizing, sensationalizing tropes of the
modern culture industry. The nexus of sexual abuse and invasive curiosity
that underpins an uninhibited capitalism appears set to continue, moreover, in both east and west. The depiction of the young woman discovered dead and naked in an east German stream at the start of the
narrative, whose corpse Leon pokes with stick to see "ob die Haut reißen
würde" (*RR*, 28), is reworked at the end of the text when a father experiments along with his son on the body of a "Babyrobbe" in order to
find out whether its skin will tear when jabbed. At the close of the novel,
accordingly, it seems that the space the women have created in the eastern
moorlands will continue to need to be defended against the cruel intru-
sions of those intent on domination.[67]

As its title suggests, *Simple Storys* (1998) by east German writer Ingo
Schulze is stitched together from a collection of brief narratives, plainly
told, with linear and uncomplicated plots. Some of the stories are related
in the first person, others in the third, and several consist of dialogue.
Each account is preceded by a short summary of the action, a contrivance
that often obscures rather than enlightens, given its typically cryptic nature. Characters are also introduced in these preliminary passages, totaling
twenty nine, a number that appears to have no significance. The novel
proceeds by means of an incremental accumulation of information,
glimpses, and allusions. Some thirty characters come into contact with
one another in a variety of contexts such that the reader is invited to infer
relationships of mutual advantage, love, and betrayal. Yet the overall picture remains opaque and incomplete. The "simple stories" belonging to
the text's various characters are, in truth, all fragments of a complex and
rapidly changing social reality. Similar to *Regenroman,* this book presents

an east German cosmos that cannot easily be reduced to western stereotypes or simply bought out.

The novel opens with the Meurers, two elderly ex-GDR citizens on their first visit to Italy. A fellow-traveler (only in the touristic sense, it turns out), climbs a cathedral wall to deliver a litany of accusations against Ernst Meurer. Nothing more is mentioned of the couple until much later in the text, or of the mysterious Zeus who plagues them. Instead, we are introduced to their son, Martin, who rides a taxi with a Korean woman, with whom he almost begins an affair. In the meantime, Conni Schubert is raped by a businessman from the west, or it least it seems that way. Later, Lydia and Patrick are chased by a car, yet appear unfazed. The Meurers obtain a "Wochenendhaus" from Neugebauer who is determined to ensure that they keep quiet about his past, and a politician, Frank, is doing well, whilst his wife, Barbara is loved by Hanni, who may have been in the *Stasi*. Subsequently, Martin's real father meets him in Munich, and offers religion as a substitute for the many missed years of paternal care following his escape west. Martin's own son, Tino, lives with his sister-in-law, Danni, and her lover, Edgar, who is betraying her with Utchen. Christian — who owns the newspaper for which Danni works — watches England v. GDR soccer matches whilst masturbating as a means of taking his mind off the new tax law, and taunts Edgar with his communist past. Several foreigners feature, including Raffael and Orlando, whose taxi firm is attacked and wrecked by local neo-Nazis, Tahir, from ex-Yugoslavia, and the poet Enrico, who changes his name to Heinrich.

On a first reading, Schulze's text appears to participate in the post-unification debate about conformity and guilt in the GDR, and about the continued passivity in the present of those who lived there. Was Ernst Meurer simply a *Mitläufer* or was he a disguised reformer, believing that more could be achieved inside the party? Or was he a committed communist who sacked Zeus, otherwise known as Dieter Schubert, from his teaching post? Is Schubert's censure of Meurer not undermined by his own many infidelities? Nor do the questions end here. Meurer's passivity is paralleled with the post-*Wende* conformity of his son Martin, who travels to work in the west German city of Stuttgart and advertises *Nordsee* dressed in diving gear, and with Jenny, who accompanies him in "Gleichschritt" (the closing image of the novel).[68] Martin may even be responsible for his wife's death, insofar as his taxi flirtation proceeds from the loss of his driver's license. His wife, Andrea, is killed on her bike by a car that may have been driven by Barbara. Is Martin, we might ask, any better than his father, or is his own history of neglect responsible for his inability to take care of Tino? Is Barbara's politician husband Frank to blame for the violence that all seem to take for granted, exemplified by

the neo-Nazi thugs from whom he fails to protect his wife and by the attack on Maik, Jenny's western boyfriend?

Schulze's novel refuses to offer clear-cut answers to precisely the
questions of conformity and guilt which it seems to raise but which in fact
more likely reflect the concerns of the *outsider* determined to impose a
coherent narrative on the former GDR. What is more important to
Schulze are the stories individuals tell and the structures of memory that
they generate for themselves. Accordingly, Ernst's wife asks herself why
she is telling her story and decides: "Weil man so schnell vergißt" (*SIM*,
23). Yet what she remembers has nothing to do with Dieter Schubert,
but with the moment during which she and her husband both thought of
their garden. To the outsider, this might appear to be a relativization of
complicity, and yet this would be to presume Ernst's guilt in the absence
of any real evidence. Judgments of this kind impose a reading of the ex-
GDR that serves the purposes of those attempting to define it from without rather than the interests of those who lived through and within it.

The density of social relations depicted in the novel, and the way its
form reminds the reader of his or her *lack* of access, resists the incorporation of the east German province. The stories related are not always edify-
ing or even honest, but they do belong to the people who tell them.
Occasionally, moreover, they transmit an intuition of depth absent from
the "new" eastern landscapes defined by Aral gas stations and the
Commerzbank. More generally, the novel's narrative construction may intimate a form of resistance to the colonizing impulses of neo-liberal capitalism. The text adopts several major tropes of cultural globalization —
the universal brands of identification, surface and sentiment imported, in
the 1990s, into Germany as *Neue Lesbarkeit* — but localizes them: the
German "misspelling" of its title is evidence of this.[69] Contained within
these *Simple Storys*, there are certainly narratives which tell of submission
to the recent colonization of the east. Yet even these point to a localized
inflection of the idiom of the colonizers insofar as they adapt the American short story in the style of Hemingway or Raymond Carver[70] or, less
inspiring, of the confessional talk show to an east German perspective. All
in all, this is a collection of east German tales that bends dominant aesthetic paradigms, both poignant and trashy, to suit the purposes of those
on the margins who, endlessly, speak of their *own* "normality."

Emerging Writers in the East

In the first few years of the new millennium, it was possible to spend almost every evening attending "open-mike" readings by young writers,
poets, and DJs in a bar, café, or club somewhere in east Berlin. Tuesday
nights meant *LSD: Liebe statt Drogen* in *Zosch* on Tucholskystraße. On

Wednesdays it was the turn of the *Surfpoeten* in the *Mudd Club* in the Große Hamburger Straße, and then on Thursdays the *Chaussee der Enthusiasten* in the *RAW-Tempel* in the Revaler Straße. On Sundays, *Dr. Seltsams Frühschoppen* in the *Kalkscheune* near Friedrichstraße railway station was followed by the *Reformbühne Heim und Welt* in the *Kaffee Burger*, only a short walk away from Alexanderplatz. Promoted via collective and personal websites, word-of-mouth, and by sympathetic journalists (including some of their own members), names such as Ahne, Jochen Schmidt, Jakob Hein, and Falko Hennig were quickly establishing themselves as representative of a network of *Vorlesebühnen* in east Berlin combining literature, performance, disco, and dance. Along with Wladimir Kaminer, the Russian-Jewish immigrant and author of a number of collections of short stories and a novel *Militärmusik* (2002), these young writers were creating a literary scene in the east which was more accessible than the more mainstream "Berlin writing" associated with figures such as Judith Hermann and other emerging, mainly west German authors. In 2001, Kaminer edited a set of stories written by collaborators at the *Reformbühne* and elsewhere entitled *Frische Goldjungs*. This was a new east German utopia of sorts, an ideal of community and solidarity in which a whole range of more or less well-known writers appeared on each other's sets, wrote forewords for one another, and advertised their friends in the media. It was a resurrected east German underground that was suitably irreverent and up-to-date, providing pithy snapshots of life in the new Berlin in short texts written for performance on stage and later collated for publication. Thus the website of the *Surfpoeten,* as of late November 2003, proudly proclaimed: "Mit all ihren Auftritten kämpfen die Surfpoeten auch für eine bessere Welt, in der es Essen umsonst für alle gibt, keinen Zwang für Lohnarbeit, billiges Bier und vieles, was sonst noch gut ist" (www.surfpoeten.de). The allusion to the regret experienced by many for the fading of utopian dreams after the end of the GDR is comic and yet evocative. For most of those reading in Friedrichshain, Prenzlauer Berg, and Mitte — mostly from the east, some from the west — these parts of the city offered a link back to a past that might inflect the present with an alternative, perhaps more subversive sensibility.

Jochen Schmidt's collections *Triumphgemüse* (2000) and *Müller haut uns raus* (2002) — the latter marketed as a novel despite the fact that it is more properly a series of short texts — are representative in style and content of the work of writers performing on the *Vorlesebühnen* of east Berlin some ten years after unification. The piece "*New York is fun!*" in *Müller haut uns raus,* for example, anticipates Jakob Hein's *Formen menschlichen Zusammenlebens* (2003). Both portray the fascination of young east Germans socialized in the GDR with a world in which a milkshake can be named after Elvis Presley ("*New York is Fun!*")[71] or there can be such mysteries as the "New York Shark — Home of the Whopper" spotted by Hein's youthful narrator on his travels throughout the United States.[72] Interspersed with photographs of iconic American scenes such as advertising billboards, street art, tenement blocks, subway stations, and slums, and with references to the 1991 Gulf War, Hein's short novel alludes at the way in which the America, and the west more generally, became real for east Germans after 1990. Yet even as he speaks of new freedoms, the narrator also points forward to the imminent erasure of a previous identity. "Während meiner Abwesenheit schien Berlin amerikanisch geworden zu sein" (*FM*, 148), he notes.

Hein's texts do not reinscribe *Ostalgie*. In *Mein erstes T-Shirt* (2001) the author brings together a series of short episodes describing his socialization in the GDR, and pieces depicting the "normality" of adolescence in the East German state are set alongside descriptions of police harassment of young people on their way to punk concerts or just before the fall of the Wall. Moreover, those east Germans who rushed to cut out the hammer and sickle from the middle of the GDR's flag in a gesture of belated opposition in the autumn of 1989 are summarily dismissed: "Heute jammern sie, daß sie genau dieses Loch in ihren Herzen spüren."[73] What Hein's work demonstrates instead is that it is possible to insist upon the "normality" of a childhood lived out in the GDR — an alternative "normality" to that now on offer in the united Germany — without promoting nostalgia. A chapter entitled "Die schlimmsten Jahre" (an allusion to Reiner Kunze's 1978 exploration of youth in the GDR, *Die wunderbaren Jahre*), for instance, begins with a quotation by Jochen Schmidt: "'Die DDR war für Jochen Schmidt keine Angsterfahrung.' Jochen Schmidt" (*M*, 45), and focuses not on state repression but on the agonies of school for the narrator as an oversensitive adolescent. Elsewhere, however, there are references to the *Stasi* as well as a satirical report on elections in the GDR. It is significant that the conclusion to this report: "und ich muß mir immer meine eigene politische Meinung bilden" (*M*, 128) suggests not so much nostalgia for a system in which political decisions were made easy by instructions from above than a self-ironizing admission that, now at least, he can choose. This, of course, may simply be a choice between equally bad options.

Falko Hennig's *Alles nur geklaut* (1999) presents a darker impression of what it was like to grow up in the GDR but nevertheless insists, as do Hein's texts, on the integrity of the experience and upon its centrality to the way his protagonist engages with the present. As a teenage boy, the narrator's response to a state in which everything was "merkwürdig"[74] was to become a consummate thief. Indeed, his minor infractions were part of game in which he was able to expose the true impotence of the powers-that-be and his disdain for the values they upheld. Yet his criminality was as much an expression of universal adolescent discontent as it was directed against the GDR in particular. The small-minded chicaneries of the police, school authorities, and Party officials are duly recorded, but it is clear that his rebellion remained unfocused and generalized. His obsessive pilfering allowed for no distinction between "guten und bösen Diebstählen" (*AG*, 62), and his admiration for the West German pop singer Rio Reiser — for the GDR leadership a rather uncomfortable supporter of the *true* ideals of East German socialism — was rooted in Reiser's "Gegenschaft zu den Mächtigen, die genau passte für jedes Land der Welt und so auch für die DDR" (*AG*, 112). In fact, it is only in the months before the final collapse of the regime that the narrator begins, retrospectively, to assign some larger significance to his thieving. Commenting on the absurdity of the requirement to submit a formal application in order to take advantage of "visa-free" travel to Hungary and Romania, he observes: "Nein, nein, wir haben kein Gefängnis, stattdessen haben wir hier dieses Haus mit vielen kleinen vergitterten Räumen, in die wir die Leute einsperren, wir nennen es 'Haus für den gefängnisfreien Haftvollzug'" (*AG*, 144). The implication, of course, is that it is scarcely surprising that people should behave as criminals in a state that insists on treating them as such.

Predictably perhaps, the narrator's petty dishonesty persists after 1989 and following his move to west Germany. For example, he claims unemployment benefit whilst working and steals from supermarkets "ganz normal" (*AG*, 232). All systems are equally bad, it is implied. Moreover, the particular skill learnt by those young east Germans born into a state bent on controlling their every thought but too incompetent to do so is an ability to create an existence on the margins of society and to preserve a degree of skepticism vis-à-vis the promises of those in charge. This was most likely the meaning of the comment made by Hennig's friend and colleague Jakob Hein in an interview with *Die Welt* in late 2002: "Mir fällt es durch die DDR-Erfahrung leichter, Ideologie zu erkennen."[75] In Hennig's text, in the same way, the narrator is less than impressed by what the values propagated in the west. The people, he says, are not as nice as those in the east (*AG*, 162), and the FRG's much vaunted tolerance is all but invisible: he is arrested at gunpoint by the local police for a trivial traffic offense. Subsequently, the narrator sets off on a tour of western Europe and then America. In the United States, significantly, he comes across drug abuse, broken families, a more systematic criminality and, again, the willingness of local police to resort to intimidation. At the conclusion of his travels, he summarizes his experiences: "Das war Amerika, warum sollte es anders sein, als irgendein anderes Land?" (*AG*, 218).

At the start of the second decade after unification, a new generation of east German writers was emerging which, at first sight, appeared to be following in the footsteps of those older authors, well-known before the disintegration of the GDR, for whom the "old" system at least represented a noble idealism absent in the new, united Germany. Unlike Christa Wolf, Volker Braun or Christoph Hein (Jakob Hein's father), however, these younger writers are as familiar with the west as with the east. Certainly, Wladimir Kaminer's description of Jakob Hein might also be applied to Hennig, Schmidt, and many of their peers: "Westgeld in der linken Hosentasche und Ostgeld in der rechten. Also: ein Weltmensch made in DDR."[76] Eastern experiences are frequently presented in western forms, producing a subversive mix. Some of these writers, accordingly, display a predilection for the portrayal of a surface reality reminiscent of the pop narratives of west German authors such as Benjamin von Stuckrad-Barre. In André Kubiczek's *Junge Talente* (2001), for instance, a young man goes to East Berlin in the late 1980s and describes both the pop music of the period — much of it from the west — and his encounters with the dissident culture of the Prenzlauer Berg scene. In related fashion, other young east German writers might initially appear to embrace a literary style consistent with the *Neue Lesbarkeit* so typical of west German writers such as Judith Hermann whilst in reality bringing what might be seen as an east German sensibility to bear. Julia Schoch's *Der Körper des Salamanders* (2001), for example, tells of life in the GDR and of travels in Bulgaria and Romania. Katrin Dorn's *Lügen und Schweigen* (2000), in like manner, sets its family drama in the east German province and depicts the enduring rifts caused by a father's frustrated desire to leave the GDR in the 1950s. In these texts, therefore, as in the work of Hein and Hennig and of others performing on the *Vorlesebühnen* in east Berlin — and similar to Ingo Schulze's *Simple Storys* — narrative forms associated with the globalization of Anglo-American models are given an eastern inflection.

In her autobiographical essay *Zonenkinder* (2002), Jana Hensel, born in 1976 and a member of a generation native to the ex-GDR but too young to remember it with precision, anticipates the way the east German state will continue to exercise the imagination of those who can draw on their experience of *both* communism in the east and western capitalism: "Wie wir uns den neuen Reichstag anschauen und stolz durch die Glaskuppel laufen, so mögen wir eben auch das Russische Ehrenmal im Treptower Park."[77] This version of a present-day German "normality" makes sense to those whose biographies are shaped by their experiences of a very different society. Consequently, it resists the attempts by west German conservatives to appropriate the former GDR as a reservoir of the "antiquated," "pre-modern" German traditions they seek for their construction of a "longitudinal normality" in the present as much as the efforts of those on the left who would simply discount the east German experience — often as a reaction to their previous overinvestment in the communist state — in their search for a "latitudinal normality" that posits the Berlin Republic, with its western orientation, simply as an extension of the "old" FRG. At the same time, memories of the ex-GDR challenge the "ahistorical normality" of the modern-day consumer society. In our next chapter, we turn to fiction by authors from the west and examine the impact of their socialization in the "old" Federal Republic on the way these writers dealt with the challenges of unification, "normalization" and globalization. Here too we see that a state formerly dismissed by many of its citizens as dull, uninspiring, and provincial — or even as potentially repressive — may suddenly be re-evaluated by those seeking to undermine a conservative campaign to locate a new German "normality" in the traditions of the eighteenth and nineteenth century on the one hand, or, on the other, the contemporary dissolution of local identity within the "normality" of globalized capitalism.

Notes

[1] Iris Radisch, "Der Herbst des Quatschocento: Immer noch, jetzt erst recht, gibt es zwei deutsche Literaturen: selbstverliebter Realismus im Westen, tragischer Expressionismus im Osten," in Andreas Köhler and Rainer Moritz, eds., *Maulhelden und Königskinder: Zur Debatte über die deutschsprachige Gegenwartsliteratur* (Leipzig: Reclam Verlag, 1998), 180–8, 181. Hereafter *DHQ*.

[2] Iris Radisch, "Zwei getrennte Literaturgebiete: Deutsche Literatur der neunziger Jahre in Ost und West," in Heinz Ludwig Arnold, ed., *DDR-Literatur der neunziger Jahre* (Munich: *text + kritik*, 2000), 13–26, here 23.

[3] Wolfgang Emmerich, "Für eine andere Wahrnehmung der DDR-Literatur," in Wolfgang Emmerich, *Die andere deutsche Literatur* (Opladen: Westdeutscher Verlag, 1994), 190–207, here 190.

[4] Volker Braun, "Das Eigentum," in *Neues Deutschland*, 4–5 (August) 1990, 1. Reprinted in Carl Otto Konrady, ed., *Von einem Land und vom anderen: Gedichte zur deutschen Wende* (Frankfurt a.M.: Suhrkamp, 1993), 51.

[5] For a more detailed reading of this poem, see Ruth Owen, *The Poet's Role: Lyric Responses to German Unification by Poets from the GDR* (Amsterdam: Rodopi, 2001), 201–3.

[6] Heiner Müller, "Selbstkritik," in Heiner Müller, *Werke*, Frank Hörnigk, ed., vol. I, *Gedichte* (Frankfurt a.M.: Suhrkamp, 1998), 236.

[7] See Rolf Jucker, "SchriftstellerInnen der DDR als Verräter und Aufklärer zugleich: Zu Christa Wolf, Sascha Anderson, Rainer Schedlinski und Heiner

Müller," in Osman Durrani, Colin Good, and Kevin Hilliard, eds., *The New Germany: Literature and Society after Unification* (Sheffield: Sheffield Academic Press, 1995), 1–13. See also Werner Mittenzwei, *Die Intellektuellen: Literatur und Politik in Ostdeutschland 1945–2000* (Leipzig: Faber & Faber, 2001).

[8] See Wolfgang Emmerich, *Kleine Literaturgeschichte der DDR: Erweiterte Ausgabe* (Leipzig: Aufbau Verlag, 2000), 469–77. See also David Bathrick, *The Powers of Speech; The Politics of Culture in the GDR* (Lincoln and London: U of Nebraska P, 1995), 219–42.

[9] Thomas Rosenlöcher, *Die verkauften Pflastersteine* (Frankfurt a.M.: Suhrkamp, 1990), 13 and 14.

[10] Thomas Rosenlöcher, *Die Wiederentdeckung des Gehens beim Wandern: Harzreise* (Frankfurt a.M.: Suhrkamp, 1991), 11.

[11] Thomas Rosenlöcher, *Ostgezeter* (Frankfurt a.M.: Suhrkamp, 1997), 17.

[12] Helga Königsdorf, *Gleich neben Afrika* (Berlin: Rowohlt, 1992), 9.

[13] See Simon Ward, "'Zugzwang' or 'Stillstand'? — Trains in the Post-1989 Fiction of Brigitte Struyzk, Reinhard Jirgl, and Wolfgang Hilbig," in Stuart Taberner and Frank Finlay, eds., *Recasting German Identity* (Rochester: Camden House, 2002), 172–89.

[14] Wolfgang Hilbig, *Die Kunde von den Bäumen* (Frankfurt a.M.: Fischer, 1996 [1994]), 81.

[15] See Volker Wehdeking, "Die literarische Auseinandersetzung mit dem Themenkomplex Staatssicherheit, Zensur und Schriftstellerkontrolle," in Volker Wehdeking, ed., *Mentalitätswandel in der deutschen Literatur zur Einheit (1990–2000)* (Berlin: Erich Schmidt Verlag, 2000), 43–55. See also Paul Cooke, "From *Opfer* to *Täter*? Identity and the *Stasi* in Post-*Wende* East German Literature," in Martin Kane, ed., *Legacies and Identity: East and West German Literary Responses to Unification* (Bern: Peter Lang, 2002), 51–66.

[16] See Paul Cooke, "The Stasi as Panopticon: Wolfgang Hilbig's <<*Ich*>>, in Paul Cooke and Andrew Plowman, eds., *German Writers and the Politics of Culture: Dealing with the Stasi* (Basingstoke: Palgrave, 2003), 139–53.

[17] Wolfgang Hilbig, *Das Provisorium* (Frankfurt a.M.: Fischer, 2000), 263. See Paul Cooke, "East German Writing in the Age of Globalisation," in Stuart Taberner, ed., *German Literature in the Age of Globalisation* (Birmingham: Birmingham UP, 2004), 25–46.

[18] Wolfgang Emmerich, *Kleine Literaturgeschichte der DDR*, 504.

[19] Christoph Hein, *Willenbrock* (Frankfurt a.M.: Suhrkamp, 2001 [2000]), 248.

[20] See Denis Tate, "Günter de Bruyn: The 'Gesamtdeutsche Konsensfigur' of Postunification Literature?," *German Life and Letters* 50:2 (1997): 201–13.

[21] Christoph Brumme, *Nichts als das* (Frankfurt a.M.: Fischer, 1996 [1994]), 175–76.

[22] Kerstin Hensel, *Im Schlauch* (Frankfurt a.M.: Suhrkamp, 1993), 60.

[23] Kerstin Hensel, *Tanz am Kanal* (Frankfurt a.M.: Suhrkamp, 1994), 80.

[24] For a fuller analysis of *Tanz am Kanal,* see Reinhild Steingröver, "'Not Fate Just History': Stories and Histories in *Tanz am Kanal* and *Gipshut,*' in Beth Linklater and Birgit Dahlke, eds., *Kerstin Hensel* (Cardiff: U of Wales P, 2002), 91–106. See also Jennifer Ruth Hosek, "Dancing the (Un)Stated: Narrative Ambiguity in Kerstin Hensel's *Tanz am Kanal*" in the same volume, 107–19.

[25] See Corey Ross, *The East German Dictatorship* (London: Arnold, 2002), 32- 36.

[26] Christa Wolf, *Medea. Stimmen* (Frankfurt a.M.: Luchterhand, 1996), 99.

[27] Georgina Paul, "Schwierigkeiten mit der Dialektik: Zu Chista Wolfs *Medea. Stimmen,*" *German Life and Letters* 50:2 (1997): 227–40, here 238.

[28] Christa Wolf, *Leibhaftig* (Munich: Luchterhand, 2002), 5. Hereafter *LH.*

[29] Brigitte Rossbacher, "(Re)visions of the Past: Memory and Historiography in Monika Maron's *Stille Zeile Sechs,*" *Colloquia Germanica* 27:1 (1994): 13–24, here 16.

[30] Monika Maron, *Stille Zeile Sechs* (Frankfurt a.M.: Fischer, 1991), 142.

[31] Monika Maron, *Animal Triste* (Frankfurt a.M.: Fischer, 1996), 30.

[32] Monika Maron, "Writers and the People," *New German Critique* 52 (1991): 36–41, here 38 and 41.

[33] Monika Maron, *Pawels Briefe* (Frankfurt a.M.: Fischer, 1999), 129. Hereafter *PB.*

[34] See my "'ob es sich bei diesem Experiment um eine gescheiterte Utopie oder um ein Verbrechen gehandelt hat': Enlightenment, Utopia, the GDR and National Socialism in Monika Maron's Work from *Flugasche* to *Pawels Briefe,*" in Carol Anne Costabile-Heming, Rachel J. Halverson, and Kristie A. Foell, eds., *Textual Responses to German Unification* (Berlin: Walter de Gruyter, 2001), 35–57.

[35] Andrew Plowman, "Escaping the Autobiographical Trap," in Paul Cooke and Andrew Plowman, eds., *German Writers,* 227–42, here 233.

[36] Gerhard Richter, "Verschüttete Kultur — Ein Gespräch mit Monika Maron," *GDR Bulletin* 18:1 (1992): 2–7, here 4.

[37] See Helmut Schmitz, "Denouncing Globalisation: Ingo Schramm's *Fitchers Blau,*" in Stuart Taberner, ed., *German Literature,* 145–67.

[38] Ingo Schramm, *Fitchers Blau* (Berlin: Volk & Welt, 1996), 44. Hereafter *FB.*

[39] For a more detailed exploration of Schramm's work, see Paul Cooke, "Escaping the Burden of the Past: Questions of East German Identity in the Work of Ingo Schramm," *Seminar* 40:1 (2004): 35–49.

[40] Martin Kane, "'Zuweilen verliere ich mich in fantastischen Zusammenhängen.' Fritz Rudolf Fries' Extravaganza *Die Nonnen von Bratislava,*" in Clare Flanagan and Stuart Taberner, eds., *1949/1989: Cultural Perspectives on Division and Unity in East and West, German Monitor* 50 (Amsterdam: Rodopi, 2000), 161–75, here 165.

[41] Matthias Biskupek, *Der Quotensachse* (Berlin: Ullstein, 1998 [1996]), 13.

[42] See Gisela Shaw, "'Keine Macht aber Spielraum' oder 'Das Ende einer Sprachlosigkeit': Brigitte Burmeisters Roman *Unter dem Namen Norma*," in Clare Flanagan and Stuart Taberner, eds., *On Division and Unity*, 199–213. See also, Alison Lewis, "The Stasi, the Confession and Performing Difference: Brigitte Burmeister's *Unter dem Namen Norma*," in Paul Cooke and Andrew Plowman, eds., *German Writers*, 155–72.

[43] Gisela Shaw, "'Keine Macht aber Spielraum,'" 172.

[44] Thomas Rosenlöcher, *Ostgezeter* (Frankfurt a.M.: Suhrkamp, 1997), 24–25.

[45] Thomas Brussig, *Helden wie wir* (Berlin: Volk & Welt, 1995), 7. Hereafter *HWW*.

[46] Stephen Brockmann, *Literature and German Unification* (Cambridge: Cambridge UP, 1999), 158.

[47] See Kristie Foell and Jill Twark, "'Bekenntnisse des Hochstaplers Klaus Uhltzscht': Thomas Brussig's Comical and Controversial *Helden wie Wir*," in Paul Cooke and Andrew Plowman, eds., *German Writers*, 173–94.

[48] For a more detailed reading of *Helden wie wir*, see Stefan Neuhaus, *Literatur und nationale Einheit* (Tübingen: A. Francke Verlag, 2002), 471–82.

[49] See Paul Cooke, "Performing *Ostalgie*: Leander Haußmann's *Sonnenallee*," *German Life and Letters* 56:2 (2003): 156–67.

[50] Thomas Brussig, *Am kürzeren Ende der Sonnenallee* (Berlin: Volk & Welt, 1999), 7. Hereafter *AKE*.

[51] Author Hans Christoph Buch claimed that in the film version the GDR was "zum Musical stilisiert mit Erich Honecker als 'Fiddler on the Roof,'" Hans Christoph Buch, "Schönen Gruß von Charlie Chaplin," *Tagesspiegel*, 18 November 1999, 49.

[52] Thomas Brussig, *Leben bis Männer* (Frankfurt a.M.: Fischer, 2003 [2001]), 46–47. Hereafter *LM*.

[53] See Patricia Hogwood, "After the GDR: Reconstructing Identity in Post-Communist Germany," *Journal of Communist Studies and Transition Politics* 16:4 (2000): 45–68, here 58–59.

[54] See Paul Cooke, *Representing East Germany since Unification: From Colonization to Nostalgia* (Oxford: Berg, forthcoming, 2005). I am grateful to Dr. Cooke for the information on *Ostalgie* and consumer culture contained in these paragraphs.

[55] Jens Sparschuh, *Der Zimmerspringbrunnen* (Munich: Goldmann Verlag, 1997 [1995]), 15.

[56] Jens Sparschuh, *Eins zu Eins* (Cologne: Kiepenheuer & Witsch, 2003), 59. Hereafter *EZE*.

[57] Wolfgang Hilbig, "Kamenzer Rede," in *Preis- und Dankreden* (Rheinsberg: Kurt Tucholsky Gedenkstätte, 1996), 13–16, here 16.

[58] Karl Heinz Bohrer, "Kulturschutzgebiet DDR?," *Merkur*, 44 (1990): 1015–18, here 1015.

[59] Stephen Brockmann, *Literature and German Unification* (Cambridge: Cambridge UP, 1999), 41–44.

[60] Günter Grass, "Viel Gefühl, wenig Bewußtsein," in Günter Grass, *Deutscher Lastenausgleich. Wider das dumpfe Einheitsgebot: Reden und Gespräche* (Frankfurt a.M.: Luchterhand, 1990), 13–25, here 17.

[61] Julia Schröder, "Was noch kommen kann," *Stuttgarter Zeitung*, 8 October 2002, iii.

[62] See Ingrid Sharp, "Male Privilege and Female Virtue: Gendered Representations of the Two Germanies," *New German Studies* 18:2 (1994/5): 87–106.

[63] Karen Duve, *Regenroman* (Berlin: Eichborn, 1999), 153. Hereafter *RR*.

[64] Matthias Altenburg, "Kampf den Flaneuren: Über Deutschlands junge, lahme Dichter," in *Der Spiegel*, 12 October 1992; reprinted in Andreas Köhler and Rainer Moritz, eds., *Maulhelden*, 72–85, here 75.

[65] Peter Graves, "Karen Duve, Kathrin Schmidt, Judith Hermann: 'Ein literarisches Fräuleinwunder,'" *German Life and Letters* 55:2 (2002): 196–207, here 198–89.

[66] Beth Linklater, "'Philomela's Revenge': Challenges to Rape in Recent Writing in German," *German Life and Letters* 54:3 (2001): 253–71, here 261.

[67] See Paul Cooke, "East German Writing in the Age of Globalisation," in Stuart Taberner, ed., *German Literature*, 25–46.

[68] Ingo Schulze, *Simple Storys* (Berlin: Berlin Verlag, 1998), 303. Hereafter *SIM*.

[69] See Paul Cooke, "Beyond a *Trotzidentität?* Storytelling and the Postcolonial Voice in Ingo Schulze's *Simple Storys*," *Forum for Modern Language Studies* 39:3 (2003): 290–305.

[70] In addition to Hemingway, Anderson, and Raymond Carver, Peter Michalzik also notes the influence of Robert Altman's filmic reworking of Carver, *Short Cuts* (1993). Peter Michalzik, "Wie komme ich zur Nordsee? Ingo Schulze erzählt einfach Geschichten, die ziemlich vertrackt sind und die alle lieben," in Thomas Kraft, ed. *aufgerissen: Zur Literatur der 90er* (Munich: Piper, 2000), 25–38, here 31.

[71] Jochen Schmidt, "*New York is fun!*," in Jochen Schmidt, *Müller haut uns raus* (Munich: C. H. Beck, 2002), 296–304, here 301.

[72] Jakob Hein, *Formen menschlichen Zusammenlebens* (Munich: Piper, 2003), 79. Hereafter *FM*.

[73] Jakob Hein, *Mein erstes T-Shirt* (Munich: Piper, 2001), 56–57. Hereafter *M*.

[74] Falko Hennig, *Alles nur geklaut* (Munich: Goldmann, 2001 [1999]), 54. Hereafter *AG*.

[75] "Generation Trabant. Angekommen im neuen Deutschland?," *Die Welt*, 9 November 2002, *Feuilleton*, 1–2, here 1.

[76] Wladimir Kaminer, "Vorwort," in Jakob Hein, *Mein erstes T-Shirt*, 6.

[77] Jana Hensel, *Zonenkinder* (Reinbek bei Hamburg: Rowohlt, 2002), 134.

3: Literature in the West

Eine unerwartet liebenswerte Republik
— Sten Nadolny, *ER oder ICH*

THE PUBLICATION IN 1995 OF Günter Grass's *Ein weites Feld* was, Daniela Dahn claims, a "nationales Ereignis" without parallel "in der Kulturgeschichte der Bundesrepublik Deutschlands."[1] Indeed, a quarter of a million copies of this nearly eight hundred page novel had been ordered prior to its release.[2] Three chapters, moreover, had appeared in *Neue deutsche Literatur,* a journal based in the ex-GDR, and some five thousand advance copies had been sent out to reviewers by Grass's publishing house, Steidl. A literary sensation appeared to be in the offing. Nineteenth-century novelist Theodor Fontane was to be resurrected as Fonty, a seventy-year-old citizen of the former East Germany whose biography would include almost incidental collaboration with the French resistance during the war and, later, with the *Stasi* as well as sporadic refusals to conform before and after 1990. Also featured would be Fonty's "shadow" Hoftaller, a.k.a. Tallhover, the man who had spied on Fontane and who was made famous by Hans Joachim Schädlich's 1986 novel *Tallhover.* This rather ambivalent figure was to be Fonty's partner in extensive dialogues on the unifications of 1870–71 and 1990 and in discussions of Fontane's eager embrace of the liberal cause in 1848, his activities as a Prussian agent reporting on German émigrés in London, and Fonty's own inconsistencies. In addition, Fonty, possibly like Fontane, would turn out to have at least one illegitimate daughter. The stage was set for the novel of the decade.

What followed was a media controversy seen by many as comparable to the *Literaturstreit* initiated by Ulrich Greiner's attack on east German writer Christa Wolf following the appearance of *Was bleibt* (1990).[3] A computer-generated image of Marcel Reich-Ranicki tearing the novel to shreds in a play on the words *Verriss* and *Zerriss* was featured on the cover of the *Der Spiegel.*[4] A short time later, Reich-Ranicki reiterated his criticism on his television show *Das literarische Quartett.* Iris Radisch, in like fashion, dismissed the novel as "unlesbar" and declared that with this "verplapperten Thesenroman" Grass had given up writing literature."[5] It was above all, Stefan Neuhaus maintains, "die zu positive Bewertung der DDR-Vergangenheit und die zu kritische Sicht der bundesdeutschen 'kapitalistischen' Gesellschaft"[6] which seemed to frustrate Grass's many critics both in the media and amongst politicians and other public figures. The title of Radisch's piece, "Die Bitterfelder Sackgasse," referring to the directive handed down by the GDR leadership in 1959 that authors should go out into the factories and write about the triumphs of East German socialism, lends weight to this assertion.[7]

For Thomas Schmid, Grass's *Ein weites Feld* constituted nothing less — and nothing more — than "eine Revue seiner Vorurteile."[8] Indeed, Grass had condemned both the speed and means of German unification in a series of essays and speeches. When Fonty declares that the anti-Semitism suffered by his friend Freundlich had to do with the new "dummdreisten Stolz auf Deutschland,"[9] therefore, this was taken to be "an expression of Grass's own thoughts, as articulated in his dictum "Wir kommen an Auschwitz nicht vorbei."[10] Much the same ideas had been expressed, critics noted, in Grass's *Unkenrufe* (1992), in which a seemingly innocent plan to repatriate the bodies of deceased Germans to the (now) Polish lands from which they had been expelled in 1945 quickly comes to be regarded by the local population as yet another instance of territorial and racial conquest, driven this time by the economic might of the newly united Germany.[11] Fonty's insistence, furthermore, that unification was an "Anschluß, der Beitritt genannt wird" (*WF*, 457) was considered to be a *post factum* confirmation of sentiments uttered by the author in 1990: "Ich lehne den Einheitsstaat ab und wäre erleichtert, wenn er [. . .] nicht zustande käme."[12] In addition, readers most probably understood the novel's critique of "colonization" by the west as a continuance of Grass's vilification of those "profitorientierten Kolonialherren"[13] who rushed in to buy up east German enterprises at bargain-basement prices after 1990.

Grass's *Ein weites Feld* (1995) is certainly, as Julian Preece contends, a "pro-GDR" book which takes seriously an east German affection "born of familiarity and habit for institutions and commodities."[14] In so doing it may well "humanize" the *Stasi* with its refusal unambiguously to condemn Hoftaller. Equally, it may well draw provocative parallels between the unifications of 1870–71 and 1989–90 as events from which disaster would inevitably flow. Yet, as Neuhaus points out, the novel *also* implies criticism of the GDR in, for example, its references to the harassment endured by Fonty after the departure of his sons for the west or to the authorities' efforts to present the 1953 workers' uprising as a western plot.[15] For all its sympathy for those in the former GDR who had been confronted with dilemmas that their western compatriots had been spared, Grass's novel is by no means entirely one-sided.[16]

More significant in the context of our present chapter, however, is what Grass chooses *not* to depict. West Germany, both before and after unification, is virtually absent from the text. The same is true of Hans Christoph Buch's 1994 novel *Der Burgwart der Wartburg,* in which the narrator is reborn throughout German history to spy on leading intellectual figures including Luther, Goethe, and Brecht in order to illustrate the country's depressing tradition of "fehlgeschlagener Revolutionen" up to and including 1989.[17] Indeed, both texts confirm a widespread prejudice of the 1990s: there are no stories to tell with regard to the "old" Federal Republic, or at least none which attest to any world-historical consequence. West Germany, in fact, appeared to be drearily irrelevant compared with East Germany. How could west German writers compete? Or, as the protagonist of Hans Pleschinski's autobiographical *Bildnis eines Unsichtbaren* (2002), asks: "Was will ich denn als Westdeutscher erzählen?"[18]

In this chapter, we look at fiction by west German writers from the early 1990s onwards, beginning with F. C. Delius, Martin Walser, and Uwe Timm and moving on to the generation of '78. West German novelists *do* have stories to tell about the "old" FRG. In the first years after unification, these were often concealed within narratives ostensibly about the former GDR; later, West Germany comes into focus in its own right. This prepares the way for a discussion of the "new pop literature." At the close of this chapter, the efforts of the younger generation to shape a contemporary German "normality" are set alongside the work of ethnic-minority writers, and particularly Feridun Zaimoğlu. These authors bring their own unique biographical experience to bear on the question of what it means to be German in a world in which identity has become increasingly fluid and difficult to define.

West Germany: Imperialist and Arrogant?

Patrick Süskind, author of *Das Parfum* (1985), a novel that many observers have seen as the highpoint of literary culture of the 1980s in West Germany, anticipated the disappearance of the "old" Federal Republic in a contribution to *Der Spiegel* in mid-September 1990: "Ja, und ein wenig traurig bin ich, wenn ich daran denke, daß es den faden, kleinen, ungeliebten, praktischen Staat Bundesrepublik Deutschland, in dem ich groß geworden bin, künftig nicht mehr geben wird." For members of Süskind's generation in particular, "wir vierzigjährige Kinder der Bundesrepublik,"[19] this would be an especially difficult leave-taking. West Germany may well have been more of a bureaucratic arrangement than a "real" country capable of inspiring any true passion, but it was the state into which those born in the early postwar years had grown up and which this same generation — the student rebels of the late 1960s — had largely succeeded in shaping in its own image. It was not only the GDR that was destined to vanish on 3 October 1990. The "old" Federal Republic would also cease to exist.

Süskind's declaration of affection for a state which he readily acknowledges to be lackluster and dull anticipates the wave of nostalgia for the former West Germany that emerged in the mid-1990s. In a period of rapid social, political, and economic change, many would look back at the "old" Federal Republic as a time of stability and reassuring predictability. This might be the case even when the emphasis appeared to be on the mundane routine of working-class life in the early FRG, such as in Ralf Rothmann's *Milch und Kohle* (2000): "Hier ist Stadt: Asphaltierte Straßen, nette Nachbarn, ein Fernseher, jeden Tag Tanz bei 'Maus,'"[20] or on the banal materialism of the 1950s' economic miracle as presented, for example, in Michael Kumpfmüller's *Hampels Fluchten* (2000). In the first few years after unification, however, established west German writers, in common with eastern colleagues, were more likely to see the Federal Republic in a negative light. Above all, they would focus on the colonization of the ex-GDR by west German capitalism and on west German condescension.

A striking example of this trend is provided by F. C. Delius's short narrative *Die Birnen von Ribbeck*, which appeared in 1991, that is, just after unification. Similar to Grass's *Ein weites Feld* and Jens Sparschuh's *Eins zu Eins* (2003), Delius's text invokes Theodor Fontane. A group of west German tourists travel to the east German village of Ribbeck and decide to plant a pear tree in memory of the nineteenth-century author who had written a ballad about Herr von Ribbeck and the pear seed planted in the old man's grave. To the narrator, a longtime inhabitant of the village, these new arrivals appear as "Besatzer."[21] Their attempts to colonize the cultural heritage of the village completely disregard the way Fontane's legacy had been inflected by the local population during the years of the GDR: "gegen das Kriechen vor den Lügen faßten wir endlich selbst einen Plan heimlich beim Bier, einen Birnbaum zu setzen an die alte Stelle" (*DBR*, 39). This was a protest against both the destruction caused by Russian tanks tearing through the village — the tree would create an obstacle in their path — and the suppression by the GDR authorities of criticism of the Soviet Union's actions in East Germany. Instead, the west Germans appropriate Fontane's legacy by associating themselves with the village's previous aristocratic landlords, as praised in the author's ballad. Bearing all manner of gifts, including biro pens, they seek to win favor and fail to comprehend that the giving of such trinkets to the "naïve natives" merely reinforces the colonial relationship.

Delius's narrative was criticized at the time of its publication by reviewers who felt that its particular illustration of what Florentine Strzelczyk terms the "neo-kolonialistische Inbesitznahme"[22] of the ex-

GDR was itself a form of colonization. For Reinhard Baumgart, for example, the presentation of a putatively authentic eastern voice by a western author "wenn auch gut, ja bestens gemeint" was nonetheless "ein Akt der Kolonisierung."[23] East Germans, it was argued, were again being "exoticized" for a western audience. Yet this analysis of the work, Karoline von Oppen reveals, was not shared by its east German readers. Nor is it sustained, she contends, by a careful inspection of its narrative strategies and its "mocking scrutiny" of the "role of ethnographer."[24] Thus von Oppen points to Delius's appearance in his own text — "was macht der da hinten, ein Tonbandgerät, na gut" — although she does not mention the link made by the narrator between this form of observation and the activities of the *Stasi* in previous times: "die Stasi ist weg und abgetaucht" (*DBR*, 17). Just as striking, she argues, is the fact that the much-vaunted dialogue between east and west never takes place. The west Germans disappear from the narrative a mere six pages into the text, satisfied that they have "learnt" all there is to know about the natives.[25]

A story that is ostensibly about east Germany hence simultaneously implies a critique of the "old" FRG — a subject on which the west German writer is certainly qualified to write. The same is also true of Delius's *Der Spaziergang von Rostock nach Syrakuse* (1995), which describes the efforts of a GDR citizen, Paul Gompitz, to follow in the steps of the philosopher Johann Gottfried Seume who journeyed from the Baltic Sea to Italy in 1802. What begins as a condemnation of the obstacles placed in his way by the refusal of the powers-that-be to allow him to travel west soon largely gives way to a critical assessment of the "old" Federal Republic. Once again, West German clichés are exposed as Gompitz quickly realizes, in conversations in Prague with two tourists from the other side of the inner German border, that it is easier to conform to their image of the GDR: "besser dummer stellen als du bist."[26] Later, he notes a distinct lack of solidarity (*DS*, 45) and is irritated by the misplaced idealism with regard to the GDR expressed by two West German youths he meets (*DS*, 47–48). What is most galling for Gompitz once he finally succeeds in sailing from East Germany to Denmark in 1988, however, is the way the authorities in West Germany appear incapable of understanding that he wishes to return to the GDR after he has completed his excursion to Syracuse. His impression of the ideological distortion informing western views of the GDR is later confirmed by newspaper reports that turn his "Bildungsreise" into a more sentimental "Traumreise" (*DS*, 100).

The narrator and his excitable interlocutor certainly express greater respect for the integrity of Gompitz's experiences than the journalists for whom he simply embodies the desire to enjoy the pleasures of consumption and self-gratification taken for granted in the west. Yet their own fascination with the figure of Gompitz is no less ideological in origin. For them, Gompitz represents what was "good" about the former GDR, that is, its range of subcultures in which "interessante Leute" of all kinds could create niches away from the prying eyes of the state and achieve a form of utopian self-sufficiency impossible in the west. Gompitz, for the narrator and his conversation partner, incorporates the "true" ideals of the ex-GDR and, by extension, offers a vision of sociability and solidarity against which they might measure the Federal Republic. "Aber hier muß man mitlügen und hochstapeln, wenn man aufsteigen will" (*DS*, 109), Gompitz is reported as saying some time after his arrival in the west.

Similar to *Die Birnen von Ribbeck*, Delius's 1995 novel might be accused of colonizing east German experiences. Here too, however, the narrative form introduces an element of self-reflexivity. Gompitz's story is related via a dialogue between the narrator and a friend, both from the west, with the friend's interjections, rendered in italics, serving as stimulus for the continuation of the saga. First and foremost, this alerts the reader to the risk that this GDR tale may tend to exoticize, sensationalize or otherwise misappropriate Gompitz's story. As the text proceeds, in fact, the friend's interjections increasingly tend to demand greater pace and drama and to express less and less regard for Gompitz's motives. The narrator is even driven, towards the end of his account, to correct his friend's use of the word "Traumreise" (*DS*, 123), the very same term used, of course, in the press during Gompitz's time in West Germany.

F. C. Delius's *Die Birnen von Ribbeck* and *Der Spaziergang von Rostock nach Syrakuse* relate east German tales in order to speak of the former West Germany and of West German materialism. At the same time, they introduce an element of self-reflexivity vis-à-vis the idealization of the former GDR by sections of the West German left and pertaining to their skepticism towards the "old" Federal Republic. We return to this in a subsequent section examining the rethinking of the early FRG and the events of '68: the "ahistorical normality" of the globalized consumer society has led many on the left to rexamine their hostility to the "old" FRG and to reevaluate its achievements. Next, however, we turn to the work Martin Walser, a writer who tells tales from east *and* west in order to uncover what he sees as malevolent continuities between the "old" FRG and the new Germany. Walser's standpoint is rooted in a *conservative* anti-capitalism. For this writer, any new German "normality" would need to be rooted in older, more "authentic" traditions.

West Germany: Philistine and Provincial?

Martin Walser's critique of the "old" FRG most likely develops out of his rejection of the *de facto* acceptance by its social and political elites, certainly from the late 1960s, of the finality of German division. In a 1972 novel, *Die Gallistl'sche Krankheit,* Walser's eponymous protagonist had already expressed what were most likely the author's own views: "Sachsen ist mir vertraut, ohne daß ich je dort war. Wie oft denke ich an Magdeburg!"[27] In the years that followed, he would refer repeatedly to his perception of the provisionality of the FRG and to his sense of alienation. In an essay published in 1979, he noted: "Alle anderen sind vielleicht erfüllt, zukunftshell und wohlgemut. Bundesrepublikaner für immer."[28] Later, the author would project his own sense of being split onto Wolf, the protagonist of the 1987 novella *Dorle und Wolf.* "Geteilt wie Deutschland" himself,[29] Wolf cannot understand why his fellow West Germans fail to grasp that they too are "lauter Halbierte" (*DW,* 313) and, in court, justifies his spying for the GDR as a patriotic act intended to prevent the technological chasm between East and West Germany from becoming an eternal barrier to unification.

For Wolf, the "old" FRG is "alles, was er sein kann und sein soll. Souverän und endgültig" (*DW,* 398). In Walser's fiction from the late 1980s onwards, in fact, the FRG is presented as a somewhat artificial bureaucratic entity in which commerce and constitutional legalism are promoted over community, memory, and identity.[30] In the 1991 novel *Die Verteidigung der Kindheit,* for instance, Alfred's obsession with the objects that provide a precarious link to a childhood spent in Dresden before the devastation of the city's baroque glories in February 1945 and his fascination with the Pergamon Altar in East Berlin are framed as acts of resistance against the erasure of Germany's cultural heritage by the Allies and against the philistinism of the Federal Republic.[31] He feels that, in the GDR, at least, elements of Germany's cultural legacy are preserved, albeit by chance — this is an example of a *conservative* idealization of an East Germany sheltered from American influence. In the FRG, the only part of the German past that concerns the authorities are the twelve years of Nazi tyranny. By their efforts to further a self-serving "Wiedergutmachungsillusion,"[32] the FRG's intellectual and political elites have destroyed all traces of more positive German traditions.[33]

Walser's 1993 *ohne einander* and his 1998 *Ein springender Brunnen* intervene in the debates on "political correctness" of the early and mid-1990s launched by the so-called intellectual New Right.[34] The critique made by Sylvio, one of the chief characters of *ohne einander,* of the "Verurteilungskultur" which infuses the German media in the 1990s,[35] for instance, resembles Botho Strauß's article in *Der Spiegel* of 1993, "Anschwellender Bockgesang," in which Strauß indicts the "bigotte Frömmigkeit des Politischen, des Kritischen und All-Bestreitbaren."[36] It also anticipates Walser's attack in his 1998 *Friedenspreisrede* on the "Meinungssoldaten" in the media who, "mit vorgehaltener Moralpistole," denigrate those who resist what he sees as the left's "instrumentalization" of Auschwitz to win political arguments.[37] In *Ein springender Brunnen,* moreover, a series of narratorial intercessions criticize a discourse of coming-to-terms with the past which generates a "gereinigte, genehmigte, total gegenwartsgeeignete Vergangenheit."[38] Indeed, the novel's very premise — that a boy growing up in the 1930s might be concerned with things *other* than Nazism — is in itself an attack on "political correctness." In *Tod eines Kritikers* (2002), the fictional murder of a Jewish critic modeled on Marcel Reich-Ranicki challenges readers to question the limits imposed on the imagination by present-day sensitivities regarding anti-Semitism.[39]

Walser's *Friedenspreis* speech and *Ein springender Brunnen* are subjected to more detailed analysis in a subsequent chapter dealing with 1990s' writing on the Nazi past. More germane to our present discussion is the way the artificial, constitutionalist character of the FRG precludes any possibility of a truly emotional attachment to a German national identity. In *Die Verteidigung der Kindheit,* then, the criticism of the postwar order suggested by Alfred's elision of the present for the sake of past glories indicts the banality of the Federal Republic. This censure is extended in *Finks Krieg,* which appeared in 1995. Here, the eponymous hero battles with little success against the rationalist, bureaucratic state, with its alliances of convenience and legalistic labyrinths, in an attempt to reverse his dismissal from the civil service. Ultimately, he is defeated by the nexus of church, parties, and state working in concert to ensure a mutually beneficial distribution of power.

In Walser's *Lebenslauf der Liebe* (2001), the social and political context is, as Martin Lüdke suggests, "nahezu vollständig ausgeblendet."[40] Its protagonist, Susi Gern, appears to be far more concerned with the failures of her love life than with the monumental events that shaped the fifteen-year period in which the novel is set, that is, from the mid-1980s to the millennium. There are, it is true, allusions to the stock market crash of 19 October 1987 and the "Marktfundamentalismus" of the late 1980s and 1990s.[41] Yet they are background detail in a plot focussed primarily on Susi's efforts to compensate for the infidelity of her husband Edmund, the miserable routine of buying off those inconvenienced by her retarded daughter and the pain caused her by her son's sordid affairs, financial impropriety, and prostitution racket. Indeed, the novel is primarily an account of her pathetic emotional dependence on Edmund and her sorry efforts to persuade the men she picks up via small ads to desire her.

Insofar as an image of the Federal Republic emerges at all, it is a portrait of its dulling lack of ambition. Susi, similar to Fink, surely impresses the reader with her stubborn denial of unpalatable realities — these represent a victory of sorts for subjectivity — and yet in many ways she and her husband are products of their age and of the FRG. For all his sexual experimentation, Edmund is utterly bourgeois, concerned mainly for his reputation and the consequences of his misguided investments. Susi, likewise, is a reluctant bohemian. In reality, she is entirely out of her depth. Endowed with sudden prosperity following the economic miracle of the 1950s, she is as materialistic as her peers. Spiritually, however, she is entirely disorientated. In a society lacking deeper values, all that is left is a thoroughly conventional idealization of love. Yet this too seems destined to be sullied by the confusion of real emotion with the immediate gratification of casual sex. It is significant, therefore, that the only man who remains true to her is a Muslim. With her second husband, Khalil, she magically returns to a state of innocence: "Sie ist vergangenheitslos [. . .] Khalil ist ihr erster Mann" (*LL,* 406). The west, it would seem, and the Federal Republic in particular, has sacrificed the aspirations of social cohesion, fidelity, and spirituality to the banality of greed.[42]

Walser's conservative anti-capitalism, with its attack on the Federal Republic, before and after unification, as a state that draws its legitimacy from its prosperity, shares much with the left-wing critique of the West German consumer society. Yet Walser decries not only the FRG's fetishization of economic success but also the way its intellectual elites appeared, from the 1970s, at least, to have abandoned an emotional attachment to the nation in favor of a discourse of German self-negation. For both left and right, the FRG was to be damned for its focus on wealth rather than "values." For the left, the "correct" values would include a sustained engagement with the Nazi past and the denial of national identity. For Walser, what Helmut Peitsch has described as his "kulturell-utopischen Nationalismus"[43] is always paramount. A new German "normality," accordingly, may only be established via a re-imagining of the German heritage seemingly obliterated by the philistine Federal Republic.

Günter Grass, as we have seen, continued throughout the 1990s to ascribe to the conventional left-wing position that any celebration of "Germanness" was dangerous. Other established writers who had previously been skeptical of the "old" FRG and its economic priorities, however, began to express a greater affection for a state which, in retrospect, now appeared to have delivered more than merely material comfort. This unexpected fondness for the "old" FRG implied an acknowledgment that West Germany, for all its faults, and after many setbacks, had entrenched respect for human rights, mutual tolerance, and the principle of equality before the law. As such, it had been quite unlike any previous — or concurrent — German state.

Rethinking the Early Federal Republic

Uwe Timm's 1993 novella *Die Entdeckung der Currywurst* takes one of the great icons of the modern Federal Republic — the curried sausage to be found at fast-food stands throughout the country — and transforms it into a symbol of the reconstruction of the western part of the divided German nation in the early postwar years. Indeed, the *Currywurst*, with its addition of an exotic blend of spices to the traditional staple of sausage meat, is presented as the embodiment of the incipient *Wirtschaftswunder* of the late 1940s. Most obviously, the availability of *Currywurst* in itself signals the end of shortages of the war years and the postwar period. More poignantly, however, the mixture of "foreign" spices in the curry powder symbolizes the FRG's opening-out to the world, in its outlook as much as in its imminent success as a trading nation.

The *Currywurst*, however, also serves a further, vital function: that of allaying melancholia. Frau Brücker, whose story is recounted by the narrator, tells of the way she invented the *Currywurst* in a process of trial and error as a means of reviving the taste buds of her lover, Bremer, the navy deserter whom she takes into her house towards the end of the war. Despite his unwillingness to be sacrificed by the Nazi leadership in a last futile battle against the invading Allies, Bremer continues to refight the lost campaigns of the eastern front. Fearful that he might fall into lethargy if she were to disabuse him, and concerned for the impact this might have on her first experience of sexual satisfaction, Brücker pretends that the British occupation troops are now allied with the Germans against the Soviet Union and insists that he remain hidden in her house so that he will not be reconscripted. All the while, the two of them continue to experiment with different spices, including ginger, "ein Gewürz gegen die Schwermut,"[44] in order to reinvigorate the defeated man's taste for life.

Timm's narrative is unusual insofar as it displays a degree of sympathy for the feelings of loss and disorientation experienced by the common German soldier, and indeed by the population as a whole, in the wake of the collapse of the Nazi regime in May 1945. The concern shown by Frau Brücker for her lover's melancholia with regard to the lost war is presented not as a desire to avoid confronting Nazi misdeeds but as a canny recognition of the need to introduce him slowly to the new realities of the postwar present, including the loss of territory and the fact of occupation. Her own shock realization of the extent of Nazi atrocities is subsequently presented as a model both for Bremer and the rest of her compatriots. Forced to contemplate images of concentration camp victims, she at first refuses to believe her eyes but is then resolute: "Der Krieg ist aus [. . .] Wir haben ihn verloren, total. Gott sei Dank" (*DEC*, 174). Melancholia, it seems, must precede the resolve to face up to the past.

Timm's narrator, who is marked as the author's alter ego, takes the story of the much older Lena Brücker and makes it his own, using the excuse that her narrative was so rambling "daß ich hier auswählen, begradigen, verknüpfen und kürzen muß" (*DEC,* 20). What the narrator is attempting, in truth, is a reconstruction of the pre-history of the FRG which would allow his generation — a generation more prone to denouncing the persistence of both Nazi ideology and personnel in the West Germany of the 1950s and 1960s — to find more positive traditions. Along with Frau Brücker, we are introduced to Holzinger, the cook who gives local Nazi leaders a dose of food poisoning and halts their interminable speeches. The narrator's grandmother, moreover, is credited with preventing some SS men from beating up a Russian POW; later, in the mid-1950s, she protested against West German rearmament. Authoritarian structures and the ideology of militarism persist after the war (this, in fact, is the theme of Timm's short narrative of 2003, *Am Beispiel meines Bruders,* as discussed in subsequent chapters). At the same time, however, there are alternative voices, voices of dissent and resistance, with which the narrator and his generation might identify and which may allow for a more differentiated view of the first years of the FRG.

F. C. Delius's *Der Sonntag, an dem ich Weltmeister wurde* (1994) effects a similar re-evaluation of the early FRG history. In this case, however, it is the German soccer world cup victory in 1954 that is presented as the instant after which the author's own generation was first able to identify with the Federal Republic. A sporting triumph that has usually been seen as reinforcing a conservative *Restauration* in the fledgling West German state, a boost to Chancellor Konrad Adenauer's efforts to restore Germany to international respectability, is reinterpreted as a moment of inspiration for the narrator in his efforts to break free of the suffocating conformity expected of him by his father, a pastor, and his mother, the dutiful wife.

The German victory against the Hungarians in the stadium at Bern is viewed by the narrator not as an excuse for a new nationalism — expressed in the newspaper headlines *wir sind wieder wer.* Nor is it presented as a moment when those members of his parents' generation who continued to insist on the injustices they suffered as a result of the lost war, those who had been bombed out or considered themselves "zu Unrecht vertrieben,"[45] might feel themselves to have been avenged, if only on the sports' field. Instead, it is the moment when the narrator loses his stutter, begins to speak in his own voice and starts to internalize the values of the new Germany. In his reconstruction of Herbert Zimmermann's famous radio commentary, he describes how two versions of the national anthem were sung simultaneously, "die verbotene erste und die erlaubte dritte Strophe." The first verse runs thus: "*Deutschland,*

Deutschland über alles" whereas the third contains the words *"Einigkeit und Recht und Freiheit."* The narrator's class had only recently been taught the third verse, in June 1954, the first anniversary of the workers' uprising in East Berlin (*DSA,* 116), in the course of the FRG's efforts to discredit the GDR. Yet these are the words with which he identifies, a statement of commitment that has nothing to do with fending off communism but everything to do with the way the German team played: "das Prinzip des Gehorchens oder Fügens oder Anpassens oder Wegtauchens galt hier nicht" (*DSA,* 110). At last, the narrator has found a set of values that he can make his own and has taken possession of this new state, the Federal Republic of Germany.

The rethinking of the early years of the "old" Federal Republic by members of the generation of '68 necessarily implies a rethinking of 1968 itself, and of the student movement. This trend too, which has been described in some detail by Ingo Cornils,[46] is reflected in a number of literary texts of the 1990s. Elsewhere, Cornils has referred to the manner in which "the process of literary representation as a continuation of the political struggle" came to be replaced "by one of remembering and reevaluation, perhaps even historicisation."[47] Literary representations of the student movement focusing on its political successes and failures — as found, for example, in Peter Schneider's *Lenz* (1974) — began to give way to more intimate recollections. These concentrate on first sexual experiences, on growing-up, and on the way the protagonist's voyage of self-discovery informs his (the main characters are almost always male) perception of his social and political context rather than the other way around. This development encourages both a lighter tone and a less dogmatic view of the state's inadequacies.

Delius's *Amerikahaus und der Tanz um die Frauen* (1997) recounts the story of Martin, a student in Berlin in the mid-1960s, who is caught up in the demonstrations against the war in Vietnam. Far from telling of his ideological commitment to the "cause," however, this novel picks up where *Der Sonntag, an dem ich Weltmeister wurde* left off and details the difficulties faced by the shy pastor's son following his move from the provinces to the city. Quite simply, *Amerikahaus und der Tanz um die Frauen,* as the two parts of its title imply, exposes the way revulsion at Nazi crimes, transposed onto images of American military action in Vietnam, combined with adolescent anxieties to produce an explosive rejection of the prevailing order. At the end of the novel, riots in Berlin in late 1966 are confused in Martin's mind with a recent sexual experience: "Krawall, Rahel, Krawall, Rahel."[48] In losing his virginity to Rahel, an Israeli, moreover, he protests against guilt inherited from his parents: "die sogenannte Unschuld, wie lächerlich, nein, deine Schuld hast du verloren" (*AT*). In *Himmelfahrt eines Staatsfeindes* (1992), the third in a trilogy with *Ein Held der inneren Sicherheit* (1981) and *Mogadischu Fensterplatz* (1987), Delius had already depicted the way the exaggerated media response to this moral fervor would, in the 1970s, push some student radicals further in the direction of terrorism.

In Uwe Timm's *Rot* (2001), the narrator looks back at his participation in far-left political activism in the late 1960s from the perspective of the late 1990s. Similar to Ulrike Kolb's *Frühstück mit Max* (2000), Erasmus Schöfer's *Ein Frühling irrer Hoffnung* (2001) and Leander Scholz's narrative *Das Rosenfest* (2001) — the latter a fictionalization of the relationship between *Rote Armee Fraktion* members Baader and Ensslin — Timm's *Rot* raises the questions of whether violence was, or may still be, a legitimate means of bringing about the realization of the student movement's heady ideals. Thomas Linde, onetime "professional revolutionary" turned jazz critic and funeral orator, offers up an improvised obituary for the radical politics to which he once dedicated himself. Along the way, he endeavors to explain to his girlfriend Iris what might have motivated his former comrade Aschenberger to plan to blow up the *Siegessäule* in central Berlin. Twenty-one years his junior, she has little understanding of "direct action." Whereas Linde dreams of carrying out Aschenberger's plan with the explosives left for him by his recently deceased friend, Iris would substitute a multi-media show for the intended protest against German militarism.

Even as he composes a requiem for his dead friend, the narrator also supplies a graveside oration for the generation of '68 to which they both belong and for the state against which they and their peers once revolted but with which they ultimately became so closely identified. Their parents had entrenched West Germany's capitalist orientation and economic configuration, but it was the "68ers" who would imbue it with its defining social and political values. Whereas the narrator's father and his two uncles "haben die Bundesrepublik aufgebaut,"[49] it was the student radicals who imposed upon the Federal Republic an ideological superstructure in which respect for human rights, the rule of law, and basic social equity made life bearable if far from perfect. Indeed, the student movement, to cite the title of Matthias Kopp's 1993 film essay, was *erfolgreich gescheitert*.[50] At the end of the 1990s, the majority of Linde's former comrades appear disillusioned — their marriages are failing and they are tormented by growing older — but they have preserved something of their ideals even *within* the compromises they have made with the system. Edmond, now a millionaire wine merchant, employs only ex-radicals in his business; Linde's ex-wife lives with an Angolan asylum seeker, and two friends work in the former East Germany as schoolteachers and accept a reduction in hours in order to create an additional post.

The narrator's depiction of the uneasy, often fraught accommodation between the West German state and the generation of '68 is both a proud statement of the student movement's lasting impact and an admission of its errors. The "68ers" were right to protest against the state's overreaction to terrorism in the 1970s and against the decree banning former radicals from the civil service, that is, the *Berufsverbot,* but wrong in their blinkered support for the ex-GDR. A key turning point for the narrator, therefore, came when he attended the trial of Erich Honecker in the early 1990s and found himself sitting next to a woman whose life had been ruined by the regime (*RO,* 409). Above all, however, the tone is one of measured nostalgia. Indeed, the fading away of the generation of '68 — the narrator too has been diagnosed with cancer — coincides with the drawn-out exit of the "old" Federal Republic and with the inauguration of the Berlin Republic.

Aschenberger's plan to blow up the *Siegessäule* was slated to be carried out on the day in 1999 on which the government would officially move to Berlin, Germany's capital city once more. His would have been a protest, therefore, against the incipient Berlin Republic, with the ruins of the *Siegessäule* — a symbol of Prussian triumphs over Denmark, Austria, and France — intended as a reminder of the hubris of German militarism in the past and as a warning against the incremental expansion of out-of-area operations by the *Bundeswehr* after 1990 and especially following the election of the Red-Green coalition. The form of the protest, moreover, an *anti*-memorial, would have offered a vivid contrast to what Aschenberger and the narrator regard as the new Germany's creeping culture of self-congratulation. The countless memorials being erected at the end of the 1990s to commemorate the extermination of European Jews, for Aschenberger and Thomas Linde, represent not so much an internalization of the lessons of the past as a desire to consign it to history. And if the Holocaust were no longer to anchor an attention to liberal values of self-criticism and restraint, what kind of country would this new Germany be? The fear is that the focus on consumption would be all that remained of the West German legacy.

The Consumer Republic? The Rebirth of "Pop"

The "normalization" of the post-unification Federal Republic entails, as far as the likes of Aschenberger and Thomas are concerned, the erasure of hard-won values of self-criticism and historical awareness by the primacy of materialism. In essence, the achievements of the "old" FRG — only now appreciated — appear to have given way to the "ahistorical normality" of globalized consumerism. Linde's lover Iris and her husband Ben, members of the generation born from the mid-1960s to the mid-1970s, are as unburdened by the Nazi past and indifferent to political protest as they are determined to enjoy the material benefits of advancement in their respective careers. Iris, the narrator tells us, combines that "wozu sie Lust hat, mit dem, was ihr Nutzen bringt" (*RO*, 32) and Ben, though made uncomfortable by the consequences for friends at work of the reports he writes on their performance, appears to believe that there can be no alternative to the doctrine of profit and productivity propagated by neo-liberal capitalism. Both, moreover, are baffled by Linde's asceticism and lack of rootedness in property and profession. Indeed, his self-confessed "Bindungslosigkeit" (*RO*, 280) appears dated to the young couple and, increasingly, to Linde himself.

The disdain for materialism broadcast by those "68ers" who, as a result of their "march through the institutions," came to hold key positions in education, politics, and the media, perhaps almost inevitably made an *embrace* of the consumer society the primary expression of dissent for subsequent generations in their own efforts to assert themselves. Accordingly, two *west* German cohorts, the "78ers" and the so-called Generation Golf, were defined in the course of the 1990s in sociological studies and journalistic investigations with reference to their attitudes both to consumerism and the "68ers." In chapter one, we mentioned "78ers" such as Matthias Politycki (born 1955), Dagmar Leupold (1955), Matthias Altenburg (1958) and Maxim Biller (1960). To these might be added, amongst others, Thomas Lehr (1953), Rainald Goetz (1954), Thomas Meinecke (1955), Ulrich Peltzer (1956), Dorothea Dieckmann (1957), Michael Wildenhain (1958), Max Goldt (1958), Silvia Szymanski (1958), Andreas Neumeister (1959), Michael Kleeberg (1959), Ulrich Woelk (1960), Norbert Niemann (1960) and Heiner Link (1961). With regard to the Generation Golf, Florian Illies's book of that name (2000) offered *eine Inspektion* — thus its subtitle — of the twenty-something generation and its attachment to brands. Ownership of a Volkswagen Golf, for Illies, had become the number one goal. In 2003, Illies followed this first survey with *Generation Golf II*, a more pessimistic volume which, in the aftermath of the terrorist attacks of 11 September 2001 and the Gulf War of 2003, announced the end of the consumption-fuelled insouciance of the early to mid-1990s: "Alles ist vorbei. Die New Economy. Die Spaßgesellschaft. Die Popliteratur."[51]

In the course of the 1990s, in fact, pop literature had become a crucial focus of the campaign by both the "78ers" and the Generation Golf to emancipate themselves from the perceived hegemony of the former student radicals who seemed to dominate post-1990 Germany. Pop, of course, as Hubert Winkels notes, is notoriously difficult to define.[52] As far as the renaissance of pop literature in the late 1980s and 1990s is concerned, however, it is possible to isolate, broadly speaking, three major trends. Thus we might refer to the "advanced pop" of Goetz, Neumeister or Meinecke, in which the club scene of the 1970s and 1980s is theorized and reproduced in an abstract, impressionistic stream of consciousness. Alternatively, we might point to the nostalgic invocations of the trends and fashions of 1980s' West Germany offered by Generation Golf writers Frank Goosen (born 1966) or David Wagner (1971), or — our third trend — to the focus on the designer labels of the 1990s to be found in Karen Duve (1961 in East Germany, then grew up in the FRG), Sibylle Berg (1962, also in East Germany), Elke Naters (1963), Tim Staffel (1965), Sven Lager (1965), Christian Kracht (1966), Alexander von Schönburg (1969), Joachim Bessing (1971), Alexa Hennig von Lange (1973) and Benjamin von Stuckrad-Barre (1975). Just as the pop movement of the 1960s seemed to many — including Martin Walser, at that time a left-wing proponent of a socially-engaged literature — to lack political relevance, so would each of these more recent pop forms be dismissed by its critics as self-satisfied.[53] In reality, however, the impression of superficiality often disguises a more profound concern with key questions of selfhood and "Germanness" in an age in which global brands and a hegemonic global culture appear to be erasing local identity. At its best, the pop literature of the 1990s, famously "das was Martin Walser nicht ist,"[54] provides an insight into the ambiguities inherent in the process of German "normalization."

"Das Ja zur modernen Welt erschien uns dabei vorübergehend als die denkbar größte Möglichkeit zu politischer Dissidenz," avers Thomas Meinecke in the foreword to *Mode und Verzweiflung* (1998), a selection of his contributions to the magazine of the same name that he co-founded in 1978. Too young to be counted amongst the "Hippies" of '68 but too old to be part of the punk craze of 1977 — the year of the Sex Pistols hit "God Save the Queen" — this "flanierende Haufen hedonistischer Partisanen"[55] began to subvert the self-righteous moralism of the "68ers." In the 1990s, this became a major literary trend. Ulrich Woelk's *Rückspiel* (1993), for example, examines the dogmatism of a veteran of '68 from the perspective of his younger brother whereas Michael Wildenhain's *Erste Liebe — Deutscher Herbst* (1997), set at the height of the terrorism alerts of the mid-1970s, elevates the experience of first love over politics. Other "78ers," however, were more interested in reproducing the *sensory* experience of contemporary popular culture in what initially appears as an entirely immanent language of celebration and imitation. This is what Moritz Baßler has referred to as the attempt to "archive" the present in a "Literatur der zweiten Worte," a manifestly *a*political contrast with the social critique of the "68ers."[56] Rainald Goetz takes this to an extreme in novels, plays, performance pieces, and CDs beginning with *Irre* (1983) and including, in the 1990s, *Celebration. Texte* *und Bilder zur Nacht* (1998), *Katarakt* (2000), *Rave* (1998), *Jeff Koons* (1998), *Dekonspiratione* (2000), *Jahrzehnt der schönen Frauen* (2001), *Heute Morgen* (2001), and the "internet-diary" *Abfall für alle* (1999). A "Bejahung," Winkels suggests, of recreational drug-taking, raves, and fashion, Goetz's work reproduces "jenen Sound der Unmittelbarkeit, der an den Augenblicken des Glücks im gelebten Leben sich anzuschließen sucht."[57] Yet even as it alludes to MTV and VIVA or celebrates the art of the "DJ mix" and the "Euphorie" of dance music,[58] a novel such as *Rave* simultaneously attacks the dulling uniformity of the pressure to be "in" as well as those who have become part of the media scene and integrated into the mainstream book industry. A note of self-reflexivity is introduced, then, as the narrator alludes to the pose inherent in the endeavor to theorize on the subject of the "Welt des Populären" from the position of "irgendeiner geistigen Pop-Elite" (*RA*, 176–77). Goetz himself is published by Suhrkamp, as are Neumeister and Meinecke, as part of this traditionally highbrow publishing house's efforts to extend its brand appeal.[59] It is probable, therefore, that he is included in this (self-)criticism.

"It's all drugs, shagging, fighting and sunburn" (*RA,* 141). This quotation from Irvine Welsh acknowledges the debt owed by the "advanced" pop literature of the 1990s to Anglo-American influences such as Welsh and Bret Easton Ellis with their juxtaposition of the value-free hedonism of popular culture with a darkly pessimistic vision of the baseness of human instincts. Equally, the work of Goetz, Meinecke, and Neumeister, in particular, is replete with allusions to fashionable cultural theorists from the USA, France, and Great Britain. In *Rave,* for example, Gilles Deleuze is cited during an attack on the self-delusion of the "pop elite" in its search for "Signalen von irgendwie widerständiger Intelligenz" (*RA,* 34). In Meinecke's *Tomboy* (1999), alternatively, it is rather the "dekonstruktivischen Werken jüngerer, mehrheitlich US-amerikanischer Feministinnen"[60] which guide the efforts of the protagonist, Vivian, to arrive at a theoretically-grounded understanding of her own complex subjectivity. Yet the highly manneristic feel of references of this kind draws attention to the way they have been imported from without. In *Tomboy,* the half-German, half-American Vivian thus stands in for a generation that can conceive of itself only as an unstable hybrid and in relation to the "global American otherness, in aller Welt imaginiert, in aller Welt beschworen" (*TB,* 209). In the end, this self-alienation can only be repressed via a total and unthinking immersion in the immediacy of consumerism. "Was werden wir tragen?" (*TB,* 251), Vivian asks herself at the close of the novel.

Pop culture provides a way out of the dilemmas of German identity and yet, in facilitating this escape, it also threatens to erase any sense of being rooted in a particular society or tradition: once again, we glimpse the familiar anxiety regarding the "ahistorical normality" of the globalized consumer society. Meinecke thematizes this dilemma in his *Church of John F. Kennedy* (1996), in which Wenzel Assmann searches out the traces of a German immigrant culture in the southern states of the USA, an attempt "einer deutschen Identität auf die Spur zu kommen" *within* a now dominant American discourse which, Charis Goer argues, remains "unvollendet."[61] Others such as Andreas Neumeister, on the other hand, choose to *inflect* an only apparently hegemonic Anglo-American pop culture with a German sensibility. In his *Gut laut* (1998), a survey of pop music from the Munich Olympics of 1972 onwards, for example, Neumeister's narrator almost obsessively lists his passion for the hits of the 1970s and 1980s but his memories of the impact they had on him is, as Hubert Winkels notes, "im Münchner Boden tief verwurzelt."[62] The German past lingers even in the world of international pop music — the narrator constructs a "German chart" of pop songs including "Public Enemy: Hitler Day" and the "Sex Pistols: Belsen was a Gas"[63] — but now there is an alternative trajectory of German identity, and of a German "normality," one that runs parallel to the consolidation of the Federal Republic in the 1970s, encompassing the "Sound of Mjunik" (*GL,* 58), influential bands such as Kraftwerk and the global phenomenon of *Krautrock.*

Looking back from the late 1990s, Neumeister's narrator summarizes the good fortune he has enjoyed: "daß uns Nachkriegselend und Nachkriegsfolgeelend großteils erspart geblieben sind, bin ich froh, daß uns das esoterische 68er-Renegatentum erspart geblieben ist" (*GL,* 176). For the narrator, the West Germany of the 1970s and 1980s was a benign place to grow up. Affluence and the achievement of a certain distance from the Nazi past meant that the FRG had become reassuringly dull. This was an unremarkable western society in which young people could indulge in the pleasures of consumerism without feeling any special responsibility for the crimes of the past or the injustices of the present. For the "78ers," West Germany was happily provincial, modest in its ambitions, concerned primarily with the economic security of its citizens, and anxious to avoid risks and grand social and political experiments.

Neumeister's *Ausdeutschen* (1994) had already expressed nostalgia for the imminent loss of this West German provinciality upon unification in 1990. Thus the narrator provides a countdown to the disappearance of West Berlin, a city which throughout the text stands in for the comfortingly circumscribed status of the "old" Federal Republic as a whole: "Westberlin als West-Berlin hatte noch eine Frist von dreizehn Stunden."[64] Other novels of the 1990s by "78ers," including Thomas Lehr's *Nabokovs Katze* (1999), Ulrich Peltzer's *"Alle oder keiner"* (1999), and Dorothea Dieckmann's novel *Damen & Herren* (2002), similarly cast back to the 1970s and 1980s. In *Nabokovs Katze*, a young man sets out for Berlin and Mexico, via a series of erotic encounters, but never loses, or even wishes to lose, his innocence of the ways of the world outside the West German province. Matthias Politycki's *Weiberroman* (1993), which tells of its narrator's affairs with various women and traces shifts in fashion into the 1980s, likewise alludes to a West German "normality." The same may be said of Politycki's novel *Ein Mann von Vierzig Jahren* (2000), with its — as Iris Radisch puts it — "etwa hausbackenen und detail-verliebten Rekonstruktion einer Jugend in den sechziger und siebziger Jahren."[65] The reassuring, and often comic, everyday banality of the pre-1990 FRG is also the predominant theme in Norbert Niemann's 1998 *Wie man's nimmt:* "Alles ist normal. *Wir sind alle ganz normal.*"[66]

In Frank Goosen's *liegen lernen* (1999), a novel with echoes of Nick Hornby's *High Fidelity* (1995), "Generation Golf" protagonist Helmut reflects back on the cosy provinciality of the Kohl era: "Auf den Illustrierten waren entweder nackte Frauen oder Atompilze, manchmal beides, und man wußte oft nicht, was schlimmer war."[67] Comparable re-frains are to be found in David Wagner's *Meine nachtblaue Hose* (2000), in which the youngsters of the 1980s are exercised by the contest of "Adidas gegen Puma."[68] According to Andrew Plowman, these texts, and novels such as Jess Jochimsen's *Das Dosenmilch-Trauma: Bekenntnisse eines 68er-Kindes* (2000) or Jürgen Noltensmeier's *Geburtenstarke Jahrgänge* (2002), embody both an attempt by the Generation Golf to distance itself from the "68ers" and nostalgia for the "old" FRG. This pe-culiarly *west* German nostalgia has been termed *Westalgie* by the British critic, by analogy with the *Ostalgie* discussed in a previous chapter. In-deed, the insistence upon a previous "normality" as an alternative to the kinds of "normality" being promoted in the present informs both *Ostalgie* and *Westalgie*. *Westalgie* thus entails, Plowman argues, regret for the pass-ing of the "old," pre-unification FRG before it was exposed to the shock of economic globalization.[69] To this extent, these novels contribute to a trend which encompasses both "78ers" and the Generation Golf. As evi-dence of this, Plowman refers to the series in the *Süddeutsche Zeitung* of 2001, *Das war die BRD,* with pieces by, amongst others, "78er" writer Maxim Biller and "78er" filmmaker Doris Dörrie,[70] and to the RTL TV program *Die achtziger Jahre* of 2002. In the course of this wave of nos-talgia, the fashion icons of the 1980s were associated with an exuberant pleasure in advertising which, in an era in which the dominance of the brand name appears complete, now seems charmingly innocent.

Goosen and Wagner, along with "78ers" including Lehr, Peltzer, Dieckmann, Politycki or Niemann, express skepticism about the *radical-ization* of the consumer society in the 1990s. Other authors, however, especially of the younger generation, appear more ready to embrace the hegemony of brand names and designer labels which, at the end of the decade, seemed to many observers to mark the victory of the "ahistorical normality" of economic neo-liberalism. Rising stars such as Benjamin von Stuckrad-Barre, Christian Kracht, Alexa Hennig von Lange, Elke Naters or Karen Duve hence quickly came to be seen to exemplify the "Liebe zum Oberflächlichen" typical of the Generation Golf as described by Florian Illies in 2000. For these writers, and for their generation as whole, Illies suggested, what counted above all was "der Marktfetishismus, die völlige Distanzlosigkeit zur Scheinwelt der Werbung."[71]

The choice of the Hotel Adlon — a prime example of the effort in the 1990s to "recreate" at least the *façade* of Berlin's former elegance[72] — as the location for their collective musings on the new pop culture was most likely a gesture of postmodern irony on the part of Alexander Schönburg, Stuckrad-Barre, Kracht, Joachim Bessing, and Eckhart Nickel. The ensuing volume, *Tristesse Royale* (1999), moreover, embodies a celebration of their own vain affectation which hints that superficiality may in fact be the *only* appropriate aesthetic stance in the new Berlin Republic. The obsession with "Lifestyle" (*TR*, 27), it is implied, has turned this latest generation into model citizens of a country in which celebrity culture is more significant than politics: "Wir werden von vorne und von hinten entertained" (*TR*, 138). It should come as no surprise, then, that some would choose to rebel precisely by means of an *exaggerated* affirmation of consumerism. The fact that this pose is so unremittingly self-conscious transforms it into a new form of dandyism. The "pop elite" parody their own slavish worship of fashion and thereby expose the hollowness of the roles they perform.

The dandy refers time and again to his feelings of *ennui* and seeks extreme solutions to his sense of his own superfluity. Stuckrad-Barre, for example, claims that his only hope of salvation would be "eine Art Somme-Offensive," an act of glorious self-sacrifice. Yet the *modern* dandy is all too aware that, in truth, he has nothing in common with the young Britons "die im Herbst 1914 [. . .] die Klassenzimmer von Oxford und Cambridge verließen, um lachend in den Krieg gegen Deutschland zu ziehen" (*TR*, 137–38). The world has been pacified by the globalization of the consumer ethos. There are no higher ideals such as patriotism in the pursuit of which the dandy might rouse himself from his lethargy. All that remains, as the narrator of Stuckrad-Barre's *Blackbox* (2000) puts it, is the tedium of ceaseless acquisition in which the individual is "schön frei, somit aber auch schwierig leer."[73]

Vincent Vega, the character played by John Travolta in Quentin Tarantino's cult movie *Pulp Fiction* (1994), reports to his fellow hit man Jules at the start of the movie that the French have a different description for the quarter pounder hamburger: "They wouldn't know what the fuck a quarter pounder is. They call it 'royale with cheese.'" Quite possibly a reference to *Pulp Fiction,* the title *Tristesse Royale* may, in similar fashion, point to a European or, in this case, German modulation of an Anglo-American pop culture — a feeling of emptiness, or *tristesse,* regarding the substitution of an "authentic" local sensibility for the immediate, yet anonymous, gratifications of a hegemonic consumerist ethic. This in fact is the dominant mood of Christian Kracht's *Faserland* (1995), arguably the most influential pop novel of the 1990s and one that replicates the "ahistorical normality" of globalized consumerism only to undermine it.

Telling of its narrator's journey from northern Germany to its extreme south and finally to Switzerland, Kracht's novel establishes two parallel thematic trajectories. On the one hand, we are introduced to the world of the pop elite or, more accurately, to the world of those who aspire to belong to this world. For example, Karin, one of a number of women with whom the narrator *almost* sleeps, has met Maxim Biller but felt "ein klein wenig Angst" in his presence;[74] the narrator himself may have heard of cultural theorists Deleuze and Metz but fails to understand them: "obwohl ich mir natürlich diese Namen merke, wie ich mir ja alles merke" (*F,* 39). For those for whom the display of "pop credibility" does not come easily, the pressure to "fit in," to wear the *right* clothes and to say the *right* things with the correct degree of self-conscious irony, is intolerable. The narrator's bouts of nausea attest both to his self-revulsion, that is, his disgust at the way in which he plays a part in order to conform, and, simultaneously, to his anxiety that his self-projection might fail to convince.

The narrator's travels through Germany are only apparently motivated by the quest for the most fashionable clique or the trendiest club. In truth, his is a search — predictably unsuccessful — for authenticity. Indeed, he is surrounded by imitation and simulation, whether it be the "gefärbten Kontaktlinsen" worn by Karin (*F,* 22) or the caresses of the black supermodel that he receives at a hip party he attends: "aber das Ganze ist so unwirklich und irgendwie auch nicht echt" (*F,* 41). This introduces the novel's second strand: a series of flashbacks to childhood which point to the narrator's desire for moments of authenticity, spontaneity, and innocence. Here, colors are often significant. The image of Karin's brown hair set off by a "buntes Halstuch" made by the fashion house Hermes is juxtaposed with the "bunten Plastikschaufeln" with which the narrator built sandcastles as a boy on holiday at the beach. What he sees in the present seems jaded and clichéd whereas the memory it sparks is more vivid, original, and unaffected: "Ich hatte eine orange-farbene Schaufel, das weiß ich noch genau" (*F,* 22). Elsewhere it is the smell of "Bohnerwachs" that recalls the pain of first love, in this case his infatuation with Sarah, the girl who did "Ballett" and had "wunder-

schöne, lange braune Haare." Yet even this memory is soiled by his incipient boyhood awareness of the way love and sex will later provoke
anxieties regarding performance and self-projection. He remembers how
he threw up in the bed in the guest room at her parents' house and defe-
cated into their sheets (*F*, 32–33).

Kracht's *Faserland* is a pop novel which, far from unambiguously en-
dorsing the world of brands and designer labels it depicts, in fact exposes
the dilemma of the sensitive individual sickened by his own participation
in consumer society and yet bereft of any alternative set of values which
might promote integrity. The narrator's incessant pose, as Anke Biendarra
suggests, plainly serves "zur Maskierung eines Gefühls einer metaphysischen Leere."[75] His rejection of the hackneyed moralism of the
"68ers" is, as Illies declared in his *Generation Golf*, surely "befreiend"[76]
and yet it also raises the unsettling question of what the narrator, and his
entire generation, is to do with this freedom. The references to pensioners
(*F*, 20; 93), taxi drivers (*F*, 38; 94) as "Nazis," or to a "Betriebsratsvor-
sitzender" as an "SPD-Nazi" (*F*, 53), on account of their poor fashion
sense, embody, as Frank Finlay argues, an attack on the "68ers." The
"misuse" of the word "Nazi" transforms it into a "term of aesthetic
abuse" and trivializes the legacy of coming-to-terms with the past initiated by the student movement.[77] Yet this provocation is an empty gesture.
It is impossible *genuinely* to refute the anti-fascism that is so essential to
the legacy of the "68ers." When the narrator glimpses his reflection in a
"Glasvitrine" containing a trailer for a newly released movie *Stalingrad*
(1993, directed by Josef Vilsmaier) with the *Wehrmacht* helmet from the
poster superimposed on his head, he feels moved to comment that he is
lucky to live "im demokratischen Deutschland, wo keiner an irgendeine
Front muß mit siebzehn." Such ideas may well be "SPD-Gewäsch" (*F*,
97), the kind of sentiment that might be uttered by an insufferably self-
righteous "68er," but this makes them no less true.

The affectation of a lack of interest in politics or, perhaps more accurately, of a provocatively "hip" political incorrectness — a penchant for
consumerism over causes — is presented as a reply to the smugness of the
"68er" generation. This response, though, leaves its proponents feeling
rootless and self-alienated. Their internalization of the pose of superficiality breeds precisely that: superficiality. Nor can their fetishization of surface be cast as a subversion of the mainstream. The pop elite's ironic
appropriation of the kitsch and the trashy is integrated into the emerging
aesthetic of the fledgling Berlin Republic. The "Bord-Treff" (*F*, 82) in the
intercity train on which the narrator travels is simply trite. The truth is
that the "new" Germany is a bland country full of people "die gute Autos
fahren müssen und gute Drogen nehmen und guten Alkohol trinken und

gute Musik hören müssen, während um sie herum alle dasselbe tun, nur eben ein ganz klein bißchen schlechter" (*F,* 153).

In the course of his travels, Kracht's narrator ends up in Heidelberg. Here, he catches a glimpse of a more "authentic" Germany amongst the "ganz alten Gebäude" of this medieval university town and in particular on the banks of the river Neckar, the so-called "Neckarauen": "So könnte Deutschland sein, wenn es keinen Krieg gegeben hätte und wenn die Juden nicht vergast worden wären. Dann wäre Deutschland wie das Wort Neckar" (*F,* 85). Heidelberg was spared Allied bombing during the war only because the Americans wished to locate their headquarters in the city. Although marred by a "miesen Pizza Hut und irgendwelchen Sport-artikelläden" and a huge "Fußgängerzone" (*F,* 85), the city provokes in the narrator a sensation of non-simultaneity, that is, a brief glimpse of lost innocence. For the most part, however, the destruction of the German heritage is so total that it is impossible for the younger generation to ground itself historically: all that is left is the ephemerality of pop.

Kracht's bestseller *Faserland,* quite unexpectedly, is not so very different, in its nostalgia for German traditions, at least, from the resolutely *un*fashionable work of Martin Walser. Certainly, as Mathias Mertens maintains, "Das Pop-Literarische, das Bret-Easton-Ellis-hafte ist nur Tarnung, damit niemand merkt, wie altertümelnd hier erzählt wird."[78] Just as in Walser's *Die Verteidigung der Kindheit* (1991), the search for authenticity leads Kracht's narrator into a potentially revisionist rereading of the Nazi past. The manner in which the narrator identifies with the "ordinary" soldier depicted on the film poster for *Stalingrad* may thus be an indirect reference to the debates on what *Germans* suffered that we will be looking at in chapter five. Similarly, the Allied bombing campaign during the Second World War is equated with the eradication of German culture: "und ich muß plötzlich an die Bomben-nächte im Zweiten Weltkrieg denken und an den Hamburger Feuersturm und wie das wohl war, als alles ausgelöscht wurde" (*F,* 47). In Kracht as in Walser, moreover, there persists the hope, however faint, that it might be possible to tap into a more "original" German dialect. Kracht's narrator seeks this in Switzerland, "ein Teil Deutschlands, in dem alles nicht so schlimm ist" (*F,* 151) and a place in which the locals speak "aus dem Innersten der Sprache heraus" (*F,* 155). The youthful protagonist of Walser's *Ein springender Brunnen* (1998) also endeavors "sich einfach der Sprache an[zu]vertrauen,"[79] but is more confident of achieving this within the German literary tradition. Whereas Johann immerses himself in Klopstock, Goethe, Schiller, Hölderlin, Nietzsche, and Stefan George, Kracht's narrator fails to find the grave of Thomas Mann. The truth is that Walser's protagonist, born, like his author, in 1927, has known something other than the consumer culture of the present and has a richer source of memories than Kracht's modern-day *flâneur,* a figure condemned to imitate rather than originate.

One of the most pressing issue for writers of the younger generation is the question of how to inflect their fiction with markers of local difference within an Anglo-American pop aesthetic and in the absence of viable German traditions. In Kracht's *Faserland,* this question is expressed via the tension between his narrator's hyper-affirmation of globalized consumer culture and feelings of self-alienation and self-revulsion. At the same time, as Kracht's *1979* (2001) insinuates, the attempt to escape a hegemonic American *style* into authenticity is doomed to fail. The narrator, described as "leer" and "ganz ohne eine Vergangenheit,"[80] hopes, in the course of his personal experience of the Iranian revolution, Tibetan Buddhism, and a Chinese labor camp, to purge himself of his western decadence but is incapable of transcending his own self-indulgent pose and of achieving total self-negation.

Other pop authors such as Karen Duve, Elke Naters, Alexa Hennig von Lange, Tanja Dückers, Sibylle Berg, Tim Staffel or Silvia Szymanski inflect their consumer reality with what Norbert Niemann has termed a "Poetik der Verarmung." This reduction of the German language to a highly stylized, self-conscious simulation of Anglo-American slang, hinting at the hollowing-out of local identity, paradoxically insinuates a German sensibility of rootlessness and self-alienation within global pop culture.[81] Many of the writers named above emerged from the so-called "Trash" and "Slam" scenes of the early 1990s — open competitions in which non-established artists would perform short pieces for *ad hoc* audiences[82] — and became known as a result of volumes such as *Poetry! Slam! Texte der Pop-Fraktion* (1996), *Trash-Piloten — Texte für die 90er* (1997), and *Social Beat, Slam Poetry: Die außerliterarische Opposition meldet sich zu Wort* (1997; 1999, 2001). The first of these was co-edited by Andreas Neumeister, who also features in the selection of pieces published from the internet forum managed by Elke Naters and Sven Lager, *The Buch: Leben am pool* (2001); this demonstrates the continuities between certain "78ers" and younger pop writers. Common to both "Trash" and "Slam" is an emphasis on the spoken work and on life on the margins, misfits, sex, drugs, abuse, and self-abuse. As "78er" Heiner Link puts it in his foreword to *Trashpiloten:* "Nicht das Ergebnis ist Trash, der literarische Ansatz ist es."[83] Unlike former journalists Kracht and Stuckrad-Barre, accordingly, this version of pop is not primarily concerned with the deceptions of the "Medienwelt"[84] or with a meta-critique of its "Klischeesprache" delivered "in genau denselben sprachlichen Klischees,"[85] as presented, for example, in Stuckrad-Barre's *Soloalbum* (1998). It is a less mediated form which, via its derivation from "Trash" in particular, refers back to the punk wave of the 1970s[86] and, in keeping with this precedent, displays what Link terms an "auffällige Schreiblust/Wut/Intensität."[87]

Enno Stahl, himself a practitioner of "Trash" literature, including *Trash Me!* (1992) and *Pewee Rocks* (1997), and editor of the 1996 collection *German Trash,* argues that the "Slam" scene has "sicher nichts mit den dandyistischen Autorinnen und Autoren zu schaffen, die in den Feuilletons gemeinhin für Pop-Literatur stehen." The same applies to "Trash": "Trash enthält sich kritischer Anmerkungen zum Projekt menschlicher Zivilisation nicht."[88] In chapter one, we noted the harsher tone of Elke Naters's *Lügen* (1999) and Karen Duve's *Dies ist kein Liebeslied* (2002). Here, we might point to Hennig von Lange's *Relax* (1999), *Ich bin's* (2000), *Ich habe einfach Glück* (2001) and *Lelle* (2002), or to the novels by Silvia Szymanski such as *Chemische Reinigung* (1998), *Kein Sex mit Mike* (1999), *Agnes Sobierajski* (2000) and *652 Kilometer nach Berlin* (2002) as further examples of this phenomenon. In each case, an obsessive interest in drugs and casual sex barely conceals a deeper anxiety with regard to the brutality that marks relationships based on mutual exploitation. Fashion accessories, in Hennig von Lange's *Ich bin's,* which begins with its female protagonist's desperate efforts to obtain a pair of Nike Airmax training shoes, as in Naters's *G.L.A.M* (2001), can only momentarily camouflage the dissolution of the self. "Ich werde fett," reports the narrator of the autobiographical *G.L.A.M,* moments after she has admired a bikini by Burberry, "von Kate Moss auf der Anzeige getragen; knapp, klassisch dreieckig."[89] In Naters's *Mau-Mau* (2002), which tells of five friends who spend their holiday on a paradise island comparing suntans, the impression of "fun" similarly conceals a more profound emptiness.

Maxim Biller, at the meeting of authors he convened in April 2000, delivered a bitter denunciation of the "moralischen Gleichgültigkeit einer ganzen Gesellschaft" and of its "Schlappschwanz-Literatur."[90] Just over a year later, in August 2001, Matthias Politycki similarly attacked the "Simplifizierer und Schubladianer" of the "pop faction."[91] Yet, as we have seen above, these younger writers are in fact by no means uncritical of the consumer society in which they live and write. Kracht's invocation of German traditions, it is true, is far removed from Karen Duve's depiction of a young woman's struggle with bulimia in *Dies ist Kein Liebeslied.* Nevertheless, both novels speak of the escape from a problematic German identity into an Anglo-American pop culture and of the sense of rootlessness that ensues. Duve's narrator is enchanted by an English pop song, "vor dem mein ganzer Widerstand in sich zusammenbrach,"[92] but finds a *German* equivalent for the hit "'This is not a love song, this is not a love song'" (*DKL,* 198) by the English band PIL in "Kein Liebeslied" by Die Prinzen. Elsewhere she implies that Goethe's *Werther* began a dismal

German tradition of self-negation that she continues in the present: "Aber ich finde, daß Goethe sehr wohl die Verantwortung für sein empfindsames Gewinsel trägt. Ist eine Zeit widerwärtig, so muß man sich eben gegen sie stellen" (*DKL,* 163).

German pop writers of the 1990s, unsurprisingly, portray the new social and political reality of the Berlin Republic, its attempts to define an identity of its own and its uneasy relationship with economic globalization. An emphasis on the *description* of a present-day reality, however, should not be confused with an *acceptance* of the neo-liberal dogma driving cultural homogenization and global consumerism. Indeed, the vision of everyday life in Germany offered by young pop authors is often more nightmarish than celebratory. Tim Staffel's *Terrordrom* (1998), for instance, reinvents Berlin *Mitte* with its "Regierungsgebäuden, Botschaften, etc." as a "deregulated" space in which the pop entertainment culture would be taken to its extreme and in which shoppers would be free to indulge in an orgy of killing. Pop literature, it seems, unlike the free-for-all consumer society it depicts, is perhaps *not* "just for fun. Spaß."[93]

Thomas Assheuer, in an article of 11 April 2001 in *Die Zeit,* predicted the imminent demise of the "new German pop literature." Six months later, following the terrorist attacks on New York and Washington on 11 September, a range of critics, including Volker Hage in *Der Spiegel* (8 October), declared the *Spaßgesellschaft* of the 1990s and, with it, pop, to be definitively over. Indeed, Neumeister's collage of fragments and slogans *Angela Davis löscht ihre Website,* which appeared a year later in 2002, seemed to embody the unnerving opacity of the new reality. David Wagner's 2002 collection of short stories *Was alles fehlt* and Frank Goosen's *Pokorny lacht* (2003) similarly hint at the newly somber mood of the Generation Golf: the entertainer Pokorny is haunted by the death of a girl that he may have helped to cause. At the same time, however, the uncertainties of the new millennium may also simply have coincided with the feeling of many of the most prominent authors of the younger generation that the time had come to "graduate" from the pop scene. "Ich will nicht ewig eine Pop-Autorin sein. Dieser Stempel nervt mich," proclaimed Alexa Hennig von Lange.[94] Four years later her transformation was complete following the publication of *Woher ich komme* (2003), a thoughtful portrait of incest, guilt, and familial dysfunction. In 2003, Hennig von Lange was joined by Tanja Dückers with *Himmelskörper,* an account of the sinking of the refugee ship *Wilhelm Gustloff* at the end of the Second World War.

Ethnic-Minority Writing: Feridun Zaimoğlu

Many of Germany's increasingly prominent authors from Turkish, Jewish, Eastern European, Asian or African backgrounds incorporate pop elements, both to signal their distance from the literary as well as the political mainstream and to underscore the way in which they, like pop, transcend borders and subvert fixed categories.[95] Here, we might point to Sarah Khan (half-Pakistani), Silvia Szymanski (half-Polish), Wladimir Kaminer (a Russian Jew), or Maxim Biller (born of Czech-Jewish parents). Members of the German-speaking population of Romania such as Herta Müller or Richard Wagner, on the other hand, or Terézia Mora and Libuše Monikova, hailing from the German-speaking areas of Hungary and the Czech Republic, respectively, often embed themselves in an archaic, highly "writerly" tradition rich in philosophical and literary allusion which, intentionally, is not entirely attuned to modern-day Germany. Authors from minority groups, moreover, perhaps almost by definition, display a heightened awareness vis-à-vis the question of what it is to be German. As such, the suggestion that with "the increasing presence of minority literatures that affirm heterogeneous, multicultural points of view, the concept of a national literature of any stripe is losing ground" — advanced in this case by Ernestine Schlant — may not be entirely accurate.[96] Writers from ethnic-minority backgrounds do not necessarily establish *rival* literatures which then replace *German* writing. They more likely inflect and expand the ongoing debate concerning the definition of Germanness itself.[97]

Emine Sevgi Özdamar and Zafer Şenocak engage with the question of German identity by drawing parallels between Turkish and Ottoman history in texts such as *Mutterzunge* (Özdamar, 1990)[98] and *Gefährliche Verwandtschaft* (Şenocak, 1998). Part of what Leslie Adelson has called the "Turkish turn" in contemporary German writing,[99] these texts (in the case of *Mutterzunge,* the first two stories) open up the question of German identity by setting the German past, especially the Nazi period, alongside Turkish and Ottoman history. Şenocak's novel, for instance, in which Sascha Muchteschem explores the histories of both a German-Jewish grandfather who emigrated to Turkey in 1934 and a Turkish grandfather implicated in the massacre of the Armenians in 1915, posits "genealogies and subject positions that do not lock the individual into specific plots or identities."[100] In this way, *Gefährliche Verwandtschaft* undermines the tendency in present-day German culture to attempt to impose a static version of the past. Not only does the ritual intonation of German crimes lead to a fundamentally dishonest form of commemoration — "Wir trauern nicht nach unseren Empfindungen. Sondern nach dem Kalender"[101] — it may also reinforce the exclusion of the ethnically-other. The Holocaust, perversely, may underwrite a German identity whose boundaries are, in any case, already always vigilantly patrolled: "Wenn aber heute die Frage gestellt wird, wer ein Deutscher ist und wer nicht, schaut man auf die Türken. An ihnen werden die Grenzen des Deutschseins getestet" (*GV*, 90).

It is certainly possible to raise objections to the narrator's motives in exploring his grandfather's problematic past: "Ich werde die Erde unter den Füßen meines Großvaters aufreißen, ihn freischaufeln von seiner Schuld" (*GV*, 40), or to the perhaps facile notion that the presence of Turks in German society might bring into existence a "Trialog" between "Deutschen, Juden und Muslimen," and releasing all parties from their "traumatischen Erfahrungen" (*GV*, 89). Yet, as Katharina Hall argues, the value of *Gefährliche Verwandtschaft* lies in the manner in which "any simplistic notion of German versus Jewish identity is destabilised; the careful demarcation lines between the German and Turkish 'other' are blurred."[102] This plea for hybridity had been outlined in Şenocak's *Atlas des tropischen Deutschlands* (1992).[103] *Der Erottomane* (1999), a "literary reflection on the politics of writing across national boundaries,"[104] similarly complicates German and Turkish identities. In his *Zungenentfernung* (2001), however, the author is more pessimistic, decrying, as Tom Cheesman notes, "the enduring condition of quarantine in which [Turks in Germany] dwell, regardless of cosmetic changes to the citizenship law."[105]

Leslie Adelson writes of "some vague linkage between 'things Jewish' and 'things Turkish'" in fiction by selected Turkish-German authors "as they negotiate the German present."[106] (Elsewhere she also notes Sten Nadolny's association of present-day attitudes towards Turks with German anti-Semitism in his 1990 novel *Selim oder die Gabe der Rede*).[107] Most obviously, of course, as Şenocak notes, both the Jew and the Turk have long aroused hostility — and fear — in Europe: "Der Türke hat neben dem Juden jahrhundertelang den Feind Europas repräsentiert."[108] Maxim Biller's *Esra* (2003) goes farther. The narrator, a Jew of Czech parentage, living in Germany, falls in love with a Turkish woman, Esra, whom he imagines to be a descendent of the "false" Jewish prophet Shabbetai Zvi. This sets the scene for an exploration of the way in which racist stereotypes are all too quickly adopted from the "host" culture — Esra complains: "'Manchmal bist du sehr deutsch,'" to which he responds: "'Und du . . . du bist sehr orientalisch'"[109] — and of the way victims may become persecutors. Most striking of all, however, are hints of a growing consciousness on the part of the narrator of his own rootedness in Germany: "ich mochte zum Beispiel das flache und neblige Ostfriesland oder die Strecke zwischen Frankfurt und Köln, entlang des Rheins, dessen ruhige, breiter Strom mich verstehen ließ, warum manche Deutsche ihre Heimat so liebten" (*E*, 186). Despite his repeated protestations that he and Esra are "anders" and his attacks on "die Deutschen," he is only truly at home in Germany. Prague belongs to his past and "Israel kam auch nicht in Frage" (*E*, 88).

Feridun Zaimoğlu's *German Amok* (2002), like Biller's *Esra,* sets out from the premise that its ethnic-minority protagonist is a permanent, if ambivalent, member of an increasingly multicultural society. To this extent, its Turkish-German narrator, who remains nameless, appears to have left behind the (self-)marginalization of the "Kanaken" — "wops" — who populate Zaimoğlu's best-known literary-political intervention, *Kanak Sprak: 24 Mißtöne vom Rande der Gesellschaft* (1995). *Kanak Sprak* is about discovering or, more accurately, stylizing a voice for the "outsider" — "Hier hat allein der Kanake das Wort"[110] — by "translating," as Tom Cheesman suggests, "interviews conducted in a mixture ('crossing') of Turkish and German into a highly original literary German bearing a strong authorial stamp, featuring rap rhythms and rich in vernacular metaphors" in order to create a "parody identity, a flagrantly artificial and intentionally slippery construct" which challenges stereotypes of Turkishness and Germanness.[111] The same can be said of the 1997 novel *Abschaum,* a more obviously fictional work. *German Amok,* on the other hand, for its wild invention, brutal imagery, and delight in the perverse, equips its narrator — like his author a self-confessed *Abitur-Türke* — with a fashionably "urbane" idiom appropriate to his position as a member of the Berlin Republic's artistic elite.

German Amok, in a sense, simply updates *Kanak Sprak.* Certainly, the novel reflects on what Cheesman has referred to as contemporary Germany's "diversity envy," that is, the way the Republic's ethnic minority writers, its "naturally cosmopolitan migrants,"[112] are lionized as the only hope of salvation for a national culture struggling to assert itself in a global marketplace that places a premium on hybrid and postcolonial voices. His colleague Daniel thus suffers from the fact that he is "too" German: "Ihm fehlt die Marktgängigkeit, er ist nicht nichtdeutsch, nicht amerikanisch schwul, nicht ethnisch different."[113] The current fashionability of those who *are* "ethnisch different" is evidenced by the desires of a German woman who makes her own, highly suspect contribution to the multicultural dialogue: "Ausländer rein in meine Jungfrauenmöse." In his own perverse internalization of German racism, the narrator later refers to this woman as "nicht lebenswert" and "unfickbares totes Fleisch" (*GA,* 17–18). Indeed, such cynicism may be understandable. The fact that he is invited to the "right" parties, exhibitions, and gallery openings does not mean that he will ever be more than an "exotic" and, most likely, passing attraction. The so-called "Kunstfotze" who dominates the Berlin art scene, accordingly, repeatedly forces her Turkish protégé to abase himself by satisfying her need for "oral gratification."

What is most significant about *German Amok*, however, and most indicative perhaps of a convergence between the concerns of minority writing and "mainstream" fiction, is the way the novel positions its representation of German society's sudden enthusiasm for its ethnic minorities within a broader analysis of the impact of globalization, neo-liberalism, and cultural colonization. Ethnicity, as a result, becomes ever more incidental within the overall development of the plot. The "Gebetsvorsteher Hodscha Seyfeddin," who, contradicting his own Muslim values, is on the lookout for a German woman to be his sex slave (*GA*, 38), as much as the "Drogenethnos" (*GA*, 45) who peddle narcotics outside the narrator's house, or the Germans who buy from them, all reject "society" in favor of egotism. The narrator, in like manner, exploits his minority identity when it suits him but is otherwise indistinguishable from those arround him. In fact, all of the characters in the novel are as indifferent to any sense of their own particularism as they are to the multicultural ideal. The only things that truly count are self-advancement, profit, and the individual's bitter struggle to survive.

Zaimoğlu's vision of the Berlin Republic at the start of the new millennium returns us to the texts by the older, established generation of authors reviewed at the outset of this chapter. Most striking of all, the trope of western colonization of east Germany resurfaces. The narrator travels into the east German province with his collaborators Pink and Daniel in order to introduce the ex-GDR "*Horden und Haufen der Untertanen*" (*GA*, 112) to "civilization" via an exhibition of their art. Their cultural imperialism, however, is dismissive of the (from the point of view of the present) relatively benign, if arrogant, west German capitalism of the early 1990s depicted in the work of Delius or Timm. Instead, the narrator, Pink and Daniel now form the ideological avant-garde of the unrestained neo-liberalism which, by the late 1990s, was beginning to permeate both east *and* west Germany. The eastern landscape is already littered with the "*riesigen Einkaufskomplexe und Megastores vor den Toren der Städte*" (*GA*, 114) associated with economic globalization, and now the moment has arrived for the new colonial subjects, the "Ostbrut" (*GA*, 162) which inhabits the "primitive" east, to be re-educated: "*Man muß die Einöde jenseits der Mauern gnadenlos durchkapitalisieren.*" Indeed, the incorporation of the east into the new global order would set an example for the final social and economic transformation of the western part of the once divided nation: "*Im anderen Land; die charakterliche Nichteignung seiner Menschen für den richtigen Umgang mit Kapitalflüssen und herrlich ungelenkter Parasitenwirtschaft ist ein Fluch*" (*GA*, 112–13). The italicization of the narrator's comments throughout this entire section most likely signals his insight into his own role as a propagandist for the new social and economic reality.

The title of Zaimoğlu's *German Amok* prefigures the novel's depiction of the new Germany. This is a country in which the liberal-democratic order has given way to the deregulated free-for-all of the new economic Darwinism. The artists gathered in the east German province produce a range of concepts for the show they are to perform for the local population, including a "Pornowall" (*GA*, 151) — an ironic allusion to the GDR's so-called "antifaschistische Schutzwall" — a fascist-nationalistic extravaganza to be rounded off by the (simulated) gassing of the audience (*GA*, 219), and, in a display of western "superiority," a play in which the actors would simply turn their backs on their eastern spectators. The latter scheme would rework Volker Braun's famous "unification poem": "Da bin ich noch/ mein Land geht in den Westen/ Krieg den Hütten Friede den Palästen"[114] into a pithier, triumphalist version: "Ost Hütte — West Palast" (*GA*, 149). Common to all the artists' aesthetic visions, however, is a rejection of values, of idealism, a glorification of violence, and a proclamation of the individual's right to instantaneous gratification, whether this be sexual, material or psychological, even at the expense of society.

Zaimoğlu's *German Amok* presents an impression of a Germany "free" of the "unproductive" obligations imposed upon it by the legacy of Nazism, specifically the obligation to protect the weak and the marginalized. Perhaps predicting this outcome, Clarissa, the narrator's retarded and self-mutilating girlfriend, the only person, in fact, for whom he seems to feel any residual responsibility — even as he abuses her — kills herself. The political liberalism which shaped the "old" West Germany, as much as the utopian socialism of the former GDR, appears to be giving way to an ethical and moral vacuum. This is a country in which "sich die Aufklärung ausgependelt hat" (*GA*, 135). The ideals of social and gender equality, ethnic and cultural diversity, and freedom of sexual expression have been emptied of content. Identities — minority identities as much as any other — are simply created, marketed, bought, and sold.

In this chapter, as in our previous chapter, we have been concerned with the "normalization" of the new Germany in east and west and particularly with the way economic globalization, towards the end of the 1990s, provoked a rethinking of the ideals and achievements of the former GDR and the "old" West Germany. For a number of writers, these two German states, retrospectively, at least, each in their own way and often perhaps only *potentially,* embodied values either of social equality and solidarity or of respect for basic rights and democratic accountability. Alternatively, a childhood lived out in one or other of the GDR or the "old" FRG may be remembered with a certain affection or nostalgia. In both cases, it may be that authors of various generations and provenances are attempting to construct a sense of where they come from, and of what has shaped them, in response firstly to the way Germany, after 1990, was called upon to abandon its provinciality and play a bigger role on the world stage and, secondly, to the homogenizing impulses of globalization. As well as undermining the "ahistorical normality" of globalized consumerism, their inflection of the present with markers of their pasts challenges both the "longitudinal normality" promoted by conservatives such as Martin Walser and the "latitudinal normality" of those who prefer to focus on post-1990 Germany's commitment to "universal" values rather than on lived experience, local specificity, and attachment to the particular.

In our next three chapters, we look at the way German authors have continued to respond to the challenge of the Nazi past. The upsurge in writing about this period from the mid-1990s onwards provides further evidence, as we shall see, of the ongoing debate on the legacy of '68 and of the relevance of values of self-criticism, universalism, and the rejection of patriotism derived from the student movement's refashioning of Enlightenment thinking. In our next chapter, we turn to the issue of "political correctness" and examine literary responses to the efforts of conservatives in the early 1990s to re-envision the Nazi past. This is not the end of the story, however. Tracing the continued impact of Nazism on the process of German "normalization," a further chapter assesses the way, at the end of the 1990s, Germans began to revisit their own suffering at the close of the Second World War. This leads directly into our subsequent discussion of literary depictions of the present-day relationship between Germans and Jews.

Notes

[1] Daniela Dahn, *Westwärts und nicht vergessen. Vom Unbehagen in der Einheit* (Berlin: Rowohlt, 1997), 54.

[2] Wolfgang Gabler, "Der Wenderoman als neues literarisches Genre," in Wolfgang Gabler and Nikolaus Werz, eds., *Zeiten-Wende — Wendeliteratur* (Weimar: Edition I, 2000), 70–93, here 76.

[3] See Oskar Negt, *Der Fall Fonty: Ein weites Feld von Günter Grass im Spiegel der Kritik* (Göttingen: Steidl, 1996). See also Heinz Ludwig Arnold, ed., *Blech getrommelt: Günter Grass in der Kritik* (Göttingen: Steidl, 1997).

[4] *Der Spiegel,* 21 August 1995.

[5] Iris Radisch, "Die Bitterfelder Sackgasse," *Die Zeit,* 25 August 1995, 111.

[6] Stefan Neuhaus, *Literatur und nationale Einheit* (Tübingen: A. Francke Verlag, 2002), 446.

[7] See Julian Preece, "Seven Theses on 'Der Fall Monty,'" in Clare Flanagan and Stuart Taberner, eds., *1949/1989: Cultural Perspectives on Division and Unity in East and West, German Monitor* 50 (Amsterdam: Rodopi, 2000), 215–30.

[8] Thomas Schmid, "Ein wüstes Feld," *Wochenpost*, 24 August 1995, *Literatur*, 40–1, here 40.

[9] Günter Grass, *Ein weites Feld* (Göttingen: Steidl, 1995), 365. Hereafter *WF*.

[10] Günter Grass, *Schreiben nach Auschwitz* (Munich: Deutscher Taschenbuch Verlag, 1990), 42.

[11] See Julian Preece, *The Life and Work of Günter Grass* (New York: Palgrave, 2001), 180–87.

[12] Günter Grass, "Kurze Rede eines vaterlandslosen Gesellen," in Günter Grass, *Ein Schnäppchen namens DDR* (Frankfurt a.M.: Luchterhand, 1990), 7–14, here 8.

[13] Günter Grass, "Ein Schnäppchen namens DDR," in *Ein Schnäppchen*, 39–60, here 45.

[14] Julian Preece, *Günter Grass*, 226.

[15] Stefan Neuhaus, *Literatur und nationale Einheit*, 452.

[16] See Julian Preece, "The Stasi as Literary Conceit," in Paul Cooke and Andrew Plowman, eds., *German Writers and the Politics of Culture: Dealing with the Stasi* (Basingstoke: Palgrave, 2003), 195–212.

[17] Hans Christoph Buch, *Der Burgwart der Wartburg* (Frankfurt a.M.: Suhrkamp, 1994), 43.

[18] Hans Pleschinski, *Bildnis eines Unsichtbaren* (Munich: Hanser, 2002), 175. See Andrew Plowman, "'Was will ich denn als Westdeutscher erzählen?': The 'old' West and Globalisation in Recent German Prose," in Stuart Taberner, ed., *German Literature in the Age of Globalisation* (Birmingham: Birmingham UP, 2004), 47–66.

[19] Patrick Süskind, "Deutschland, eine Midlife-crisis," *Der Spiegel*, 17 September 1990, 118–25, here 125 and 123.

[20] Ralf Rothmann, *Milch und Kohle* (Frankfurt a.M.: Suhrkamp, 2000), 29.

[21] F. C. Delius, *Die Birnen von Ribbeck* (Reinbek bei Hamburg: Rowohlt, 1993 [1991]), 32. Hereafter *DBR*.

[22] Florentine Strzelczyk, *Un-Heimliche Heimat. Reibungsflächen zwischen Kultur und Nation* (Munich: iudicium, 1999), 260.

[23] Reinhard Baumgart, "Deutsch-deutsche Sprechblasen: Friedrich Christian Delius' Beitrag zur deutschen Einheit," *Die Zeit*, 22 March 1991, 13.

[24] Karoline von Oppen, "'Wer jetzt schwarzweiss malt, hat keine Ahnung': Friedrich Christian Delius's *Die Birnen von Ribbeck* and the Predicament of 'Wendeliteratur,'" *German Life and Letters* 54:4 (2001): 352–65, here 362.

[25] Karoline von Oppen, "'Wer jetzt schwarzweiss malt . . .," 362–3.

[26] F. C. Delius, *Der Spaziergang von Rostock nach Syrakuse* (Reinbek bei Hamburg: Rowohlt, 1999 [1995]), 36. Hereafter *DS*.

[27] Martin Walser, *Die Gallistl'sche Krankheit* (Frankfurt a.M.: Suhrkamp 1972), 112.

[28] Martin Walser, "Händedruck mit Gespenstern," in Martin Walser, *Deutsche Sorgen* (Frankfurt a.M.: Suhrkamp, 1997), 213–27, here 224.

[29] Martin Walser, *Dorle und Wolf,* in *Deutsche Sorgen,* 276–405, here 304. Hereafter *DW.*

[30] See my "'Deutsche Geschichte darf auch einmal gutgehen': Martin Walser and the 'German Question' from *Ehen in Philippsburg* to *Ein springender Brunnen,*" in Helmut Schmitz, ed., *The Future of Vergangenheitsbewältigung* (Aldershot: Ashgate, 2001), 45–64.

[31] See Stuart Parkes, "Looking forward to the Past: Identity and Identification in Martin Walser's *Die Verteidigung der Kindheit,*" in Arthur Williams and Stuart Parkes, eds., *The Individual, Identity and Innovation. Signals from Contemporary Literature and the New Germany* (Bern: Peter Lang, 1994), 57–74.

[32] Martin Walser, *Die Verteidigung der Kindheit* (Frankfurt a.M.: Suhrkamp, 1991), 315.

[33] See Alison Lewis, "The 'Phantom-Pain' of Germany: Mourning and Fetishism in Martin Walser's *Die Verteidigung der Kindheit,*" in Peter Monteath and Reinhard Alter, eds., *German Monitor, Kulturstreit − Streitkultur* (Amsterdam: Rodopi, 1996), 125–44.

[34] See my "A Matter of Perspective?: Martin Walser's Fiction in the 1990s," in Martin Kane, ed., *German Literature after Unification* (Bern: Peter Lang, 2002), 145–69.

[35] Martin Walser, *ohne einander* (Frankfurt a.M.: Suhrkamp, 1993), 175.

[36] Botho Strauß, "Anschwellender Bocksgesang," *Der Spiegel* 8 February 1993, 202–7, here 205.

[37] Martin Walser, "Erfahrungen beim Verfassen einer Sonntagsrede," in Frank Schirrmacher, ed., *Die Walser-Bubis-Debatte* (Frankfurt a.M.: Suhrkamp, 1999), 7–17, here 15 and 13.

[38] Martin Walser, *Ein springender Brunnen* (Frankfurt a.M.: Suhrkamp, 1998), 282.

[39] See Bill Niven, "Martin Walser's *Tod eines Kritikers* and the Issue of Anti-Semitism," *German Life and Letters* 56:3 (2003): 299–311.

[40] Martin Lüdke, "Die Frau weint, der Mann schläft," *Frankfurter Allgemeine Zeitung,* 19 July 2000, 20.

[41] Martin Walser, *Der Lebenslauf der Liebe* (Frankfurt a.M.: Suhrkamp, 2002), 189–90. Hereafter *LL.*

[42] See my "The Triumph of Subjectivity: Martin Walser's Novels of the 1990s and his *Der Lebenslauf der Liebe* (2001)," in Stuart Parkes and Fritz Wefelmeyer, eds., *Martin Walser, German Monitor* (Amsterdam: Rodopi, 2004), 429–46.

[43] Helmut Peitsch, "Vom Preis nationaler Identität. *Dorle und Wolf*," in Heike Doane and Gertrud Pickar Bauer, eds., *Leseerfahrungen mit Martin Walser, Houston German Studies* 9 (Munich: Fink, 1995), 171–88, here 178.

[44] Uwe Timm, *Die Entdeckung der Currywurst* (Cologne: Kiepenheuer & Witsch, 1998 [1993]), 161. Hereafter *DEC*.

[45] F. C. Delius, *Der Sonntag, an dem ich Weltmeister wurde* (Reinbek bei Hamburg: Rowohlt, 1996 [1994]), 87. Hereafter *DSA*.

[46] See Ingo Cornils, "Successful Failure? The Impact of the German Student Movement on the Federal Republic of Germany," in Stuart Taberner and Frank Finlay, eds., *Recasting German Identity* (Rochester: Camden House, 2002), 109–26.

[47] Ingo Cornils, "Long Memories: The German Student Movement in Recent Fiction," *German Life and Letters* 56:1 (2003): 89–101, here 91.

[48] F. C. Delius, *Amerikahaus und der Tanz um die Frauen* (Reinbek bei Hamburg: Rowohlt, 1999 [1997]), 154. Hereafter *AT*.

[49] Uwe Timm, *Rot* (Cologne: Kiepenheuer & Witsch, 2001), 129. Hereafter *RO*.

[50] See Ingo Cornils, "Successful Failure?," 109.

[51] Florian Illies, *Generation Golf zwei* (Munich: Karl Blessing Verlag, 2003), 62.

[52] Hubert Winkels, "Grenzgänger: Neue deutsche Pop-Literatur," *Sinn und Form* 51:4 (1999): 581–610, here 581.

[53] See Martin Walser, "Über die Neueste Stimmung im Westen," *Kursbuch* 20 (1970): 19–42.

[54] Johannes Ullmaier, *Von Acid nach Adlon und zurück* (Mainz: Ventil, 2001), 12.

[55] Thomas Meinecke, *Mode und Verzweiflung* (Frankfurt a.M.: Suhrkamp, 1998), 8.

[56] Moritz Baßler, *Der deutsche Pop-Roman* (Munich: Beck, 2002), 184.

[57] Hubert Winkels, "Grenzgänger," 596 and 598.

[58] Rainald Goetz, *Rave* (Frankfurt a.M.: Suhrkamp, 2001 [1998]), 69. Hereafter *RA*.

[59] See Thomas Ernst, *Popliteratur* (Hamburg: Rotbuch Verlag, 2001), 60–61.

[60] Thomas Meinecke, *Tomboy* (Frankfurt a.M.: Suhrkamp, 1998), 9. Hereafter *TB*.

[61] Charis Goer, "Cross the Border — Face the Gap. Ästhetik der Grenzerfahrung bei Thomas Meinecke und Andreas Neumeister," in Heinz Ludwig Arnold, ed., *Pop-Literatur, Text + Kritik* (Munich: Richard Boorberg Verlag, 2003), 172–82, here 177.

[62] Hubert Winkels, "Grenzgänger," 594.

[63] Andreas Neumeister, *Gut laut* (Frankfurt a.M.: Suhrkamp, 1998), 21. Hereafter *GL*.

[64] Andreas Neumeister, *Ausdeutschen* (Frankfurt a.M.: Suhrkamp, 1994), 22.

[65] Iris Radisch, "Zwei getrennte Literaturgebiete. Deutsche Literatur der neunziger Jahre in Ost und West," in Heinz Ludwig Arnold, ed., *DDR-Literatur der neunziger Jahre* (Munich: text + kritik, 2000), 13–26, here 24.

[66] Norbert Niemann, *Wie man's nimmt* (Munich: Hanser, 1998), 432.

[67] Frank Goosen, *liegen lernen* (Frankfurt a.M.: Eichborn, 2000 [1999]), 35.

[68] David Wagner, *Meine nachtblaue Hose* (Berlin: Fest, 2000), 154.

[69] See Andrew Plowman "'Was will ich denn als Westdeutscher erzählen?': The 'old' West and Globalisation in Recent German Prose," in Stuart Taberner, ed., *German Literature*, 47–66.

[70] See Andrew Plowman, "'Westalgie'? Nostalgia for the 'old' Federal Republic in Recent German Prose," *Seminar* 40:3 (2004): 249–61.

[71] Florian Illies, *Generation Golf* (Frankfurt a.M.: Fischer, 2002 [2000]), 27–28.

[72] See Catherine Slessor, "Gehry's Geode," *Architectural Review* 210.1254 (2001): 48–54.

[73] Benjamin von Stuckrad-Barre, *Blackbox* (Berlin: Goldmann, 2002 [2000]), 11.

[74] Christian Kracht, *Faserland* (Munich: Deutscher Taschenbuch Verlag, 2002 [1995]), 16. Hereafter *F*.

[75] Anke S. Biendarra, "Der Erzähler als 'Popmoderner Flaneuer' in Christian Krachts Roman *Faserland*," *German Life and Letters* 55:2 (2002): 164–79, here 170.

[76] Florian Illies, *Generation Golf*, 155.

[77] Frank Finlay, "'Dann wäre Deutschland wie das Wort Neckarrauen': Surface, Superficiality and Globalisation in Christian Kracht's *Faserland*," in Stuart Taberner, ed., *German Literature*, 189–208, here 196.

[78] Mathias Mertens, "Robbery, assault, and battery," in Heinz Ludwig Arnold, ed., *Pop-Literatur*, 201–17, here 208.

[79] Martin Walser, *Ein springender Brunnen*, 404.

[80] Christian Kracht, *1979* (Munich: Deutscher Taschenbuch Verlag, 2003 [2001]), 34.

[81] Norbert Niemann, "Realismus der Verarmung," *Süddeutsche Zeitung*, 21 October 2000, *Feuilleton*, 17.

[82] See Boris Preckwitz, "ready — steady — slam. Notizen zum *Poetry Slam*," *Weimarer Beiträge* 49:1 (2003): 70–79, here 72.

[83] Heiner Link, *Trash-Piloten. Texte für die 90er* (Leipzig: Reclam, 1997), 16.

[84] Horst Spittler, "Die Dichter der 'Generation Golf,'" *literatur für leser* 25:3 (2002): 189–96, here 190.

[85] Mathias Mertens, "Robbery, assault, and battery," 211.

[86] See Martin Büsser, "'Ich stehe auf Zerfall.' Die Punk- und New-Wave-Rezeption in der deutschen Literatur," in Heinz Ludwig Arnold, ed., *Pop-Literatur*, 149–57, here 151.

[87] Heiner Link, *Trash-Piloten*, 14.

[88] Enno Stahl, "Trash, Social Beat und Slam Poetry," in Heinz Ludwig Arnold, ed., *Pop-Literatur,* 258–78, here 262 and 273.

[89] Elke Naters, *G.L.A.M* (Cologne: Kiepenheuer & Witsch, 2001), 16 and 15.

[90] Maxim Biller, "Feige das Land, schlapp die Literatur. Über die Schwierigkeiten beim Sagen der Wahrheit," *Die Zeit,* 13 April 2000, 47–49, here 47 and 49.

[91] Matthias Politycki, "Simplifizierer und Schubladianer," *die tageszeitung,* 27/28 October 2001, 13.

[92] Karen Duve, *Dies ist kein Liebeslied* (Berlin: Eichborn, 2002), 66. Hereafter *DKL.*

[93] Tim Staffel, *Terrordrom* (Berlin: Ullstein, 1999 [1998]), 197.

[94] "'Ein schnelles, kurzes Leben.' Alexa Hennig von Lange im Interview," in *KulturSpiegel,* 27 June 1999, 46.

[95] A number of encyclopedias reveal the diversity of backgrounds represented by minority authors presently writing in German. Carmine Chiellino's *Interkulturelle Literatur in Deutschland* (2000) thus includes sections on writers originally from, or who parents were from, Italy, Spain, Greece, the ex-Yugoslavia, Portugal, Turkey, the former Soviet Union, Eastern Europe, Brasil, Latin America, or from both Arab and African countries and Asia, or of German ancestry from Russia and Rumania. Irmgard Ackermann's *Fremde Augenblicke: Multikulturelle Literatur in Deutschland* (1996) and Mary Howard's *Interkulturelle Konfigurationen* (1997) are less comprehensive but nonetheless impressive. In 2000, Jamal Tuschick drew attention to the wealth of minority authors amongst the younger generation with a collection of original pieces in *Morgen Land. Neueste deutsche Literatur.*

[96] Ernestine Schlant, *The Language of Silence: West German Literature and the Holocaust* (New York: Routledge, 1999), 4.

[97] For a more detailed examination of this tension, see Azade Seyhan's *Writing Outside the Nation* (Princeton: Princeton UP, 2001) and Petra Fachinger's *Rewriting Germany From the Margins: "Other" German Literature of the 1980s and 1990s* (Montreal: McGill-Queen's UP, 2001).

[98] See Margaret Littler, "Diasporic Identity in Emine Sevgi Özdamar's *Mutterzunge,*" in Stuart Taberner and Frank Finlay, eds., *Recasting German Identity,* 225–40.

[99] Leslie A. Adelson, "The Turkish Turn in Contemporary German Literature and Memory Work," *Germanic Review* 77:4 (2002): 326–38.

[100] Katharina Gerstenberger, "Difficult Stories: Generation, Genealogy, Gender in Zafer Şenocak's *Gefährliche Verwandtschaft* and Monika Maron's *Pawels Briefe,*" in Stuart Taberner and Frank Finlay, eds., *Recasting German Identity,* 242–55, here 248.

[101] Zafer Şenocak, *Gefährliche Verwandtschaft* (Munich: Babel, 1998), 61–62. Hereafter *GV.*

[102] Katharina Hall, "'Bekanntlich sind Dreiecksbeziehungen am kompliziertesten': Turkish, Jewish and German Identity in Zafer Şenocak's *Gefährliche Verwandtschaft,*" *German Life and Letters* 56:1 (2003): 72–88, here 81.

[103] Zafer Şenocak, *Atlas des tropischen Deutschlands* (Berlin: Babel, 1992), 13.

[104] Katharina Gerstenberger, "Writing by Ethnic Minorities in the Age of Globalisation," in Stuart Taberner, *German Literature*, 209–28, here 217.

[105] Tom Cheesman, "Ş/ß: Zafer Şenocak and the Civilization of Clashes," in Tom Cheesman and Karin Yeşilada, eds., *Zafer Şenocak* (Cardiff: U of Wales P, 2003), 144–59, here 146.

[106] Leslie A. Adelson, "Touching Tales of Turks, Germans and Jews: Cultural Alterity, Historical Narrative and Literary Riddles of the 1990s," *New German Critique* 80 (2000): 93–124, here 102.

[107] Leslie A. Adelson, "Turkish Turn," 326.

[108] Zafer Şenocak, "Feindbild Türkei, " in Zafer Şenocak, *War Hitler Araber? IrreFührungen an den Rand Europas* (Berlin: Babel, 1994), 75–78, here 75.

[109] Maxim Biller, *Esra* (Cologne: Kiepenheuer & Witsch, 2003), 115.

[110] Feridun Zaimoğlu, *Kanak Sprak: 24 Mißtöne vom Rande der Gesellschaft* (Hamburg: Rotbuch, 1995), 18.

[111] Tom Cheesman, "Akçam — Zaimoğlu — 'Kanak Attak': Turkish Lives and Letters in German," *German Life and Letters* 55:2 (2002): 180–95, here 184 and 187.

[112] Tom Cheesman, "Akçam — Zaimoğlu — 'Kanak Attak.'" 182.

[113] Feridun Zaimoğlu, *German Amok* (Cologne: Kiepenheuer & Witsch, 2002), 151. Hereafter *GA*.

[114] Volker Braun, "Das Eigentum," reprinted in Carl Otto Konrady, ed., *Von einem Land und vom anderen: Gedichte zur deutschen Wende* (Frankfurt a.M.: Suhrkamp, 1993), 51.

4: Confronting the Nazi Past I: "Political Correctness"

> Wenn das Tante Lenchen sagt, sie war
> eine Nationalsozialistin, dann soll sie
> das bitte auch behaupten dürfen, oder?
> — Andreas Maier, *Wäldchestag*

AT THE CLOSE OF HANNS-JOSEF ORTHEIL'S *Abschied von den Kriegs-teilnehmern* (1992), the narrator — a writer who shares a great deal of his biography with Ortheil — relates how he went to Prague in the autumn of 1989 to deliver a letter to an East German couple who, along with hundreds of their compatriots, had taken refuge in the West German embassy and were demanding to be allowed to travel to the FRG. He tells of how he bribed an enterprising East German within the embassy compound to find the addressees of the letter, written by friends who had crossed from Hungary to Austria. On handing it over to the exhilarated defectors, he insists that they travel to Vienna and be reunited with their friends, and with him, as soon as they made it to the West. This would be "eine ganz unglaubliche Freude, namenlos, eine namenlose Freude," for all concerned.[1]

"Eine namenlose Freude" — the unification of East and West Germans embodied for the narrator, in late 1989, at least, a joy so improbable, so unthinkable as to be unidentifiable. Yet he may also have been alluding to the prospect of a joy whose name Germans had, for so long, not *dared* to pronounce, that is, delight in national unity and a desire for redemption of the past, sentiments summarized by Martin Walser in 1993: "deutsche Geschichte darf auch einmal gutgehen."[2] At the same time, some worried that this jubilation might contain something more sinister. Günter Grass, for example, famously accused Walser of possessing "zu viel Gefühl und zu wenig Bewußtsein,"[3] and, just before unification in 1990, insisted: "Wir kommen an Auschwitz nicht vorbei."[4] For Grass, the fear was that unification would provoke a new nationalism and a wish to draw a line under the National Socialist period, to consign it to "history." In this chapter, we begin by reading *Abschied von den Kriegs-teilnehmern* as a novel that predicts the central question addressed by much of the writing on National Socialism from the mid-1990s onwards: whether it is appropriate to "historicize" the experience of those who lived through it and to "normalize" the German past (and thus German identity) in the present. We look then at debates on "political correctness" in the mid-1990s and literary works by Peter Schneider and F. C. Delius. Finally, we turn to Walser's 1998 *Ein springender Brunnen,* a semi-autobiographical narrative which caused controversy on account of its efforts to "filter" Nazism from its protagonist's childhood experiences.

The Caesura of 1989

The pleasure taken by Ortheil's narrator in the events of 1989 is paralleled with his successful negotiation of the trauma handed down by his parents, the *Kriegsteilnehmer* of the novel's title. This trauma derives from two primary sources: the loss of four sons in the war — causing his mother's recurrent loss of speech and neurotic concern for her surviving son, and his father's combat experiences in Poland and around Berlin, to which he reacts with a fear of travel eastwards, towards the region in which the war was at its most brutal, German crimes most heinous, and German suffering, in the closing months, most acute. The melancholic despair endured by both parents, Helmut Schmitz suggests, "wird von Ortheil als Heimatvertreibung beschrieben."[5] Here, *Heimatvertreibung* is also understood as an expulsion from the comfort of the familiar and as an intrusion of monumental events beyond the parents' control, and understanding, such as Nazism, war, defeat, and loss.

The narrator's focus on his father's past recalls the West German *Vaterroman* of the 1970s and 1980s, in which the generation of '68 confronted their fathers with their wartime deeds, silence, and authoritarian practices.[6] Indeed, as a young man, the narrator was angered by his father's unwillingness to speak of Auschwitz (he had been stationed nearby) and tried to force him to confess to having known of the camp's existence (*AK,* 105). Yet, as Schmitz argues, Ortheil's novel refuses any comprehensive "Verurteilung des Vaters."[7] The narrator, in fact, repeats his father's stories of how a friend had been killed at his side, how he had almost been left for dead himself (*AK,* 114–17), or how his patrol had been trapped near Russian lines (*AK,* 282–84). He then goes on to describe his reactions to these accounts in retrospect: "Ich hatte zu Gott gebetet, meinen Vater von seiner Vergangenheit zu erlösen und ihm alle Erinnerungen abzunehmen" (*AK,* 285). Unlike the *Vaterroman,* the son in the present novel does not desire to inflict memory upon a father in denial of a shameful record. Instead, he wishes to absolve a father traumatized by wartime suffering, that is, by the loss of *Heimat,* of memory itself. He accepts his father's self-characterization "als Opfer des Krieges" (*AK,* 108).

The cause of the narrator's melancholy thus differs from that of his peers in the earlier wave of *Väterliteratur*. In both instances, despair derives from "Mitwisserschaft" (*AK*, 285), and yet the knowledge to which this narrator is party, the "haltloser Trauer" (*AK*, 64–65) from which he desires release, does not concern his father's complicity in the perpetration of atrocities, but the suffering of both his parents in the war. The losses they suffered had obtruded upon the "normal" development of their remaining son, not least in the way he was compelled to narrate, time and time again, the excursions into nature undertaken with his father. These, Schmitz argues, may represent the "zwanghafte Wiederholung der Heimatvertreibung und der ständigen Heimkehrversuche im Krieg."[8] Eventually, the ritual nature of such excursions, and their retelling, had overpowered the son, inducing feelings of alienation that led him to flee his father's funeral for America and San Domingo, a journey that, in psychic terms at least, never took him very far.

Reviewing the novel at the time of its publication, Thomas Anz drew attention to the fact that it is "im Plusquamperfekt erzählt."[9] This suggests the way the narrator's self-examination reflects on an earlier, apparently abnormal self and anticipates the emergence of a new normality. As so often in post-1968 reflections on the Nazi past and its influence on postwar Germany, the figure of the son stands in for the fledgling Federal Republic, and for many of his own generation. His "normalization," therefore, anticipates, and perhaps even sums up, the debates of the 1990s on the "normalization" of the newly unified Germany. Most pertinent of all is the fact that the narrator's revisioning of the Nazi past begins with a re-signification of *Heimat*. Previously, he had visualized his "heimatlichen Landschaften" (*AK*, 298) with his father in the foreground, an indication of the extent to which his father, and *his* memories, had dominated the son's mental landscapes. In the course of his travels, however, he works through the images of *Heimat* that fill his nightmares and finally takes possession of them: "all diese Bilder haben sich zurückverwandelt zu Kindheitsbildern!" (*AK*, 300). The innocent normality of childhood memory replaces the obsessive repetition of loss. And "normality" means that the narrator can now tell the stories he wishes, and in a manner of his choosing. What writers must do, the novel hints, is abandon their ineffective stammering — "Kotzkrieg, Kotzkrieg" (*AK*, 350) — and tell their own, authentically "German" stories.

"Ordinary" Germans — A Matter of Perspective?

The title of *Abschied von den Kriegsteilnehmern*, as much as its plot, suggests that the end of the GDR coincided with a taking-leave from the generation that had dominated postwar German society with their accounts of conformity, complicity, and suffering. Equally, as Schmitz notes, it alludes to Schirrmacher's "Abschied von der Literatur der Bundesrepublik,"[10] a major contribution to the debates on the future of German literature discussed in chapter one. The perhaps natural wish to bid farewell, both to the Nazi past and a literary enterprise preoccupied by it, may, however, be problematic. A presentation of the past that depicts the Nazi era as equivalent to any other period in history might, it could be argued, bring about a relativization of German crimes of the kind that many observers had seen, for example, in Andreas Hillgruber's book *Zweierlei Untergang: Die Zerschlagung des Deutschen Reiches und das Ende des europäischen Judentums* (1986),[11] which had provoked controversy with its empathetic historicization of the motivation of German soldiers fighting a rearguard action against the Red Army,[12] or in Helmut Kohl's efforts in 1985 to gain American President Reagan's absolution for fallen German soldiers buried in Bitburg cemetery, including *SS* men.

The father in *Abschied von den Kriegsteilnehmern* is, of course, no *SS* man, but an "ordinary" German. Indeed, a focus on the convoluted biographies of Germans simply "caught up" in the circumstances of their time was characteristic of writing on the Nazi past from the early to mid-1990s. By the start of the new millennium, however, the notion of the "ordinary" German no longer necessarily referred exclusively, or even primarily, to those uninvolved in any direct way in atrocities or massacres. It could also incorporate those who took part in the killing but who were otherwise, to cite the German title of Christopher R. Browning's influential historical study of Reserve Police Battalion 101, *Ordinary Men*. What emerges towards the end of the 1990s, accordingly, is a far more complex picture of individuals' differing degrees of complicity, and of the causes of this complicity. In Ortheil's novel, the father is more or less absolved. In Uwe Timm's short narrative *Am Beispiel meines Bruders* (2003), in contrast, the author's older brother, a *Waffen-SS* volunteer killed in 1943, is seen as typical of an age group led into error by misplaced idealism and a depressing blindness to the cruelty around them, and, in a throwback to the *Vaterroman,* by the pedagogical and political failure of their fathers: "Um eine eigene Geschichte und um die Erfahrbarkeit eigener Gefühle betrogen, bleibt nur die Reduktion auf Haltung: Tapferkeit."[13]

Novels such as Ortheil's and Timm's, and, as we shall see in our next chapter, Marcel Beyer's *Flughunde* and Bernhard Schlink's *Der Vorleser* (both 1995), re-evaluate the motives and choices of "ordinary" Germans — whether bystanders or perpetrators — in both literature and historical writing throughout the 1990s. On more than one occasion, Timm's *Am Beispiel meines Bruders* hence refers directly to Browning, citing the German title of his *Ordinary Men,* published in 1993 as *Ganz normale Männer.* Browning, of course, famously insists on the obligation to see "the perpetrators in human terms" and on the need to "attempt to empathize."[14] Schlink, in an interview with Volker Hage, echoes this point and stresses the didactic value of such empathy: "Wir hätten doch mit den Tätern schon lange abgeschlossen, wenn es wirklich alle Monster wären, ganz fremd, ganz anders, mit denen wir nichts gemein haben."[15] This is perhaps reminiscent of the premise of Peter Schneider's 1987 *Vati,* in which Dr. Mengele's son visits his father in South America and attempts to discover what motivated him to persecute so many — if we accept that Mengele was no monster but someone with whom we might, potentially, at least, empathize, we must ask about the motives of those far less infamous. More prosaically, it is likely that the interest in "ordinary" individuals reflects the desire, expressed by Ortheil's narrator, to write "German" stories and "normalize" the past. Whatever the case, the friction between historicization and relativization resonates throughout in the tension between the desire to understand individuals' actions within the context of social expectations and pragmatic choices during the Nazi period and the fear that this approach might excuse the culpability of real people — in sins of commission or of omission alike — or, many would argue, deny the existence of personal responsibility.

The notion of historicization raises further issues. Specifically, many discussions on the presentation of the Nazi past since the early 1990s have revolved around the question of perspective, or focalization, that is, the standpoint from which the story is told. Examples from the early 1990s are Ludwig Harig's *Weh dem, der aus der Reihe tanzt* (1990) and Ulla Berkéwicz's *Engel sind schwarz und weiß* (1990); at the end of the decade and beyond, Martin Walser's *Ein springender Brunnen* (1998) and Günter Grass's *Im Krebsgang* (2002) suggest radically opposed solutions to what is only superficially an aesthetic problem. In each case, historicization almost inevitably involves adopting the point of view of individuals caught up in events. To be sure, to locate the behavior of people in the past within their range of expectations and choices is to see history through their eyes and to bracket out knowledge or values that are alien to their period. Historical fiction does this as a matter of course. The difficulty arises when this technique is applied to the National Socialist period. Any depiction that restricts itself to the perspective of a blissfully unaware protagonist and lacks even an implicit condemnation of Auschwitz might seem to chip away at the moral foundations of conventional readings of Nazism.

Helmut Schmitz argues that Harig's *Weh dem, der aus der Reihe tanzt* manages to avoid these dangers insofar as it "contextualises the 'normality' of adolescence in the 1930s and early 1940s [. . .] with the ultimate goal of Nazi politics, war and extermination."[16] The narrator sets his childhood memories of his time in the Hitler Youth alongside his present knowledge of the period's totality. Berkéwicz's *Engel sind schwarz und weiß,* with "its close personal narration," to cite Schmitz in a separate piece on this author and Schlink, similarly reproduces the "Nazi-speak" adopted by its protagonist, Reinhold, and yet undermines it by introducing conflicting and contrasting voices.[17] Something comparable happens in Marcel Beyer's *Spione* (2000), in which four cousins use old photographs as the starting point reconstructing their grandfather's time in the Legion Condor, including his part in the obliteration of Guernica. This novel, one of a number from the late 1990s, including W. G. Sebald's *Austerlitz* (2001, building on his *Die Ausgewanderten,* 1992) and Monika Maron's *Pawels Briefe* (1999), to explore the tension between photographic evidence, the imaginative reconstruction of the past and the pursuit of historical truth, most likely responds to the "Crimes of the *Wehrmacht*" exhibition of the mid- to late 1990s.[18] In common with Ulla Hahn's *Unscharfe Bilder,* which appeared in 2003, *Spione* tests the boundaries between empathy with those caught up in the Nazi military machine and the desire to confront them with documentary evidence of their past. In Beyer's novel, the cousins attempt to understand their grandfather's deeds — "jetzt schauen wir mit seinen Augen"[19] — yet ultimately refuse to excuse him. Judith Kuckart's *Lenas Liebe* (2002), likewise, essays an empathetic reconstruction of the history of Julius Dahlmann, her mother's onetime lover, and the secret he possesses about Auschwitz, but perhaps loses focus as it digresses into ruminations on love and the memory of love.

Ortheil's *Abschied von den Kriegsteilnehmern* breaks with the moral fervor of the '68 generation. Indeed, this novel is perhaps the first of its kind to point to the blind spot of the *Vaterromane* of the 1970s and 1980s, which, as Klaus Briegleb notes, had typically avoided any reflection on the "Ursprungsphänomen '1968.'" As such, the work predicts the wave of narratives that appeared from the mid-1990s, including F. C. Delius's *Amerikahaus und der Tanz um die Frauen* (1997), Hans-Ulrich Treichel's *Der Verlorene* (1998), Ulrike Kolb's *Frühstück mit Max* (2000), Erasmus Schöfer's *Ein Frühling irrer Hoffnung* (2001) and Uwe Timm's *Rot* (2001), which probe the question of whether, as Bernhard Schlink claims, the "68ers" were guilty of sublimating feelings of alienation and youthful anxiety "in dem moralischen Pathos" of political activism and condemnation of their parents' involvement in Nazism.[20] Novels by Judith Kuckart, *Wahl der Waffen* (1990), and Ulrich Woelk, *Rückspiel* (1993), concentrate more specifically on the impact of this moral fervor on a subsequent generation,[21] whereas Leander Scholz, in *Das Rosenfest* (2001), sets out to trace links between the student movement and the emergence of the Red Army Faction. Yet the plea for a more differentiated historicization of the past and a more questioning depiction of the student radicals contained in Ortheil's text and those that followed could not be more different from the infinitely more antagonistic attacks on the generation of '68 launched by conservatives as part of their campaign in the mid-1990s against "political correctness." On the one hand, then, we have those now willing to concede the need for historicization — including, as we shall see, Peter Schneider and F. C. Delius — but determined that the effort to understand the motives and actions of the "ordinary" German be balanced by a critical appraisal of where these fit into the overall picture of perpetration and guilt. On the other, we have those, for example Martin Walser, for whom the rejection of all "political correctness" facilitates a pursuit of "pure" historicization unencumbered by posterior knowledge of how the individual, the local, or the peripheral were all related to the centers of Nazi power. In effect, this is a conflict between an interpretation of the past which, while it demonstrates empathy with individual Germans, nevertheless places Nazi crimes at the heart of the way Germans see themselves in the present and one which seeks to "normalize" the past in order to relativize its centrality to the struggle to shape national identity. In neither case, therefore, and despite all claims to the contrary, is historicization entirely unconnected to present-day political aims and agendas.

"Political Correctness"

"Aber das Insistieren, das meine Generation damals mit rebellischem Stolz und nicht ohne moralische Kraft eingeübt hat, hat sie dann auch noch beibehalten, als es seine Funktion verloren hat," writes author and lawyer Bernhard Schlink in his philosophical treatise *Vergangenheitsschuld und gegenwärtiges Recht* (2002).[22] Coming some twelve years after unification, these comments were perhaps no longer controversial. Yet only four years *previously*, in late 1998, the coming-to-power of the SPD-Green coalition, led by Gerhard Schröder and Joschka Fischer — two former student radicals — had been greeted in sections of the conservative media, and by a number of intellectuals and social commentators, with what Ingo Cornils refers to as a "plethora of new books, essays and editorials" challenging the "cultural hegemony" of the generation of '68 and what was seen as its claim to the "exclusive right to interpret the past in the Federal Republic."[23] The more extreme elements amongst the critics of the "68ers" in the Government would later attempt to discredit Fischer as a "street fighter" during the student protests.

These attacks came towards the end of a decade in which a bitter clash on the subject of "political correctness" had been imported from the United States and given a particularly German twist. Sally Johnson and Stephanie Suhr thus describe the manner in which the "discourse of 'political correctness'" arrived in the FRG via translations and reviews of American texts such as Robert Hughes's 1993 *Culture of Complaint* and was quickly domesticated by a range of German-speaking journalists and in a number of books including Michael Bonder's *"Political Correctness": Ein Gespenst geht um die Welt* (1995) and *"Politische Korrektheit" in Deutschland: Eine Gefahr für die Demokratie* (1995) by Michael Behrens and Robert von Rimscha. Subsequently, special editions of three academic journals were swiftly produced, examining the ideological and linguistic manifestations of the debate,[24] in addition to a book by Diedrich Diederichsen, *Politische Korrekturen* (1996). The primary concern of those complaining of "political correctness," Johnson and Suhr argue, even overshadowing international debates on feminism, racism, and environmentalism, was with "the purported taboo surrounding German historical consciousness" which, conservatives claimed, was "stifling democratic discourse and preventing Germany from shaking off the past and progressing towards a new, more positive self-identity."[25] This is without a doubt what Martin Walser had in mind when, in a 1994 interview, he criticized the "journalistischen Wächter der 'political correctness.'"[26] In his 1998 *Friedenspreisrede,* as will be discussed presently, Walser further referred to the abuse of the past for contemporary political purposes.

Similar attacks, of course, had been the mainstay of the so-called intellectual New Right that flourished in the early 1990s. Botho Strauß, in his 1993 *Spiegel* essay, "Anschwellender Bocksgesang," for example, depicted the liberal media as the primary pillar of the "telekratischen Öffentlichkeit" which, he continued, had institutionalized the "unblutigste Gewaltherrschaft und zugleich der umfassendste Totalitarismus der Geschichte."[27] Ulrich Schacht, on the other hand, editor of the volume *Die selbstbewußte Nation* (1994), often held to have launched the intellectual New Right, indicted the power of the media and its supposed (ab)use of Auschwitz in a far more concrete fashion: "Wer Faschist ist, bestimmen in diesem Land inzwischen Redakteure und Journalisten 'seriöser' Medien."[28] This formed part of a wide-ranging assault on the media, exemplified by the advertisements commissioned by right-wing historians and political thinkers Rainer Zitelmann, Karlheinz Weißmann, and Heimo Schwilk, and a number of others — not all associated with the New Right — in the *Frankfurter Allgemeine Zeitung* in April 1995, shortly before the fiftieth anniversary of the end of the Second World War. These full-page spreads attacked what they portrayed as the taboo on discussing the suffering of the *Vertriebenen,* those Germans "abandoned" to communism as a result of the *Ostpolitik* inaugurated by Willy Brandt, and, most important, the "national question."[29]

Later in the decade the media outcry following the entreaties by the Austrian author Peter Handke for greater understanding for the Serbian position during the wars in the ex-Yugoslavia, the "Crimes of the *Wehrmacht* exhibition" organized by Hannes Heer of the Hamburg Institute for Social Research, and the final stages of discussions surrounding the construction of a Holocaust memorial in Berlin, were all accompanied by accusations of political piety and premeditated instrumentalization of the past. Similarly, remarks by FDP vice-chairman Jürgen Möllemann just before the 2002 Federal elections, in which he insisted on his right to criticize Israel and implied that Jews might sometimes be responsible for anti-Semitism, exploited the belief of many voters that an oppressive philo-Semitism had been imposed on them by politicians afraid to voice the real views of their constituents.

"Political correctness," Johnson and Suhr contend, is "typically constructed" by its opponents "as an inhibitive discursive force" even as they themselves attempt to close down, and preclude, "the kind of open debate" which they "purportedly desire."[30] In what comes next, we look at literary texts by two authors concerned with the controversy over "political correctness" and the presentation of genocide that seek to expose precisely this tendency. Following this we look at Walser's *Ein springender Brunnen* as a novel that conjoins our discussion of historicization with the debate on whether certain perspectives on the past are, or should be, taboo.

Peter Schneider and F. C. Delius

Peter Schneider's *Eduards Heimkehr* (1999) and F. C. Delius's *Die Flatterzunge* (1999) both respond to discussions of the ritual culture of accusation that many observers perceived in German society even as each employs, as we shall see, a quite different tone and style. Schneider's novel, the sequel to his 1992 *Paarungen,* is concerned with the tension between the endeavor to expose responsibility and the need for social integration. The central question Schneider's novel raises is whether an overzealous approach to the *Aufarbeitung* of the Nazi past is being duplicated, with negative consequences for the "inner unity" of the new Federal Republic, in the post-unification obsession with the role of "ordinary" Germans during the GDR dictatorship. Delius's narrative, on the other hand, limits itself to revealing the private resentments of at least some of those who decry "political correctness." Implicit in both texts, however, is the realization that the moral fervor of the "68ers" may be no longer appropriate to efforts to represent the Nazi past and, in particular, the actions of "ordinary" Germans. Schneider's novel, therefore, lacks the abstract moralizing once common in works by his generation. Delius's text, alternatively, revels in satirizing its own narrator's persecution complex following his ignominious return to Germany following some tactless comments in Israel even as it — similar to *Eduards Heimkehr* — also critiques "politically-correct" overreactions.

Schneider's protagonist, Eduard, returns to Berlin after a lengthy absence in the United States and ruminates upon what kind of "normality" is being established in a city in which wild accusations of profiteering from Jewish misfortune can be leveled against individuals — including the narrator himself — attempting to clarify the legality, and indeed the morality, of their grandparents' acquisitions of Jewish property. Just as many of the allegations of repression and distortion of the past are motivated by predictably contemporary interests — not least the desire of the *west* German squatters to colonize the *east* German block to which Eduard may have a claim — so are the variety of vicious witchhunts directed against Eduard's east German colleagues in his scientific research institute the product of political power struggles in the post-unification era. The narrator's reflections on these and other matters are embedded within a consideration of topical discussions on the extent to which criminality has a genetic or a sociological cause.

Eduard's grandfather is absolved of complicity in the dispossession of Jews in the 1930s; indeed, it is hinted that he may have been an Oskar-Schindler figure, who bought the disputed property in order to protect the interests of his Jewish business partner. The excavation of the past, it would appear, is susceptible to instrumentalization. The implied criticism of an excessive zeal for *Aufarbeitung* may lend credence to Helmut Peitsch's positing of a shift in Schneider's politics from a left-wing critical enlightenment to a partial endorsement, at least, of the stance on "political correctness" embraced by neo-conservatives in the early 1990s.[31] Certainly, in an essay in his volume *Vom Ende der Gewißheit* (1994), Schneider reflects on his new, unexpected status as a *Renegat*.[32] Other pieces in this collection — and in his 1992 *Extreme Mittellage,* a set of reflections on the fall of the Wall — display, moreover, impatience with left-wing orthodoxy concerning the Nazi past and East Germany. Auschwitz, Schneider asserts, had been declared an eternal barrier to unification, with no regard to the pain caused by division, whereas the GDR had been recklessly idealized as a utopian alternative to a "latently fascist" FRG.

Yet, as Andreas Michel argues in a plea for a careful differentiation between the views expressed by Schneider and essays by intellectuals associated with the New Right such as Botho Strauß and Ansgar Graw, the author's thinking does *not* display a rejection of critical enlightenment *per se*. It is, Michel maintains, rather "enlightenment *utopianism*" (my italics) that he refuses, not a considered discourse of reason and *Kritik*.[33] *Eduards Heimkehr* does not seek to question the critical excavation of the past. Rather, it warns against the perils of a *misdirection* of enlightenment zeal, of the dangers posed by a utopian radicalism that may turn into fanaticism, and which fails to reflect on its own, possibly egotistical motives. Indeed, a similar point is communicated in Schneider's short story "Skizze eines Enthüllers" (2003) which portrays Burk's self-destructive obsession with the evident cruelty of the German psychiatric profession during the Nazi years.[34]

In *Eduards Heimkehr*, the protagonist's intolerance of the present-day tendency to excuse anti-social behavior on the grounds of deprivation, trauma or predisposition points not to his conservative instincts, but to a conventional, Enlightenment belief in individual accountability. To this extent, he mirrors Schneider's own "Skepsis," expressed in an essay of 1993, towards the "Erklärungsansätze" offered by sections of the liberal media to explain the racist attacks sweeping Germany in the early 1990s: "Sie tragen dazu bei, die Opfer zu entwirklichen und die Täter in den Mittelpunkt der Aufmerksamkeit zu stellen."[35] Schneider concedes "daß es so etwas wie das Böse gibt und daß es jederzeit unten dem dünnen Firnis der Zivilisation hervorbrechen kann," but contends that the response to this realization cannot be a melancholic dismissal of Enlightenment but a "militante Demokratie."[36] For Schneider, the need for critical engagement with questions of individual responsibility remains as pressing today as it ever was.

The central character in Delius's *Die Flatterzunge,* a mediocre *Posaunist,* stands guilty as charged: on tour in Israel he signed a bar tab with the name Adolf Hitler.[37] The scandal is uncontainable, and his dismissal immediate. He returns in disgrace to Berlin to ruminate on his botched relationships and professional failure and to indulge his Jericho-complex. Thus he imagines himself in 1200 BC helping to bring about the collapse of the walls of Jericho. This he associates with the fall of the Berlin Wall — there is an echo of Thomas Brussig's comically egomaniac figure Uhltzscht: "vielleicht gelte ich in den USA als der Mann, der die Mauer umstürzte mit seiner Posaune" (*FZ,* 125) — an event which, he hints, marks the end of Germany's forty years of enforced contrition.

Delius exploits his protagonist, whose fate is based on a "true story" of 1997,[38] in order to demonstrate the manner in which genuine concerns about "political correctness" and the apparent ritualization of Holocaust remembrance may all too easily metamorphose into an irrational, possibly retrogressive, antipathy to Germany's ongoing engagement with the Nazi past. The author is concerned, to cite a review by Jörg Magenau, "zugleich mit der moralischen Schieflage deutscher Erinnerungspolitik *und* den störenden Untertönen im deutschen Wohlbefinden."[39] Indeed, Delius's *Die Flatterzunge* in many ways appears to be a response to the kind of sentiments expressed, for example, by Botho Strauß, in his "anschwellender Bocksgesang" essay, or perhaps in his autobiographical treatise *Die Fehler des Kopisten* (1997). In the latter work, accordingly,

Strauß inveighs against the requirement for public figures, artists, and intellectuals endlessly to reiterate "ihre Opposition zu Hitler, dem lebendigsten Toten aller Zeiten. In diesem Sinn ist unsere gesamte aufgeklärte Gesittung in Wahrheit eine okkulte Obsession."[40]

Delius's narrator is, on occasion, blessed with genuine insight regarding the shortcomings of the discourse of memorialization. For example, he quite plausibly suggests that the tone of the debates on the design of the Holocaust memorial threatens to distract from the perpetrators, rather than inscribe their crime into the fabric of the new Germany: "Im Streit um das richtige Gedenken werden die Verbrecher immer blasser" (*FZ*, 47). The commemoration of the Holocaust, he implies, has become a matter of "das richtige Gedenken," a search for a suitably elegant political and aesthetic solution. This would not be a memorial, but a concreting-over of the past. Equally damaging, the discussions may be a form of relativization, a means of diverting attention away from the crimes, or a way for those involved to distance themselves from their perpetrators.

This line of thought does not stop here, however. The narrator's generally valid criticism of the way an insistence on the need for public commemoration of the Holocaust can become ritualized, or even unconsciously instrumentalized as a barrier to an unmediated confrontation with the past, descends into moral relativism: "Vielleicht spinne ich, aber . . . steckt doch nicht in jedem von uns, nicht nur uns Deutschen, der Bruchbruchteil eines Nazis, auch wenn wir noch so demokratisch, noch so prosemitisch, noch so aufgeklärt sind?" (*FZ*, 76). The implication is twofold: the discourse of remembrance is not only a form of psychological evasion, it also denies the reality of human nature. The democratic, philo-Semitic, impeccably enlightened culture of contrition is but a thin veneer that disguises the ugly truth that hatred of the other is the norm. How, then, can an individual — or a nation — be condemned for simply behaving in keeping with human nature, for acting on instincts as ancient as they are irrepressible? Tribunals can legislate against genocide, but they cannot eliminate the craving to indulge the evil in the human psyche: "Einmal der Teufel sein. Der Böseste aller Bösen. Ein sehr menschlicher Wunsch" (*FZ*, 104). Here, the romanticized fascination with evil may be a parody of the likes of Karl Heinz Bohrer, Hans Jürgen Syberberg, Botho Strauß, or Martin Walser.

If evil is all too human, then so are the emotions that drive individuals to cast off the constraints of civilization and enlightenment: failure, humiliation, and the desire for revenge. And if these emotions are human, they must be understandable. The focus is widened to include all the setbacks the narrator has had to endure. Everything is attributable to circumstances, he claims, invoking an extreme form of moral relativism: "Aber wie soll man mein Verbrechen verstehen und verurteilen, wenn man die Kette meiner Niederlagen und Aufstiege nicht kennt" (*FZ*, 13). Here, the word "Kette" implies a sequence of events over which the narrator has little control. His crime is as much reflex as willed; he is as much a victim as a perpetrator: "Aber ich bin doch das Opfer, das jüngste Opfer dieser Scheiß-Nazis, dachte ich" (*FZ*, 82). As a German, his biography is always overdetermined, in a culture of ritualized remembrance, by the Nazi past. His outburst, it seems, is aimed against the reminders of national shame and humiliation that so oppress him.

A sense of ignominy and of failure, feelings of victimhood, and a reflex rejection of "political correctness" — these are the symptoms of a crisis of confidence within liberal thought. The fetishistic internalization of Enlightenment tenets of tolerance, historical awareness, and critical self-examination induces an unsustainable self-reflectiveness. In a café, the narrator worries that a rose-seller might think that he refused to buy from him because he is black (*FZ*, 82). Others, he supposes, must suffer from the same pressure to be "politically-correct." He suggests that the orchestra would not have dared to fire him if he were homosexual (*FZ*, 112). The result of this unrelenting anxiety, perhaps predictably, is the desire to run amok: "Ich träume von einer Karriere als Amokläufer" (*FZ*, 112).

Delius's trombonist is undermined by gentle satire. Towards the end of the novel, his efforts to render his suffering as a consequence of "political correctness" in poetic form strike a self-pitying note that is at the same time opportunistically self-aggrandizing:

> Ich bin der Böseste der Bösen / ich bin der Böseste gewesen / mit den eisern-bösen Besen / werden wir die Sache lösen / bin besonders bös gewesen / bin der Hitler selbst gewesen / einmal ist in mir gewesen / eine Stimme, laut gewesen / hat verwirrt mir meinen Sinn / gesagt, daß ich der Hitler bin / Hitler sein. Das darf ich nicht / Hitler sein, das will ich nicht [. . .] das wolln wir in Deutschland nicht / und erst recht im Ausland nicht / schlimmer kann es nicht mehr werden / als ein Hitler sein auf Erden. (*FZ*, 136–37)

This passage is both ridiculous — witness the childish petulance of "bin besonders bös gewesen" and the comically inappropriate register of "wolln" and "auf Erden," recalling a tradition of Romantic poetry of which he is unworthy — dangerously delusional, and also self-defeating in its overstatement: "Schlimmer kann es nicht mehr werden / als ein Hitler sein auf Erden." The narrator's subsequent review of his own work — "weniger als die Hälfte scheint mir gerichtstauglich" (*FZ*, 137) — does little to bolster his credibility.

Schneider and Delius concede important points to those who detect a damaging overzealousness in the contemporary discourse of coming to terms with the past. At the same time, and herein lies the significance of the novels just considered, each of them insists that historicization must be balanced by an awareness of the need to foreground the unalterable fact of German crimes. What Delius and Schneider fear is a Berlin Republic in which the chief achievement of the "old" FRG — a critical attitude towards the Nazi period — is sacrificed. To this extent, these "68ers" are anxious to combat the twin perils of a "longitudinal normality" which seeks to reject "political correctness" and to relativize the Nazi past and an "ahistorical normality" which tends towards a sentimentalization of the individual's rejection of politics *in toto* in favor of an egotistical "self-expression." The same might be said, of course, of Uwe Timm, whom we examined alongside Delius in chapter three.

In our next section, we examine one of the most important literary texts of the 1990s, Martin Walser's *Ein springender Brunnen,* which appeared in 1998. The goal that Walser set himself in composing this novel, and which made it so controversial at the time of its publication, was to give value to the longing to experience the past as it delivers itself "wie von selbst."[41] For this author, freedom from a view of the past disastrously distorted by contemporary contingencies and exigencies follows from a celebration of language's transcendent potential, that is, of the capacity of poetic language in particular to transcend the banal and purely immanent claims of "political correctness." For his critics, however, Walser's fascination with the limited perspective of his youthful protagonist unavoidably leads to the bracketing out of Nazi atrocities in the name of precisely the kind of unreflected "longitudinal normality" rejected by Delius, Schneider, and other "68ers."

Martin Walser's *Ein springender Brunnen*

In Zafer Şenocak's *Gefährliche Verwandtschaft* (1998), Sascha Muchteschem claims that Germans attempting to shape their new "normality" with obsessive reference to the Nazi past are traitors to their own history, "wie sie überhaupt Verräter an ihrer Geschichte waren, und dies nur, um den Amerikanern zu gefallen."[42] The narrator of Arnold Stadler's *Ein hinreissender Schrotthändler,* for which he won the *Büchnerpreis* in 1999, is more indirect in his laconic description of a nation that appears to have sacrificed any hope of an authentic relationship to its past. Thus the Berlin Republic touted by the newly elected chancellor, Gerhard Schröder, is portrayed as pure pastiche, a trite blend of global fads and adopted styles. So unsure are the narrator and his wife of their identity, in fact, so uncertain of their liberal values in the age of "political correctness," that they allow a complete stranger into their home. Adrian is an English-speaker, a foreigner whose name invokes the Adriatic, and who — in a further anomaly — wears Adidas jogging trousers with "schwarz-rot-goldenen Seitenstreifen."[43] In truth, the nation's multi-cultural banality is exemplified by this recent arrival, the personification of the modern, American-style throw-away consumerism alluded to in the novel's title. To refuse him entry would smack of nationalism, even racism — and so the narrator and his wife rush to service his every need. Gabi, indeed, even "ließ sich [. . .] mehrfach von ihm durchficken," and this, almost inevitably, "am Tag der deutschen Einheit" (*HS*, 228).

The narrator's irreverence extends to his whimsical allusions to the ritual practice of coming-to-terms with the past. In dialogue with his wife, who hails from Hamburg and projects the middle-class, liberal superiority of the Republic's urban elites, he promises, insincerely, to raise the issue of his provincial origins with his psychiatrist: "um es und mich aufzuarbeiten, sagte ich '*aufzuarbeiten*' — wollte ich eigentlich vergessen oder erinnern, erinnern, um vergessen zu können — oder umgekehrt?" (*HS*, 36). The very term *Aufarbeitung* is a fad, a psychological disorder, perhaps even a symptom of the liberal crisis of "political correctness." Elsewhere, on his way to a reunion of childhood friends, he sings the "Kreenheinstetter Heimatlied," a local anthem banned during what he flippantly refers to as the "3. Reich." Luckily, he and his friends were "mit der dritten Strophe zu Ende" just as their bus pulled up at their hotel: "Das war 'timing,' ja, wir hatten noch ein Gefühl für die Zeit" (*HS*, 43). The third verse of this *regional* song of praise is just as unwelcome in the Federal Republic as it was in the Hitler period. Instead, the universalist values of a *different* third verse, that is, the third stanza of the anthem of the FRG — "*Einigkeit und Recht und Freiheit*" — must prevail over the particularist sensibilities of local traditions.[44] For Stadler's narrator, however, in contrast to the narrator of Delius's *Der Sonntag, an dem ich Weltmeister wurde* (1994) whose reception of this stanza we discussed in chapter three, the FRG's anthem signals only a dulling, "politically correct" conformity and the absence of any real emotional attachment to *Heimat*.

Martin Walser's *Ein springender Brunnen*, published a year previous to Stadler's *Büchnerpreis*-winning novel, in the summer of 1998, would seem, at first glance, to have little in common with *Ein hinreissender Schrotthändler*. Stadler's novel is set in 1998, at the time of the Federal elections won by the SPD-Green coalition; his protagonist is a weak-willed conformist craving acceptance into the urban middle-classes yet beset by his provincial origins and profoundly melancholic bent. Walser's text, on the other hand, is the semi-autobiographical tale of a young boy's passage from the formlessness of childhood to self-realization, in the manner of Goethe's *Dichtung und Wahrheit*, within the world of poetry and the imagination. This takes place, it just so happens, between 1932 and 1945, that is, very nearly contemporaneously with National Socialism, in Wasserburg on the *Bodensee*. The link between the two novels, however, lies in their shared commitment to a vision of a provincial Germany, which, untainted by Nazism, appears as the repository of *true* German values. This is *Heimat* as imagined within the Romantic oppositions of nature and city, authenticity and the deceptions of modernity, community and society.

In fact, Walser's implacable hostility to what he has termed the "Tugendterror der 'political correctness,'"[45] his dismissal of the artificiality of the Federal Republic, before and after unification, his location of authenticity in the regions, and in language, especially dialect, and, in particular, his complaints about the ritualization of Holocaust commemoration, predetermine his admiration for Stadler. Certainly, Walser has been one of Stadler's most consistent champions in his efforts to carve out a niche in a literary scene that, following the debates on *Unterhaltsamkeit* and *Neue Lesbarkeit*, was hostile to the author's intermingling of metaphysical reflection and arcane allusion. An afterword to Stadler's 1994 *Mein Hund, meine Sau, mein Leben* extols a tone that ranges "vom Aufrufen und puren Nennen zum lakonischen Konstatieren und zuletzt zum in allen Präzisionen blühenden Erzählen,"[46] and the 1999 novel is commended in *Der Spiegel* for its "schreienden Humor."[47] Throughout Stadler's oeuvre, Walser proposes, the author repeatedly returns to a "Quelle einer Verzweiflung, die er auf eine sie entblößende Art verbergen muß"[48] — the destruction of *Heimat* and the demise of authenticity.

Walser's *Ein springender Brunnen* sets its own attempt to recuperate an authentic *Heimat,* rooted in the province, far from the center of Nazi power, alongside ruminations on the contemporary instrumentalization of the past. To this extent, it both prefigures and elaborates on the substance of the controversial speech Walser was to make on receipt of the *Friedenspreis des deutschen Buchhandels* on 11 October 1998 in the *Paulskirche* in Frankfurt in front of 1200 guests, including the then *Bundespräsident* Roman Herzog. Indeed, his appeal for an end to what he decried as the "Instrumentalisierung unserer Geschichte zu gegenwärtigen Zwecken"[49] and his allusion to Holocaust remembrance as "Drohroutine [. . .] Einschüchterungsmittel oder Moralkeule" (*EES*, 20) reignited the debate on "political correctness." Of especial significance here, however, is Walser's response to the rebuke delivered by literary critic Marcel Reich-Ranicki and his reproach that *Ein springender Brunnen* "fails" to mention Auschwitz: "Nie etwas gehört vom Urgesetz des Erzählens: der Perspektivität. Aber selbst wenn — Zeitgeist geht vor Ästhetik" (*EES*, 19).

In *Ein springender Brunnen*, Walser works to reinstate the primacy of perspective over politics, to ensure that *Ästhetik* precedes *Zeitgeist*. In philosophical terms, this means favoring the transcendent over the merely immanent.[50] This recalls Karl Heinz Bohrer's aesthetic program, which Jan-Werner Müller describes as a "conception of aesthetics as pure presence, instead of representation, i.e. the idea of the immanent, self-reflexive sign that pointed to nothing beyond itself, and was radically divorced from 'reality,' and therefore, *inter alia,* politics."[51] Put more simply, the novel prefers the ideal of poetry to the banality of the "everyday" in which individuals pursue their selfish interests, sacrifice subjectivity to conformity, and engage in intrigue for the sake of short-term advantage.

The reinstatement of perspective over *Zeitgeist* initiates a defense of subjectivity. Thus the novel's contraction of perspective to what its adolescent protagonist could have known of his environment at the time at which the story is told clashes with the present-day discourse of *Vergangenheitsbewältigung* into which the book was launched, and in the context of which it would be received, irrespective of Walser's wishes. The immanent conditions of *both* the "narrative present" and the "actual present," of the period during which the story takes place and the time of the novel's reception, are subordinated to Johann's restricted point of view. This provides cover for his choice to lose himself in art and the imagination — the horrors of Nazism, and, ultimately, of Auschwitz, were simply not as "present" to him as they would be to people more than fifty years later at the time of the book's publication — as well as for the book's more generalized defiance of the obligation to subject the Hitler era to a critical unpicking of guilt and complicity.

Yet Walser's novel does not simply indulge in an unreflected historicization of the Nazi period. It attempts something far more sophisticated: a critique of the way modernity has shattered the life-affirming naïveté that underpins community, tradition, and memory. Here, Walser parts company with Bohrer, who, Müller argues, "does not see art as a form of 'compensation' for the disorientation characteristic of modernity."[52] For Bohrer, the work of art does not contain any "metaphysische Instanz," "im Sinne eines transzendenten Verständnisses."[53] *Ein springender Brunnen,* on the other hand, sets out to transcend the disastrous split in the human subject that accompanied the project of modernity. This is achieved by means of framing the narrator's lovingly detailed reconstruction of Johann's childhood — the *historicizing* passages which make up the larger part of the text and which relegate Nazism to the margins — within a series of meta-narrative, apparently authorial interventions.

In the opening pages of the novel, the narrator confirms that "solange etwas ist, ist es nicht das, was es gewesen sein wird" (*SB*, 9). The conventional perspective is inverted to imply the viewpoint of the past upon its own future, a future in which historical experience will no longer be "true" to itself but subject to the exigencies of the present. This insight laments the delegitimization of historicization — the longing to recreate the past *wie es eigentlich gewesen* — and forewarns of the challenges the novel will confront within what its narrator, and its author, appear to perceive as the present-day tendency to render history normative for didactic purposes: "Je normierter dieser Umgang, um so mehr ist, was als Vergangenheit gezeigt wird, Produkt der Gegenwart" (*SB*, 282). The instrumentalization of the past, the narrator declares, inaugurates what he lavishly describes as a "komplett erschlossene, durchleuchtete, gereinigte, genehmigte, total gegenwartsgeeignete Vergangenheit. Ethisch, politisch durchkorrigiert. Vorexerziert von unseren Gescheitesten, Einwandfreisten, den Besten." Yet in addition to the attack on "political correctness," and on the intellectuals who enforce it, these lines also display a melancholic regret with regard to the fractured subject of modernity. In the place of transcendence, "innocent" metaphysical awe, modernity imposed reason, and knowledge, and with knowledge, guilt. The constitutional state replaced the emotional ties that bind individuals to *Heimat,* and to *Nation*. The past, and memory itself, it is argued, came to be corrupted by a critical excavation serving only "gegenwärtigen Zwecken."

The narrator's aim in *Ein springender Brunnen* is to relate the past in such a way that it becomes "auf ihre Weise gegenwärtig" (*SB*, 9), that is, *gegenwärtig* in the sense of "authentically accessible" to us, *wie es eigentlich gewesen,* rather than as a mere adjunct of the *Gegenwart* from which it is viewed. This would be "ein interesseloses Interesse an der Vergangenheit" in which the past "uns entgegenkäme wie von selbst." At the same time, he concedes that this may be no more than a "Wunschdenkensziel" (*SB*, 283). Indeed, if the schizophrenic disintegration of the self cannot be resolved, if time cannot be turned back to the "wholeness" that preceded modernity, then the only remaining option is to *imagine* such a return. *Heimat* is projected by means of language, relocated in art and the imagination as a metaphysical ideal, not of this world, but transcendent of it, and in the cultural traditions that pit subjectivity against reason and conformity. Modernity will be transcended within the aesthetic; language will be freed of its misappropriation by "political correctness" and move closer to the things it describes.

In order to accomplish this, the German language, and German traditions, must first be liberated of another misappropriation: the Nazi exploitation of notions of *Heimat* and German culture in pursuit of the Nazis' ideological aims, *their* subordination of the past "zu gegenwärtigen Zwecken," that is, *their* "political correctness." The best way to achieve this is by situating National Socialism itself within the trajectory of modernity. Indeed, this has been proposed by conservative historians such as Ernst Nolte since the early 1980s;[54] in 1994, young "New Right" historians Michael Prinz and Rainer Zitelmann published their *National-sozialismus und Modernisierung*. This rethinking of the Hitler period turns upside down the conventional premise whereby Nazism is viewed as a *response* to the ravages of modernity, and in particular to its destruction of community. Consequently, those aspects of German culture previously discredited as forerunners to Nazi thought, especially Romanticism with its patriotic bent and seemingly anti-modern impulse, can be rehabilitated and relocated *in opposition* to Hitler.

Nazism hence appears in *Ein springender Brunnen* as a motor of modernization. It descends unbidden upon the provinces from the cities, imported by the "Zugezogenen," including Nazi luminaries "Ribbentrop und Streicher" (*SB*, 229); indeed, the vast majority of party members in the novel speak *Hochdeutsch*. The compliance of the villagers comes, accordingly, from resignation rather than enthusiasm. The crisis of modernity in the early 1930s — financial collapse, unemployment, the disintegration of community — pushes them into making pragmatic rather than judicious choices. Johann's mother offers her inn to the local Nazis as a meeting place in order to stave off financial ruin, not because she is committed to the cause. Hers is a short-term calculation of self-interest, a very *modern* reaction to a crisis itself rooted in modernity. Yet her inability to grasp the more profound imperative to resist the Nazis simply hastens the destruction of that which she aims to defend.

Johann chooses to follow his father rather than his mother, but only after he has rejected the worldly temptations of National Socialism, represented by Adolf, son of a wealthy and influential local Nazi, for whom he experiences an occasional homoerotic attraction, and Anita, the girl whose obvious charms distract him from his quest for poetic transcendence. Hence he moves from reading the work of Rabindranath Tagore (1861–1941), the Indian lyricist who had been a favorite of his father, to Zarathustra (B.C. 628–551), the Iranian poet who founded Parsism, an injunction to make an ethical choice between good and evil, between the wicked spirit Angra Manju and the God Ahura Masda. These two poets exemplify the ideals embraced by his father in his attachment to Theosophy, the contemporary popular movement which looked to Eastern thinking to unite science and philosophy in order to achieve an "ethical life" and the "truth of being." For Johann's father, poetic transcendence and aesthetic integrity offered a more spiritual response to the disruptions of modernity. For Johann, art opens up the route to an authentic sense of self: "Wenn er las *Nacht ist es: nun reden lauter alle springenden Brunnen*, hatte er das Gefühl, seine Stimme singe ganz von selbst" (*SB*, 164). The quotation here, repeated in the novel's title, is from "Das Nachtlied" in Nietzsche's *Also sprach Zarathustra*.

Johann is attracted to Klopstock, Goethe, Schiller, and Hölderlin. Above all, he is drawn to Stefan George and Nietzsche. George, proponent of "art for art's sake," friend of Verlaine, Mallarmé, and Hofmannsthal, and editor of the *Blätter für die Kunst,* perfectly embodies the concept of art as transcendent. The fact that George went into Swiss exile in 1933 conveniently sets him against the Nazis, as does his belief in a "German-Jewish elective affinity," aptly described by Ritchie Robertson.[55] Nietzsche, on the other hand, must be actively cleansed of the taint of Nazism: "Obwohl in dem, was der Schaführer so betonungslos dahinsagte, manchmal Wörter wie aus Zarathustrasätzen vorkam, spürte Johann, daß das alles andere als Zarathustrasätze waren" (*SB,* 344). The Nietzsche that Johann admires propounds the superiority of the individual's perspective, and, to cite Robert Solomon, the promise of "*self-creation,* ethics as aesthetics."[56] It is not the Nietzschean notion, misappropriated by National Socialism, of the *Übermensch.*

"Ohne Heimat ist der Mensch ein elendes Ding, eigentlich ein Blatt im Wind," claims Johann in an essay responding to the task set by Nazi schoolteacher, Ernst Heller, "Wieviel Heimat braucht der Mensch?" (*SB,* 249). He continues with some daring: "Aber jeder muß wissen, daß nicht nur er Heimat braucht, sondern andere auch [. . .] Die weiße Rasse tut, als wäre sie etwas Besseres. Solange sie andere Rassen vernichtet, ist sie etwas Minderes, ist sie schlimmer als jede andere Rasse" (*SB,* 252). For Johann, *Heimat* implies *Gemeinschaft:* without community, the individual is as forlorn as a "Blatt im Wind." Yet this is not the Nazi *Volksgemeinschaft.* It is *Heimat* as the repository of German traditions of artistic transcendence, subjectivity, and individualism. These embody a quintessentially *German* sensibility, a Romantic defiance of the philistine excesses of modernity which is as opposed to Nazism as it is to the contemporary instrumentalization of the past. In truth, Johann most likely never wrote the essay on *Heimat.* The narrator simply imagines that he did, or that his *Schutzengel* called upon him to do so.

Johann's defense of individual perspective is rooted in language; it is a search for "eine eigene Sprache" (*SB,* 402), a yearning "sich einfach der Sprache an[zu]vertrauen" (*SB,* 404). His projection of *Heimat* is an act of will, a feat of the imagination in which reality — mundane and ephemeral — is far less significant than the utopian alternative anticipated in the aesthetic. "In der Sprache," Walser claimed in a 1997 interview with Heribert Vogt, "liegt eine Utopie, denn sie hat bis jetzt noch jede Scheußlichkeit von dieser Welt weggebracht." And this was precisely the problem for many of his critics. Language is certainly "voller kritischer Instrumente und Waffen," as Walser suggests, yet the "Spott und Hohn hinsichtlich des Entgegenstehenden und der Machthaber"[57] that inhere in it do not necessarily engage directly with prevailing injustices. Rather, they may legitimize a retreat from the "real" into the ostensible authenticity of introspection.

Johann's fascination with the aesthetic causes him to look away from the horrors of the period in which his self-discovery occurs. "So gestimmt konnte Johann von nichts Schrecklichem Kenntnis nehmen" (*SB*, 388–89), the narrator informs us. With regard to Jewish suffering, Johann cannot regret something in which he was not involved and which was so distant from his own experience. Enforced contrition would be fraudulent. Indeed, a culture of ritualized remorse, Walser proposed in his *Friedenspreisrede*, inevitably leads to the desire to "wegschauen" (*EES*, 17–18). The only "genuine" response to the Holocaust, he implies, is one compatible with the *individual's* conscience — and this, of course, cannot be subject to any normative analysis or required to justify itself.

"Normalization"

"If personal conscience is seen as the main instrument of remembering," Kathrin Schödel argues in her analysis of Walser's *Ein springender Brunnen* and his *Friedenspreisrede*, "memory becomes merely a depoliticized and ahistorical process of self-examination." This, Schödel continues, encourages "an apologetic view of general human weakness."[58] Bill Niven describes the same process as a "privatization" of guilt and shame.[59] Since at least the early 1990s, in fact, Walser's work has promoted an arguably apologist understanding of human behavior. The 1993 novel *ohne einander*[60] and *Tod eines Kritikers* (2002), for example, challenge the Enlightenment presumption of a universal ethical code by which individuals should be judged. Both pit a very "human" desire to fantasize about indulging the darker side of our nature against the constraints of "political correctness." In each text, an adversary is murdered, albeit in the imagination. In the case of *Tod eines Kritikers*, the fictional murder of a character unmistakably modeled after the famously acerbic Jewish critic Marcel Reich-Ranicki caused a public scandal.[61]

The form of historicization preferred by Walser may actually *dehistoricize* the past insofar as it detaches the individual's experience from any overarching social and political context. An essential correspondence between experience and memory of it is obsessively reiterated as a means of freezing time at the moment before the loss of innocence can no longer be postponed and the naïve, truly *undivided* individual fragments into the tortured subject of modernity. Johann had *always* registered the persecution of Jews, even if only at the periphery of his vision — he witnesses the expulsion of the half-Jew Wolfgang from the National Socialist *Jungzug* (*SB*, 133–34) — but he simply did not *want* to see it. Even in 1945, he wishes to continue this self-delusion to delay the moment at which awareness of the Holocaust would force him to turn against himself and to question his childhood memories: "Er wollte nicht gezwungen sein. Zu nichts und von niemandem" (*SB*, 401). The most deleterious aspect of modernity, for Johann, is not the mechanized mass killing. It is rather *knowledge* of this event.

Walser is well aware that knowledge of German crimes cannot be erased; nor has he ever proposed this. The fact that, as Schödel notes, his 1998 speech was "applauded by the far right and may well have contributed to an atmosphere in which anti-Semitic attacks became more frequent" is surely regrettable, but it was not his intention, even if he might be thought to have a responsibility to anticipate such misappropriations of his words.[62] For Walser, what is at stake is a "longitudinal normalization" which places the Hitler period within a chronological sequence extending back to the very beginnings of the German past, and which dismisses attempts to interpret the entirety of the German historical experience through the prism of the twelve years of National Socialism as teleological. *Heimat,* for Walser, is essentially about tradition, the permanence of the nation and "Germanness." To interpret German history solely in the aftermath of the Holocaust, he proposes in his eulogy for Victor Klemperer, the German-Jewish professor of Romance Literature whose wartime diaries caused such a stir on their belated publication in 1995, is nothing other than "Auskunft NACH Auschwitz."[63]

The debate on "ordinary" Germans continued throughout the 1990s and into the new millennium. Moreover, as discussed at the beginning of this chapter, it expanded to include not only those who were bystanders, or were at the periphery, but also those who were directly involved in the worst crimes. In part, this was encouraged by high profile events such as the "Crimes of the *Wehrmacht*" exhibition that toured the country in the mid-1990s, was withdrawn in late 1999 following criticism of its inaccuracies, and then reinstated after a substantial reconceptualization. Certainly, photographs of *Wehrmacht* soldiers allegedly involved in the executions of Jews, partisans, and POWs provoked a discussion about the involvement of those "ordinary" recruits believed (by large sections of the population) to have been free of any direct guilt. Likewise, historical works such as American political scientist Daniel Jonah Goldhagen's *Hitler's Willing Executioners* (German translation, 1996), which responded to Browning's *Ordinary Men* (1992) with a sweeping condemnation of German anti-Semitism in all sections of society, led many to reconsider their parents' or grandparents' possible complicity in Nazi atrocities.

At the same time, the reassessment of the legacy of "1968" and, in particular, the growing sense that the form of coming to terms with the past promoted by the generation of '68 may have been overzealous contributed to what Niven has aptly described as an "ongoing process of broadening understanding" with regard to its texture.[64] Indeed, the texts by Schneider and Delius examined above exemplify this development. As critical as they are of right-wing efforts to repudiate the project of *Vergangenheitsbewältigung* as "political correctness," they also concede the need to temper the imperative to judge with a degree of common sense and a willingness to differentiate. The title of Hahn's *Unscharfe Bilder* (2003), in fact, implies precisely this. An archetypal "68er," although only sixteen at the height of the student protests, the narrator learns in the course of discussions with her father provoked by her discovery of what appears to be his image in the "Crimes of the *Wehrmacht*" exhibition to view his time on the Russian front as less clear-cut and more ambiguous than she might have wished. At the close of the novel, she realizes that the photograph does not show her father, yet does not know what to make of his admission that he executed a partisan in cold blood. Can she accept his plea that he felt compelled by his superior, the Nazi Katsch? And what is she to make of the fact that he then saved Wera, also a partisan, from being raped and killed by Katsch and spent the rest of the war as a deserter? In the end, an uneasy truce exists between the generations. The narrator is unable to forgive entirely, but nor does she judge as harshly as she might once have. Thus Hahn's *Vaterroman* returns to the origins of the genre insofar as it interrogates the deeds of a father complicit in Nazi crimes. As it does this, however, it also integrates the historicist agenda of Ortheil's *Abschied von den Kriegsteilnehmern*.

Post-unification debates on historicization, "political correctness" and how to view both bystanders and perpetrators do not take place within an exclusively *German* discourse of coming-to-terms with the National Socialist past. They also draw on, and react to, the globalization of Holocaust, that is, the surge in international interest in the mass murder of Europe's Jews and in ethnic cleansing in the former Yugoslavia, in Rwanda, and elsewhere throughout the 1990s. In the process, Enlightenment principles of the primacy of reason, mutual tolerance, and humankind's capacity to learn from the past were thrown into doubt. This represents a second strand within the questioning of '68 initiated by the debates on "political correctness." What emerges is a darker impression of human nature and a tendency to contextualize German perpetration within a long, global history of genocide. German "normalization" might in fact imply the country's gradual approximation to the tendency, itself evolving in the course of the 1990s, for people in the west to both restate Enlightenment values such as the inalienability of human rights, anti-racism, and the need for rational solutions to disputes and, at the same time, concede a lack of confidence in the viability of those very same values. Critical reason, therefore, exists in tandem with the insight that to pass final judgment may be a misreading of human nature. On the one hand, this represents a welcome complication of the way Germans view the past. On the other hand, however, a form of historicization that is allied with an apologist view of human nature may lead to the relativization of guilt. Indeed, the new Germany appears to vacillate between the endeavor to balance condemnation and perspective and a tendency to judge nothing and forgive all.

This discussion about how best to present perpetrators evolved at the end of the 1990s into a debate on how to represent German wartime suffering. This development too is reflected in Hahn's *Unscharfe Bilder* in a passage in which the father speaks:

> Warum hatte Rattke nicht verstehen wollen, daß Grass mit seinem "Krebsgang" nicht die Nazimorde gegen deutsches Unglück rechnen wollte? War es denn niemals möglich, auch das ganze Bild zu sehen? Das Unheil des ersten Weltkriegs, das Terrorregime der Nazis zunächst gegen die deutschen Demokraten, gegen die Juden und schließlich gegen ein Europa, das sich nach Frieden sehnte? Und dann auch noch das, was er am eigenen Körper erfahren hatte, ohne jemals selbst etwas entscheiden zu können; er, ein Teil der deutschen Kriegsmaschine und ihr Opfer zugleich. Mußte man aus dem Mosaik immer nur die Steine einer Farbe auswählen? Gab nicht erst das ganze Bild einen Sinn?[65]

The father argues that, in order to truly understand the Nazi past and the actions of those who killed in Hitler's name, or at least tolerated such crimes, it is necessary to see the whole picture. And this may include a consideration of the extent to which they too were victims, of Nazi propaganda, coercion, or the pressure to conform, or of Anglo-American air raids, Soviet rapes and arbitrary executions, and mass expulsions. In our next chapter we examine the way the theme of German suffering was apparently rediscovered in the late 1990s and moved to the center of novels concerned with the Nazi past. Once more, we will see that a critical consciousness determined to balance a fuller picture of German suffering with a restatement of the temporal and logical precedence of German perpetration — this is exemplified by Grass's *Im Krebsgang,* the novel cited in Hahn's text — competes with a less rigorous, and perhaps even sentimentalized, presentation of what Germans undoubtedly endured in the war years and after.

Notes

[1] Hanns-Josef Ortheil, *Abschied von den Kriegsteilnehmern* (Munich: Piper, 1999 [1992]), 407. Hereafter *AK*.

[2] Martin Walser, "Deutsche Sorgen 1," in Martin Walser, *Deutsche Sorgen* (Frankfurt a.M.: Suhrkamp 1997), 430–38, 438. See my "'Deutsche Geschichte darf auch einmal gutgehen': Martin Walser, Auschwitz, and the 'German Question' from *Ehen in Philippsburg* to *Ein springender Brunnen*" in Helmut Schmitz, ed., *The Future of Vergangenheitsbewältigung* (Aldershot: Ashgate, 2001), 45–64.

[3] Günter Grass, "Viel Gefühl, wenig Bewußtsein," in Günter Grass, *Gegen die verstreichende Zeit. Reden, Aufsätze und Gespräche* (Hamburg: Luchterhand, 1991), 13–27, 24.

[4] Günter Grass, *Schreiben nach Auschwitz* (Munich: Deutscher Taschenbuch Verlag, 1990), 42.

[5] Helmut Schmitz, *Der Landvermesser auf der Suche nach der poetischen Heimat. Hanns-Josef Ortheils Romanzyklus* (Stuttgart: Verlag Hans-Dieter Heinz, 1997), 230.

[6] Examples of *Väterliteratur* include: Bernhard Vesper's *Die Reise* (1977), Ruth Rehmann's *Der Mann auf der Kanzel* (1979), Peter Härtling's *Nachgetragene Liebe* (1980), Christoph Meckel's *Suchbild* (1980), Brigitte Schwaiger's *Lange Abwesenheit* (1980) and Peter Schneider's *Vati* (1987).

[7] Helmut Schmitz, *Der Landvermesser,* 249.

[8] Helmut Schmitz, *Der Landvermesser,* 220.

[9] Thomas Anz, "Westwärts," *Die Zeit,* 2 October, 1992, 11.

[10] Helmut Schmitz, *Der Landvermesser,* 252, footnote 71.

[11] Andreas Hillgruber, *Zweierlei Untergang: Die Zerschlagung des Deutschen Reiches und das Ende des europäischen Judentums* (Berlin: Seidler, 1986).

[12] See Charles Maier, *The Unmasterable Past* (Cambridge, MA: Harvard UP, 1988).

[13] Uwe Timm, *Am Beispiel meines Bruders* (Cologne: Kiepenheuer & Witsch, 2003), 31.

[14] Christopher R. Browning, *Ordinary Men: Reserve Police Battalion 101 and the Final Solution in Poland* (New York: HarperPerennial, 1998 [1992]), xx.

[15] Volker Hage, "Gewicht der Wahrheit," *Der Spiegel,* 29 March 1999, 242–43, here 243.

[16] Helmut Schmitz, *On Their Own Terms: German Literature and the Legacy of National Socialism after Unification* (Birmingham: Birmingham UP, 2004), 167.

[17] Helmut Schmitz, "The Return of the Past: Post-Unification Representations of National Socialism: Bernhard Schlink's *Der Vorleser* and Ulla Berkéwitz's *Engel sind schwarz und weiß*," in Clare Flanagan and Stuart Taberner, eds., *1949/1989:*

Cultural Perspectives on Division and Unity in East and West, German Monitor 50 (Amsterdam: Rodopi, 2000), 259–76, 262.

[18] See Bill Niven, *Facing the Nazi Past* (London: Routledge, 2002), 143–74.

[19] Marcel Beyer, *Spione* (Frankfurt a.M.: Fischer, 2002 [2000]), 35–36.

[20] Bernhard Schlink, "Die Gegenwart der Vergangenheit," in Bernhard Schlink, *Vergangenheitsschuld und gegenwärtiges Recht* (Frankfurt a.M.: Suhrkamp, 2002), 145–56, here 147.

[21] See Ingo Cornils, "Long Memories: The German Student Movement in Recent Fiction," *German Life and Letters* 56:1 (2003): 89–101.

[22] Bernhard Schlink, "Die Gegenwart der Vergangenheit," 146–47.

[23] See Ingo Cornils, "Successful Failure? The Impact of the German Student Movement on the Federal Republic of Germany" in Stuart Taberner and Frank Finlay, eds., *Recasting German Identity* (Rochester: Camden House, 2002), 109–26, 109.

[24] *Das Argument* 213 (1996), *Deutsche Sprache und Literatur* 78 (1996) and *Muttersprache* 1 (1997).

[25] Sally Johnson and Stephanie Suhr, "From 'Political Correctness' to '*Politische Korrektheit*': Discourses of 'PC' in the German Newspaper *Die Welt*," *Discourse and Society* 14:1 (2002), 49–68, 52.

[26] Martin Walser, "Reise ins Innere. Oder wie man erfährt, was man erlebt hat," in Martin Walser, *Stimmung 94* (Eggingen: Edition Isele, 1994), 37–57, 51–52.

[27] Botho Strauß, "Anschwellender Bocksgesang," in *Der Spiegel*, 8 February 1993, 202–7, reprinted in Botho Strauß, *Der Aufstand gegen die sekundäre Welt* (Munich: Hanser, 1999), 55–79, here 68.

[28] Ulrich Schacht, "Stigma und Sorge. Über deutsche Identität nach Auschwitz," in Heimo Schwilk and Ulrich Schacht, eds., *Die selbstbewußte Nation* (Frankfurt a.M.: Ullstein, 1994), 57–68, 59.

[29] "Gegen das Vergessen," *Frankfurter Allgemeine Zeitung*, 7 April 1995.

[30] Sally Johnson and Stephanie Suhr, "From 'Political Correctness' to '*Politische Korrektheit*,'" 63.

[31] Helmut Peitsch, "'Vereinigung': Literarische Debatten über die Funktionen der Intellektuellen" in Hans Hahn, ed., *Germany in the 1990s, German Monitor* (Amsterdam: Rodopi, 1995), 39–65, 56.

[32] Peter Schneider, "Die Intellektuellen als Grenzschützer," in Peter Schneider, *Vom Ende der Gewißheit* (Berlin: Rowohlt, 1994), 97–120.

[33] Andreas Michel, "Convergences? Peter Schneider's Critique of the Left-Liberal Consensus and the Emergence of the German New Right," *Colloquia Germanica*, 31:3 (1998): 237–58, 255.

[34] Peter Schneider, "Skizze eines Enthüllers," in Peter Schneider, *Das Fest der Missverständnisse* (Reinbek bei Hamburg: Rowohlt Verlag, 2003), 26–51.

[35] Peter Schneider, "Rassismus und Erklärungssucht" in Peter Schneider, *Die Diktatur der Geschwindigkeit* (Berlin: Transit, 2000), 123–26, 123–24.

[36] Peter Schneider, "Rassismus," 126.

[37] F. C. Delius, *Die Flatterzunge* (Reinbek bei Hamburg: Rowohlt, 1999). Hereafter *FZ*.

[38] See Henryk Broder's satirical essay "Jedem sein Adolf" on the way this incident was reported in Germany (in Henryk Broder, *Jedem das Seine*, [Augsburg: Öllbaum, 1999], 93–96).

[39] Jörg Magenau, "Posaunen gegen Berlin," *Frankfurter Allgemeine Zeitung*, 28 August 1999, *Literatur*, 42. My emphasis.

[40] Botho Strauß, *Die Fehler des Kopisten* (Munich: Deutscher Taschenbuch Verlag, 1999 [1997]), 114.

[41] Martin Walser, *Ein springender Brunnen* (Frankfurt a.M.: Suhrkamp, 1998), 9. Hereafter *SB*.

[42] Zafer Şenocak, *Gefährliche Verwandtschaft* 42 (Munich: Babel, 1998), 42.

[43] Arnold Stadler, *Ein hinreissender Schrotthändler* (Cologne: Dumont, 1999), 9. Hereafter *HS*.

[44] See my "'Nichts läßt man uns, nicht einmal den Schmerz, und eines Tages wird alles vergessen sein.' The Novels of Arnold Stadler from *Ich war einmal* to *Ein hinreissender Schrotthändler*," *Neophilologus*, 87 (2003): 119–32.

[45] Martin Walser, "Über freie und unfreie Rede," in *Deutsche Sorgen*, 468–85, 473–74.

[46] Martin Walser, "Das Trotzdemschöne." "Nachwort" to Arnold Stadler, *Mein Hund, meine Sau, mein Leben* (Frankfurt a.M.: Suhrkamp, 1996), 156 and 160.

[47] Martin Walser, "Über das Verbergen der Verzweiflung," *Der Spiegel* 29/1999, 161–62, here 161.

[48] Martin Walser, "Über das Verbergen der Verzweiflung," 161.

[49] Martin Walser, *Erfahrungen beim Erfassen einer Sonntagsrede* (Frankfurt a.M.: Suhrkamp, 1998), 18. Hereafter *EES*.

[50] See my "A Manifesto for Germany's 'New Right'? — Martin Walser, the Past, Transcendence, Aesthetics, and *Ein Springender Brunnen*," *German Life and Letters* 53:1 (2000): 126–41.

[51] Jan-Werner Müller, *Another Country: German Intellectuals, Unification and National Identity* (New Haven: Yale UP, 2000), 181.

[52] Jan-Werner Müller, *Another Country*, 53.

[53] Karl Heinz Bohrer, "Zeit und Imagination: Das absolute Präsens der Literatur," in Karl Heinz Bohrer, *Das absolute Präsens* (Frankfurt a.M.: Suhrkamp, 1994), 143–83, 177.

[54] See Hans Hahn, "'Es geht nicht um Literatur': Some Observations on the 1990 'Literaturstreit' and its recent Anti-intellectual Implications," *German Life and Letters* 50:1 (1997): 65–81, 69–70.

[55] Ritchie Robertson, *The "Jewish Question" in German Literature, 1749–1939* (Oxford: Oxford UP, 2001 [1999]), 370–42.

[56] Robert C. Solomon, "Introduction: Reading Nietzsche," in Robert C. Solomon and Kathleen M. Higgens, eds., *Reading Nietzsche* (New York/Oxford: Oxford UP, 1988), 3–12, 10.

[57] Martin Walser, "Die Utopie in der Sprache." in Martin Walser, *"Ich habe so ein Wunschpotential." Gespräche mit Martin Walser* (Frankfurt a.M.: Suhrkamp, 1998), 121–29, 128.

[58] Kathrin Schödel, "Normalising Cultural Memory? The 'Walser-Bubis-Debate' and Martin Walser's Novel *Ein springender Brunnen*," in Stuart Taberner and Frank Finlay, eds., *Recasting German Identity*, 69–87, 72–73.

[59] Bill Niven, *Facing the Nazi Past*, 188.

[60] See my "The Final Taboo?: Philosemitism, the *Meinungsindustrie,* and the New Right in Martin Walser's *Ohne Einander*," *Seminar* 37:2 (2001): 154–66.

[61] See Bill Niven, "Martin Walser's *Tod eines Kritikers* and the Issue of Anti-Semitism," *German Life and Letters* 56:3 (2003): 299–311.

[62] Kathrin Schödel, "Normalising Cultural Memory?," 71.

[63] Martin Walser, *Das Prinzip Genauigkeit: Laudatio auf Victor Klemperer* (Frankfurt a.M.: Suhrkamp, 1995), 33.

[64] Bill Niven, *Facing the Nazi Past*, 5.

[65] Ulla Hahn, *Unscharfe Bilder* (Munich: Deutsche Verlagsanstalt, 2003), 27.

5: Confronting the Nazi Past II: German Perpetrators or German Victims?

> *Das hört nie auf. Nie hört das auf.*
> — Günter Grass, *Im Krebsgang*

IN ULLA HAHN'S *UNSCHARFE BILDER* (2003), Hans Musbach tells his daughter of a meal at which he was present in the early 1970s during which a colleague's son publicly attacked his father for his wartime service in North Africa. Provoked by the young man's scornful self-righteousness, another colleague then proceeded to act out the final agonies endured in the Balkans by a dying German soldier whose testicles had been cut off by partisans. "'Ich dachte, Sie wollten wissen, wie es war,'" concluded the older man with evident bitterness at the end of this description of a traumatic episode that had been by no means out of the ordinary, but over which a veil of silence appeared to have been drawn.[1]

Hahn's novel recapitulates, on occasion perhaps rather too obviously, many of the issues central to the sudden "rediscovery" of German wartime suffering towards the end of the 1990s. Had the "68ers" been too harsh in their judgment of their fathers' generation? Did the moral fervor of their condemnation conceal, perhaps, a desire to rearticulate "die eigene Unschuld" or to style themselves "als Opfer der Täter-Väter"? Had there been a lamentable unwillingness to even attempt empathy with the actions of those caught up in the Nazi period? "Hatten sie jemals Nachsicht und Mitgefühl empfunden, zu verstehen versucht?"[2] Finally, does the need to tell of German suffering necessarily relativize the history of German crimes? Might it indeed be the case, as British correspondent Jason Cowley declared in his review of Günter Grass's 2002 novella *Im Krebsgang* for *The Guardian* that "normalisation," a "complex and tortuous process," will never "be complete without an acceptance of Germany's own suffering"?[3] This would be part of what Bill Niven has termed an "ongoing process of broadening understanding" regarding the Nazi past: Germans in the present would integrate an understanding of what their predecessors had suffered into a recognition of the offenses against human rights in which these had been complicit.[4]

In what follows, we start out from a discussion of post-unification debates on the nexus between perpetration and victimhood — with brief reference to earlier periods as a means of indicating that the subject of German wartime suffering had scarcely been taboo — and trace the manner in which a post-unification shift in sensibilities regarding the Nazi past and events in the ex-Yugoslavia and beyond inspired many to re-examine the motives and actions of "ordinary" Germans during the Hitler years. As in our previous chapter, it is apparent that two forms of historicization are to be detected: a critical consciousness that seeks to paint a more textured picture of the Hitler period by *including* the story of German suffering on the one hand and, on the other, a more ambivalent reading of the past which perhaps promotes a relativization of Nazi crimes. The danger is that the undoubted anguish endured by Germans during the war years may be depicted in a manner which blurs the boundaries between perpetration and victimhood and generates a generalized narrative of human suffering. Alternatively, or perhaps even consequently, suffering itself, both German *and* Jewish, may be sentimentalized and turned into a commodity to be marketed by the globalized culture industry. These issues become particularly pressing when we look at the increased interest in seemingly "absolute" victims towards the end of the 1990s, that is, Germans who were not directly involved in crimes but who suffered the brutal consequences of a war launched by their leaders.

Discourses of Victimhood in the 1990s

Discussion of what Germans suffered as a result of the Allied bombing campaign against their cities, the indiscriminate killings and mass rapes carried out by the Red Army, and the expulsions from East Prussia, the Sudetenland, and Silesia throughout 1945, did not begin in the 1990s, of course. In the 1950s, German suffering had been a major issue in the domestic politics of the incipient FRG. At that time, too, as Aleida Assmann has suggested, many chose to focus on what they had endured at the hands of the Allies as a means of excusing their actions — or inaction — during the war, and to see their anguish as equivalent to the victimhood of former enemies, Jews and other persecuted groups.[5] In later years, as Helmut Schmitz points out, it is possible to detect "the continuous presence of East Prussia below the official literary culture of the Federal Republic in the East Prussian *Heimat*-novels of Arno Surminski, Heinz Piontek, Christine Brückner or Horst Bienek," the memoirs of expellees such as Marion Gräfin Dönhoff, onetime co-editor of *Die Zeit,* and in "an untold number of popular coffee-table books with titles like *Der Kampf um Schlesien, Heimat in Feindesland. Ostpreußische Schicksale 1945* and *Tragödie Ostpreußen 1944–1948.*"[6] For the majority of Germans in the postwar period, and into the 1960s and 1970s, all were equally entitled to remember what had been done to them, unburdened by difficult questions of prior responsibility.

In the early 1990s, the issue of German victimhood was most often associated with the neo-conservative intellectuals who had emerged in the wake of unification and who vocally attacked what they perceived as the left-wing hegemony over interpretations of the past. Many of the contributions to the volume *Die selbstbewußte Nation* (1994), edited by Ulricht Schacht and Heimo Schwilk, for instance, refer to the suffering inflicted upon Germans by the Allies during the war and, in the form of partition, after 1945. Martin Walser, furthermore, had long campaigned against what he called the "Strafprodukt Teilung,"[7] and his condemnation of these forty years of "victimization" grew more strident after unification. Similarly, there was a proliferation of accounts of the firestorms unleashed upon German cities by Allied air raids,[8] the treatment of German POWs,[9] and the rapes and shootings committed by the Soviet armies in the course of the mass expulsions of 1945,[10] penned by both neo-conservative thinkers and more mainstream historians. In similar vein, doyens of the conservative revival Rainer Zitelmann, Karlheinz Weißmann, and Heimo Schwilk ran advertisements attacking the liberal media for their supposed indifference to the *Vertriebenen* and those Germans abandoned to communism.[11]

This attention to German victimhood was most often seen as a throwback to the *Historikerstreit* of the mid-1980s, and in particular to Andreas Hillgruber's book *Zweierlei Untergang: Die Zerschlagung des Deutschen Reiches und das Ende des europäischen Judentums* (1986).[12] Memories were also evoked of Helmut Kohl's handling of President Reagan's visit to the cemetery at Bitburg in 1985 which caused such a scandal when it was revealed that graves of *SS* troops were amongst those to be honored at a ceremony intended as a gesture of reconciliation. Indeed, Kohl must have been gratified by Reagan's clumsy comments just before his departure for West Germany: "Those young men are victims of Nazism also [. . .] They were victims just as surely as the victims in the concentration camps."[13] Yet, by the mid-1990s, the theme of German suffering was beginning to mutate. To an extent, this may be attributed fairly straightforwardly to the passing of time: fifty years had elapsed since the end of the war, the cohort of people directly involved was disappearing, and it seemed appropriate to document their stories. The publication of the diary of Willy Peter Reese, a soldier on the Russian front, *Mir selber seltsam fremd: Die Unmenschlichkeit des Krieges. Russland 1941–44* (2003), collated by Stefan Schmitz, reporter at the *Stern* magazine, might be cited here as one example among many. As noted in our previous chapter, public events such as the "Crimes of the *Wehrmacht* exhibition" also provoked a resurgence of interest in the real experiences of the wartime generation. In addition, a majority of Germans, born long after the war, especially of the younger generation, no longer felt obliged endlessly to restate German culpability for the Holocaust or believed that the recognition of such responsibility meant that their grandparents' suffering should be disregarded.

More generally, the brutal conflicts which attended the break-up of the troubled, multi-ethnic Yugoslavia caused intellectuals in particular to think anew about human nature, about the prevalence of evil, and about their previous confidence in the inevitable triumph of reason. The concentration camps, mass rapes, and arbitrary killings inflicted by Serbs, Croatians, and Bosnians upon one another in the early 1990s, and, later in the decade, Slobodan Milošević's efforts to "ethnically cleanse" Kosovo of Albanians, reminded Germans of their own past, both of their nation's brutality towards others and the way their grandparents had been driven from their homes in the east by the Soviets and others. The western response, when it finally came, evoked similar memories. Thus the NATO bombing campaign against Serbia during the Kosovo conflict of early 1999 recalled the Allied onslaught on German cities. More broadly, as Bill Niven argues, events in the former Yugoslavia, as well as in Rwanda and Burundi in 1994, stimulated "concern at other genocides" and brought about a "release of pressure on Germany." This may have opened up a "space in which the rediscovery of German suffering can thrive."[14] Germans, then, began to reflect on the universal nature of human cruelty and suffering.

For writer Hans Magnus Enzensberger, events in Bosnia were put into context by a Ugandan dramatist during a discussion of the civil war in that country. It was not a sudden outbreak of reason that caused a cessation of the slaughter, the Ugandan claimed, but "Erschöpfung."[15] This insight fitted with Enzensberger's view that events in the former Yugoslavia were part of a global picture of ethnic hatred, conflict, and migration. His 1992 treatise, *Die große Wanderung,* for instance, reflected on the manner in which, following the artificial stability of the Cold War, human nature had returned to form: "Gruppenegoismus und Fremdenhaß sind anthropologische Konstanten."[16] To believe otherwise is "universalistische Rhetorik" (*GW,* 55) and "ethische Selbstüberforderung" (*GW,* 55). This is initially reminiscent of Botho Strauß's 1993 essay "Anschwellender Bocksgesang": "Rassismus und Fremdenfeindlichkeit sind 'gefallene' Kultleidenschaften, die ursprünglich einen sakralen, ordnungsstiftenden Sinn hatten."[17] Yet Enzensberger is far "konkreter" than Strauß, as Gustav Seibt notes.[18] His response hence reflects the melancholic resignation of the disenchanted left-wing critic whereas Strauß displays his joy in the irrepressibility of human nature *in spite of* the deadening effects of moral edification. Nonetheless, the convergence in their conclusions is striking.[19]

Despair at the apparent immunity of the human psyche to reason and the gospel of mutual tolerance — this was the response of large sections of the left to the explosion of ethnic hatred in the former Yugoslavia, in the former Soviet block, and in Africa. Closer to home, of course, the towns of Solingen and Moelln became synonymous with the revival of right-wing extremism and xenophobia. The 1990s, consequently, were a period of crisis for left-liberal thought. The discrediting of utopian socialism, the resurgence of the intellectual right, and attacks on "political correctness" called into question both the left's commitment to realizing the "unvollendete Projekt der Moderne"[20] — the project of critical *Aufklärung* — and its apparent supremacy over interpretations of the Nazi past. In sum, the achievement of the generation of '68 in establishing their brand of critical engagement, with the Nazi past and the unreconstructed present, as the dominant social paradigm was being interrogated; as Jan-Werner Müller argues, the "68ers" had become "intellectually most defensive after 1989."[21] This was most evident — only apparently paradoxically, Ingo Cornils proposes — following the 1998 election victory of the SPD-Green coalition.[22] The accession to power of Schröder and Fischer was thus accompanied by what Heinz Bude describes as a "demonstrative Abkehr von den Ideen von 1968."[23]

At the end of the decade, the campaign against critical enlightenment was being most energetically waged by philosopher Peter Sloterdijk.[24] Sloterdijk's *Regeln für den Menschenpark,* a rejoinder to Heidegger's *Brief über den "Humanismus,"* caused particular controversy on its publication in 1999 in the wake of its author's determinedly "politically incorrect" comments in a public lecture on genetic engineering. Certainly, the implications of Sloterdijk's uninhibited attack on left-liberal German intellectuals and their insistence, in the wake of the Holocaust, and in spite of all evidence to the contrary, on viewing "den Menschen als *animal rationale,*" are far-reaching.[25] For Sloterdijk, the bankruptcy of humanism, the failure of its "zähmenden, dressierenden, bildenden Mittel" (*RM,* 39), is evident in the desperately misguided belief, especially in the aftermath of the Holocaust, that the only way to rescue the "European soul" was "durch eine radikalisierte Bibliophilie" (*RM,* 15). The immunity of the masses to a humanist program of moral training means, he claims, that the only real purpose to political thought is to define the "Regeln für den Betrieb von Menschenparks" (*RM,* 48). This is all the more necessary, he avers in his short volume *Die Verachtung der Masse* (1999), in view of the fact that the majority of the population is a "programmbezogene Masse."[26] For Sloterdijk, and much of the right, a form of cultural pessimism was adopted that mixed melancholic fascination with the scenes of slaughter with pleasure in discrediting the left's naïve idealism.

The crisis of liberal thought in the mid-1990s opened up space for the right to re-introduce the taboo topic of German victimhood. At the same time, the repudiation of the critical enlightenment of the "68ers" may have encouraged a form of moral relativism. If human beings were simply incapable of rational behavior in extreme circumstances, and in the absence of social restraints, they might be seen as victims of their inalterable nature or their environment. Evil could be explained but it could not be judged. And perpetrators might even be deserving of empathy, to a degree at least. This was perhaps also related, paradoxically, to the globalization of the culture of commemoration and the interest in genocide, starting with the Holocaust. The "Globalisierung des Gedenkens,"[27] Michael Jeismann argues, means that Auschwitz has come to be seen in metaphysical terms as the embodiment of evil *per se*. It is "a *global* paradigm for evil which both fascinates and repels in its refusal to fall within the parameters of rational explanation," to cite Caroline Gay.[28] Yet this development may also imply a dehistoricization of events, and, Jeismann proposes, a "Universalisierung des Opfers."[29] All those touched by genocide, including perpetrators and bystanders, can claim to be victims of a universal *human* weakness.

In what follows, we look at "ordinary" Germans as perpetrators in Marcel Beyer's *Flughunde* and Bernhard Schlink's *Der Vorleser* and consider whether they are victims — of circumstances or their own dispositions. We distinguish, once again, between a critical historicization in Beyer's novel and a more ambivalent image of the relationship between broader context and guilt in Schlink's internationally acclaimed work. Subsequently, we turn to Günter Grass's *Im Krebsgang,* and to his presentation of the suffering of Germans whose complicity may have extended only to a very generalized support for Nazism.

Perpetrators as Victims? — Marcel Beyer's *Flughunde*

The protagonist of Marcel Beyer's novel *Flughunde,* one Hermann Karnau — sound technician, amateur researcher into the physiognomy of human speech, and occasional babysitter to the six young children of Joseph Goebbels — is, he claims almost at the onset of his narrative, "ein Mensch, über den es nichts zu berichten gibt."[30] Indeed, he thinks himself so insignificant that when he listens into himself, he hears "nichts, nur einen dumpfen Widerhall von Nichts, unten aus der Bauchhöhle vielleicht, das Fiebern, das Rumoren meiner Innereien" (*FH,* 17). So far removed is he from the decisive events of his time, he says, that he exists only as a weak echo of his own inconsequentiality. And yet, for all that, he seems strangely ill at ease: "das Rumoren meiner Innereien."

Karnau is not one of life's protagonists — he desires only to eavesdrop. He is the archetypal conformist, but one temperamentally predisposed to evidence the present and render it corporeal in the sound recordings he makes. At the same time, however, he recognizes that sound is synonymous with the individual's inescapable entanglement with the quotidian realities of human history: perpetration, complicity, spinelessness, and moral failure. It is, as Ulrich Schönherr points out, "an acoustic fingerprint, as it were, storing and documenting the individual biography of its subject."[31] Sound literally resonates with the impossibility of not expending energy. Every action, every movement transforms a proportion of the energy invested into sound, a reverberation of the deed itself, a "Schalldruck" (*FH*, 15), the effects of which reach beyond the physical source and impact on other bodies. The visual is insubstantial. It may suggest detachment from events and even foster the illusion that it is possible to remain forever as a mere observer. Sound, conversely, betrays the slightest movement in time with events, the merest hint of complicity.

Beyer's protagonist desires nothing more than to remain silent. The human voice, he notes, is a conduit into the soul and yet it also bears the marks of its use: "So bilden die Narben auf den Stimmbändern ein Verzeichnis einschneidender Erlebnisse, akustischer Ausbrüche, aber auch des Schweigens." To voice consent, just as to voice dissent, is to participate in history and to suffer the imprint of this entanglement. Karnau maintains, in fact: "man dürfte wohl kaum sprechen" (*FH*, 21). Certainly, it seems that he envies the "Taubstummen," the crippled soldiers, who are impervious to the military band that demands submission to its beat. He wonders how it would be to be like them, to have "keine erkennbare Vergangenheit," and to exist beyond sound, beyond history itself: "Nichts, das mir widerfährt, nichts in meiner Erinnerung könnte zu einer Geschichte beitragen" (*FH*, 18). The desire for obscurity is implied in the childhood fantasy to which he returns as an adult. He dreams of the "Flughunde," the secretive bats with their predilection for the cover of night, and of the womb-like protection they embody.

Yet the compulsion to narrate memory and contribute "zu einer Geschichte," to partake both in history itself and its telling, is as much a part of human experience as the complicity that inevitably inheres in each of these activities. Karnau's awareness of this fact explains his fascination with the as yet uncorrupted speech of the children placed in his custody. The narrator fetishizes their voices, idealizing the "Freiheit" of which they are not even conscious and the "Natürlichkeit" that will later fade, "unweigerlich" (*FH*, 74). They embody the blamelessness to which he no longer has access, the "kindliche Offenheit" that he lacks. Yet they too will learn conformity. To speak as an adult is to be guilty, to play a part in history, and to have that collusion recorded. The children are to be protected as long as possible: their lack of guile must be preserved. He declares that they must never be recorded, "wenn man sich nicht am Umkippen der Kinderstimmen in das verkrampfte Sprechen schuldig machen will" (*FH*, 63).

Karnau does, of course, record the children's voices, both in Goebbels's home and then, more frequently, in Hitler's bunker in the days before he poisons them. In fact, he undertakes a whole series of actions which he had previously abjured. It seems that the license granted individuals such as Karnau to pursue obsessions that would otherwise be taboo makes it impossible for him to resist. He is no fanatical Nazi, but he is also by no means, as Ulrich Schönherr proposes, a "critic of totalitarian culture."[32] Circumstances simply align his obsession with the biology of the human voice with the Nazis' fantasy of linguistic purity. Consequently, he is recruited for an *SS* special research group set up to experiment with "Modifikationen des artikulatorischen Apparats" (*FH*, 143) with the aim of achieving an "uncontaminated" German sound. He describes this assignment as somewhat dubious — this is most likely more a comment on its scientific viability than on its morality — but accepts the position in order to escape conscription.

A similar combination of obsession and calculation had previously motivated his decision to volunteer for the grotesquely named "Entwelschungsdienst" in Alsace. "Die Klanglandschaften zu Hause sind ausgekostet" (*FH*, 83), he notes, and this region, long the source of conflict between Germany and France and now incorporated into the Reich, promises new opportunities to pursue his fascination with the human voice. What is most important, for Karnau, is that fact that his working conditions are "hervorragend." Yet the freedom to pursue his obsession comes at a price: "als Gegenleistung dafür muß ich unvorstellbare Anblicke über mich ergehen lassen: Verhöre, furchtbar, Prügelstrafe bis auf das Blut" (*FH*, 84). His complicity is manifest, and yet, he implies, it is always reluctant. He denounces a colleague as an "Untergrund-Franzosen" in order to conceal an error that might have resulted in his being transferred just as he is about to take the opportunity of visiting the local German university with its collection of skulls, but insists that this deed was not willed: "Und es entfuhr mir, ohne erst zu überlegen" (*FH*, 86–87).

Is Karnau a victim of his circumstances, or, more accurately, of the interaction of circumstances and his innate disposition? Does *Flughunde* promote a form of moral relativism in which the perpetrator's misdeeds appear understandable, to be an inevitable function of human weakness, obsession, and the force of events? An interpretation of this kind certainly seems plausible, at least initially. And yet in order to fully understand the novel it may be necessary to read against the grain of Karnau's narrative. We may need to induce his voice to say, once again, more about him than he intends to divulge.

The unraveling of Karnau's narrative perspective begins with his fetishization of the children's voices. The children of propaganda minister Joseph Goebbels, as might be expected, speak on the radio in support of their father. Hence Karnau's concern for their innocence is, he suggests, "lächerlich naiv" (*FH*, 90). Nonetheless, he insists:

> Niemand sollte eine Gelegenheit erhalten, in ferner Zukunft, über den Tod der Kinder hinaus oder den Tod der Kinderstimmen, nachdem diese unabwendbar in Erwachsenenstimmen umgeschlagen sind, auch nur einen einzigen Laut von ihnen zu hören. (*FH*, 92–93)

This passage contains several points of slippage, moments of unintended self-revelation, which undermine Karnau's continued over-investment in the children's voices. For example, the seemingly redundant "in ferner Zukunft" invites the reader to edit the sentence in such a way as to make the expression integral to a more ominous sentiment, one that perhaps reveals something of Karnau's unconscious: "Niemand sollte eine Gelegenheit erhalten, in ferner Zukunft, über den Tod der Kinder hinaus [. . .] auch nur einen einzigen Laut von ihnen zu hören" (*FH*, 92–93). This truncated sentence seems to detach itself from its context and point forward to the manner in which, in 1992, "in ferner Zuknuft," the discovery of Karnau's recordings of the children as they chattered in their beds in Hitler's bunker will reveal that he was the one who poisoned them. In the immediate context, his desire to prevent the recording of their voices derives from his wish to protect them from the reproaches that their naïve enthusiasm for Nazism might provoke in later listeners. More generally, it may reflect his fear that the concord of sound and complicity will record his own guilt and make it permanent.

The same sentence may also, however, be edited as follows: "Niemand sollte eine Gelegenheit erhalten [. . .] über den Tod der Kinderstimmen [hinaus], nachdem diese unabwendbar in Erwachsenenstimmen umgeschlagen sind, auch nur einen einzigen Laut von ihnen zu hören." This form of editing suggests an alternative, or perhaps additional, motive for Karnau's poisoning of the children in Hitler's bunker. At the instant before the "Tod der Kinderstimmen," they must be silenced. Yet it is not the loss of innocence that comes with the passage from childhood to adulthood that Karnau truly fears. Helga, the eldest, is in fact already in her early teens and had already been described by Karnau as "aufgeweckt" and "wißbegierig" (*FH*, 56) when she was only eight years old. He fears the loss of the *illusion* of innocence that would follow if they were to fall into the hands of the Russians now only meters from the bunker. Certainly, all the adults dread the physical violation of the children. Yet they also worry that the veneer of innocence which the children afford the regime will be destroyed.

The children do not survive to become adults. The reader, of course, knows they are destined to be murdered from the very start of the text — those unaware of the novel's basis would have gleaned this information from the dust cover. As such, the alternating chapters in which the story is related from Helga's perspective are suspended, as it were. This is a voice from beyond the grave, a fictionalization of Helga's speech which — in a novel about the conservation of sound — itself takes on the uncanny quality of a recording. And, as noted at the beginning of our discussion of the novel, such recordings evoke the familiar, a fleeting sensation of presence, as much as they mark the trauma of loss. Here, this sensation perhaps refers to Karnau's fetishization of Helga's voice. The chapters apparently narrated by her, embedded within Karnau's story, are most likely created by him, a transcription and fictionalization of the recordings he furtively makes of her and her siblings, elaborated in order to give the impression of presence where there is now only absence. Time is arrested at the moment before the loss of that which is so adored. The fullness of that moment, the life that inhabits it — the girl's innocence — is frozen. Indeed, the ensuing loss must be repressed.

Fetishization attempts to exclude, or rather squeeze out, any trace of dissonance from the image it has created of the object of its adoration. Anything that points beyond the moment at which the image is frozen undermines the illusion of hypostasis, reminds of the transience of the fetishized object — the fact that all things are subject to change — and points to the return of that which has been repressed: the knowledge that the suspension of a single moment cannot delay, in reality, the loss that is imminent. As far as Helga's voice is concerned, these traces of dissonance are the moments at which the child's propensity to record details of her environment as a function of her natural curiosity shows signs of developing into a more critical awareness of what is taking place around her. In short, Helga's narrative contains moments of adult judgment that gesture forwards to her impending loss of innocence. Her insight into her father's obsessiveness, his lust for mastery and control, when he drives his new sports car ever faster in order to dislodge a spider, is one such moment. On another occasion she asks her father about "Entwelschung" (*FH*, 125); here, she is not as persistent as when she refers to biology lessons in which Ayran skulls are measured as "Unsinn" (*FH*, 163), or when she pleas silently with her father at a rally (most likely the infamous *totaler Krieg* demonstration of 1 September 1944) to hurry and finish (*FH*,

169). Similarly, she begins to note the quite routine way in which adults dissemble. She gradually becomes aware of her mother's telephone calls with a Norwegian (*FH*, 207), her father's affair with an opera singer (*FH*, 134–36), and, vitally, his lies about German military successes (*FH*, 206–7).

Helga's voice must be silenced before it is transformed "unabwendbar" into an "Erwachsenenstimme," and the state of innocence before this transformation preserved, or rather conserved. Conservation, in archaeological terms, implies the attempt to freeze time; in the lexicon of physics, it is a matter of minimizing the outflow of energy — here, both meanings apply. The child's perspective, which excludes all that is peripheral to her vision, must not be allowed to become blurred; innocence must not be dissipated within the confusions of adulthood. Above all, Helga's point of view must be fixed at the instant at which it provides most sustenance for Karnau's mythologization of his own essential innocence, his endeavor to see himself as a victim of circumstances and of the inevitable complicity of adulthood. For Helga, at the moment of her death, Karnau is the man who — paradoxically — had treated her as an adult, introduced her to new words (*FH*, 56–57), allowed the children to play with his dog, and bought them chocolate in the bunker.

As might be expected, it is a sound recording that, after the war, confronts Karnau with the truth that it was he who killed the children. Fittingly, this return of the repressed occurs following a series of reflections on the way in which Germans could not bear to hear their own voices in the immediate postwar period, preferring instead to adopt the "flächendeckende Stimmveränderung" (*FH*, 230–31) imposed upon them by the Allies in their rush to recruit collaborators in the Cold War against the Soviet Union. Yet there can be no such thing as a "vergangene Stimme," Karnau insists: complicity is inscribed on the vocal chords as "verhängnisvolle Narben" (*FH*, 231–32). These ruminations, which beg the question of his own handling of the past, subsequently trigger his descent into his own unconscious. He seeks out the "Stimmensammlung" that he carried "von Umzug zu Umzug in jede neue Wohnung, ohne sie jemals wieder abzuhören" (*FH*, 233) and begins listening to the recordings. In what follows, he — and the reader — is transposed back to the children's final days in Hitler's bunker, that is, their last days alive in April 1945.

Yet Karnau has one recording too many. He has "nicht neun, sondern insgesamt zehn Platten" (*FH*, 300). This tenth recording, the material evidence that demands to be heard, the "surplus" that disrupts the repression of the past, confronts Karnau with the moment immediately *after* the death of the children, that is, with the moment which his fetishization of their voices was intended to defer indefinitely. "Ein

Schlürfen, das sich insgesamt sechsmal wiederholt" follows Helga's question: "Ist das Herr Karnau, der jetzt zu uns kommt?" (*FH*, 300–301). Karnau was present at the murder of the six children; he brought the poison to their room and helped administer it. Even worse, he recorded the entire event. The sounds the children make as they die, recorded even as the Nazi regime is disintegrating, are no more sacred to Karnau, the fanatical collector of human voices, than the splutterings of wounded soldiers at the front that he once crawled out to record, or the agonizing screams of the prisoners upon whom he used to conduct his experiments.

Beyer's novel is surprisingly "moral." Far from presenting Karnau as propelled into complicity by his circumstances and his unalterable natural disposition, it warns of the facility with which victimhood may be invoked as a means of masking perpetration. It is probably significant in this respect that the narrative recommences in 1992 with the discovery of the underground laboratories in which Karnau had conducted experiments. The recent unification of Germany might be considered to mark a break with the past, a new era in which involvement in National Socialism might be seen more sympathetically. Yet the third person narrator, who intervenes briefly but decisively at this point, refuses to allow Karnau's pretence that he was simply a watchman to stand unchallenged. In truth, *Flughunde* is perhaps as much about the present as about the past. The "verhängnisvolle Narben" left by the Nazi period, Karnau claims, remain inscribed on the vocal chords, that is, on history itself, "so daß die alte Stimme noch verfügbar bliebe, und sich bis heute manchmal ganz unerwartet Gehör verschafft, da sie aus tieferen Schichten hervorbricht" (*FH*, 232). Here, the allusion to modern-day neo-Nazis is obvious: today's "normality," it seems, may be disrupted at any moment by voices from the past.

Perpetrators as Victims? — Bernhard Schlink's *Der Vorleser*

The unexpected success of Bernhard Schlink's *Der Vorleser* following its publication in 1995 has been described in any number of newspaper reviews, publishers' briefs, and academic articles. Schlink's story of the illicit love affair between a fifteen-year-old boy and a woman twenty years his senior, and of the subsequent revelation that she had been a concentration camp guard in an outpost of Auschwitz, seemed to grip readers throughout the world. By April 1999, Claudia Kühner testifies, five hundred thousand copies of the novel had been sold in Germany, seven hundred fifty thousand in America, two hundred thousand in Britain, and one hundred thousand in France.[33] These figures have continued to rise rapidly since. In addition, the novel has been translated into twenty-five languages, featured on the Oprah Winfrey show, and was, at one time, being considered by director Anthony Minghella as a possible movie project. It is also a set text in schools, both in Germany and abroad.[34]

Contrasting with the positive reception that the novel has enjoyed, particularly in the United States and Great Britain, is the way it has been discussed in academic articles. Objections have been raised, specifically, to the suggestion that Hanna's illiteracy pushed her into joining the SS. Ernestine Schlant, for example, insists that "illiteracy cannot serve as an explanation for cooperating in and committing criminal acts,"[35] an argument echoed in a piece by Sally Johnson and Frank Finlay which exposes the myth that literacy is related to moral judgment.[36] William Collins Donahue even contends that the novel's presentation of a perpetrator as a victim of circumstances might "undermine ethics entirely."[37] Helmut Schmitz is perhaps marginally more positive in his assessment of Michael's reflections on the psychological roots of the overly zealous attacks on the wartime generation instigated by the generation of '68. Yet its "Historisierung des Kinderanteils an der 'zweiten Schuld,'" Schmitz argues, "erzeugt quasi einen Ausschluss der Opferperspektive."[38] Omer Bartov goes still farther. Schlink, the historian claims, depicts Michael as a "victim's victim" and "postwar German society" as a "spiritually dead victim of its own crimes."[39] The novel, it is maintained, not only excludes Jewish victimhood — it even claims it for Germans.

There can be no doubt that Schlink's narrator *does* invite sympathy, but as much for Hanna as for himself. In part two of the novel, set in the early 1960s at the time of Hanna's trial for her failure to release the prisoners she was guarding on a forced march towards the end of the war from a burning church set alight by an Allied air raid, Michael's narrative implies a searing indictment of the court's procedures. "So sitzen mußte weh tun,"[40] he comments when he sees her in the dock; and yet his attack on the court is not restricted to its lack of concern for Hanna's physical well-being. The trial is depicted as a cynical game in which Hanna does not know the rules. Indeed, her *essential* innocence — her childlike ignorance of the pretences that adults deploy in pursuit of their own ends — is always emphasized: "Sie kalkulierte und taktierte nicht" (*DV*, 128). Her naïveté makes it all too easy for her female co-defendants' lawyers to trick her into accepting responsibility for their joint actions. She finally admits to having written the official report on the events that led to the deaths of almost all of their charges.

Hanna, of course, cannot read or write, and could not have composed the report. This revelation, which comes to Michael as an epiphany whilst out walking, presents him with a means of relativizing her guilt. Not only is she a victim of the court's need to find somebody guilty, she is also a victim of her circumstances. "Hanna," Michael claims, "hat sich nicht für das Verbrechen entschieden. Sie hatte sich gegen die Beförderung bei Siemens entschieden und war in die Tätigkeit als Aufseherin hineingeraten" (*DV,* 128). The shame she felt at her disability, he suggests, moved her to turn down promotion at Siemens; only then did she "fall" into her involvement in the criminal institution of the camp. Here, Michael appeals directly to the reader, in the guise of reporting questions he posed to friends: "Stell dir einfach vor, daß der Angeklagte sich schämt" (*DV,* 133).

Bill Niven is right to point out that the most familiar objection to this portrayal of Hanna as victim misses the mark. Michael does not in fact make a link, he argues, between "real" literacy and moral literacy, nor does he insinuate that if only Hanna had been able to read she would have known better, or even claim that she should be forgiven because her disability exempts her from moral judgment. Rather, he implies that *shame* is what leads Hanna to quit her job and join the *SS.* Drawing on the work of Aleida Assmann, Niven goes on to claim that the novel portrays the way the Nazi regime allowed Germans to take refuge in conformity and complicity as a means of compensating for shame, whether this arose from individual failure or national humiliation, whilst creating an ethos in which they could act out their resentments. Hanna's possible guilt, as such, may be explicable as a coincidence of interests between her desire to avoid shame, her innate brutality, and opportunities for employment within the Nazi apparatus of terror.[41]

This "explanation" of the circumstances of perpetration is familiar, of course, from our discussion of *Flughunde.* Are we to read "against the grain," therefore, as we did in that novel? Are there loose threads in Michael's account that we are *supposed* to pull at in order to unravel the multiple excuses he makes for Hanna's actions? Certainly, there are a number of indications that we are supposed to question Michael's narrative. The text is littered with hints that Michael's presentation of his ex-lover is distorted by nostalgia and by his yearning not to disrupt the image he presents of the happiness they enjoyed together. "Warum macht es mich traurig, wenn ich an damals denke? Ist es Sehnsucht nach vergangenem Glück? Ist es das Wissen, was danach kam und daß danach nur ans Licht kam, was schon da war?" (*DV,* 38), he asks, even before it is revealed that she was a concentration camp guard. Equally, only the most obtuse reader would overlook the many implausibilities in his story, not least the multiple occasions on which the adult narrator fails to mention Hanna's illiteracy during his account of his youthful affair. For example, the narrator reports that she had to ask his name despite the fact that his school books are lying on the table, surmises that a piece of paper on which he had told her he would return soon to their hotel room must have been carried away by a gust of wind, and fails to see the irony of her reaction to his father's library: "Sie ließ ihren Blick über die Bücherregale wandern [. . .] als lese sie einen Text" (*DV*, 60). On not one of these occasions, nor on many others, does the narrator — now in possession of all the facts — mention her illiteracy. To do so would be to undermine the cardinal principle of historicization: that *posterior* knowledge detracts from the authenticity of the moment. Most damning of all, perhaps, is Michael's suppression of the sentiments expressed by his law tutor, the professor responsible for their seminar and a former exile from the Nazis. The professor's words are duly reported — "Sehen Sie sich die Angeklagten an — Sie werden keinen finden, der wirklich meint, er habe damals morden dürfen" (*DV*, 87) — and yet promptly repressed: "Wessen hat uns der Professor belehrt?" (*DV*, 125).[42]

Thus, certain aspects of Michael's narrative seem to invite skepticism. Yet his more abstract ruminations appear to lay claim to a greater "truth-value." These passages, told from the perspective of the present day, reflect in general terms on the enterprise of excavating the past. In performing this function, they project an authority that is denied those sections, riddled with implausibilities, in which Michael recounts the details of his affair with Hanna. Now and again, he will retreat from the more radical implications of these philosophical interventions, and yet this, as Donahue points out, is "rather like asking the jury to ignore a sensational outburst."[43] The point has been made and the retraction is simply a matter of form. In any case, the novel consequently appears to contain two narrative voices, as it were, sometimes fused, occasionally in conflict with one another, but which on the whole co-exist within an ambivalent dialectic. This is what Donahue dubs the "postmodern valorization of ambiguity."[44] Michael's attempts to present Hanna as a victim are undermined by a series of gaps in his narrative which invite exposure of his repression of her crimes. Yet, at the same time, the very purpose of this kind of critical scrutiny is itself challenged. In his more philosophical passages, therefore, Michael develops a critique of the generation of '68, its self-appointment as judge and jury with regard to the Nazi past, "political correctness," and of the Enlightenment belief in reason and the improvability of human nature.

"Je furchtbarer die Ereignisse waren, über die wir lasen und hörten, desto gewisser wurden wir unseres aufklärerischen und anklägerischen Auftrags" (*DV*, 88). Such is the narrator's view, some twenty-five years after the events — "das sind spätere Gedanken" — of the "auftrumpfende Selbstgerechtigkeit" (*DV*, 162–63), with which he and his fellow students set about exposing their parents' guilt. The culture of ritual condemnation and contrition, Michael further suggests, is responsible for the sensation of "Betäubung" that suffuses the trial. This sense of being anaesthetized is initially a numbed reaction to the "Furchtbarkeit der Ver-nichtung der Juden" (*DV*, 99). Later, it became the individual's only permitted response to the horror of a crime "vor dem er nur in Ent-setzten, Scham und Schuld verstummen kann" (*DV*, 100). To explore the circumstances of the Holocaust, to ask questions about the motives of its perpetrators or the conditions that had made it possible — to historicize it — was taboo. To turn it into an object of discussion would be to diminish its aura or to question the essential "truth" of its dreadfulness. Yet this internalized "Betäubung," it is suggested, ultimately evolves into a reflex feeling of over-exposure to Auschwitz, to the pictures of the camps, eyewitness reports, and blockbuster movies that have become part of our everyday.

Throughout her incarceration, in an uncanny continuation of their routine during their love affair, Hanna had received recordings of Mi-chael's voice reading classics of German literature. His choice of texts, evidence of a "bildungsbürgerliches Urvertrauen" (*DV*, 176) that he has now forsaken, bear witness to his belief, at that time, that Hanna might learn to think morally. Indeed, she learns to read by listening to his re-cordings holding the book, borrowed from the prison library, in her hand. Hanna's moral rehabilitation, we are to assume, was to come via the "radikalisierte Bibliophilie" that Sloterdijk, as discussed earlier, sees as being at the core of the doomed endeavor to reshape human nature and eliminate evil.[45] Confirmation of this appears to be offered by the fact that she subsequently begins, of her own volition, to read the emerging corpus of works by Holocaust survivors, texts by Wiesel, Borowski, and Levi as well as academic studies on the Holocaust. What is significant, however, is the fact that Michael ultimately sees her suicide as an indictment of the project of moral instruction — critical enlightenment — and of his own, earlier belief in the improvability of human nature. In the wake of the Holocaust, despair drives humanism towards the radicalization of its core impulse of critique and self-critique. For Michael, learning to read and write is what destroyed Hanna. This is true not only figuratively, but also literally. The spontaneity, "animal" instinctiveness and lack of restraint that so excited Michael as a boy, the absolute contrast she offered to the guilt-ridden culture in which he grew up, disappears as soon as she "learns" to think morally. The "essential" Hanna, once so full of life and verve, is, in his perception, replaced by a dowdy old woman, bereft of sexual magnetism, and turned in on herself in pious — and suitably sanc-timonious — self-analysis.

While it is unfair to expect authors to be consistent in their responses to questions posed by readers, Schlink's public comments are nonetheless revealing. In an interview in *The New York Times*, Schlink thus appeared to encourage a critical reading of Michael: "He never confronts himself or his guilt, his entanglement."[46] Yet elsewhere he has expressed concern at the continued moralizing of the generation of '68, much as Michael does. "Denken Sie nur an den moralisierenden Ton, den es bis heute gibt," he bids his interlocutor in an interview in the year 2000 with reference to current attitudes towards the Nazi past and the plight of ethnic Albanians in Kosovo: "Mir ist er unheimlich, dieser selbstgerechte moralische Eifer."[47] Here, he most likely has in mind Joschka Fischer's call for military intervention to prevent a "second Auschwitz." In truth, Schlink's inconsistencies may reflect the ambiguities of *Der Vorleser* as a whole in its questioning of the project of critical enlightenment associated with the generation of '68 and its related tendency towards the relativization of German perpetration within an all-encompassing and undifferentiated understanding of "victimhood."

"Ordinary" Germans as Victims?

In a series of lectures in Zurich in 1997, W. G. Sebald pointed to the apparent "failure" of German authors to address in their fiction the obliteration of German cities by Allied airforces during the latter part of the war. In the debate that followed, many observers referred to the manner in which discussion of German wartime suffering since the 1960s, that is, following the Auschwitz trials and the era of the student movement, had been considered taboo lest it distract from the genocidal campaign against Jews, sentimentalize German pain, or fuel an ugly nationalism. Reinhard Baumgart, for example, spoke of a "Wunde [. . .] die gar keine sein sollte, die nicht zu schmerzen wagte, die sich selbst ihrer Narben schämt."[48] Sebald, in fact, traces the beginnings of the taboo back to what he calls the "Larmoyanz" of the generation of German authors associated with the *Gruppe 47* in the immediate postwar period.[49] Writers such as Alfred Andersch and Hans-Werner Richter were, he claims, too concerned with their experiences at the front to think about the effects of Allied bombing. Heinrich Böll was to be considered an exception insofar as he touched upon the subject in his *Der Engel schwieg* — although his description of the bombed-out city of Cologne was considered too horrific in 1949–50, and was only published in 1992. On the whole, Sebald argued, the literary efforts of this generation, merely replicated the "individuelle und kollektive Amnesie" (*LK*, 18) of the immediate postwar period.

In his "Nachschrift" to the lectures, written in response to criticisms leveled by various commentators in the media, Sebald acknowledged the existence of a number of novels portraying the bombing of German cities, not least Gert Ledig's long-forgotten 1955 *Die Vergeltung* (which was then re-released in 1999). He also conceded that a proportion of the many letters he had received after the publication of the lectures were "von dem Bedürfnis motiviert, die Deutschen endlich einmal als Opfer dargestellt zu sehen" (*LK,* 92). Certainly, some Germans no doubt took a degree of satisfaction in Sebald's description, for example, of the bombing of Hamburg in the summer of 1943, during which incendiary devices were used to create a firestorm in a city already highly combustible following a period of hot, dry weather: "Drei Stunden lang brannte es so. Auf seinem Höhepunkt hob der Sturm Giebel und Hausdächer ab, wirbelte Balken und ganze Plakatwände durch die Luft, drehte Bäume aus ihrem Grund und trieb Menschen als lebendige Fackeln vor sich her" (*LK,* 36). Sebald insisted, however, that the vast majority of Germans "weiß heute, so hofft man zumindest, daß wir die Vernichtung der Städte, in denen wir einst lebten, geradezu provozierten" (*LK,* 119). The effectiveness of the project of coming-to-terms with the past meant that it might now be possible for the story of German suffering to be told without fear that this would relativize German crimes. Even so, author Dieter Forte argued that Sebald had displayed an overly cautious "Distanz zum wirklichen Schrecken" marked by a "gutmütigen und freundlichen professoralen Bemühen."[50] Without doubt, Forte's own portrayal of the bombing raids in his *Das Muster* (1992), *Der Junge mit den blutigen Schuhen* (1995) and *In der Erinnerung* (1998) are extremely hard-hitting. His aim, as set out in an essay written around the time of the Kosovo conflict, was to confront those "die keinen Krieg kennen" with the reality of war. For Forte, it was time to break the "Schweigen der Opfer: Erdulden und ertragen," for the sake of preventing further "adventurism."[51]

Hans-Ulrich Treichel may have had in mind the discussions sparked by Sebald's lectures during an interview on his short prose work *Der Verlorene,* which was published in 1998. For Treichel, it was an adequate portrayal of the *Vertreibung* from East Prussia, the Sudetenland, and Silesia that was absent from the literary canon: "Vielleicht weil man über die Verbrechen der Russen nicht sprechen wollte, um die deutschen Verbrechen nicht zu relativieren."[52] Again, the implication was that it might now be time to focus on the much neglected theme of German suffering, and specifically upon that which Volker Hage has referred to as the "bislang weitgehend tabuierten Erzählterrains — der Traumata der Flucht als Folge des verlorenen Krieges."[53] In the published version of his *Frankfurter Poetikvorlesungen* (2000), accordingly, Treichel discussed the way the fall of the Berlin Wall came to be associated in his mind with his mother's revelation in 1991, a few weeks before her death, that she and his father had lost a son during their flight from the Red Army: "Ich habe den Verlust Westberlins, wenn ich die Wiedervereinigung einmal so nennen darf, in gewisser Weise verschoben verarbeitet, in dem sich mir plötzlich der Verlust meines älteren Bruders im Jahr 1945 aufdrängte."[54] The "loss" of West Berlin is regretted — the city, Rhys Williams notes, offered many of Treichel's generation (he was born in 1952) "access to the student movement and the alternative scene"[55] — as a symbol of the imminent "normalization" of Germany. The luxury of living "apart from history" would finally disappear and Treichel's generation would now have to bear the full burden of the German past.[56] And that would mean confronting the "taboo" — indeed politically explosive — story of German suffering as much as the reality of German perpetration.

Treichel's *Der Verlorene* confronts the moral blindspot of the generation of '68. It explores the way the students' eagerness to dissociate themselves from National Socialism rendered them indifferent, and even hostile, to the suffering their parents had endured in the course of the Allied bombing campaign and to the mass rapes and random killings that accompanied the expulsions of 1945. Their flight from a West German present which they saw as hopelessly complicit with the past into the alternative scene — or into the historical limbo of West Berlin — was simultaneously a flight from the burdens of national identity. This rejection of Germanness meant that their criticisms of their parent's generation required little in the way of *self*-analysis: any understanding of the complexity of events soon gave way to an assertion of absolute moral certainty. And yet, unlike Schlink's *Der Vorleser*, Treichel's narrative does *not* suggest that a more critical attitude towards the generation of '68 necessarily has as its corollary a more "sympathetic" view of the historical entanglement of "ordinary" Germans, that is, one which presents German suffering whilst eliding German perpetration. The narrator's railings against his parents' obsession with the "prodigal" son "lost" on one of the many treks westwards reveals a great deal about the adolescent rebellion of a generation spoilt by affluence and radicalized by a history it could barely grasp. He is a "zu dick geratener pubertierender Knabe,"[57] bloated by the prosperity of the *Wirtschaftswunder* that he so detests, and his moral outrage may, in truth, be motivated by selfishness: "Ich wollte nicht mit Arnold teilen" (*V,* 61). At the same time, the parents' efforts to frame themselves as "pure" victims are undermined by the use of irony and the novel's refusal to sentimentalize their loss.[58] Their construction of a pristine "Kühlhaus" hence becomes an extended metaphor for the deep freezing of their past, including both guilt and trauma (*V,* 76). Elsewhere, they fail to grasp the grotesque implications of a hearse driver's avid endorsement of the "Leistungsfähigkeit der Öfen" (*V,* 106) installed in a new crematorium in which, he claims, the bones are burnt so clean that it is possible to chew them.

Günter Grass's *Im Krebsgang,*[59] published in February 2002 amid great fanfare, initially appears to promote a more self-indulgent, less even-handed perspective: the refusal of the generation of '68 to contemplate German suffering is characterized as a "Versäumnis" which is "bodenlos."[60] The novella, moreover, is subtitled "in memoriam," a gesture that pays tribute to German victims. Accordingly, it seemed to many of the novella's reviewers that Grass had moved away from his previous focus on German perpetration and was now pandering to the culture of sentimentalized German victimhood that emerged during the 1990s. Joachim Günter, for example, suggested that *Im Krebsgang* confirmed Germany's "Eintritt in die internationale Opferkultur."[61] And this was not all. "Hätte Martin Walser dieses Buch fabriziert," Christian Florin declared, "[wäre es] von den Torpedos der politischen Korrekheit versenkt worden."[62]

Grass's novella was certainly popular: by March 2002, more than 300,000 copies had been sold.[63] Moreover, the specific theme of this most recent work by Germany's Nobel Prize-winning author — the torpedoing in the Baltic of the *Wilhelm Gustloff,* a former *Kraft durch Freude* liner packed with 7,000 refugees and a number of military personnel, by a Soviet submarine in January 1945 — became the focus of massive media interest. It was hailed, inaccurately, as the first attempt to deal with German suffering since Sebald's *Luftkrieg und Literatur* — Walter Kempowski's *Das Echolot: Fuga furiosa,* a multi-volume work of letters and diary entries written by German troops and civilians fleeing the Russians in early 1945 or bombed in Dresden was overlooked (the first volume appeared in 1993, the second in 1999).[64] Notwithstanding this imprecision, *Stern* magazine published a supplement on the sinking,[65] and *Der Spiegel* of 4 February 2002 advertised its lead story with the arresting caption: "die deutsche Titanic." The TV historian Guido Knopp then rushed into print a short manuscript, *Der Untergang der "Gustloff,"* which related, "wie es wirklich war."[66] Finally, *Im Krebsgang* inspired a four-part special edition of *Der Spiegel* magazine on "Deutsche als Opfer."[67] The following year, the same publication produced its *Als Feuer vom Himmel fiel,* edited by Stephan Burgdorrf and Christian Habbe. This was a far less well documented version of historian Jörg Friedrich's 2002 account of the Allied bombing raids, *Der Brand. Deutschland im Bombenkrieg,*[68] which, five years after Sebald's lectures, presented a vivid and graphic impression of the suffering of German civilians.

"Eigentlich, sagt er, wäre es Aufgabe seiner Generation gewesen, dem Elend der ostpreußischen Flüchtlinge Ausdruck zu geben" (*IK,* 87). This confession is delivered by the narrator Paul Pokriefke on behalf of his fictional *Arbeitgeber,* the latest in a long line of Grassian alter egos. It is a *mea culpa* that motivates the novella's account of German suffering at the end of the war, specifically the flight from the east and the sinking of the *Gustloff.* The *Arbeitgeber,* accordingly, "directs" Paul — son of Tulla Pokriefke, who had been introduced in *Katz und Maus* (1961), incorporated into *Hundejahre* (1963), and falsely reported in *Die Rättin* (1986) as lost on the *Gustloff*— to make good his oversight and to tell the story of the ship's destruction and of his own birth on its decks as it went under.[69] In parallel, Paul tells the story of his own "failure," as a journalist, a husband, and a father. He begins with the murder of Wilhelm Gustloff, Nazi activist in Switzerland, on 4 February 1936 by David Frankfurter, a Jew. He goes on to relate the story of his work as a journalist with the *Springer Verlag* and the *taz*, then switches to the naming of the *Kraft durch Freude* liner after Gustloff in 1936, and speaks of Tulla, her fate in January 1945, of life in the GDR, and of the campaign to resurrect a monument near Schwerin dedicated to Gustloff by the Nazis and smashed to pieces by GDR authorities. Along the way, he recounts the tale of Alexander Marinesko, captain of S 13, the submarine that sank the *Gustloff*, and an incorrigible drunk who fell out of favor with Stalin after the war. Last but not least, he narrates the sequence of events that led his son Konrad to shoot dead Wolfgang, a young man who had passed himself off as a Jew in their often heated, sometimes jocular exchanges in the chat room linked to the webpage www.blutzeuge.de set up by Konrad in honor of the German "martyr" Gustloff. Throughout the text, Paul moves back and forth between these narrative strands, "etwa nach der Art der Krebse" (*IK*, 8).

Paul's narrative offers a modicum of redress for the fact that German suffering had been "jahrzehntelang tabu" (*IK*, 31–32). As such, it participates in what Bill Niven, as already cited, has described as the "process of broadening understanding" within the discourse of *Vergangenheitsbewältigung* in post-1990 Germany. It responds to Sebald's *Luftkrieg und Literatur* lectures — the *Arbeitgeber*, speaking for Grass, concedes that his generation of writers neglected German suffering, but argues "die eigene Schuld [war] übermächtig und bekennende Reue in all den Jahren vordringlich" (*IK*, 99) — gives reasons for the failure of the generation of '68 to address the issue, and enlists a member of this generation to compensate for the author's "negligence." Yet the question remains: does the depiction of German suffering, however timely, relativize German perpetration? Does *Im Krebsgang* encourage the kind of discursive ambiguity that we saw in *Der Vorleser*, or does it — like *Flughunde* and *Der Verlorene* — contribute to a more differentiated view of perpetration and victimhood without blurring the boundaries between the two?

The answer to this question lies in the *Arbeitgeber*'s suggestion, again transmitted via Paul, that the left's true folly was not so much that it ignored "so viel Leid" but that it abandoned "das gemiedene Thema den Rechtsgestrickten" (*IK*, 99). Far from colluding in an obfuscation of victimhood, or promoting a form of ambiguity that might bolster the right's efforts to "normalize" German history, Grass's novella instead appropriates the theme of German suffering for the left. The anguish endured by

Germans in the final stages of the war is integrated into the hierarchy of cause and effect — the insistence that German perpetration is always logically prior to German victimhood — promoted by the left since the 1960s. The critical excavation of the past is extended so as to encompass the experiences of individual Germans. In this way, the blind spot within the discourse of *Vergangenheitsbewältigung,* the tendency towards abstraction, generalization, and depersonalization attacked by Walser in his 1998 *Friedenspreisrede,* is overcome.

The story of the sinking of the *Gustloff* hence comprises three intertwined strands, each of which contextualises the other two. First, Paul's acceptance of his metaphorical "simultaneity" with German suffering, implied by the coincidence of the demise of the *Gustloff* with his birth, makes it possible for him — belatedly — to display empathy with individual Germans. This sets the background against which the second strand, his report on the sinking of the ship and the deaths of so many of its passengers, is to be read. Third, he portrays the excesses of the Red Army during its rapid advance westward, including the massacre at Nemmersdorf, the East Prussian village taken by the Russians in October 1944 and recaptured by elements of the German 4th Army. Throughout his description of German suffering, however, Paul is careful to make sure that Soviet brutality appears neither unprovoked, nor always fully proven. This more differentiated picture allows him to balance compassion for individuals with a restatement of German perpetration.

It is only once Paul is able to concede that his birth coincided with the demise of the *Gustloff,* and that his first cry merged with the "Schrei der Zigtausend" (*IK,* 177) who died that very instant, that he can display empathy for the pain suffered by his mother and millions of other Germans expelled from their homelands by the Soviets. Previously, he had preferred to think of himself as a "Findelkind" (*IK,* 142); in common with many of his generation, he sought to deny his biographical link to a past defined by complicity even if this meant eliding what his predecessors had endured. In the present, however, he understands that the story of German suffering must be told, if for no other reason than to compensate, albeit too late, for his failure as a father, that is, for his failure to provide a sense of historical and biographical continuity for his son. Above all, the recounting of the story of the sinking of the *Gustloff* must not be left to his mother Tulla. Unlike Tulla, Paul is determined that his narrative, while paying due respect to the human tragedy that inescapably followed from ship's destruction, will also situate it within the overall context of a war that was started, supported, and prosecuted by "ordinary" Germans.

Paul is initially resolved not to stumble into the error of over-identification that so often accompanies attempts at historicization. He will not, he says, endeavor

> mir Schreckliches vorzustellen und das Grauenvolle in ausgepinselte Bilder zu zwingen, sosehr mich jetzt mein Arbeitgeber drängt, Einzelschicksale zu reihen, mit episch ausladender Gelassenheit und angestrengtem Einfühlungsvermögen den großen Bogen zu schlagen und so, mit Horrorwörtern, dem Ausmaß der Katastrophe gerecht zu werden. (*IK*, 136)

There will be, he says, no excessive focus on individuals, epic narration, or overwrought compassion. He will not essay an illusory and yet melodramtic realism that evokes sentimentality rather than dispassionate reflection. And yet, ultimately, individual fates are so compelling that he cannot help but relate them. His self-admonition: "aber ich darf keine weiteren Storys erzählen" (*IK*, 139), sounds ever more unconvincing. He tells of lifeboats so packed that they capsize, of wounded soldiers left to die, women trapped in the "Promenadendeck" (*IK*, 138), and Dr. Richter who delivered Tulla's baby on the rescue boat *Löwe*. Finally, he goes on to speak of the "allseits beliebten Bordfriseur, der seit Jahren die immer seltener werdenden silbernen Fünfmarkstücke gesammelt hatte" (*IK*, 139). Tragically, if predictably, the hairdresser is drowned under the weight of his prized collection.

This willingness to display empathy with the agony borne by individual Germans is a new departure for Paul. Yet this "local" compassion is relativized by his account of the Soviet advance into Germany. The brutality of the Red Army is swiftly conceded, in particular the massacre at Nemmersdorf, and yet the narrator is quick to highlight the manner in which Nazi propaganda exploited rumors of the way German women had been raped by Russian soldiers and nailed naked to a barn door (*IK*, 101). Similarly gruesome accounts, he claims, are to be found at www.blutzeuge.de. In this way, a parallel is intimated between Nazi propaganda — the last word in manipulation — and present-day allusions to Soviet brutality. Political instrumentalization is at work in both cases, Paul insinuates, with the aim of presenting ordinary Germans as absolute victims (*IK*, 101). This suggestion is then reinforced by his comment that images of German suffering at the hands of the Soviets, such compelling "bebilderten Satzfolgen," might well appear to many of the website's anonymous visitors "wie auf gegenwärtiges Geschehen gemünzt, wenngleich das ohnmächtig zerfallende Rußland oder die Greuel auf dem Balkan und im afrikanischen Ruanda nicht benannt wird" (*IK*, 102). The fate of Germans fleeing the Soviets in 1944–45, Paul intimates, may be all too swiftly conflated with the suffering of the victims of displacement and genocide in Chechnya, the Balkans or Rwanda, with no regard for prior German guilt.

Paul presents additional, equally damaging proof of his son's intention to mislead via his website. The narrator asks why Konrad's site makes no mention of the missing "Rettungsboote" or the "eingeschifften tausend U-Bootsmatrosen und dreihundertsiebzig Marinehelferinnen" (*IK,* 103). The first of these omissions reveals Konrad's reluctance to admit that German incompetence played a part in the scale of the tragedy; the second relates to the controversy about whether the *Gustloff* was a legitimate military target or whether its sinking was a war crime. Only in the course of his trial does Konrad declare that he has finally come to understand "daß der Kommandant von S 13 das für ihn namenlose Schiff zu Recht als militärisches Objekt gewertet habe" and that the "real" criminal was Admiral Dönitz (*IK,* 192), who allowed the ship to function both as military transport and refugee vessel. For Paul, on the other hand, there had never been any doubt that the ship was a valid target. His son's efforts to suggest otherwise, he maintains, reveals "sein Bedürfnis nach einer sauberen Opferbilanz" (*IK,* 104). Above all, Paul is determined that neither his son nor his mother should be allowed to separate out the undeniable horror of what Germans went through in the closing months of the war — for Tulla, "alles andere zählte nicht" (*IK,* 157) — from the wider historical context.

Far from promoting a transformation from the "Täter- zur Opfergesellschaft," as Harald Welzer puts it,[70] the depiction of German suffering in Grass's novel is remarkably conventional. It reasserts the left-liberal position with minor amendments designed to satisfy contemporary sensibilities. Similar to Grass's works *örtlich betäubt* (1969) and *Aus dem Tagebuch einer Schnecke* (1972), two texts that also deal with the enduring impact of the Nazi past in the present,[71] *Im Krebsgang* marks the author's resolve to intervene in an ongoing debate in an immediate, even didactic manner. The same is true, in fact, of his 1992 novel *Unkenrufe,* in which Reschke's desire to compensate for the German suffering endured as part of what he refers to as the "Jahrhundert der Vertreibungen" is presented as understandable but potentially dangerous.[72] His plans to repatriate elderly Germans, once deceased, to cemeteries in the (now) Polish lands they once inhabited may lead, it is feared, to a second occupation of Germany's neighbor. This would be a form of nationalism fuelled by superior economic strength. In *Im Krebsgang,* on the other hand, Grass is worried less by a misguided post-unification patriotism or even the specter of neo-Nazism than by what he sees as the sentimentalization of victimhood within a particular inflection of the contemporary discourse of normalization. Towards the end of the novella, Konrad smashes his model of the *Gustloff* (*IK,* 215), and discovers that his hands bleed,

Christ-like. As the narrator concludes: "Das hört nie auf. Nie hört das auf" (*IK*, 216).

In mid-2004, at the time the present book was being completed, it was certainly true that the debates on the German past, and the controversies on how to depict it, were as lively and controversial as ever before. Volker Hage's anthology of literary depictions of the bombing of Hamburg, *Hamburg 1943: Literarische Zeugnisse des Feuersturms* (2003), for example, was a belated contribution to the debate on Sebald's *Luftkrieg und Literatur,* demonstrating that the topic had never been taboo.[73] What is more, it seemed that the wave of literary portrayals of German wartime suffering begun in the late 1990s had not even begun to crest. Nor was this a phenomenon restricted to authors of a certain age or provenance. Tanja Dückers, a young western author known for her short stories and her "Berlin novel" *Spielzone* (1999), published her *Gustloff* narrative *Himmelskörper* in 2003, the same year Reinhard Jirgl, an older writer from the east renowned for his complex, modernist texts, brought out *Die Unvollendeten,* the chronicle of three women expellees. Jörg Bernig, a less well-known figure, had also approached the subject of mass expulsions, this time from the Sudentenland, in *Niemandszeit* (2002), as had the more established Peter Härtling in his 1998 *Große, kleine Schwester.*

Uwe Timm's *Am Beispiel meines Bruders* (2003) similarly reveals the extent to which the representation of German wartime suffering remained as topical as it was controversial. Timm, as narrator of the story of his older brother's wartime record as a member of the *Waffen-SS* (Timm was born in 1940, his brother was killed in 1943), concedes the need for a proper historicization but draws attention to the danger of a return to the 1950s when German suffering was obsessively discussed in the family "ohne daß sich die Frage nach der Schuld stellte, nach Chronologie und Kausalität der Grausamkeit."[74] It is undoubtedly the case, he concedes, that only from today's perspective is it possible fully to grasp the "Kausalketten, die alles einordnen und faßlich machen" (*ABM*, 38), and yet he refuses to allow his brother's references to the fire-bombing of Hamburg to go unchallenged: "Es wird von ihm niedergeschrieben, ohne auch nur einen Augenblick eine Verbindung zwischen den zerstörten Häusern in der Ukraine und der zerbombten Häusern in Hamburg zu sehen" (*ABM,* 93). Nor will he accept that his brother was unaware of the atrocities against partisans, Russian POWs, and civilians: "so muß er doch mit den Opfern der Zivilbevölkerung konfrontiert worden sein, den Hungernden, Obdachlosen, den durch Kampfhandlungen Vertriebenen, Erfrorenen, Getöteten." In fact, the narrator's insistence upon this indifference most likely represents the most accurate historicization of his brother's war: "Von ihnen ist nicht die Rede, vermutlich erschien ihm dieses Leid, diese Zerstörungen und Todesopfer normal, also *human*" (*ABM*, 27–28).

Timm, in a manner reminiscent of the *Vaterroman,* describes the authoritarian structures of the German family — the passivity of the mother, the illiberalism of the father, and the conformity of the children — in a narrative which incorporates a degree of sympathy for the older brother but which reaffirms the underlying critique instigated by the generation of '68. Historicization, for Grass and Timm, at least, hence implies an emphasis on the depressing banality of Nazi crimes. Yet unlike Schlink, arguably, they refuse to resign themselves to the "inevitability" of evil, or to see it, with Sloterdijk or Strauß, as part of human nature which it is pointless to judge. If historicizing the past reveals that authoritarianism, prejudice, and indifference were the "norm," they suggest, then it is surely worth fighting for a different kind of "normality."

And Jewish Victims . . . ?

In her investigation of *Ein springender Brunnen* and *Der Vorleser,* Kathrin Schödel acknowledges that "eine differenzierte Sicht der Tätergeneration" is "wünschenswert." At the same time, however, there may be a risk "dass hier eine deutsche Sichtweise etabliert wird, die sich als die scheinbar freiere, authentischere und einfühlsamere der Erinnerung der Opfer überlegen gibt." This, Schödel suggests, may correspond to the "momentanen 'Zeitgeist' in Deutschland."[75] A very contemporary concern with the fates of individuals thus blurs distinctions between the perpetrator nation and those it persecuted and may even tend to present German suffering as more authentic. This was certainly the perception of many observers following the publication of Jörg Friedrich's *Brandstätten* (2003), a collection of extremely graphic photographs of the aftermath of Allied bombing raids on German cities. Moreover, the emphasis on German suffering may function as a form of displaced identification which allows Germans, in the present as much as in the past, to associate themselves with Jewish victimhood and escape the shame of perpetration. As the protagonist of Judith Kuckart's *Die schöne Frau* (1994), who is forced to confront the fact that her mother had been a "product" of the *Lebensborn* program, puts it: "Bin ich denn die einzige, die lieber ein Kind aus Theresienstadt wäre, mit schattenhaften, aber jüdischen Familienverhältnissen? Denn Opfer sind bessere Menschen als Täter?"[76]

In our next chapter, we look at novels, diaries, and memoirs by both Jewish and non-Jewish authors. We investigate the points raised above and consider whether it possible for non-Jewish Germans to write on behalf of their Jewish compatriots, to tell the story of their persecution, without appearing to appropriate their suffering as displaced identification or as a means of escaping the stigma of German crimes. More specifically, can the German-Jewish symbiosis be resurrected? Or is this too a chimera, another ambiguity in the present-day discourse of "normalization"?

Notes

[1] Ulla Hahn, *Unscharfe Bilder* (Munich: Deutsche Verlagsanstalt, 2003), 65.

[2] Ulla Hahn, *Unscharfe Bilder,* 255.

[3] Jason Cowley, "Forgotten Victims," *Guardian,* 27 March 2002, 27.

[4] Bill Niven, *Facing the Nazi Past* (London: Routledge, 2002), 5.

[5] Aleida Assmann and Ute Frevert, *Geschichtsvergessenheit, Geschichtsversessenheit: Vom Umgang mit deutschen Vergangenheiten nach 1945* (Stuttgart: Deutsche Verlags-Anstalt, 1999), 140–41.

[6] Helmut Schmitz, *On Their Own Terms: German Literature and the Legacy of National Socialism after Unification* (Birmingham: Birmingham UP, 2004), 266.

[7] Martin Walser, "Über Deutschland reden: Ein Bericht," in Martin Walser, *Deutsche Sorgen* (Frankfurt a.M.: Suhrkamp, 1997), 406–27.

[8] See Karlheinz Weißmann, *Rückruf in die Geschichte* (Berlin: Ullstein, 1993).

[9] See Albrecht Lehmann, "Die Kriegsgefangenen," *aus politik und zeitgeschichte,* 10 February 1995, 13–14.

[10] See Alfred Theisen, "Die Vertreibung der Deutschen — ein unbewältigtes Kapitel europäischer Geschichte," *aus politik und zeitgeschichte,* 10 February 1995, 20–33.

[11] "Gegen das Vergessen," *Frankfurter Allgemeine Zeitung,* 7 April 1995. See Zitelmann's comments on 8 May 1945 in *Wohin treibt unsere Republik?* (Frankfurt a.M.: Ullstein, 1995), 87. Stefan Berger's *The Search for Normality* (Oxford: Berghahn, 1997) offers a useful guide to the New Right.

[12] Andreas Hillgruber, *Zweierlei Untergang: Die Zerschlagung des Deutschen Reiches und das Ende des europäischen Judentums* (Berlin: Seidler, 1986).

[13] Quoted in Mary Fulbrook, *German National Identity after the Holocaust* (Cambridge: Polity Press, 1999), 94.

[14] Bill Niven, "The Globalisation of Memory and the Rediscovery of German Suffering," in Stuart Taberner, ed., *German Literature in the Age of Globalisation* (Birmingham: Birmingham UP, 2004), 229–46.

[15] Hans Magnus Enzensberger, "Bosnien, Uganda," in Hans Magnus Enzensberger, *Zickzack* (Frankfurt a.M.: Suhrkamp, 1999 [1997]), 89–94, here 94.

[16] Hans Magnus Enzensberger, *Die große Wanderung* (Frankfurt a.M.: Suhrkamp, 1994 [1992]), 13. Hereafter *GW.*

[17] Botho Strauß, "Anschwellender Bocksgesang," in *Der Spiegel,* 8 February 1993, 202–7; reprinted in Botho Strauß, *Der Aufstand gegen die sekundäre Welt* (Munich: Hanser, 1999), 55–79, here 75.

[18] "Die Ohnmacht der Schriftsteller," *Frankfurter Allgemeine Zeitung,* 6 October 1993; reprinted in Franz Josef Görtz, Volker Hage, and Uwe Wittstock, eds., *Deutsche Literatur 1993* (Stuttgart: Reclam, 1994), 305–8, here 307.

[19] See Jay Julian Rosellini for a comparison of Enzensberger's thought in the 1990s with that of Strauß and Martin Walser. *Literary Skinheads? Writing from the Right in Reunified Germany* (West Lafayette: Purdue UP, 2000), 80–95.

[20] Thus the title of Jürgen Habermas's 1980 essay, "Die Moderne — Ein unvollendetes Projekt," in Jürgen Habermas, *Kleine politische Schriften I–IV* (Leipzig: Reclam, 1991), 444–64.

[21] Jan-Werner Müller, *Another Country: German Intellectuals, Unification and National Identity* (New Haven: Yale UP, 2000), 121.

[22] See Ingo Cornils, "Successful Failure? The Impact of the German Student Movement on the Federal Republic of Germany," in Stuart Taberner and Frank Finlay, eds., *Recasting German Identity* (Rochester: Camden House, 2002), 109–26.

[23] Heinz Bude, *Generation Berlin* (Berlin: Merve Verlag, 2001), 24.

[24] Sloterdijk's dismantling of the Enlightenment began with his 1983 *Die Kritik der zynischen Vernunft.*

[25] Peter Sloterdijk, *Regeln für den Menschenpark* (Frankfurt a.M.: Suhrkamp, 1999), 24. Hereafter *RM.* Heidegger's 1946 essay attacks Western humanism and the tradition of "metaphysical subjectivism" as the cause of the disasters of the twentieth century.

[26] Peter Sloterdijk, *Die Verachtung der Masse* (Frankfurt a.M.: Suhrkamp, 1999), 17.

[27] Michael Jeismann, *Auf Wiedersehen Gestern* (Stuttgart: Deutsche Verlags-Anstalt: 2001), 190.

[28] Caroline Gay, "Remembering for the Future, Engaging with the Present: National Memory Management and the Dialectic of Normality in the Berlin Republic," in William Niven and James Jordan, eds., *Politics and Culture in Twentieth-Century Germany* (Rochester: Camden House, 2003), 201–26, here 202.

[29] Michael Jeismann, *Auf Wiedersehen Gestern,* 186.

[30] Marcel Beyer, *Flughunde* (Frankfurt a.M.: Suhrkamp, 1996 [1995]), 16. Hereafter *FH.*

[31] Ulrich Schönherr, "Topophony of Fascism: On Marcel Beyer's *The Karnau Tapes,*" *Germanic Review* 73:4 (1998): 329–48, here 334.

[32] Ulrich Schönherr, "Topophony of Fascism," 331.

[33] Claudia Kühner, "Ein Buch geht um die Welt," *Rheinischer Merkur,* 16 April 1999, 18.

[34] My own critical edition appeared in July 2002 (London: Duckworth).

[35] Ernestine Schlant, *The Language of Silence: West German Literature and the Holocaust* (New York: Routledge, 1999), 213.

[36] Sally Johnson and Frank Finlay, "(Il)literacy and (Im)morality in Bernhard Schlink's *The Reader*," *Written Language and Literacy* 4:2 (2001): 195–214.

[37] William Collins Donahue, "Illusions of Subtlety: Bernhard Schlink's *Der Vorleser* and the Moral Limits of Holocaust Fiction," *German Life and Letters* 54:1 (2001): 60–81, here 63 and 77.

[38] Helmut Schmitz, "Malen nach Zahlen? Bernhard Schlinks *Der Vorleser* und die Unfähigkeit zu trauern," *German Life and Letters* 55:3 (2002): 307.

[39] Omer Bartov, "Germany as Victim," *New German Critique* 80 (2000): 29–40, here 30–31.

[40] Bernhard Schlink, *Der Vorleser* (Zurich: Diogenes, 1997 [1995]), 96. Hereafter *DV*.

[41] Bill Niven, "Bernhard Schlink's *Der Vorleser* and the Problem of Shame," *Modern Language Review*, 98:2 (2003): 381–96, here 384–86.

[42] For a discussion of *Der Vorleser* as a novel about the legal difficulties of dealing with perpetrators, see Beate M. Dreike, "Was wäre denn Gerechtigkeit? Zur Rechtsskepsis in Bernhard Schlinks *Der Vorleser*," *German Life and Letters* 55:1 (2002): 117–29.

[43] William Collins Donahue, "Illusions of Subtlety," 69.

[44] William Collins Donahue, "Illusions of Subtlety," 77.

[45] Peter Sloterdijk, *Regeln für den Menschenpark*, 15.

[46] Dinitia Smith, "Seeking guilt, finding fame," *New York Times*, 30 March 1999, E-1.

[47] Bernhard Schlink, "Ich lebe in Geschichten,," interview in *Der Spiegel*, 24 January 2000, 180–84.

[48] Reinhard Baumgart, "Das Luftkriegstrauma der Literatur," *Die Zeit*, 20 April 1999, 55.

[49] W. G. Sebald, *Luftkrieg und Literatur* (Munich: Hanser, 1999), 17. Hereafter *LK*.

[50] Dieter Forte, "Luftkrieg im Literaturseminar," in Dieter Forte, *Schweigen oder sprechen* (Frankfurt a.M.: Fischer, 2002), 31–36, here 33 and 34.

[51] Dieter Forte, "Schweigen oder sprechen," in *Schweigen oder sprechen*, 69–70, here 69 and 70.

[52] "RP-Interview mit dem Leipziger Autor Treichel," *Rheinische Post*, 25 September 1998, 29.

[53] Volker Hage, "Auf der Suche nach Arnold," *Der Spiegel*, 23 March 1998, 244–49, here 249.

[54] Hans-Ulrich Treichel, *Der Entwurf des Autors. Frankfurter Poetikvorlesungen* (Frankfurt a.M.: Suhrkamp, 2000), 46.

[55] Rhys Williams, "'Mein Unbewußtes kannte . . . den Fall der Mauer und die deutsche Wiedervereinigung nicht': The Writer Hans-Ulrich Treichel," *German Life and Letters* 55:2 (2002): 208–18, here 212.

[56] For an examination of the dynamics of guilt and shame as experienced by the different generations represented in *Der Verlorene,* see David Clarke, "Guilt and Shame in Hans-Ulrich Treichel's *Der Verlorene,*" in David Basker, ed., *Hans-Ulrich Treichel* (Cardiff: U of Wales P, 2004), 61–78.

[57] Hans-Ulrich Treichel, *Der Verlorene* (Frankfurt a.M.: Suhrkamp, 1999 [1998]), 139. Hereafter *V.*

[58] See my "Hans-Ulrich Treichel's *Der Verlorene* and the 'Problem' of German Wartime Suffering," *Modern Language Review* 97 (2002): 123–34.

[59] See my "'Normalization' and the New Consensus on the Nazi Past: Günter Grass's *Im Krebsgang* and the Problem of German Wartime Suffering," *Oxford German Studies* 31 (2002): 161–86.

[60] Günter Grass, *Im Krebsgang* (Göttingen: Steidl, 2002), 99. Hereafter *IK.*

[61] Joachim Günter, "Opfer und Tabu. Günter Grass und das Denken im Trend," *Neue Zürcher Zeitung,* 23 March 2002, 33.

[62] Christian Florin, "Die Toten morsen SOS," *Rheinischer Merkur,* 22 February 2002, 21.

[63] *Der Spiegel,* 25 February 2002, 37.

[64] In 2001, Kempowski published an additional volume on the bombing of Dresden: *Der rote Hahn: Dresden im Februar 1945* (Munich: Goldmann, 2001).

[65] Online at: http://www.stern.de/kultur/spezial/gustloff/artikel_46097.html (accessed 20 May 2002).

[66] Guido Knopp, *Der Untergang der "Gustloff"* (Munich: Econ Taschenbuch, 2002). Econ is a subsidiary of Ullstein Verlag, which published works by New Right historians in the early 1990s. Knopp is generally balanced, although he occasionally sentimentalizes German suffering.

[67] *Der Spiegel,* 25 March 2002; 30 March 2002; 8 April 2002; 15 April 2002.

[68] Jörg Friedrich, *Der Brand. Deutschland im Bombenkrieg* (Munich: Propyläen, 2002).

[69] The torpedoing of the *Gustloff* had been adumbrated in *Hundejahre,* but it was only in 1999, with the publication of *Mein Jahrhundert* (Göttingen: Steidl, 1999), that Grass returned to the theme.

[70] Harald Welzer, Online at: http://www.nzz.ch/2002/04/03/fe/page-article 81DU6.html (accessed 20 May 2002).

[71] See my "Feigning the Anaethestisation of Literary Inventiveness: Günter Grass's *örtlich betäubt* and the Public Responsibility of the Politically Engaged Author," *Forum for Modern Language Studies* 34:1 (1998): 71–81.

[72] Günter Grass, *Unkenrufe* (Göttingen: Steidl, 1992), 37.

[73] Hage also wrote afterwords for the re-publication of Gert Ledig's *Die Vergeltung* (1999) and *Faustrecht* (2001).

[74] Uwe Timm, *Am Beispiel meines Bruders* (Cologne: Kiepenheuer & Witsch, 2003), 131–32. Hereafter *ABM.*

[75] Kathrin Schödel, "Jenseits der *political correctness*— NS-Vergangenheit in Bernhard Schlinks *Der Vorleser* und Martin Walsers *Ein springender Brunnen*," in Stuart Parkes and Fritz Wefelmeyer, eds., *Martin Walser, German Monitor* (Amsterdam: Rodopi, 2004), 307–23, here 319.

[76] Judith Kuckart, *Die schöne Frau* (Frankfurt a.M.: Fischer Verlag, 1999 [1997]), 228.

6: A German-Jewish Symbiosis?

Weil die Deutschen und die Juden in
Auschwitz ein Paar geworden sind,
das auch der Tod nicht mehr trennt.
— Barbara Honigmann,
"Selbstporträt als Jüdin"

IN MAXIM BILLER'S *HARLEM HOLOCAUST* (1990), the German narrator
pictures how the American-Jewish author Warszawski is caught up in
the guilt-induced yet self-serving philo-Semitism of his German girlfriend. "Ihr Volk tut mir ja so schrecklich leid!," she screams while
receiving oral sex from him, "worauf sie in seinen hungrigen jüdischen
Schlund hineinejakulierte."[1] The narrator — whose "Jewish" name
Rosenhain is ironic given that his grandfather wrote anti-Semitic tracts
and his great-uncle tortured Jews in the Berlin headquarters of the *SS*
(*HH*, 8–9) — similarly ingratiates himself with Warszawski and yet also
exploits him in pursuit of his own "Gier nach Schuld und Entsühnung"
(*HH*, 9). In the end, the text turns out to be a product of Rosenhain's
paranoia. One Hermann Warschauer of Columbia University had taken it
upon himself to ensure the posthumous publication of this "Dokument
eines selbstzerstörischen Talents und der großen deutschen Krankheit"
(*HH*, 61).

The symptoms of Rosenhain's "deutsche Krankheit" are an excessive
philo-Semitism combined with a paranoid conviction that Jews, especially
Warszawski, are more astute and sexually potent than Germans. In a rerun
of anti-Semitic clichés, Rosenhain catalogues the prodigious talents of the
Jew and frames himself as the naïve, yet sincere German who is the victim
of the more worldly, more cosmopolitan and more savvy interloper. At
the core of this fake philo-Semitism is the desire to enlist the Jew in his
mythologization of a pre-Holocaust productive interaction of German
and Jewish culture. This would be a "longitudinal normality" designed to
erase the Nazi past and to glorify a German-Jewish relationship that was,
in truth, always already fraught. If Jews would only reciprocate the affection shown them by Germans, the likes of Rosenhain might be released
from the burden of the Nazi past. Warszawski's refusal to acknowledge
"die von so vielen propagierte deutsch-jüdisch Symbiose" (*HH*, 50) thus
provokes resentment. His oeuvre, a postmodern engagement with survi-

vor guilt, is dismissed by Rosenhain as a self-indulgent mass of "Schleifen und Verschachtelungen" (*HH*, 40). In reality, however, the American author's style is most likely simply too "Jewish" for an "uncomplicated" German sensibility.

In our next section, we illustrate what Jack Zipes has described as the post-unification "fascination for things Jewish."[2] Following that, we ask whether literary endeavors to commemorate murdered Jews need always equate to a desire to elide the Holocaust for the sake of a resurrected German-Jewish symbiosis that might seem to assuage past guilt. Present-day German writers clearly display none of the traits of the "*Philosemiten, die sogenannten Judenfreunde,*" who, Rafael Seligmann proposes, more often than not reveal themselves to be "rabiate Konservatoren jüdischer Ängste und eines daraus resultierenden Regressionsverhaltens"[3] — this description might fit Rosenhain. At the same time, they do offer insight into Germany's efforts to define its new "normality."

Jews and Post-Unification Germany

"'Deutchland und die Juden — eine seltsame Liebesaffäre,' schreibt die 'Newsweek,' der 'Tagesspiegel' zitiert es stolz," reports the narrator of Delius's 1999 novel *Die Flatterzunge,* the failed trombonist who had secured his notoriety by signing a bar tab in an Israeli hotel with the name of Adolf Hitler.[4] Real-life journalist Jane Kramer, writing in *The New Yorker,* had already made much of the significance of philo-Semitism to the self-image of the new Germany. "Germans," she proclaimed in 1995, were engaged "in an elaborate exercise in 'solidarity,' if not identification, with Hitler's victims."[5] Since the late 1980s, the talk show host Lea Rosh had been leading a campaign for a major Holocaust memorial in Berlin.[6] Berlin's new Jewish museum, designed by Daniel Libeskind, moreover, had attracted massive public interest even before any exhibits had been deposited — Michael Blumenthal claims that 330,000 visitors "paid 8 marks for the privilege to see this empty structure" in 1999 and 2000.[7] And local towns were staging exhibitions to celebrate their "lost" Jewish histories at the same time as new monuments were being erected apace.

Jewish communities across the nation, and especially in Berlin, were growing rapidly, largely as a result of immigration in the early 1990s from the former Soviet Union.[8] Germans rushed to visit newly reinstated synagogues in their cities and learn about Jewish customs;[9] many visited concentration camps in the east, above all Auschwitz. Journalist Henryk Broder thus describes how, on ascension day 1995, the former *Vernichtungslager* in Poland was the chosen destination for the self-appointed "'geschichtsbewußte Motorradfahrerinnen und -fahrer'" of the "Berliner Motorrad-Club" — this was truly "Auschwitz für alle."[10] Closer to home, the *Neue Synagoge* in the Oranienburg district of Berlin was popular, even though the conflict between Israelis and Palestinians in the Middle East meant that it required the protection of armed police units, surely an uncanny spectacle for Jewish and non-Jewish Germans alike. Bookshops, furthermore, were full to bursting point with what Thomas Kraft has termed "jüdische Memorienliteratur."[11] Ruth Klüger's *weiter leben* (1992) and Victor Klemperer's *Tagebücher 1933–1945* (1995) are only the two most outstanding examples of this phenomenon. By the end of 1996, in fact, more than 150 000 hardcover copies of Klemperer's diaries had been sold and a thirteen-part television serialization was in production with the *ARD* (it was broadcast in 1999).[12] Austrian-Jewish writer Robert Schindel's début novel *Gebürtig* (1992) similarly enjoyed unexpected success.

In parallel with this cultural philo-Semitism, chieftains of the intellectual New Right pointed to German-Jewish historian Michael Wolffsohn as a patriot whose work incorporated a reconciliation of the two traditions.[13] Ignatz Bubis, then-President of the Council of Jews in Germany, had once accused Wolffsohn of being the "Vorzeigejude der deutschen Rechtsradikalen."[14] Following his death in 1999, however, Bubis was also acclaimed by former Chancellor Helmut Kohl as a *deutscher Patriot* in remarks that were widely repeated in the media, but which offended many Jews in Germany and Israel. Bubis, in fact, had made public his wish not to be laid to rest in Germany for fear that his grave might be desecrated.[15] Less than a year later, Foreign Minister Joschka Fischer was restyling Germany as the savior of Europe's "new Jews," the Kosovar Albanians, and many thousands of Germans were marching in protest against resurgent right-wing extremism and skinheads following a bomb attack on a Düsseldorf railway station in which six Jews were injured.

Philo-Semitism, of course, had been almost official policy in the FRG since its foundation in the year 1949. This bizarrely artificial situation is neatly satirized by the time-traveling narrator of Hans Magnus Enzensberger's novel *Wo warst du, Robert?* (1998): "Andererseits hatte der Lehrer eine Vorliebe für alles Jüdische, und auch im Fernsehen wurde es jedesmal hervorgehoben, daß der oder jener ein Jude war."[16] Writing in *Die Zeit* in 1965, commentator Eleonore Sterling even went so far as to suggest: "Der Philosemitismus — ähnlich wie der Antikommunismus — gehört zum Bekenntnischarakter der noch nicht verwirklichten deutschen Demokratie."[17] In his 1991 study, Frank Stern similarly highlighted the ritual quality of the "philosemitischen Habitus" and noted its instrumentalization as a "festen Bestandteil der ideologischen Legitimität der Bundesrepublik,"[18] whereas Mary Fulbrook speaks of "state-ordained philo-Semitism."[19] In the 1950s, Adenauer certainly made effective use of the reparations issue to gain legitimacy for the West German state.[20]

Later, geo-politics in the form of rivalry with the GDR (which tended to be anti-Israel) and the need to mark a clear break with the past played a part. For the Berlin Republic, finally, public avowals of reconciliation, without exception preceded by a rehearsal of the enormity of German guilt, demonstrate the way the new Germany has sought to combine contrition with its aspiration to "normalize" its relationship with Jews at home and abroad. To this end, a treaty was signed between the Federal Republic and the *Zentralrat der Juden in Deutschland* in early 2003. In it, the state pledged three million euros a year to the *Zentralrat* to assist it in its work in supporting Jewish life in the FRG and in integrating newly arrived Russian Jews.

Yet, until relatively recently, official intolerance of anti-Jewish bigotry most likely conflicted with privately-held attitudes. For a number of decades, "a peculiar situation" existed in the FRG, Anson Rabinbach proposes, "which necessitated that German leaders be *more* philo-Semitic than their constituents, legislate political morality and prohibit anti-Semitism by strict sanctions."[21] As late as the mid-1980s, research undertaken by the Allensbach Institute indicated, according to Werner Bergmann, "die Tabusierung und Latenz des Antisemitismus in der BRD."[22] In rare instances, latent anti-Semitism would become visible, as, for example, in the controversy surrounding Fassbinder's *Der Müll, die Stadt und der Tod,*[23] or during the Bitburg affair of 1985 — that is, the planned visit by President Reagan to a military cemetery where members of the *SS* were buried. On the latter occasion, Rabinbach argues, some Germans reacted "against their 'victimization' by the Jewish monopoly on the moral capital of suffering."[24]

The difference in the 1990s was that philo-Semitism seemed to have been internalized. Daniel Jonah Goldhagen received a rapturous welcome during his German tour to promote his 1996 book *Hitler's Willing Executioners,* even though the book scarcely made for comfortable reading.[25] And yet even then the true depth of such ostentatious displays of philo-Semitism has been questioned by a number of observers. Goldhagen's reception, Eve Rosenhaft suggests, may have had to do with the fact that the American was "emphatic in acknowledging that postwar Germans have shaken off the anti-Semitic traditions and qualify as good democrats."[26] By outdoing their Jewish visitor in condemning the dreadfulness of German perpetration, German audiences may have been exhibiting a new German "normality," one rooted in a reflex rejection of the Nazi past and a modish self-stylization as open, tolerant, and multi-cultural. More worrying, the intermittent desecrations of Jewish graves throughout the decade seemed to provide evidence of anti-Semitic attitudes, although incidents of this nature were by no means restricted to Germany.[27] This fed into the widespread anxiety that unification might ultimately lead to a revival of anti-Semitism.[28] Indeed, one in eight Germans, according to an opinion poll conducted by the *Spiegel* magazine in 1992, held anti-Semitic attitudes,[29] although, as Sander Gilman points out, the framing of the question presupposed that there could be no such thing as a Jewish German.[30] Valentin Senger, who had survived the war with false papers, declared in his memoirs *Der Heimkehrer* (1995): "Fünfzig Jahre danach habe ich wieder Angst."[31] Inge Deutschkron, who had evaded deportation with the help of "Ayran" neighbors, spoke in similar terms of her fears for the future of a country "in dem es wieder eine Bewegung junger Menschen gibt, die auf brutalste Weise gegen andere, ihnen nicht genehme Menschen vorgeht."[32] Deutschkron's comments referred not only to anti-Semitic outrages but also to attacks on asylum seekers and Turks in Hoyerswerda, Lübeck, Mölln, and Solingen.

A series of minor scandals, furthermore, appeared to confirm that politicians and even writers would not shy away from tapping into anti-Semitic clichés in order to score cheap political points or discredit an opponent. Helmut Kohl's claim that he was being treated "like a Jew" during the *Spendenaffäre* that followed his defeat in the 1998 elections — he had sanctioned the use of illegally-held funds to finance CDU campaigns — hence seemed to relativize the Holocaust. The same might be said of Martin Walser's assertion that the Jewish literary critic Marcel Reich-Ranicki had "trashed" "German" writing: "in unserem Verhältnis bin ich der Jude."[33] The insensitivity of Klaus von Dohnanyi's question in the debate on Walser's 1998 *Friedenspreisrede* is equally astonishing: Jewish Germans should ask themselves whether they would have behaved differently "wenn nach 1933 'nur' die Behinderten, die Homosexuellen, die Roma in die Vernichtungslager verschleppt worden wären."[34] Kathrin Schödel contends, in fact, that although there were very few "blatantly anti-Semitic clichés" in the course of the controversy ignited by Walser's speech, there were examples of "more subtle forms of exclusion."[35]

In early 2002, further uproar was caused by remarks by FDP vice-chairman Jürgen Möllemann, who insinuated that Jews might sometimes by their own actions be responsible for anti-Semitism. The brief controversy that resulted from these remarks, which were widely seen as a crude ploy to raise his party's profile for the forthcoming Federal elections, fed into the debate on "secondary anti-Semitism" — resentment of the way Jews had supposedly "profited" from the Holocaust — that had been gaining momentum since the arguments in 1999 about how much compensation German companies should pay to forced laborers, including Jews, and the publication of Norman Finkelstein's *The Holocaust Industry* in 2000.[36] This fuelled the round of soul-searching following Frank Schirrmacher's decision not to print excerpts from Walser's *Tod eines Kritikers* (2002) in the *Frankfurter Allgemeine Zeitung* on account of its allegedly anti-Semitic overtones.[37] On the eventual publication of the novel, in fact, Rafael Seligmann, who had already dismissed Möllemann as an "Opportunist," was moved to echo Ignatz Bubis at the time of the *Friedenspreisrede:* "Ich halte Walser für einen antisemitischen Brandstifter."[38] A year later, in November 2003, an utterance by CDU parliamentarian Martin Hohmann to the effect that "the Jews," on account of the actions of the Israeli government in the occupied territories, were a "Tätervolk," provoked another round of discussions.

In their introduction to a book of photographs of experimental Jewish art in Berlin, Gabriel Heimler, Britta Jürgs, and Michael Frajman observe that Jewish life in contemporary Germany tenders a strange mix of "Gedenktafeln und Sonntagsreden, Polizeischutz und immer wieder Klezmermusik."[39] Memorials and earnest orations and the police presence at major Jewish sites thus co-exist with what the narrator of Elke Naters's *Lügen*, listening to a tape cassette "mit jüdischen Gesängen oder so was ähnlichem," glibly terms "Ethnozeug."[40] Against the backdrop of unremitting anti-Semitism, it seems, Jewish life, and, for that matter, all "minority culture," is sentimentalized and commodified within a new "ahistorical normality."

Sentimentalized philo-Semitism is satirized in Bernhard Schlink's short story "Die Beschneidung" in his collection *Liebesfluchten* (2000). Here, Andi falls in love with the American Jew Sarah, envies the sense of belonging that her culture furnishes her but also finds himself censoring his hurt at the assumptions her family makes about him. He finally resolves his crisis of identity by having himself circumcised. Yet his "sacrifice" merely reinforces old stereotypes: the guileless German who falls prey to the seductive exoticism of the Jewess. "'Du hast das schwärzeste Haar, das ich jemals gesehen habe, und die frecheste Nase und den aufregendsten Mund,'"[41] he declares. At the end of the story, he leaves her immediately after having made love to her. Her error was that she declared that she could feel no difference between a circumcised and an uncircumcised lover. She fails to give him an answer to question "wohin er gehöre" (*DB*, 251), that is, confirmation that he has "crossed over" from the German to the Jewish "camp."

It might be argued that Schlink's story trivializes anti-Semitism by making it appear as an adolescent aberration, or by implying that "too much" talk about the Holocaust provokes only negative reactions. Whatever the case, the text points to the manner in which a sentimentalizing philo-Semitism "appropriates" the Holocaust for the sake of a sanitized *German* identity. This Henryk Broder describes as the "Germanisierung des Holocaust." Indeed, Broder claims, the more than five hundred proposals submitted to the competition to design the Berlin Holocaust memorial were typical of the mix of "Größenwahn und Weinerlichkeit" that underpins this new identity.[42] Maxim Biller too inveighs against the exploitation of the "Holocaust-Trauma als Mutter eines endlich gefundenen deutschen Nationalbewußtseins."[43]

Can non-Jewish Germans write about Jews, give voice to Jewish characters, or describe Jewish fates without exploiting them as a means of underpinning a form of German "normality" which either excises German perpetration from German history or sentimentalizes, even commodifies, Jewish suffering? This is the theme of our next two sections, in which we look at two very different authors, Martin Walser and Peter Schneider, and their endeavors to reimagine a German-Jewish symbiosis. Subsequently, we consider a range of German-Jewish writers with detailed reference to Seligmann and Biller. As might be expected, these authors display a good deal of skepticism about German-Jewish relations in the past — and about the philo-Semitism of the present.

Reviving the German-Jewish Symbiosis?

"Ich aß amerikanische Konserven und schrieb die Geschichte eines deutschen Juden. Da wurde es meine Geschichte," declared Wolfgang Koeppen in the foreword to his 1992 re-publication of a book that first appeared in 1948, and again in 1985, under the name Jakob Littner.[44] In effect, Koeppen claimed authorship — and ownership — of Littner's *Jewish* story, which now appeared as *Jakob Littners Roman Aufzeichungen aus einem Erdloch*. He maintained that he had been given a few "scribblings" by Littner and had turned them into a coherent narrative. This text, with Koeppen now named as its "real" author, was chosen by the Suhrkamp group to re-launch its *Jüdische Verlag* — cashing in, unquestionably, on the surge of interest in "things Jewish" in the early 1990s. Indeed, as Reinhard Zachau suggests, the book is "ohne Zweifel eines der beeindruckendsten Dokumente der Holocaust-Literatur."[45]

Yet Zachau's inquiries into the book's genesis had provided incontrovertible evidence to show that Littner had supplied Koeppen with a complete manuscript — after several years of detective work, Zachau discovered a copy of the original with a relative of Littner's in the United States. In fact, Koeppen had more or less conceded this in an interview with Margit Knapp Cazzola in 1989, in which he spoke of the uncertain "Rechtslage" of plans to publish a manuscript by a Holocaust survivor; this statement, however, did not appear in the collection of interviews edited by Hans-Ulrich Treichel and published by Suhrkamp in 1995.[46] This was an omission, that to Theodor Fiedler, who, along Zachau and Roland Ulrich, went on to publish an extensive account of the entire affair in the American journal *Colloquia Germanica*, looked suspicious.[47] In 2002, Suhrkamp finally replied with a new edition that included an account of its *Entstehungsgeschichte;* the same year, the Berlin Metropol Verlag released a competing version with an introduction by Zachau and Ulrich.

Not only had the German author effectively "appropriated" Littner's story, he had also subtly altered it. The insertion of numerous symbols of "natural catastrophe," Zachau argues, meant that "die Leidenserfahrung Littners" was robbed of "ihrer Einzigartigkeit [. . .] und ins Allgemeine verklärt" such that "das bei Littner noch klar erkennbare Opfer-Täter Verhältnis" was transformed into "ein mythisches Verhältnis." Koeppen's rewriting of Littner's text, moreover, displayed a "Tendenz, die Rolle der sogenannten 'guten' Deutschen zu betonen."[48] David Basker, without prior access to the manuscript, makes much the same point: "Germans are seen to be no better and no worse than anyone else." This mystification of personal responsibility and the blurring of distinctions between the perpetrator nation and its Jewish victims made it possible, Basker continues, for Koeppen to regard "himself as a victim of National Socialism,"[49] and this in spite of his initial enthusiasm for the Nazi regime and membership of the *Reichsschrifttumskammer.* More generally, Simon Ward argues, in this text as in his trilogy of novels satirizing the early FRG, "Koeppen connects German Jews with a German cultural tradition which lies in ruins in the wake of National Socialism."[50]

The re-publication of *Jakob Littners Roman Aufzeichungen aus einem Erdloch* came just one year after the release of Martin Walser's *Die Verteidigung der Kindheit.* This lengthy novel similarly draws on the prewar and wartime experiences of a Jewish survivor, in this case Victor Klemperer, the professor of Romance Literature who was spared deportation to the camps when Dresden was destroyed by the Royal Air Force on the night of 13 to 14 February 1945. Klemperer thus appears in various guises, both directly when the protagonist Alfred comes across him shoveling snow at the behest of his Nazi tormentors in the course of his compulsory *Arbeitsdienst* in early 1942, and indirectly in the person of Dr. Halbedl, the family doctor. This character, certainly, shares a remarkable degree of biographical detail with the author of the *Tagebücher 1933– 1945.* His marriage to an "Ayran" woman saves him from immediate transportation, although this is always cruelly precarious given that his wife, like Eva Klemperer, suffers from frequent illness. The catalog of *Verbote,* some petty, many intolerable, to which Halbedl is subject, moreover, is virtually identical with the list of 31 restrictions recorded by Klemperer.[51] Like Klemperer, Habedl is forced to inform fellow Jews of their impending deportation. Finally, Halbedl flees the Dresden *Judenhaus* during the utter confusion caused by the aerial bombardments of February 1945, much as his real-life prototype did.

A comparison of Alfred's meeting the "real-life" Klemperer and his behavior towards his fictional counterpart, Dr. Halbedl, reveals the manner in which Walser's novel, as much as the re-release of Koeppen's 1948 "fictionalization" of Jakob Littner's story, anticipates two key ideas which will come to shape the post-unification "fascination for things Jewish." First: human nature is such that Germans cannot be expected to have behaved in an exemplary fashion towards Jews *all the time* (this is part of the discussion about "ordinary Germans" covered in chapter four). Second: that it might be possible to rebuild a German-Jewish symbiosis upon the admission of guilt tempered by a plea for greater understanding of the patent fallibility of ordinary individuals and by the regret that *Germans,* retrospectively, feel for the "loss" of the immeasurable contribution made by Jews to German culture. Hence Alfred recalls, after the war, how — as a young boy — he had called out "He, Jude!" to Klemperer as the old man toiled miserably under the brutal instructions of his Nazi supervisor. He remembers the entire episode with great shame, and concedes: "In dieser Sekunde war die Propaganda des Nationalsozialismus in ihm Herr geworden. In dieser Sekunde ist er Nazi gewesen. Nie davor und nie mehr danach" (*VK,* 304). Yet this statement is as much a defense as an admission: *only* "in dieser Sekunde," he claims, did he succumb to Nazi propaganda. National Socialism and its lies are alien to him, an imposition he resists, if not always successfully — he is, after all, only human. Moreover, his behavior towards Halbedl reveals the "true" extent of his intimacy with his Jewish neighbors. The narrator reports that Alfred's family allowed Halbedl to practice medicine in their home (*VK,* 302), and, in a reworking of Klemperer's account, that they took in Halbedl's cat following the ban on Jewish ownership of pets (*VK,* 151). In reality, Klemperer's cat was put down.

Walser returned to Klemperer in his *Friedenspreisrede* in 1998. Here, he cited from his own *Laudatio* for the German-Jewish professor, *Das Prinzip Genauigkeit,*[52] published in 1995, the same year as Klemperer's *Tagebücher 1933–1945:* "Ich habe gesagt: wer alles als einen Weg sieht, der nur in Auschwitz enden konnte, der macht aus dem deutsch-jüdischen Verhältnis eine Schicksalskatastrophe unter gar allen Umständen."[53] The objective of the 1995 eulogy had been, in part, to claim Klemperer as a *German* patriot and deny the "Germanness" of Nazism. Thus Walser quoted from the diaries: "Die Nazis sind undeutsch" (*PG,* 31; Klemperer, v. I, 210) and "Ich bin deutsch, die anderen sind undeutsch" (*PG,* 32; Klemperer, v. II, 84), and noted Klemperer's "Bekenntnis zum Deutschtum, das er mitten im NS-Terror wieder und wieder formulierte" (*PG,* 21).[54] The 1998 presentation, however, went farther in contrasting the fake philo-Semitism of the postwar Federal Republic with a "genuine" respect for Jewish contributions to German culture. This appraisal of the long trajectory of German-Jewish relations rejects the "Instrumentalisierung" of the Holocaust as an "Einschüchterungsmittel oder Moralkeule" (*ESS*, 20) designed to stifle debate on a German national identity. By focusing on the much longer history of German-Jewish collaboration, Walser implies that it might be possible to re-integrate Jews into a German cultural tradition within which — with the exception of the twelve years of Nazism — they rightly felt themselves to be at home. This, as noted in chapter four, is probably the root of Johann's fascination in *Ein springender Brunnen* with Stefan George, the poet who so cherished the "German-Jewish elective affinity."[55] Indeed, the re-integration of Jews redeems German culture itself.

In his essays, speeches, and literary fiction since 1990, Walser consistently links his invocation of the German-Jewish symbiosis with a critique of the FRG both before and after unification — and this in spite of the claim in his *Friedenspreisrede* that it was precisely the abuse of the past "zu gegenwärtigen Zwecken" (*EES*, 18) he was determined to avoid. This critique, discussed in chapter three, extends to an assault on what the author sees as the philistinism, opportunism, and bureaucratic obscurantism of the modern Federal Republic. And what would the solution be? For Walser, a return to the German cultural tradition, a "longitudinal normality" in which Germans, Jewish and non-Jewish, would celebrate their shared attachment to the nation. Yet when non-Jewish German writers speak of Jews they all too often have themselves in mind. In Ruth Klüger's *weiter leben* (1992), the narrator confronts Christoph, a character clearly based on Walser, and comments: "Ihr redet über mein Leben, aber ihr redet über mich hinweg, ihr macht so, als meinet ihr mich, doch meint ihr eben nichts als das eigene Gefühl."[56]

Rescuing Jews?

It is not only in the work of Martin Walser that we see a desire to tell Jewish stories as a means of underpinning a particular vision of post-unification German "normality." In chapter two, for example, we noted how the protagonist of Monika Maron's *Pawels Briefe* (1999) hopes for a redemption of her mother's fateful political choice to support the GDR in the unquestionable innocence of her (Polish-)Jewish grandfather: "das nicht getilgte Wort, der nicht gelöschte Name Iglarz, [war] wie eine Erlösung für uns." The answer to the question posed by the Dutch TV crew — "wann werden die Deutschen wieder normal?"[57] — has to do, it is implied, with creating a social and political order in the new Berlin Republic in which the memory of Jewish victims (rather than ritualistic commemoration of the Holocaust *in the abstract*) informs the values to be upheld by the new, reunified Germany. Yet Maron's fictionalized biography of her grandfather is arguably itself an appropriation of individual fates for political purposes. Occasionally, then, the novel seems to suggest an equivalence between Nazism and the GDR.

Max Färberböck's *Aimée und Jaguar* (1998), one of the success stories of German cinema in the 1990s, is more sentimental and points towards the commodification of Jewish suffering. The film thus moves back from the present day to the wartime affair between a German woman, at the beginning a convinced Nazi, and Felice, a Jewess trying to evade deportation by concealing her identity. A nostalgic, even fetishized, identification with the Jewish woman's fate appears to offer a solution to the dilemma articulated by Lilly when she discovers Felice's secret: "Wie kannst du mich lieben?" If Germans can bring Jews to love them once more, and to forgive their crimes, the German-Jewish love affair might be resurrected.[58] The fact that the narrative opens with shots of the reconstructed *Berlin Mitte* of the late 1990s, and with a reference to the newly built *Kanzleramt* about to be occupied by Gerhard Schröder, hints at a perspective on the past rooted in the "latitudinal normality" of the Berlin Republic. An empathetic identification with Jewish victims, accordingly, is smoothly integrated into the new Germany's image of itself as liberal and tolerant.

Peter Schneider's two "Berlin novels," *Paarungen* (1992) and *Eduards Heimkehr* (1995) are more complex but may also evidence an idealization of German-Jewish relationships. The two texts deal, in part, with the close relationship between three male friends: Eduard, composer André, and East German poet Theo Warenberg (based on Schneider's friend, the East German Jewish writer Jurek Becker), who frequently ruminate on the fact that André and Warenberg are Jewish. In each book, Eduard is faced with the possibility that first one, and then the other, of his grandfathers behaved criminally during the Third Reich. This forces him to rethink his relationship with André and Warenberg, Colin Riordan notes, and "to reconsider whether the fact of their Jewishness may have played more of a role in their friendship than he had considered," that is, whether his affections result from an "artificial" philo-Semitism unconsciously adopted as a means of compensating for an inherited sense of shame. The fact that the novels simultaneously debate scientific issues related to genetics, nature versus nurture, and whether evil is part of human nature — topics which are especially controversial for Germans — raises the question of the way the past should be brought to bear on the process of establishing a social and ethical consensus in the new Germany.

In his reading of Schneider's two Berlin novels, Riordan remains unconvinced of the extent to which the author "successfully avoids the twin traps of stereotyping and philo-Semitism."[59] Might similar concerns, then, be generated in relation to Schneider's *"und wenn wir nur eine Stunde gewinnen . . .,"* a short account of the efforts of a small number of (undeniably) brave Germans to protect a German-Jewish musician, Konrad Latte, from deportation? The text, which appeared in 2001, was widely praised. Kristian Teetz, for example, claimed that its message was "daß es eben doch möglich war zu helfen,"[60] whereas Gunhild Kübler concluded: "Der Holocaust bekommt zusätzliche Einzelgeschichten, neben Tätern und Opfern und Zuschauern werden Menschen sichtbar."[61] Once again, a focus on *individuals* is typical of post-unification discourses on the past. If the debates surrounding Goldhagen's *Hitlers Willing Executioners,* the "Crimes of the *Wehrmacht*" exhibition or Walser's *Friedenspreisrede* were about "ordinary" Germans as perpetrators, then *"und wenn wir nur eine Stunde gewinnen . . ."* was about those "ordinary" Germans who had struggled to behave well.

Steven Spielberg's 1993 movie *Schindler's List* had already, of course, told the story of a German who sought to rescue Jews from the concentration camps.[62] The difference now was that a similar story was being told by a *German* author. In his introduction, Schneider antipicated the unease this might provoke, especially amongst his domestic audience: "Es hat uns fünfzig Jahre gekostet, zu begreifen, daß wir zum Volk der Täter gehören. Man verwirre uns jetzt bitte nicht mit Geschichten über die paar anständigen Deutschen!"[63] Yet the fact that some did resist demonstrated, he insisted, "die Schuld der Mitläufer, Denunzianten und passiven Zuschauer" (*UW,* 14). And it was precisely this lesson — the possibility, perhaps even duty, of opposition — that was inadequately communicated in the commemorative culture of the FRG. Where, he asked, were the *positive* examples that might inform the present?

Schneider's *"und wenn wir nur eine Stunde gewinnen . . ."* belongs to a wave of publications on German resistance and assistance to Jews, which, like the concurrent deliberations of German wartime suffering investigated in chapter four, set out, consciously or unconsciously, to reclaim the past for the purposes of shaping an identity for the fledgling Berlin Republic — even if this meant breaking with long-standing taboos.[64] In the majority of cases, these books, in common with Schneider's volume, combine the noble aims of promoting "Anstand" and affording Jewish victims their "Menschenwürde" (*UW,* 14–15) with a degree of sentimentalization. Jews all too often appear as unusually clever, even cunning, Nazis as comically simple, and "ordinary" Germans as apolitical, with a few decent exceptions. Filmmaker Margarethe von Trotta, with whom Schneider collaborated on the 1996 "unification" movie *Das Versprechen,* continued this trend with her 2003 movie *Rosenstraße.* This exploration of the "Ayran" women who saved their Jewish husbands from deportation in Berlin at the height of the war tells, in parallel, of a German woman who rescues a Jewish girl. Throughout, quotations from

Victor Klemperer's diaries abound: "Ich bin deutsch und warte, daß die Deutschen zurückkommen; sie sind irgendwo untergetaucht."[65]

Texts such as Schneider's, and indeed movies such as *Rosenstraße*, contribute to the self-image of the new Germany — reflexive, self-critical, and concerned above all with human dignity. This is a version of "latitudinal normality" as opposed to Walser's purely "longitudinal normality," and yet it is no less open to abuse. Indeed, Schneider's critical engagement with the past, outlined in our chapter on "political correctness," may all too easily descend, in this case, at least, into a sentimentalized philo-Semitism. His avowal: "Heldentum kann man nicht verlangen," a formulation with which it is hard to disagree insofar as it recognizes human frailty while suggesting the symbolic value of the smallest act of resistance, might be taken by his readers to imply the unreasonableness of expecting individuals, weak as they are, to offer more than token gestures. Those who helped Jews, notwithstanding Schneider's insistence to the contrary, are *exceptional*. Other Germans can console themselves with the thought that they might at least have been *anständig*.[66]

German-Jewish Writers and the New Germany

Skepticism on the part of Jewish authors with regard to the German-Jewish symbiosis is nothing new, of course. Edgar Hilsenrath's satire *Der Nazi & der Friseur* (1977), for example, reveals, as Jakob Hessing argues, "was wirklich geschieht, wenn eine Symbiose scheitert: Dann frißt ein Organismus den anderen auf, er verleibt ihn sich ein und setzt sich an seine Stelle":[67] the SS man Max Schulz adopts the identity of the Jew he murdered, Itzig Finkelstein, emigrates to Palestine and becomes a soldier in Israel's war of independence. Hilsenrath's grotesque comedy anticipates both the style and the tone of Maxim Biller's *Harlem Holocaust,* discussed at the onset of this chapter, and perhaps also the fiction of Rafael Seligmann. Less outrageously, but with equally serious intent, the famed Kabbalah scholar and friend of Walter Benjamin, Gerschom Scholem also frequently voiced doubts about the true nature of relations between Germans and Jews. In interview with Jörg Drews, for instance, he noted: "All diese Beziehungen, über die man so gern schreibt, über den Anteil der Juden an der deutschen Kultur — das ist alles sehr richtig, aber es hat eben nicht nur den Salon, sondern auch den Keller gegeben,"[68] a sentiment echoed by the writer Katja Behrens: "Würdest du mir deine Dachkammer anbieten? Deine Lebensmittelkarte mit mir teilen?"[69] The response of Holocaust survivors Valentin Senger and Inge Deutschkron to outbreaks of *Ausländerfeindlichkeit* and fears of a rise in neo-Nazi activity in the years after unification have already been cited at the beginning of this chapter.

At the same time, in recent years Jewish writers have flourished in Germany — or at least in the German language, as we shall see. Although it was, as Karen Remmler notes, "not until the mid-1980s" that "contemporary Jewish writers living in Germany begin to write about their lives in present-day Germany,"[70] there can be no doubt that German-Jewish writers have become an indispensable part of the literary landscape of the Berlin Republic. Indeed, Hartmut Steinecke claims that with the publication of Barbara Honigmann's *Roman von einem Kind* (1986), Esther Dischereit's *Joëmis Tisch* (1988) and Rafael Seligmann's *Rubensteins Versteigerung* (1989), there began a "neue Phase der jüdischen Literatur," which was consolidated after unification: "Seit Beginn der neunziger Jahre — und damit etwa zugleich mit der politischen Wende — nahm die Zahl der Autoren und Werke rasch zu."[71] To these three, Thomas Nolden adds a lengthy list of names, the more familiar being Katja Behrens, Robert Schindel, Valentin Senger, Henryk Broder, Robert Menasse, and Maxim Biller, and notes the establishment of a "third generation" (after Auschwitz) of German-Jewish writers in the FRG,[72] a phenomenon also identified by Remmler. In addition, Lothar Schöne might be mentioned. Although he generally objects to attempts to categorize his writing as "German-Jewish," Schöne's *Das jüdische Begräbnis* (1996),[73] with its description of the problems faced by a family seeking to have a Jewish woman buried next to her "Ayran" husband — and this in today's Germany — reflects, as Beatrix Langer rightly suggests, "ein heftiges Unbehagen an der verquälten Goodwill-Mentalität im Verhältnis zwischen offizieller deutscher und jüdischer Kultur."[74]

Indeed, Schöne's short narrative is typical of the essays and fiction of many of the writers named above. Frequently, the German-Jewish protagonists of such works experience profound irritation with the anxiously unrelenting official discourse of reconciliation combined with irrepressible feelings of alienation, marginalization, and even exclusion. The protagonist of Esther Dischereit's *Merryn* (1992), for example, states at the end of novel that she is an "integrierter Fremdkörper."[75] In similar vein, author and academic Ruth Klüger, whose *weiter leben* was one of a wave of survivor accounts to appear in the early 1990s,[76] claims that she writes "für die, die finden, daß ich eine Fremdheit ausstrahle, die unüberwindlich ist. Anders gesagt, ich schreibe für Deutsche."[77] Yet, Carmel Finnan suggests, Klüger at the same time also "attempts to reclaim her personal cultural and linguistic links with Germany."[78] The same is true of Barbara Honigmann, who, like Monika Maron, rejected her parents' commitment to the GDR, attaching instead great significance to her German-Jewish heritage. In *Eine Liebe aus Nichts* (1991), *Soharas Liebe* (1996) and *Alles, Alles Liebe* (2000), and in a number of short stories such as "Am Sonntag spielt der Rabbi Fußball,"[79] "Von meinem

Urgroßvater, meinem Großvater, meinem Vater und von mir"[80] and "Meine sefardischen Freundinnen,"[81] Honigmann thus explores various Jewish traditions as well as her own rootedness in German traditions: "in einer sehr starken Bindung an die deutsche Sprache, kehre ich immer wieder zurück."[82] For many Jewish exiles, Herta Müller suggests, the sense that "Sprache ist Heimat" is a form of "Beharren auf sich selbst."[83] Whatever the case, ties of culture and language seem to endure.

At first glance, such comments appear to lend credence to Walser's insistence upon the durability of the German-Jewish symbiosis. The same might be said of the appearance of a number of elegantly produced biographies of German-Jews following the largely unexpected success of Klemperer's *Tagebücher 1933–1945*, including, for example, the latter's *Curriculum Vitae* (1996) and Martin Doerry's widely discussed volume *"Mein verwundetes Herz." Das Leben der Lilli Jahn, 1900–1944*, an edition of his own grandmother's letters, published with his commentary in 2002. Yet Schöne, Dischereit, Honigmann, Behrens, Senger, and Broder, and particularly Seligmann and Biller, focus less on German-Jewish relations pre-1933 than on what Dan Diner has termed the "negative Symbiose" *today:* "für beide, für Deutsche wie für Juden, ist das Ergebnis der Massenvernichtung zum Ausgangspunkt ihres Selbstverständnisses geworden."[84] The presentation of German culture, and of the German-Jewish present, in the work of these authors is inevitably more fraught and often over-determined.

"Durch die Macht des Faktischen ist ihnen [Juden] Deutschland wieder zur Heimat geworden," insisted Rafael Selgmann in a 1999 article in *Die Zeit*.[85] The focus of this author — born in 1947 to German-Jewish parents in what was to become Israel, but resident in Germany since 1957 — is, as such, very much on the quandaries faced by German-Jews as they reconstruct Jewish life in what his characters often call *Nazi-Land*. How can German-Jews affirm their *German* heritage in spite of the past, and in the face of the incredulity of Israeli Jews, and proclaim a *living* Jewish identity in a country which, as Seligmann put it in 1997, seems to engage "mit obsessiver Hingabe fast ausschließlich mit toten Juden"?[86] Relations between Jewish and non-Jewish Germans, generational conflict within the Jewish community, concern for its survival in an age of inter-marriage and emigration, attitudes towards Israel and the FRG — these are the issues that dominate Seligmann's literary work.

In his essay on *Rubensteins Versteigerung* (1989), Ritchie Robertson suggests that Seligmann, in addressing the contemporary concerns just described, also revives "that once flourishing genre, the Jewish family novel," and this in order to debate the dilemma of Jewish existence in Germany since the Enlightenment, that is, a "nominal and illusory assimi-lation" in which Jews "were really cut off from their gentile fellow-citizens by the walls of an invisible ghetto."[87] Hence we see how conventional motifs of the nineteenth-century Jewish family novel — the *schemiel* (the brilliant fool), the attraction to the *Schickse* ("impure," non-Jewish woman) and the crisis of masculinity (with Jews typed as feminine) — are combined with more contemporary anxieties. The protagonist, Jonathan, berates his parents for living in Germany, but is appalled by the brutality of the Israeli army (part of Israeli "normality" is to shake off the image of the "virtuous Jew"), and wonders whether he really is a "typical" Jew when his classmates mock him for auctioning his seat next to their new, attractive female teacher. At the same time, his efforts to establish a relationship with a non-Jewish girl fail, both because his parents disapprove and on account of his own circumspection. It is only at the end of the novel that Jonathan resolves his uncertain identity: "*Ich bin ein deutscher Jude.*"[88] This sentiment most likely conveys Seligmann's own preferred solution to the "new-old" predicament of Jewish life in Germany.

Seligmann's refashioning of a German-Jewish literary genre which developed in response to the gulf between the promise of emancipation and assimilation and the reality of continued exclusion reveals something of the hollowness of philo-Semitism *and* Jewish self-ghettoization in the present, and thus of the obstacles to the resolution of German-Jewish identity in the FRG. The key difference, his work insinuates, is that the Holocaust is superimposed onto this nineteenth-century configuration. Where they once imposed an "emancipation contract" in which Jews would be rewarded for giving up their "specificity" with social and cultural acceptance, Germans now indulge in a trite and superficial fascination with Jewish "difference" in an effort to relieve their consciences and convince themselves of their tolerance. In *Die Jiddische Mamme* (1990), consequently, in a series of free-standing chapters, various characters reflect on the relations between Jews and non-Jews, and on the most recent forms of stereotyping to which Jews are subjected. More explicitly, in *Der Musterjude* (1997), Moische Bernstein — Jeans-salesman turned journalist — finds himself fêted by his editors and readers when he writes a piece that no "German" could write on "Adolf Hitler. Der Mann des 20. Jahrhunderts." Perhaps predictably, only "die wenigsten" of his readers grasp the true reason for their limitless infatuation with Moische: "weil er Jude war." In failing to identify the overwhelming irony in his exploitation of the fact that a Jew in contemporary Germany is permitted any and all liberties — even the freedom to celebrate Hitler — his readers transform Moische, as he puts it at the conclusion of the novel, "zum Juden. Zu eurem Musterjuden."[89]

From the late 1990s, we begin to perceive a subtle but still important shift in emphasis in Seligmann's writing. While he continues to satirize the ostentatious philo-Semitism displayed by many Germans, it is the issue of Jewish self-exclusion that truly dominates his later work. This theme is typically explored within the context of the upsurge in Arab-Israeli violence which accompanied the Palestinian intifada. For example, Ron, the protagonist of *Schalom, meine Liebe* (1998), is torn between Israel and Germany, a conflict personified by the two women in his life. Yael, the mother of his son Benni, exerts a constant fascination upon him, much as Israel does — "'Yael ist wie Israel,' fuhr Ron fort — 'Es . . ., sie zieht mich an — aber ich komme mit ihr und mit dem Land nicht zurecht'"[90] — and yet he always returns to his German girlfriend Ingrid. Finally, he chooses Ingrid, and hence Germany, but not until he has assured himself and Benni that the post-unification FRG is a very different prospect from the Third Reich. Benni looks at pictures of the fall of the Berlin Wall that he comes across in a coffee-table book of twentieth-century German history and wonders whether the dramatic photographs of national euphoria in 1989–90 might make Germans forget the uncannily similar images of Nazi parades in the 1930s. Yet these pictures too are to be found elsewhere in the book, and so Benni concludes: "Die Deutschen drückten sich also nicht vor ihrer Vergangenheit, wie er befürchtet hatte. Aber die Geschichte geht weiter. Die Bilder vom Fall der Mauer bewiesen, daß die Deutschen aus ihrer Geschichte gelernt hatten" (*SML,* 165). Subsequently, Ron delivers his own personal vote of confidence in the Berlin Republic: "Ich glaube nicht, daß sich der böse Geist der Vergangenheit in den Gebäuden festfrißt — der Reichstag hat sich zum Beispiel prima von einem bulgarischen Künstler einwickeln lassen" (*SML,* 239). It seems that Jews can have faith in the new German "normality" — and finally feel at home.

Seligmann's *Der Milchmann* (1999) reveals once more the manner in which the author turns to fiction as a means of intervening directly in contemporary debates both within the Jewish community and between Jewish and non-Jewish Germans. Set during the week of Israeli Prime Minister Yitzchak Rabin's assassination (on 4 November 1995) at a rally in support of negotiations with the Palestinians on his "land for peace" proposal, the novel depicts Jakob Weinberg's efforts to accept his life in Germany some fifty years after the Holocaust. In addition, Weinberg must contend with prostrate cancer, with the disappointment of a son who lacks his commercial zeal and a daughter whose life in Israel does not stop her desiring her German lover, with his own profound love for his second wife, a *Schickse,* and with demands placed on him by his *Chawejrim,* his Jewish male friends, who, like him, survived the Holocaust thanks to a mixture of cunning and ruthlessness. Along the way, Seligmann introduces his reader to debates within the Jewish community on the viability of belief in God after the Shoah, the image of the Jew as victim, and whether Israeli military prowess presents a more seductive model for Jewish identity. Simultaneously, words placed in Weinberg's mouth by his author question the authenticity of philo-Semitism — "Die deutschen Judenfreunde glichen Schmetterlingssammlern" — and partake in contemporary German discussions. "Sonderbare Propheten wie Lea Rosh, die [. . .] riesige Holocaustdenkmäler planten [. . .] reizten Weinberg mehr als Antisemiten," so the narrator declares, thereby most likely echoing his author's own opinions.[91]

Seligmann's solution to the problem of German-Jewish identity — or at least the solution suggested by his protagonists — may often appear simplistic. Like his literary predecessors Jonathan and Ron, Weinberg concludes that Germany has changed and that Jews can now be at home in the country without, however, having to repress their grief: "Deutschland war ein halbes Jahrhundert nach Hitler nicht mehr Nazi-Land — auch wenn seine Erde vom Blut der ermorderten Juden schrie" (*DM*, 326). Yet his work is nonetheless significant for the manner in which its serial assault on a range of taboos — Jewish racism, Jewish self-exclusion, or criticism of Israel, to name but a few — poses difficult questions for Jewish and non-Jewish Germans alike, and, most important of all, challenges the "new-old" stereotypes of Jews generated by present-day German philo-Semitism.[92] There are few "virtuous Jews" in Selig-mann's fiction, none of his protagonists possesses greater moral or ethical sensibilities than his non-Jewish neighbors, Israel is not free of blame for Palestinian misery, and even concentration camp survivors may owe their continued existence to an act of entirely understandable selfishness. None of this means that Germans may dismiss Auschwitz as part of a long history of human brutality in which the roles of victim and perpetrator are interchangeable. The fact that Jews are only human, Seligmann implies, with human weaknesses and moral imperfections, relativizes neither German crimes in the past nor those that he believes are being committed by the state of Israel in the present.

Seligmann's younger colleague Maxim Biller (born 1960 in Prague) is equally adept at identifying and undermining the stereotypes that underpin a hollow philo-Semitism. A regular contributor to the youth magazine *Tempo* before it went out of business in 1996 — the early pieces are collated in *Die Tempojahre* (1991) — Biller's column "100 Zeilen Haß" provoked intense controversy with its vicious attacks on media personalities, politicians, the German public, and on the hypocrisy regarding Jews in the FRG. In addition, of course, as noted in chapter one, Biller was a proponent of the *Neue Lesebarkeit* and openness to Anglo-American influences championed by, amongst others, Martin Hielscher,[93] even as he defended, at the meeting of writers he convened in Tutzing in 2000, the principle of political engagement at a time when this seemed to be out of fashion: "Ohne Moral keine Kunst, keine Literatur."[94] This *Engagement* is reflected in the essays and short stories collated in a number of volumes, including *Wenn ich einmal reich und tot bin* (1990), *Land der Väter und Verräter* (1994), and *Deutschbuch* (2001), as well as a wealth of articles in a variety of newspapers, magazines, and journals. In addition, Biller has also published two novels: *Die Tochter* (2000) and *Esra* (2003).

In *Die Tochter,* Biller expands on key themes present throughout his shorter fiction and essays, and which he will further develop in *Esra:*[95] philo-Semitism, the "identifikatorische Einvernahme der jüdischen Leidensgeschichte als Fluchtpunkt jüdischen Selbstverständnisses" (Norbert Otto Eke),[96] and the particular resonance and potential of Jewish writing in Germany.[97] The narrative tells of the Israeli Jew Motti who moves to Germany to live with a German woman, Sofie, he met en route from Tel Aviv to Munich on the way to New Delhi, and whose deferential anxiety at Israeli passport control immediately sets the scene for a novel in which Germans all too often offend with their efforts to flatter Jewish sensibilities and Jewish characters seem unable to define themselves without reference to Germans. Motti thus earns a living by exploiting the nervous desire to make amends — and the resultant sexual availability — of a number of women who come to him to learn Jewish customs and law in the hope of converting. In the meantime his relationship with his wife fails. So obsessed is she with her work as a doctoral student and a publishing assistant that she "neglects," as he sees it, to prevent him from abusing their daughter Nurit.

The text's shocking opening pages, in which we are introduced to Motti as he masturbates whilst viewing a pornographic movie featuring the daughter he has not seen for some ten years, inaugurates a series of flashbacks during which it becomes clear that he is suffering from dangerous self-delusion. He is pathologically obsessed, both with his daughter and with an incident during the Israeli invasion of Lebanon in 1982 in which he and a fellow soldier tortured and murdered a Palestinian prisoner. Consequently, the taking away of his daughter by the German authorities aggravates a persecution complex rooted in Holocaust imagery that competes with his longing to find relief from the burden of his own crime in "Sofies Totenland." For Motti, the Jew cannot be victim and perpetrator at the same time, and schizophrenia ensues.

Similar to the novels of Rafael Seligmann, Biller's *Die Tochter* undermines the cliché of the "virtuous Jew" and thereby critiques a shallow philo-Semitism. Biller also asks, as Seligmann does, whether the extent to which Auschwitz impacts upon Jewish identity formation by engendering a sense of eternal victimhood or essential innocence is not detrimental to individual Jews, and the state of Israel, unviable and even immoral. Yet Biller goes farther than Seligmann. He includes in the novel the story of a German-Jewish narrator who observes Motti and records his descent into schizophrenia. It is even hinted that the narrator — an author, who like Biller, wonders where he will find work following the demise of *Tempo* in 1996[98] — is simply another aspect of Motti's schizophrenia, or Motti a dimension of his split personality. Indeed, the entire narrative is revealed at its conclusion to have been nothing but a dream; the adolescent in the video who sparked it was not Motti's daughter but a Polish girl.

In telling Motti's story, the German-Jewish narrator reveals something of his desire to imagine a Jewish "normality" that is absent in Germany. Indeed, Germany is a country in which the narrator finds himself to be "unfähig, in einem Menschen etwas anderes zu sehen als seine deutsche Herkunft" (*DT,* 406), but which he cannot leave and about which he must write obsessively. Motti, on the other hand, appears to the narrator to be "einer von diesen ehrlichen und normalen Israelis [. . .] bei denen man — wäre das nicht das Problem mit dem Militärdienst — absolut nicht verstand, warum sie von zu Hause weggingen, von dort also, wo wir andern alle gerade noch hin wollten" (*DT,* 373). And yet this glorification of the Israeli blinds him to extent to which Motti suffers under the *abnormality* of present-day Israel and is traumatized by the perpetual war between Arabs and Jews. Or, it may be precisely *because* of Motti's murder of the Palestinian that he embodies the narrator's deformed ideal of "normality." The narrator watches Israeli films "in der Hoffnung, die Zahal-Soldaten dann mehr oder weniger live dabei zu erleben, wie sie sterben und töten, wie sie gut sind und böse" (*DT,* 391), and becomes obsessed with the "ergreifendsten von allen israelitischen Kriegsgeschichten" (*DT,* 393): the story of a soldier and his comrade who slaughter a Palestinian prisoner. In Israel, Biller's narrator seems to believe, Jews can be "normal," no longer victims, no longer *Musterjuden,* and no longer required to be "better" than other people. Yet the desire for *this* kind of "normality" may indicate the form of schizophrenia endured by those Jews struggling to define an identity within a contemporary rhetoric of German "normalization" which reserves for them a privileged space in public discourse — a new ghetto — in which they endure as the revered residue of the nation's awful past, proof of its moral renewal, and as the idealized recipients of its anxious solicitations.

By means of their literary fiction and essayistic interventions in present-day debates, Seligmann and Biller attack the taboos surrounding Jewish life in Germany after the Holocaust. Each begins with a critique of a shallow philo-Semitism and a public discourse that speaks endlessly of Auschwitz yet fails to grasp that the Holocaust cannot be instrumentalized as the foundation stone for a new German identity. A true "normality," for both Seligmann and Biller, would require sensitivity towards the past, but also a determination not to exchange discredited stereotypes for "new-old" clichés of the "virtuous Jew." "Die Juden waren auch nur

Menschen, und darunter gab es auch schlechte, und das wollen die Leute nicht sagen," insists the narrator of Katja Behrens's short story, "Arthur Mayer oder das Schweigen."[99] A true "normality" would also regard Jewish *life* in modern Germany as unexceptional, not as something which, in fetishistic fashion, "compensates" for the destruction of a German-Jewish dialogue which was in any case often more fraught than it appears in the contemporary imagination. This kind of candor, the work of Seligmann and Biller suggests, might assist Germans *and* Jews in shaping a new German "normality." As Joschka Fischer put it during the anti-Semitism debate sparked by FDP politician Jürgen Möllemann before the 2002 elections, the issue of whether Jews can "[sich] vielleicht eines Tages wieder 'zu Hause' fühlen" is no "nachrangige Frage, sondern die Glaubwürdigkeitsfrage unserer deutschen Demokratie schlechthin."[100]

Writing about Jews — W. G. Sebald

In a July 1997 article in *Zeitmagazin*, Matthias Altenburg caused a minor scandal when he declared that the subject of Jews in Germany was so delicate that he had resolved at a very early age not to approach it: "Seitdem rede ich nicht mehr über die Juden. Ich lasse das den Biller machen oder den Seligman oder den Schindel."[101] Rafael Seligmann's response in the same publication a short time later took issue with Altenburg's "kindlichen Selbstmitleid" and insinuated that the writer was trying to close his eyes to anti-Semitism — and furthermore complained that Altenburg had "circumcised" his name "um ein 'n'."[102] In a subsequent column, Altenburg asserted that Seligmann had missed the "darin enthaltende Ironie" of his previous piece but apologized for misspelling Seligmann's name.[103] Nothing more was said on the matter.

"Als deutscher Schriftsteller kann man nicht dahergehen und sagen, jetzt schreibe ich einmal über die Juden."[104] W. G. Sebald's comments in an interview cited by Gunhild Kübler perhaps reflect a similar anxiety over writing about Jews to that expressed, albeit more flippantly, by Altenburg. Yet Sebald, unlike Altenburg, chose not to leave the narration of Jewish fates to Biller, Seligmann, or Schindel, or indeed any other of the German-Jewish writers previously mentioned. In two major novels, *Die Ausgewanderten* (1992) and *Austerlitz* — the latter appeared after his death in 2001[105] — this author, who moved to Britain in 1966, presents a testimonial to Jewish lives which can be compared to the architecture of the new Jewish Museum in Berlin, as described by Bill Niven: "'voids' vertical shafts of open space intersected by corridors, what Libeskind calls 'the embodiment of absence.'"[106] Yet can literary texts composed by a German author and organized, like Libiskind's Jewish Museum "around the centres of absence — German-Jewish history as loss,"[107] commemorate Jewish suffering and *not* indulge German melancholia? There is no doubt that "the integrity of Sebald's vision allows him an unnerving aesthetic freedom," to cite Arthur Williams.[108] The issue at stake, however, is whether his writing of Jewish fates *restricts* itself to "celebrat[ing], mourn[ing] and commemorat[ing] individuals and communities lost in the Holocaust," as Katharina Hall claims.[109] Or, put differently, is Ralf Jeutter right to assert that, in Sebald's work, "memory [. . .] can never be a vehicle for [German] nostalgia"?[110] Does Sebald manage to recover the stories of his Jewish characters without mythologizing the German-Jewish symbiosis for the sake of a "latitudinal normality" or promoting the commodification and sentimentalization of Jewish suffering associated with the emergence of a new "ahistorical normality"?

Much has been made of what Hall calls the tensions in *Die Ausgewanderten* "between documentary and imaginative material, and their lack of resolution." This tension, Hall argues, is "highly productive"[111] insofar as the irreducible "otherness" of the snatches of personal reminiscence and letters scattered through the text keeps open the wounds of a traumatic history and refuses narrative closure. The same is asserted with regard to many of the photographs in the text, which, Jonathan Long contends, "frequently function as a goad to narration, acting indexically as a metonymic trace of the past that needs to be provided with a temporal context in order to 'make sense.'"[112] The argument is that the novel's four stories, each of which excavates the biography of a Jewish exile (and one story that features a relative of the author's who emigrated to America), remain unresolved but provoke the reader to step in and make a gesture of sympathy which would give meaning to a loss that, in truth, cannot be compensated, neither in reality nor in fiction. In the first story, then, Henry Selwyn, an émigré from Lithuania, commits suicide in his adopted homeland England — he has never reconciled himself to exile, nor indeed told his wife of his Jewish origins. In the second, Paul Bereyter, a schoolteacher dismissed by the Nazis because he was a quarter Jewish, kills himself on the railroad tracks in a bitter parody of the German idiom "bei der Eisenbahn enden" — a turn of phrase whose resonances can never again be as innocent after Auschwitz. In the third, Sebald's great-uncle Ambros Adelwarth goes with his Jewish employer to Palestine: both are driven mad by the abrupt intrusion of news of the Holocaust into their idyllic co-dependency. And, in the fourth, we are introduced to the painter Max Aurach who has lost his ability to speak German. Aurach's parents were killed in Riga in 1941, after his own escape to England, and the connection to his biography forever lost.

Yet it is not always obvious that the sense of loss that the narrator mourns alludes solely to the murder and exile of Jews as *Jews*. Indeed, *Die Ausgewanderten* perhaps *also* bemoans the rendering asunder of the *Ger-*

man-Jewish cultural tradition. The reader's attention is drawn, therefore, to the intimacy between German and Jew: Adelwarth and Solomon, it is implied, were lovers; Luisa Lenzberg, Aurach's mother, had an aunt who was a "wahre Germania;"[113] and Paul Bereyter was "von Grund auf Deutscher" (*DA*, 84). Each of these *German*-Jews is mourned as a representative of a cultural flowering that has been smothered. More striking still, the "Aurach narrative" features a visit undertaken by the narrator to a Jewish cemetery in Bad Kissingen, an episode based, Arthur Williams notes, on Sebald's journey to the same location, as recorded in the opening pages of his *Die Ringe des Saturn* (1995).[114] The passage in *Die Ausgewanderten* betrays a profound sense of nostalgia for the destruction of the German-Jewish symbiosis. The narrator describes how he stood in front of one of the graves and placed a stone on it, "wie es Sitte ist." The "Sitte," of course, is a Jewish custom, a gesture of respect appropriated by the German who admits that he does not know how to confront the grave's paradoxical allusion to the normalcy of Jewish *life* in Germany. Yet, as he writes these lines, he is suddenly able to formulate a response: "und jetzt, wo ich dies schreibe, kommt es mir vor, als hätte *ich* sie verloren und als könne ich sie nicht verschmerzen trotz der langen, seit ihrem Ableben verflossenen Zeit." The "sie" refers to Friedericke Halbleib (*DA*, 336–37), a writer who perished not in the camps, but in 1912, and whose gravestone is inscribed with a quill: a Jew who wrote in German and contributed to the fusion of the two traditions. Thus, it is not just the Holocaust that the narrator mourns. It may also be the one-time ordinariness of a German-Jewish co-existence in which Jews could die of natural causes.

The 2001 novel *Austerlitz* tells of its narrator's encounter with the Czech-Jewish exile Austerlitz in the Antwerp railway station during the second half of the 1960s, their chance meetings at various locations in Belgium, long walks in London, where Austerlitz worked as an academic art historian, and, after a lengthy break, the renewal of their conversations in 1996.[115] During their first meetings in the 1960s, Austerlitz is reluctant to speak of his past, or indeed of his own person at all, preferring instead to pass on to the narrator — who bears a striking resemblance to Sebald — his vast knowledge of the history of European architecture in a series of close readings of European landmark buildings and the manner in which they invoke modernity, the entrenchment of the nation-state, colonialism, and capitalism. When they encounter one another for a second time, some twenty years later, however, Austerlitz reveals that he has become preoccupied by his *own* past. The *grand récit* of modernity now concerns him less than the extraordinary twists and turns of his own biography. It is *this* story that the narrator reports in *Austerlitz:* the experiences of a Jewish boy removed from his family and taken to England from

Prague on one of the very last *Kindertransporte*. We learn that Austerlitz was placed with a Calvinist preacher named Emyr Elias and his wife in Wales, that he only discovered his true identity following Gwendolyn's death and Emyr's insanity, and that he attended Oxford University. It is only many years later, in 1993, after he hears two women discussing their experiences of the *Kindertransporte* on the radio, that he feels compelled to travel to Prague. There he meets Věra Ryšanová, the erstwhile best friend of his mother Agáta, and is told of his mother's deportation to Terezín from which, it is to be assumed, she was sent to her death in the east. Even less is known of his father's fate. Austerlitz's narrative closes with his journey to Paris where he hopes to find out what happened to his father after he had been captured and interned in southern France in 1941. Or perhaps it was 1943 — the records are incomplete. The novel ends with the narrator's own account of his return to the concentration camp at Breendonk which he had visited just after he first met Austerlitz. This completes the framing of Austerlitz's story within the narrator's: the text opens with his trips to Belgium in the mid- to late 1960s, undertaken, he says, "aus anderen, mir selber nicht recht erfindlichen Gründen."[116]

Austerlitz's decision to travel to Prague and trace his mother's history had been prefigured in comments made in conversation with the narrator as late as 1996, but reported at the beginning of the narrative: "Von meinem heutigen Standpunkt aus sehe ich natürlich, daß mir dieser Name und die Tatsache, daß mir dieser Name bis in mein fünfzehntes Jahr vorenthalten geblieben war, mich auf die Spur meiner Herkunft hätten bringen müssen" (*A*, 64–65). Almost simultaneously with the commencement of the narrator's account of what Austerlitz told him of his life, we are presented with a trajectory that endows it with redemptive potential, almost independently of whatever significance, or lack of significance, hope or melancholic despair the Jewish survivor may himself invest in his story. Austerlitz will move from ignorance of his past and the uncertain comforts of fatalism to a knowledge of the injustices inflicted upon him and his family by the Nazis. He will finally receive the message that the pageboy who stares out from the photograph on the cover of the hardback version of the novel — Austerlitz as a small boy — seeks to deliver from his past.

This is the story that the narrator tells in relaying his intermittent, frequently interrupted conversations with Austerlitz. The danger, of course, is that the German narrator, in relating Austerlitz's journey from his historical limbo to self-awareness, may — albeit unintentionally — identify, or be identified, with his Jewish subject. Austerlitz's pursuit of historical closure might all too easily be transformed into a vehicle for Sebald's own efforts, via his narrator, to counter the bouts of depression that so often afflicted him, specifically the "böse Zeit" mentioned in *Austerlitz* (*A*, 50) and more fully described in *Die Ringe des Saturn*. In the 1995 work, indeed, the author describes his own melancholic pilgrimage to sites of mass murder and environmental destruction. In ventriloquizing the Jewish refugee's experience of exile in *Austerlitz*, the narrator may thus imply an analogy with Sebald's feelings of dislocation as described in the earlier text: a generalized sense of disorientation following the disaster of modernity. As Anne Fuchs argues, the "Überschuss an Sinnhorizonten und Beschreibungsdetails" in the narrator's description of his own journey, and that of his characters, conjures up the "unbewältigte Qualität eines als katastrophal erfahrenen Geschichtsverlaufs."[117]

Yet the temptation to submerge the German experience of this catastrophe into the Jewish is always rejected — on the German side. The narrator tells his companion's story, and certainly filters it through his own concerns, but consistently signals the fact that this does not make it his, and that his rendition is a necessary literary device of which the reader should be conscious. All this he does via the insistent insertion of markers of Austerlitz's ownership of his history: "Sagte Austerlitz" (throughout); "so sagte Austerlitz, habe Alphonso gesagt" (*A*, 135); "sagte Věra, fuhr Austerlitz fort" (*A*, 240), and many other examples. The narrator thereby insinuates an ethical principle into his retelling of Austerlitz's story. The narrator is a "Konservator und Archivar," as Iris Radisch suggests, but he must not be an "Imitator."[118] Any peace of mind that comes from Austerlitz's facing-up to the past is reserved for the Jewish survivor and not for the German narrator.

Sebald's text in fact contains *two* parallel narratives: Austerlitz's and his own. In Austerlitz's story, as related to us by the narrator, we see how the Jewish survivor progresses from his repression of the past to a confrontation with the particulars of what was done to his family, and other Jews, by Germans. For all the pain that this necessarily provokes, his journey contains at least the possibility of some relief, or perhaps even release, from the historical limbo into which he had been cast. The narrator's story, on the other hand, is circular. At the very beginning of the text, then, we encounter him in the mid-1960s at Antwerp railway station from which he travels to the former concentration camp at Breendonk. Almost four hundred pages later, at the end of the narrative, he returns to this place, and reads from the copy of *Heschel's Kingdom*, by Dan Jacobson, given him by Austerlitz during their last meeting in Paris. Jacobson's account of his efforts to trace those of his relatives descended from his grandfather, Rabbi Yisrael Yehoshua Melamen, who were killed in the Holocaust, mirrors Austerlitz's quest for information about his father's fate. And there is some hope for Austerlitz: Jacobson discovers a date, a place, and a name, and even a location in which their remains are concealed. For the narrator, on the other hand, precious little has changed. The "Festung" at Breendonk may attract more visitors now — in contrast to the time of his first visit, the history of the Holocaust is no longer repressed — but its vista remains "unverändert" (*A*, 414). For the German, born into the nation of perpetrators, the meaning of this place, and of so many other similar sites, is the same as it had been thirty years before: "das waren die Familienväter und die guten Söhne aus Vilsbiburg und aus Fühlsbüttel, aus dem Schwarzwald und aus dem Münsterland, wie sie hier nach getanem Dienst beim Kartenspiel beieinander saßen oder Briefe schrieben an ihre Lieben daheim, denn unter ihnen hatte ich ja gelebt bis in mein zwanzigstes Jahr" (*A*, 33–34). At the end of his story, the contrast between the Jewish survivor, Austerlitz, whose story he recounts, and the narrator could be no greater. Austerlitz sets off to follow in the tracks of his murdered father, attempting to trace a life that has been erased from history. For the narrator, however, testimony of the itineraries followed by his forebears, and of their deeds, is apparent, throughout Europe, in the evidence of ghettos, camps, and mass graves. If Austerlitz's dilemma is that he has too *little* evidence of the past, the narrator's is that he has too *much*. Both men remain displaced, banished from home and the comforts of an unproblematic past — at the close of the text, the narrator leaves once again, "auf den Rückweg nach Mechelen" (*A*, 417) — but the nature of their exile is very different.

In *Austerlitz*, Sebald addresses the problematic question of identification with Jews raised by his own *Die Ausgewanderten* and indicates the impossibility of a "normalization" of relations between Germans and Jews which serves primarily to allow non-Jewish Germans to feel comfortable. And he does this with reference to a literary and philosophical culture that is infused, as Gunhild Kübler indicates, with "Hölderlin-, Mörike- und Stifter-Tönen,"[119] and which includes Kafka, Benjamin, and Adorno, that is, both non-Jewish and Jewish Germans. Indeed, although Sebald was fêted as "England's [. . .] greatest German writer,"[120] he was thoroughly immersed in these traditions and deeply implicated in the ongoing process of reflection on the idea of "Germanness" itself. In contrast to Martin Walser's efforts to recreate a "healthy" German cultural heritage, however, the allusion to such traditions provides no sense of relief or any escape from the burdens of the past.

In chapters one and two, we were concerned with the persistence of the former GDR and the "old" FRG in the literature of the late 1990s and the way both are invoked as part of a strategy to inflect the homogeneity of the global consumer culture. In the following three chapters, the focus was on efforts to rethink the Nazi past in order to develop a more robust identity in the present. In our final chapter, these two strands converge. We turn now to the ways writing about the "German province," for so long denigrated on account of its presumed links to the Nazi ideology of *Blut und Boden,* has been rehabilitated by a number of contemporary authors seeking to confront the apparent hegemony of globalized capitalism.

Notes

[1] Maxim Biller, *Harlem Holocaust* (Cologne: Kiepenheuer & Witsch, [1990] 1998), 44.

[2] Jack Zipes, "The Contemporary German Fascination for Things Jewish: Toward a Jewish Minority Culture," in Sander Gilman and Karen Remmler, eds., *Re-emerging Jewish Culture in Germany: Life and Literature since 1989* (New York and London: New York UP, 1994), 15–46.

[3] Rafael Seligmann, *Mit beschränkter Hoffnung* (Hamburg: Hoffmann und Campe, 1991), 109.

[4] Friedrich Christian Delius, *Die Flatterzunge* (Reinbek bei Hamburg: Rowohlt, 1999), 141.

[5] Jane Kramer, "The Politics of Memory," *New Yorker,* 14 August 1995, 48–65, here 49.

[6] Rosh also collaborated with historian Eberhard Jäckel on *Der Tod ist ein Meister aus Deutschland. Deportation und Ermordung von Juden: Kollaboration und Verweigerung in Europa* (Hamburg: Hoffmann und Campe, 1991).

[7] Michael Blumenthal, *Daniel Libeskind and the Jewish Museum of Berlin. Leo-Baeck Memorial Lecture 44* (New York: Leo Baeck Institute, 2000), 7. See James Young, *At Memory's Edge* (New Haven: Yale UP, 2000), 152–83.

[8] See Willi Jasper, Julius Schoeps, and Bernhard Vogt, eds., *Russen und Juden in Deutschland: Integration und Selbstbehauptung in einem fremden Land* (Weinheim: Athenäum, 1996). See also Jeroen Doomernik, *Going West: Soviet Jewish Immigrants in Berlin since 1990* (Aldershot: Avebury, 1997).

[9] Jewish organizations have been active in promoting the Jewish history of German cities. See, for example, www.berlin-judentum.de or the collection of photographs by Elke Nord in Ulrich Eckhardt and Andreas Nachama, eds., *Jüdische Orte in Berlin* (Berlin: Nicolai Verlag, 1996).

[10] Henryk Broder, "Auschwitz für alle!," in Henryk Broder, *Volk und Wahn* (Hamburg: SPIEGEL-Buchverlag, 1996), 210–11, here 210.

[11] Thomas Kraft, "Einleitung," in Thomas Kraft, ed., *aufgerissen: Zur Literatur der 90er* (Munich: Piper, 2000), 11–22, here 11.

[12] Hans Reiss, "Victor Klemperer (1881–1960): Reflections on his 'Third Reich' Diaries," *German Life and Letters* 51:1 (1998): 65–92, here 66.

[13] See, for example, Michael Wolffsohn, *Keine Angst vor Deutschland!* (Erlangen: Straube, 1990) and his *Meine Juden — Eure Juden* (Munich: Piper, 1997).

[14] See http://www.comlink.de/cl-hh/m.blumentritt/agr48.htm.

[15] Kohl used this phrase in a letter written to Bubis's widow. Reported by the dpa, 15 August 1999. Cited in Colin Riordan, "German-Jewish Relations in Peter Schneider's Works," in Pól O'Dochartaigh, ed., *Jews in German Literature since 1945: German-Jewish Literature, German Monitor* (Amsterdam: Rodopi, 2000), 625–36, here 634.

[16] Hans Magnus Enzensberger, *Wo warst du, Robert?* (Munich: Deutscher Taschenbuch Verlag, 2002 [1998]), 117–18.

[17] Eleonore Sterling, "Judenfreunde — Judenfeinde: Fragwürdiger Philosemitismus in der Bundesrepublik," *Die Zeit,* 10 December 1965, 30.

[18] Frank Stern, *Im Anfang war Auschwitz: Antisemitismus und Philosemitismus im deutschen Nachkrieg* (Gerlingen: Beicher Verlag, 1991), 351 and 300.

[19] Mary Fulbrook, *German National Identity after the Holocaust* (Cambridge: Polity Press, 1999), 65.

[20] See Jack Zipes, "The Vicissitudes of Being Jewish in West Germany," in Jack Zipes and Anson Rabinbach, eds., *Germans and Jews since The Holocaust: The Changing Situation in West Germany* (New York: Holmes and Meier, 1986).

[21] Anson Rabinbach, "The Jewish Question in the German Question," *New German Critique* 44 (1988): 159–92, here 167.

[22] Werner Bergmann, "Sind die Deutschen antisemitisch? Meinungsumfragen von 1946–1987 in der Bundesrepublik Deutschland," in Werner Bergmann and Rainer Erb, eds., *Antisemitismus in der politischen Kultur nach 1945* (Opladen: Westdeutscher Verlag, 1990), 108–30, here 116.

[23] Heiner Lichtenstein, ed., *Die Fassbinder-Kontroverse, oder das Ende der Schonzeit* (KönigsteIn Athenäum, 1986). See also the special edition of *New German Critique* (38) on *The German-Jewish Controversy* (Spring/Summer 1986), and Jessica Benjamin and Anson Rabinbach, "Germans, Leftists, Jews," *New German Critique* 31 (Winter/Summer, 1984): 188–95.

[24] Anson Rabinbach, "The Jewish Question in the German Question," 180. See also Anson Rabinbach, "Beyond Bitburg: The Place of the 'Jewish Question' in German History after 1945," in Kathy Harms, ed., *Coping with the Past: Germany and Austria after 1945* (Madison: U of Wisconsin P, 1990), 187–218.

[25] See Volker Ullrich, "Daniel J. Goldhagen in Deutschland: Die Buchtournee wurde zum Triumphzug," *Die Zeit,* 13 September 1996.

[26] Eve Rosenhaft, "Facing up to the Past — Again? Crimes of the Wehrmacht," *Debatte* 5:1 (1997): 105–18, here 114–15.

[27] There had been desecrations of Jewish graves in the 1970s and 1980s, of course, but such occurrences seemed more organized, widespread, and frequent in the 1990s.

[28] See Sander L. Gilman, "German Unification and the Jews," *New German Critique* 52 (1991): 173–91.

[29] *Der Spiegel,* 3 March 1992, 52–66, here 41–50.

[30] Sander L. Gilman, "Negative Symbiosis: The Reemergence of Jewish Culture in Germany after the Fall of the Wall," in Klaus L. Berghahn, ed., *The German-Jewish Dialogue Reconsidered* (Bern: Peter Lang, 1996), 207–32, here 213–4.

[31] Valentin Senger, *Der Heimkehrer* (Munich: Luchterhand, 1995), 5.

[32] Inge Deutschkron, "Mit den Jahren wuchsen die Zweifel," in Helmut Lotz and Kai Precht, eds., *Deutschland, mein Land?* (Munich: Deutscher Taschenbuch Verlag, 1999), 247–53, here 253.

[33] Willi Winkler, "Die Sprache verwaltet das Nichts," *Süddeutsche Zeitung,* 19/20 September 1998, 15.

[34] Klaus von Dohnanyi, "Eine Friedensrede: Walser notwendige Klage," *Frankfurter Allgemeine Zeitung,* 14 November 1998; collated in Frank Schirrmacher, ed., *Die Walser-Bubis-Debatte* (Frankfurt a.M.: Suhrkamp, 1999), 146–50, here 148. The title of a collection of essays on the debate collated by Johannes Klotz and Gerd Weigel most likely exaggerates the "new tone" in the Berlin Republic: *Geistige Brandstiftung: Die neue Sprache der Berliner Republik* (Berlin: Aufbau, 2001).

[35] Kathrin Schödel, "Normalising Cultural Memory? The 'Walser-Bubis-Debate' and Martin Walser's Novel *Ein springender Brunnen,*" in Stuart Taberner and Frank Finlay, eds., *Recasting German Identity* (Rochester: Camden House, 2002), 69–87, here 81.

[36] Many of the contributions to this debate are collated in Michael Naumann, ed., *"Es muß doch in diesem Land wieder möglich sein . . ." Der neue Antisemitismus-Streit* (Frankfurt a.M.: Ullstein, 2002).

[37] See Bill Niven, "Martin Walser's *Tod eines Kritikers* and the Issue of Anti-Semitism," *German Life and Letters* 56:3 (2003): 299–311. See also the collection of responses to the debate in *Der Streit um Martin Walser* (Berlin: Junge Freiheit Verlag, 2002).

[38] Elisabeth Kiderlen, "'Wie die Gänse auf dem Kapitol.' Der Schriftsteller Rafael Seligmann über Antisemitismus heute," *Badische Zeitung,* 3 May 2002, 3. The debate between various characters in the novel as to whether André Ehrl-König is in fact Jewish seems tasteless at the very least (Martin Walser, *Tod eines Kritikers* [Frankfurt a.M.: Suhrkamp, 2002], 144).

[39] Gabriel Heimler, Britta Jürgs, Michael Frajman, eds., *DAVKA: Jüdische Visionen in Berlin* (Berlin: AvivA, 1999), 7.

[40] Elke Naters, *Lügen* (Cologne: Kiepenheuer & Witsch, 1999), 78.

[41] Bernhard Schlink, "Die Beschneidung," in Bernhard Schlink, *Liebesfluchten* (Zurich: Diogenes, 2000), 199- 255, here 218. Hereafter *DB.*

[42] Henryk Broder, "Die Germanisierung des Holocaust," in *Volk und Wahn,* 214–28, here 218 and 228.

[43] Maxim Biller, "Heiliger Holocaust," in Maxim Biller, *Deutschbuch* (Munich: Deutscher Taschenbuch Verlag, 2001), 27–29, here 28.

[44] Wolfgang Koeppen, *Jakob Littners Roman Aufzeichnungen aus einem Erdloch* (Frankfurt a.M.: Jüdischer Verlag, 1992), 6.

[45] Reinhard Zachau, "Das Originalmanuskript zu Wolfgang Koeppens *Jakob Littners Roman Aufzeichungen aus einem Erdloch*," *Colloquia Germanica* 32:2 (1999): 115–33, here 119.

[46] Wolfgang Koeppen, *Einer der schreibt. Gespräche und Interviews*, ed. by Hans-Ulrich Treichel (Frankfurt a.m.: Suhrkamp, 1995), 221–26.

[47] Theodor Fiedler, "eine sehr komplizierte Rechtslage wegen der Urheberrechte," *Colloquia Germanica* 32:2 (1999): 103–4. Roland Ulrich, "Vom Report zum Roman: Zur Textwelt von Wolfgang Koeppens Roman *Jakob Littners Roman Aufzeichungen aus einem Erdloch*," in the same issue of *Colloquia Germanica*, 135–50.

[48] Reinhard Zachau, "Das Originalmanuskript," 124 and 128.

[49] David Basker, "The Author as Victim: Wolfgang Koeppen, *Jakob Littners Aufzeichnungen aus einem Erdloch*," *Modern Language Review* 92:4 (1997): 903–11, here 905 and 900.

[50] Simon Ward, "Koeppen's *Jakob Littners Roman Aufzeichungen aus einem Erdloch*," in Pól O'Dochartaigh, ed., *Jews in German Literature since 1945*, 651–63, here 659.

[51] Compare Martin Walser, *Die Verteidigung der Kindheit* (Frankfurt a.M.: Suhrkamp, 1991), 302 (hereafter *VK*) and Victor Klemperer, *Tagebücher 1933–1945*, ed. Walter Nowojski with Hadwig Klemperer (Berlin: Aufbau Verlag, 1995), vol. II, 107–8.

[52] Martin Walser, *Das Prinzip Genauigkeit* (Frankfurt a.M.: Suhrkamp, 1995). Hereafter *PG*.

[53] Martin Walser, *Erfahrungen beim Erfassen einer Sonntagsrede* (Frankfurt a.M.: Suhrkamp, 1998), 19 (hereafter *EES*). Compare with *PG*, 34–35.

[54] See my "'Wie schön wäre Deutschland, wenn man sich noch als Deutscher fühlen und mit Stolz als Deutscher fühlen könnte': Martin Walser's Reception of Victor Klemperer's *Tagebücher 1933–1945* in *Das Prinzip Genauigkeit* and *Die Verteidigung der Kindheit*" (*Deutsche Vierteljahrsschrift* 73 [1999]: 710–32). Henry Ashby Turner, in his essay "Victor Klemperer's Holocaust" (*German Studies Review* 22:3 [1999]: 385–96) is, like Walser, much more inclined to read the diaries for evidence of "ordinary" Germans' willingness to help Jews and to resist the anti-Semitic propaganda of the regime.

[55] See Ritchie Robertson, *The "Jewish Question" in German Literature, 1749–1939* (Oxford: Oxford UP, 2001 [1999]), 370–42.

[56] Ruth Klüger, *weiter leben* (Munich: Deutscher Taschenbuch Verlag, 1995 [1992]), 199.

[57] Monika Maron, *Pawels Briefe* (Frankfurt a.M.: Fischer, 1999), 104 and 10.

[58] See my "'Wie kannst du mich lieben?': 'Normalising' the Relationship between Germans and Jews in the 1990s' Films *Aimée und Jaguar* and *Meschugge*," in William Niven and James Jordan, eds., *Politics and Culture in Twentieth-Century Germany* (Rochester: Camden House, 2003), 227–43.

[59] Colin Riordan, "German-Jewish Relations," 630 and 634.

[60] Kristian Teetz, "Helden, still und tapfer," *Die Welt*, 28 July 2001, 5.

[61] Gunhild Kübler, "Stille Helden, von Mitgefühl getrieben," *Die Weltwoche*, 5 April, 2001 41.

[62] See Bill Niven, "The Reception of Steven Spielberg's 'Schindler's List' in the German Media," *Journal of European Studies* 25 (1995): 165–89.

[63] Peter Schneider, *"Und wenn wir nur eine Stunde gewinnen . . ."* (Berlin: Rowohlt, 2002 [2001]), 12. Hereafter *UW*.

[64] See, for example, *Zwei Bäume in Jerusalem* (Hoffmann und Campe, 2002), in which Cornelia Schmalz-Jacobson describes her parents' efforts to rescue Jews. It is worth noting that Schmalz-Jacobson was, at the time of the book's publication, the *Beauftragte der Bundesregierung für Ausländerangelegenheiten*. In addition to "memoirs," there have also been serious academic works, including: Beate Kosmala and Claudia Schoppmann, eds., *Solidarität und Hilfe für Juden während der NS-Zeit: Überleben im Untergrund: Hilfe für Juden in Deutschland 1941–1945* (Berlin: Metropol Verlag: 2002).

[65] Victor Klemperer, *Tagebücher 1933–1945*, vol. II, 105.

[66] The *Gedenkstätte Deutscher Widerstand* in the Stauffenberger Straße in Berlin (formerly the Bendler Block housing the *Wehrmacht* High Command) deals well with these problems — after many years of wrangling and controversy. See Bill Niven, *Facing the Nazi Past* (London: Routledge, 2002), 74–84.

[67] Jakob Hessing, "Im Exil: Zur deutsch-jüdischen Literatur," *Merkur* 567 (1996): 491–501, here 493.

[68] Gerschom Scholem, *". . . und alles ist Kabbala." Gerschom Scholem im Gespräch mit Jörg Drews* (Munich: edition text + kritik, 1980), 12.

[69] Katja Behrens, "Alles normal," in *"bin ich um den Schlaf gebracht." Literarische Texte von vierzehn Autorinnen und Autoren. Heinrich-Heine-Haus, Lüneburg 1993* (Lüneburg: Altstadt-Druck, 1993), 83–88, 88. This line does not appear in the version of the story published in *Salomo und die anderen* (Frankfurt a.M.: Fischer, 1993, 7–17).

[70] Karen Remmler, "The 'Third Generation' of Jewish-German Writers after the Shoah Emerges in Germany and Austria," in Sander L. Gilman and Jack Zipes, eds., *The Yale Companion to Jewish Writing and Thought in German Culture, 1096–1996* (New Haven: Yale UP), 796–804, here 798.

[71] Hartmut Steinecke, "Einleitung," in Sander L. Gilman and Hartmut Steinecke, eds., *Deutsch-jüdische Literatur der neunziger Jahre: Die Generation nach der Shoah, Beiheft zur Zeitschrift für Deutsche Philologie* 11 (2002): 9–16, here 9.

[72] Thomas Nolden, *Junge jüdische Literatur* (Würzburg: Königshausen & Neumann, 1995), 30–31.

[73] Lothar Schöne, *Das jüdische Begräbnis* (Munich: Deutscher Taschenbuch Verlag, 1999 [1996]).

[74] Beatrix Langner, "Gleichnis vom ewigen Juden," *Süddeutsche Zeitung*, 20 June 1996, 14.

[75] Esther Dischereit, *Merryn* (Frankfurt a.M.: Suhrkamp, 1992), 117.

[76] See Irene Heidelberger-Leonard, "Ruth Klügers *weiter leben* — ein Grundstein zu einem neuen Auschwitz-'Kanon'?," in Stephan Braese, Holger Gehle, Doron Kiesel, Hanno Loewy, eds., *Deutsche Nachkriegsliteratur und der Holocaust* (Frankfurt a.M.: Campus, 1998), 157–69.

[77] Ruth Klüger, *weiter leben*, 213.

[78] Carmel Finnan, "Autobiography, Memory and the Shoah: German-Jewish Identity in Autobiographical Writings by Ruth Klüger, Cordelia Edvardson and Laura Waco," in Pól O'Dochartaigh, ed., *Jews in German Literature since 1945*, 447–61, here 453.

[79] Barbara Honigmann, "Am Sonntag spielt der Rabbi Fußball," in Barbara Honigmann, *Am Sonntag spielt der Rabbi Fußball* (Heidelberg: Wunderhorn, 1998), 36–37.

[80] Barbara Honigmann, "Von meinem Urgroßvater, meinem Großvater, meinem Vater und von mir," in Barbara Honigmann, *Damals, dann und danach*, 39–55.

[81] Barbara Honigmann, "Meine sefardischen Freundinnen," in *Damals, dann und danach*, 63–82.

[82] Barbara Honigmann, "Selbstporträt als Jüdin," in *Damals, dann und danach*, 11–18, here 18.

[83] Herta Müller, *Heimat ist das was gesprochen wird* (Blieskastel: Gollenstein Verlag, 2001), 24.

[84] Dan Diner, "Negative Symbiose: Deutsche und Juden nach Auschwitz," *Babylon* 1 (1986): 9–20, here 9.

[85] Rafael Seligmann, "Hier geblieben! Warum tun deutsche Juden noch so, als seien sie Zionisten?," *Die Zeit*, 26 August 1995, 13.

[86] Rafael Seligmann, "Deutsche Musterjuden. Oder: Schluß mit dem Totenkult," in Michael Gerwarth, *Innensichten Deutschland* (Berlin: Parthas Verlag, 1997), 76–78, here 76.

[87] Ritchie Robertson, "Rafael Seligmann's *Rubensteins Versteigerung:* The German-Jewish Family Novel before and after the Holocaust," *Germanic Review* 75:3 (2000): 175–93, here 184 and 182. See also Ritchie Robertson, *The "Jewish Question" in German Literature*, 273–85.

[88] Rafael Seligmann, *Rubensteins Versteigerung* (Munich: Deutscher Taschenbuch Verlag, 1991 [1989]), 189.

[89] Rafael Seligmann, *Der Musterjude* (Munich: Deutscher Taschenbuch Verlag, 1999 [1997]), 146 and 390.

[90] Rafael Seligmann, *Schalom meine Liebe* (Munich: Deutscher Taschenbuch Verlag, 1999 [1998]), 162. Hereafter *SML*.

[91] Rafael Seligmann, *Der Milchmann* (Munich: Deutscher Taschenbuch Verlag, 2000 [1999]), 125. Hereafter *DM*.

[92] Seligmann's work has been controversial within the Jewish community. See Sander Gilman's "Negative Symbiosis: The Reemergence of Jewish Culture in

Germany after the Fall of the Wall" (225–32) for a discussion of the debates following *Rubensteins Versteigerung*.

[93] Biller's short story "Und wenn der Kater kommt" was the title piece of Hielscher's collection *Wenn der Kater kommt. Neues Erzählen. 38 deutschsprachige Autorinnen und Autoren* (Cologne: Kiepenheuer & Witsch, 1996), 161–73.

[94] Maxim Biller, "Feige das Land, schlapp die Literatur: Über die Schwierigkeiten beim Sagen der Wahrheit," *Die Zeit*, 13 April 2000, 47–49, here 47.

[95] Biller's *Esra* was briefly discussed in chapter three.

[96] Norbert Otto Eke, "'Was wollen Sie? Die Absolution?,'" in Sander L. Gilman and Hartmut Steinecke, eds., *Deutsch-jüdische Literatur der neunziger Jahre: Die Generation nach der Shoah, Beiheft zur Zeitschrift für Deutsche Philologie* 11 (2002): 89–107, here 90.

[97] See Biller's "Goodbye Columbus. Randlage oder: Über die Voraussetzungen jüdischer Literatur," *Frankfurter Rundschau*, 2 March 1995, 9.

[98] Maxim Biller, *Die Tochter* (Cologne: Kiepenheuer & Witsch, 2000), 200. Hereafter *DT*.

[99] Katja Behrens, "Arthur Mayer oder das Schweigen," in *Salomo und die anderen*, 67–152, here 145.

[100] Joschka Fischer, "Deutschland, deine Juden," in Michael Naumann, ed., *"Es muß doch in diesem Land wieder möglich sein . . .",* 43.

[101] Matthias Altenburg, "Flaubert und die toten Juden," *Zeitmagazin*, 4 July 1997, 6.

[102] Rafael Seligmann, "So simpel ist Antisemitismus," *Zeitmagazin*, 1 August 1997, 6.

[103] Matthias Altenburg, "Sehr geehrter Herr Seligmann," *Zeitmagazin*, 1 August 1997, 7. Both pieces are collated in Altenburg, *Partisanen der Schönheit* (Münster: Oktober Verlag, 2002), 78–81 and 81–84.

[104] Gunhild Kübler, "Dem Freund erzählen, was nicht zum Aushalten ist," *Die Weltwoche*, 15 February 2001, 41.

[105] See the edition of *Akzente* dedicated to Sebald (50:1 [2003]) for reflections on his life and work.

[106] Bill Niven, *Facing the Nazi Past*, 209. Libeskind cited from Daniel Libeskind, "Between the Lines: Das Jüdische Museum," in *Jüdisches Museum Berlin* (Berlin: Jüdisches Museum Berlin, 1999), 6–11, here 10.

[107] Bill Niven, *Facing The Nazi Past*, 210.

[108] Arthur Williams, "'Das korsakowsche Symptom': Remembrance and Responsibility in W. G. Sebald," in Helmut Schmitz, ed., *German Culture and the Uncomfortable Past* (Aldershot: Ashgate, 2001), 65–86, here 69.

[109] Katharina Hall, "Jewish Memory in Exile: The Relation of W. G. Sebald's *Die Ausgewanderten* to the Tradition of the *Yizkor* Books," in Pól O'Dochartaigh, ed., *Jews in German Literature since 1945*, 153–64, 155.

[110] Ralf Jeutter, "'Am Rand der Finsternis.': The Jewish Experience in the Context of W. G. Sebald's Poetics," in Pól O'Dochartaigh, ed., *Jews in German Literature since 1945,* 165–79, here 171.

[111] Katharina Hall, "Jewish Memory in Exile," 163.

[112] Jonathan Long, "History, Narrative, and Photography in W. G. Sebald's *Die Ausgewanderten,*" *Modern Language Review* 98:1 (2003): 117–37, here 126.

[113] W. G. Sebald, *Die Ausgewanderten* (Frankfurt a.M.: Suhrkamp, 1997 [1994]), 292. Hereafter *DA.*

[114] Arthur Williams, "Das korsakowsche Symptom," 81.

[115] See my "German Nostalgia? Remembering German-Jewish Life in W. G. Sebald's *Die Ausgewanderten* and *Austerlitz,*" *Germanic Review* 79:3 (2004): 181–202.

[116] W. G. Sebald, *Austerlitz* (Munich: Hanser, 2001), 5. Hereafter *A.*

[117] Anne Fuchs, "'Phantomspuren': Zu W. G. Sebalds Poetik der Erinnerung in *Austerlitz,*" *German Life and Letters* 56:3 (2003): 281–98, here 282.

[118] Iris Radisch, "Der Waschbär der falschen Welt," *Die Zeit,* 5 April 2001, 55.

[119] Gunhild Kübler, "Dem Freund erzählen," 41.

[120] Carole Angier, "In the Killing Fields," *Guardian,* 23 May 1998, 9. Cited in Arthur Williams, "Das korsakowsche Symptom," 66.

7: From the Province to Berlin

Alle reden von Berlin, aber was soll das sein.
— Kathrin Röggla, *Abrauschen*

WRITER AND ACADEMIC W. G. SEBALD, in his book on Austrian literature, declares: "Je mehr von der Heimat die Rede ist, desto weniger gibt es sie."[1] Elsewhere, speaking of fiction in the German language in general, he elaborates: *Heimat* is "ein *mirage,* eine Luftspiegelung." It is, of course, literature itself that is the most important instrument of this myth, deploying "ihre ganze ethnopoetische Kraft" to deliver "authentische Beschreibungen," Sebald claims, "aus einer sagenhaften Provinz."[2] *Heimat* and *Provinz* — these are two recurring themes in German-language writing, and, needless to say, of the effort to define German identity.

The tradition of writing about *Heimat* upon which Sebald draws begins, as Norbert Mecklenburg has established in a number of canonical studies, with the opposition of the province and modernity during the period of rapid industrialization towards the end of the nineteenth century. On the one side, therefore, Mecklenburg depicts a literary avant-garde which celebrated the urban, the cosmopolitan and the complexity of modern life. Opposed to this, he describes the anti-modern impulse of a body of writing stressing traditional values and community.[3] It was precisely this inherently conservative desire for order and the exclusion of all traces of difference that came to be seen as discredited from the late 1960s because of the way it seemed to function as a precursor of Nazi ideology.[4] From the time of the student protests, accordingly, anti-*Heimat* novels, plays, and films such as Volker Schlöndorff's TV production *Der plötzliche Reichtum der armen Leute von Krombach* (1970), Martin Speer's *Jagdszenen aus Niederbayern* (1966) or Franz Xaver Kroetz's *Wildwechsel* (1968) began to feature heavily in West German cultural production.[5]

More affirmative writing about the province did not entirely disappear after '68, of course, but it was regarded with suspicion by many. Martin Walser, for one, has attracted much opprobrium on account of a series of novels published from the 1970s onwards which appear to celebrate the "authenticity" of the province over the "affectations" of the Federal Republic, or indulge in nostalgia for the eastern provinces lost after the Second World War. Wolf, in *Dorle und Wolf* (1987), thinks fondly of "Memel," "Riga" and "Revel," although the narrator is adamant: "Nicht daß er's wiederhaben wollte. Den Verlust bedauern dürfen wollte er."[6] More generally, regional presses have long published works by "local" authors on "local subjects." In this chapter, however, we look at the way the province, after unification, once again became central to the efforts of a much broader assortment of very different writers seeking to imagine a German "normality." This entails an examination of the ambiguity of the very notion of provinciality. Thus *Provinz* may suggest a degree of authenticity on which it might be possible to draw in order to resist the "ahistorical normality" associated with globalization. This would be an appeal to the "longitudinal normality" of "German" traditions. Alternatively, the term *provinziell* may be deployed in a derogatory fashion precisely as a means of describing the way the bland "latitudinal normality" of the present-day Federal Republic, its tendency to imitate rather than innovate, is already so far progressed as to make it impossible to withstand its inevitable submersion within the globalized culture industry. Towards the end of this chapter, we turn to efforts in the late 1990s to overcome *this* particular understanding of provinciality by recreating the city of Berlin as a cultural focal point for the new Germany.

Botho Strauß — Theoretician of *Provinz*

In his description of the qualities associated with traditional forms of German *Heimatliteratur,* Mecklenburg isolates the "utopische Aura, die von alten und neuen zivilisationskritischen Denkmotiven gefärbt ist," a "Bewegung zur 'Rettung des Besonderen,'"[7] and what he calls a "verträumte Innerlichkeit" and a "Spiritualisierung der Provinz."[8] Yet, far from being defunct, these characteristics are precisely those that are to be found in the work of a writer who has become perhaps the most vocal champion of the virtues of *Provinz* and the scourge of all that is shallow, trite, and trivial — that is, "modern" — in the Federal Republic: Botho Strauß.

Although best known for his dramas, Strauß has nonetheless produced a corpus of literary and essayistic works since unification which combine moments of autobiographical reflection, social comment, philosophical abstraction, fragmentary insights, and fictional elements. The themes of his highly combative oeuvre, which, as Thomas Assheuer notes, amounts to a conservative reworking of the "linken Kritik an der Kulturindustrie" pioneered by the Frankfurt School,[9] are as follows: the superficiality and artificiality of the Federal Republic, the hollowness of modern life, the sanctity of language, and the desire to return to the "genuineness" of the province in order to escape the countless deceptions of the city, global media culture, and consumerism. Throughout, Strauß is indebted to what Stephen Brockmann has termed the "romantic anti-capitalist tradition" in German thought and literature.[10] In both formal and thematic terms, therefore — with a penchant for the fragmentary and the metaphysical — he alludes to Schopenhauer, Wagner, Nietzsche, Tönnies, Spengler, Heidegger, and others discredited by their association with National Socialism, in an expression of repugnance with the modern world.

Strauß's "Anschwellender Bocksgesang" first appeared in *Spiegel* magazine in February 1993 and was reprinted as the centerpiece in a collection of essays edited by Heimo Schwilk and Ulrich Schacht, *Die selbstbewußte Nation* (1994), the volume often held to represent the manifesto of the intellectual New Right in the early 1990s. The essay attacks the liberal press and a media culture of "enlightened" cynicism, that is, what the author terms the "bigotte Frömmigkeit des Politischen, des Kritischen und All-Bestreitbaren."[11] More generally, however, Strauß condemns the Federal Republic as a regulated public space in which reason is prized over emotional attachment and perpetual self-criticism esteemed more highly than attachment to tradition (*AB*, 58). The nation's verve, he claims, has been dissipated within a passionless, artificial constitutional order. Here, of course, we are reminded of Martin Walser's similar critique of the Federal Republic, as discussed in chapter three.

From early in the 1990s, Strauß's offensive against present-day Germany is linked to a broader critique of modernity in general. A series of essays in *Beginnlosigkeit* (1992) and fictional fragments in *Wohnen, Dämmern, Lügen* (1994) predict the sentiments of Strauß's first *Heimatroman* of the 1990s, *Die Fehler des Kopisten* (1997). The protagonist of this work, clearly based on the author, dismisses the modern world as "unverträumt, aufgeklärt, vollkommen unsentimental" and calls for a re-aestheticization of the cosmos, a language of spirit and sensibility.[12] This would entail a renewal of faith in beauty and its ability to transcend the merely quotidian, the banality of the immanently political and the ugly excesses of *homo economicus*. Such beauty is to be found in a return to a more "original" concept of the work of art: beauty as capable of resisting instrumentalization and of repairing the damage done by the split in human consciousness which, according to Kant, is a prerequisite of modernity. Strauß, therefore, recalls with nostalgia the enchantment of the undivided subject. His protagonists, and indeed his reader, need not reflect on their intuition of the world — a split in perception which requires individuals to subject their prejudices, beliefs, and pleasures to critical analysis — but are permitted simply to make good the "Verlust des tautologischen Urvertrauens in die Sprache: ich bin der ich bin" which so afflicts the human subject in the modern world.[13] Here, Strauß's understanding of *Anwesenheit* is influenced by thinker and literary critic George Steiner, who argues for the "authentic presence" of the work of art in a world formed by the superficiality of consumerism. Strauß, in fact, wrote the afterword for the German version of Steiner's *Real Presences*, which appeared in 1990.

The 1999 piece "Zeit ohne Vorboten" associates the "sekundäre Welt" more directly with the mediatization of the world, the internet revolution, and the loss of cultural identity. This is an essay which, more than any of other Strauß's works, betrays the influence of the German thinker who, Jan-Werner Müller argues, planted the seeds of the "nationalist postmodernism of post-unification" and sent out a "proto-postmodernist message in a bottle, which was found by ideological [neo-conservative] movements forming themselves in the late 1980s and early 1990s." The figure in question, of course, is Martin Heidegger.[14] In "Zeit ohne Vorboten," Strauß thus presents himself as an "armes deutsches Überbleibsel," as yet untouched by the psychosis of post-modern uprootedness "in den Wässern der Globalität."[15] In a world where everything has become *vernetzt,* however, there are still gaps in the system in which authentic feeling might be experienced. There is a space "für den Fluch, den ersten und rohen" (*ZV,* 97). The pain of "being-in-the-world," that foundational Heideggerian moment, offers some resistance to the blandly anaesthetizing effects of the commodity culture. In the confrontation with the fundamentals of life and death — joy, awe, longing, and loss — the individual snatches a split second of genuine experience, an instant of unmediated emotion.

Where is such identity with the essential self most likely to be experienced? For Strauß, the answer is self-evident: "Je großspuriger ('globaler') man redet und rechnet und denkt, um so gewisser findet die letze Ritzung, die das Wort vermag, in einer sehr entlegenen Provinz statt" (*ZV,* 97). In *Die Fehler des Kopisten,* the author retreats into the province with his son. It is here that he experiences the metaphysical union of word and deed: "Ich ließ ein Lamm schlachten [. . .] So wie ich mit Wörten die erzählbare Geschichte zerstückle, so teilte ich hier mit dem Beil das warme Fleisch" (*FK,* 25). Similarly, in *Das Partikular,* which tells of a failed love affair but which also gives over space to its narrator to reflect on sex, commerce, and God, it is only away from the metropolis that beauty can be felt. The island of Zehl, to which the narrator retreats, "erhebt sich allerdings schroff aus den Fluten gewöhnlicher Berührungen und Kontakte, ihre Erde zeigt das Versteinerte von lauter flüchtig Schönem."[16] Beauty, transience, and resistance: these define Strauß's *Provinz.*

In "Zeit ohne Vorboten," Strauß offers a cryptic comment on the calls for a *Neue Lesbarkeit* and *Unterhaltsamkeit* that dominated discussions of German literature in the 1990s: "Der Gegensatz zur leserfreundlichen Literatur ist nicht die leservergrämende, sondern der andere Leser. Dem das Lesen schwerfällt" (*ZV*, 103). The work of the authors to be considered next, Peter Handke and Arnold Stadler, is certainly demanding: an intentional obscurity and density is set against the platitudes of the culture industry, and of politics, society, and the media in the modern Federal Republic. In Stadler's case, an ironic appropriation of the tropes of the *Heimatroman* hints at the pain felt by the individual cast out from the comforts and security of "home" into the anonymity of the modern consumer society.

The Authenticity of the Province?

Peter Handke has been a controversial figure since his decision to declare his residency of the *Elfenbeinturm* — his indifference to the mundane, merely *political* issues of the day and allegiance to the "eternal" principles of art — at the meeting of the *Gruppe 47* in Princeton in 1966 — that is, at the height of the worldwide protests against the Vietnam War. Thirty years later, the Austrian author's supposedly apolitical stance once again caused a highly political disagreement following his publication of a travel report in the *Süddeutsche Zeitung* on 5 and 13 January 1996 on his journey to the former Yugoslavia, entitled "Gerechtigkeit für Serbien."[17]

The full title of the book which derived from the essays *Eine winterliche Reise zu den Flüssen Donau, Save, Morawa und Drina oder Gerechtigkeit für Serbien*[18] left no doubt as to Handke's attitude towards the international condemnation of Serbia's aggression against those states attempting to break away from Yugoslavia in the early 1990s. The author attacked the international media for their "defamatory campaign" against the "Land der allgemein so genannten 'Agressoren,'"[19] western governments for their hypocritical willingness to overlook the crimes committed by other parties, and the public in Germany and Austria for its sentimentalization of those fighting against Serbia. As might be expected, Handke was roundly criticized by much of the liberal press. Three years later, in 1999, the outrage caused by Handke's apparent indifference to the pain caused by Serbian expansionism was reignited when he opted to defend Slobodan Milošević during the Kosovo conflict. NATO attacks on Serbia and Kosovo, with the intention of removing Serbian forces from that province, clearly betrayed, he stated, the duplicity of the West.[20]

It was not only Handke's defense of Serbia that was provocative, however. Critics were also outraged by his invocation of a discredited German tradition which presented the province as essentially innocent, both untouched by the betrayals of modernity and ignorant of the crimes being committed beyond its borders and yet in its name. Handke's journey to the rivers of Donau, Save, Morawa, and Drina thus constituted, Hans Hahn reminds us, "an individual voyage of self-discovery, a form of 'Wiederholung': returning to the region in order to trace the origins of his Slovenian grandfather."[21] Indeed, the author admits that one of the motives for his trip was to observe the country: "Doch es lockte mich auch, einfach das Land anzuschauen" (*GS,* 13). Yet what Handke sees, Hahn continues, appears as a "heile Welt," a place of sanctuary, security, and peace, a place of blissful unawareness in which the locals, although only a short distance from Srebrnica — the city made infamous by the Serbian massacre of thousands of Muslim men on 11 July 1995 — "had heard 'nearly nothing' of the war and regretted that they were no longer able to swim in the river Drina."[22] Here, we might be reminded of Walser's *Ein springender Brunnen,* published two years later, and set in 1933–45, which propagates a similar fiction: that its provincial protagonists were mercifully disconnected, and disassociated, from the horrors taking place in the wider world. For Walser, that *Heimat* may be considered to be something "ungeheuer Beschränktes, etwas ungeheuer Provinzielles" can only be positive. In this interview of 1997, he speaks of its virtues: "das schöne Wort Kosmos. Es ist die vollkommene Geschlossenheit!"[23]

Arnold Stadler, like Handke, volubly objected to western intervention in Kosovo in early 1999. In his case, however, his recriminations were rooted less in any sympathy for the Serbian cause than in what he saw as the moral hypocrisy of those such as Foreign Minister Joschka Fischer who justified "Bombenabwürfe im Namen der Menschenrechte."[24] The author of a number of collections of poetry, including *Kein Herz und keine Seele* (1986) and *Gedichte aufs Land* (1998), studies of Brecht, Paul Celan (1989) and Hebbel (1999), travel accounts such as *Volubilis: Oder Meine Reise ans Ende der Welt* (1999) and *Ausflug nach Afrika* (1999), Hebrew translations, and six novels, Stadler — an outsider on the literary scene until he won the Büchner prize in 1999 — sees himself, like Handke, as a writer "der die Heimatlosigkeit beschreibt."[25] Yet his work resounds with the realization that *Heimat,* for his contemporaries, has no "metaphorische oder sonstige Bedeutung."[26] Nor does this author think it possible to indulge — as Handke seems to do in his accompanying text to Lisl Ponger's photo-essay *Ein Wortland: Eine Reise durch Kärnten, Slowenien, Friaul, Istrien und Dalmatien* (1998) — in a fantasy of blissful innocence. Stadler is adamant: "Ja, dieses Jahrhundert [. . .] bot eine Leben in der Nachbarschaft von Verbrennungsöfen." "Wo soll da noch Heimat sein?," he asks.[27]

Nevertheless, Stadler's fiction speaks precisely of the loss of *Heimat* and of the degradations of the modern consumer society. His novels, as he claims in an interview of 1999, depict the "Menschen auf dem Land

[. . .]. Sein langsames Aussterben, die Schmerzlaute seiner Sprache, daß seine Schweine in die Städte verfrachtet und industriell ausgeschlachtet werden wie seine alten Wörter, die das Fernsehen längst überrollt hat."[28] In *Ich war einmal* (1989), Stadler presents a life on the very margins of modernity — his own childhood in Meßkirch in Oberschwaben — in a work that defines the struggle between the conflicting desires of *Fernweh* and *Heimweh*. This theme also permeates *Feuerland* (1992), in which the narrator travels to Patagonia only to find that things are as at home, *Mein Hund, meine Sau, mein Leben* (1994), and *Der Tod und Ich, wir zwei* (1996). Throughout, the Heideggerian concepts of "In-der-Welt-Sein"[29] and "Schmerz als Grundriß" (*MH*, 13) are central, as is the notion of pain as proof of existence: "*Es tat weh und ich war da*" (*MH*, 143). In *Der Tod und Ich, wie zwei*, the narrator, an author, speaks of the pressures of finding a publisher for his "unverfilmbare Angelegenheit" in the philistine, American-style culture "der unbegrenzten Möglichkeiten."[30] Finally, he sends his manuscript to the Residenz Verlag (the novel's publisher!) but remains indifferent to the outcome: "Wenn sie nicht wollen, werde ich mich auch nicht umbringen" (*DTI*, 212).[31]

The 1999 novel *Ein hinreissender Schrötthändler* begins with its narrator opening his door to a stranger dressed in a "Adidas-Hose" with "schwarz-rot-goldenen Seitenstreifen" and holding a sports' bag.[32] This is the "enticing scrap merchant" of the title, a young man whose occupation, personality, and provenance exemplify the Berlin Republic of the newly-elected chancellor, Gerhard Schröder: despite his attire, Adrian is not German but an English-speaker whose name hints at the Adriatic. Modern Germany is pure pastiche, a blend of trite global fads and adopted identities, a nation obsessed with recycling because it can produce nothing original. The alacrity with which the narrator and his wife accept this asylum seeker into their home, moreover, hints at the Republic's anxious "political correctness." Enlightened and left-leaning — Gabi fantasizes about the photogenic Schröder during sex — and tax-aware, with a number of "Abschreibungsobjekte" in Apolda (*HS*, 57), their lives are lived out in a spiritual vacuum for which consumerism, in the shape, for example, of a "schmerzstillenden Mercedes" (*HS*, 54), offers only partial relief.

The narrator, who remains nameless throughout, originally hails from the southwestern German provincial hinterland of Kreenheinstetten but is now part of the urban middle-classes whose "politically-correct," cosmopolitan attitudes broadly define the Berlin Republic. He is a schoolteacher whose subject is "die unerfreulichste aller Fächer — Geschichte" (*HS*, 10), and who has internalized — almost — the values of the liberal, educated elite of the city of Hamburg, the north German conurbation in which his wife was born and which is now their home: "Wahrscheinlich

sagte ich doch nicht 'schwulenfeindlich,' sondern 'intolerant,' 'wenig liberal' oder 'politisch nicht korrekt'" (*HS,* 106). Yet he has become "einer,
der nicht am Leben teilnimmt" (*HS,* 123). He is an outsider who regrets
the loss of the sacrosanct. In the metropolitan culture of pragmatic conformity that he now inhabits, there is no marveling at the mysteries of being, no sense of amazement, and no feeling of awe, whether at the
majesty of God or the pity of human existence. The narrator and his
relatives once "staunten [. . .] über die Größe der Welt" (*HS,* 37) and
sustained the "Illusion, daß es etwas gibt, was es nicht gibt und nie
gegeben hat" (*HS,* 11–12). Now that he has seen the "Größe der Welt"
for himself, however, there is nothing left at which he might wonder.

Stadler's novel is most obviously a satire on the "normality" — for
this read bland conformity — of the fledgling Berlin Republic. Chancellor
Schröder's new Germany, it is implied, is superficial, lacking in historical
awareness and primarily an instrument for the reconciliation of competing
economic interests. Insofar as modern Germany has any religious or spiritual foundation at all, it is the passionless, rationalistic Protestantism of
the north of the country — what Botho Strauß describes as "die
erstickende, satte Konvention des intellektuellen Protestantismus (das
einzige geistige Originalerzeugnis der Bundesrepublik)"[33] — rather than
the catholic emphasis on immediacy, emotion, and the mystical typical of
the more provincial south. This is reminiscent of Martin Walser's critique
of the stifling banality and soulless rationality of the Federal Republic, as
discussed in chapter three. As in Walser's *Ein springender Brunnen,* there
is also an implied defense, albeit more ironic here, of those Germans who,
between 1933 and 1945, lived far from the centers of Nazi power: "Wir
in Kreenheinstetten waren keine Nazis, vielleicht auch nur, weil man uns
übersehen hat" (*HS,* 168). At the same time, as Harald Klaus suggests,
the novel reflects more generally on the phenomenon of globalization:
"Seit wir die Welt 'globalisiert' haben, sind wir nirgends mehr zu
Hause."[34] In the second part of the text, then, when the narrator abandons his wife to Adrian's worldly lustfulness in order to journey to Kreenheinstetten in search of his past, the place to which he returns is not the
Provinz that he had imagined.

Part two is altogether more melancholic, although no less ironic, than
part one. The narrator travels back to Kreenheinstetten for the funeral of
Irmelda Swichtenberg, "eine Vertriebene" whose presence in the village
paradoxically provides "ein letzter Beweis, daß es Heimat gibt" (*HS,*
136), and yet his rural refuge from the superficiality of the city no long
exists. He has no idea "wer noch lebte und wer schon tot war" (*HS,* 147)
and cannot integrate the "neuen Häuser, die keine Geschichte haben und
haben werden" into his memories of the past. Even the dialect greeting,
"Bischd au do?," a "Bestätigung in unserer Muttersprache, daß wir da

waren" (*HS,* 154), has become meaningless. Nobody is truly interested in his story of an uncle missing in the war (*HS,* 191), and the inn — once owned by his parents and sold by his brother so that he can move to Spain — no longer serves the aptly named "oberschwäbische Seele" (*HS,* 160), the celebrated local dish. The modern world has arrived, and the region has sacrificed its soul. The narrator's friends run detective agencies and real estate firms, dye their hair a modish "schwarz-rot," and fret a-bout their weight, houses, and insurance (*HS,* 157–62). They lead solitary existences, even when married — "wir sind doch alle Single heutzutage" (*HS,* 162) — worry about the "Ozonloch" (*HS,* 164), complain about their sex lives (*HS,* 177), have children called Mike and Tom, drink high-energy drinks, and, perhaps most revealing of all, drive "Geländewagen" because of their "Angst vor dem Steckenbleiben" (*HS,* 182).

What makes Stadler's text so effective is the fact that it starts out from the certainty that, in the present day, the German province is no less "modern," co-opted, or integrated than the city. The novel draws on the tradition of the *Heimatroman,* and yet even as it attacks modernity, displays its own decidedly modernist sensibilities. The entire narrative is constructed as a piece of confessional fiction designed to appeal to a contemporary fascination with salacious self-revelation. At the same time, however, the narrator, supposedly the book's author, suffers *precisely* because his sense of loss at the disappearance of *Heimat* can only be articulated, in a metropolitan culture that derides real emotions as insufficiently *urbane,* via that most affected of literary techniques: self-conscious irony. This repackages genuine feeling for the gratification of an audience for which literature is a form of "Kontaktanzeige": "Diese Anzeige, ich weiß, es gab Menschen, Männer und Frauen, die haben auf diese Anzeigen hin gewichst, die saßen zu Hause, lasen meinen Selbstbeschreibungsversuch und befriedigten sich dabei" (*HS,* 111). Fittingly, the narrator becomes a regular visitor to a psychoanalyst, the diagnostician of that most modern of illnesses: schizophrenia.

At the close of his narrative, Stadler's protagonist bemoans the impossibility of authentic communication, even between man and wife: "Eigentlich wollte ich ihr nur sagen, wie weh es tat, wie einst, als ich vom Dreirad gefallen war" (*HS,* 235). Whether it be feelings of inadequacy, personal trauma, or a sense of loss following the destruction of *Heimat,* any genuine expression of pain is disqualified: "Weil alle Stellen so schön verheilen. Nichts läßt man uns, nicht einmal den Schmerz, und eines Tages wird alles vergessen sein" (*HS,* 232). All that is left in a society in which emotions are either simulated or imported from a global culture are what the narrator still experiences, albeit only with a large dose of self-conscious humor, as those most "German" of German words: "das Geheimnis, die Vergänglichkeit, die Sehnsucht, das Heimweh!" and "deutlich und abgesetzt: Weltschmerz" (*HS*, 69). The implication is that the only genuine experience of pain now permissible is an ironic gesture of regret that the genuine experience of pain is no longer permissible.

In Stadler's *Sehnsucht* (2002), the narrator travels to Bleckede, in the Lüneburger Heide, after many years in Berlin. His motivation, as the title of the novel hints, is to revive an authentic sense of "longing," an emotion first revealed to him by his teacher, Schultze, a "Heimatvertriebener" who took his pupils to the coast of northern Germany and bid them to "alles aufsagen, was vorbei und verloren war, vor allem die Inseln" (*S*, 290). Schultze, the narrator insists, "war wohl kein Revisionist, er hatte nur vielleicht ab und zu mal Heimweh, was er verschweig," and yet "Heimweh," following the shifts in moral and social sensibilities after '68, was considered "peinlicher als Küssen unter freiem Himmel" (*S*, 287). Any mention of the lost territories was taboo — overt, even exhibitionist, sexual displays were not. Only in the 1990s did it once again become possible to speak of *Heimat*, but the same social revolution that rendered innocent memories of childhood suspect whilst destroying the sanctity of sexual intimacy had, by then, led to the emergence of a world of inauthenticity and manufactured emotions. Towards the end of *Sehnsucht*, accordingly, the narrator ends up in a sex-club, the BLUE MOON, in which he tries, disastrously, to relive *das erste Mal*. There is no way back, and the future holds no prospect of *genuine* experience.

"Nicht einmal die Erektionen läßt man uns, nicht einmal die Erinnerung daran, nicht einmal die Erinnerungen an den Schmerz unter dem Frisiermantel."[35] *Sehnsucht*, like *Ein hinreissender Schrotthändler*, as this example of fatuously inaccurate self-citation illustrates, regrets the annihilation of longing. In the modern, demystified world, anticipation has been rendered obsolete. The individual is fully informed of all available products, takes what is desired, but no longer experiences the *boundaries* which once reminded of rootedness in time and space. Longing, once located in the individual's desire to set out from home and explore what lies beyond, has been superceded — the province has gone "online": "Doch gerade diese Gegenden waren bald die ersten, die angeschlossen waren" (*S*, 62). In the Lüneburger Heide, as in the other backwaters that the narrator tours with his "Verbraucher-Vortrag" (*S*, 15), the victory of cultural homogeneity and global networking is complete.

In Stadler's novels, characters leave the province for the city only to return in an effort to re-acquire the capacity for authentic feeling. Their efforts are always unsuccessful, but there may be a certain profit to be had from failure itself. "Mir schien," remarks the narrator of *Sehnsucht* in a moment of despair at the modern world, "daß ich nichts als dieser Sehnsucht, jener ganz bestimmten Stelle, entgegenlebte, auf die nichts als Heimweh folgte" (*S*, 158). Such expressions of loss, however, occasionally extend beyond melancholia and indict the fetishization of immediacy promoted by globalized capitalism. For the cultural conservative Arnold Stadler, Germany's obsession with global consumerism necessarily degenerates into an "ahistorical normality." The only form of resistance that remains open to the individual out-of-synch with the demoralizingly pragmatic and demystified epoch in which he or she lives, therefore, is a plaintive irony.

The Federal Republic as "Provincial"

In the work of Hans-Ulrich Treichel, characters return only reluctantly to the province. More often than not they share with their author the depressing certainty that memories of a childhood passed in Germany's parochial backwoods offer no Proustian "Madeleine-Erlebnis," but only "Pappkartons" and "Altpapier," or the "Geruch von Holzwolle," as he puts it in an essay, "Lektionen der Leere: Eine Kindheit auf dem Lande: Oder wie ich Schriftsteller wurde" (2000). In place of the "fullness" conjured up by Strauß or Handke, Treichel senses only the illusion of substance: "Die Leere ist ohne Zweifel meine prägendste Kindheitserfahrung." The objects that inhabit his memories possess nothing of "vom Rilkeschen 'Ding der Dinge,'" nor anything "vom Ding Heideggers mit seiner 'verborgenen Dingheit.'"[36] The same impression of emptiness is intimated in two volumes of essays, *Von Leib und Seele* (1992) and *Heimatkunde oder alles ist heiter und edel* (1996). These detail with laconic dexterity the author's strained and yet obsessive relationship with his "ostwestfälischen Heimat,"[37] and add up a wide-ranging condemnation of the marginality of modern-day Germany and its inhibiting self-doubt. As such, Treichel indicts the flight into provinciality and adapts it as a metaphor for the inability of Germany *as a whole* to project a self-confident and distinctive identity of its own.[38]

Treichel's *Tristanakkord* (2000) initially recalls the writing of Martin Walser. Indeed, the author himself has declared that he was "in gewisser Weise auf [Walsers] *Gallistl'sche Krankheit* geprägt,"[39] and critics, including Martin Ebel, have pointed to the "Produktivität des Scheiterns" in his work, "wie wir sie von Martin Walser kennen."[40] Yet Treichel's province, as the ironic extension — *alles ist heiter und edel* — of his adaptation of the title of Walser's volume of essays *Heimatkunde* (1968) hints, has little in common with the rural landscapes depicted by the older author.[41] In *Tristanakkord,* accordingly, the backwater of Emsfelde from which the protagonist hails appears as a flat, featureless substitute for the *Heimat* irreversibly lost to Georg's parents, refugees expelled from the east after 1945, but scarcely regretted by their son. Unlike his parents, Georg draws no comfort from a sense of rootedness in a genuinely German past or in the natural beauty of the regions. For him, the province is precisely that: *provincial.* Memories of his own childhood are left behind as soon as he crosses the Ems, "der Strom des Vergessens" to study in the city for a doctorate.[42] This is his *Lethe,* the river at the edge of the underworld into which the dead plunge in order to wash away the misery of their lives as they pass over into Hades. Subsequently, it appears that he has succeeded in escaping the narrow confines of his childhood. Employed by the composer Bergmann to proofread his memoirs, Georg accompanies the international superstar to Scotland, New York, and finally to Sicily.

"Zuviel Emsfelde und zuwenig New York" (*T,* 190) — thus Georg is described by the narrator. Notwithstanding his efforts to cast off his past, he remains a product of his upbringing, ill at ease and unable to simulate the cosmopolitan sophistication of those he meets as he travels in Bergmann's wake. Indeed, he is manifestly, even hopelessly, fascinated by Bergmann, despite the fact that the latter is the most hypocritical kind of elitist, a snob who despises the mass entertainment industry but who rushes to appear on talk shows.[43] For all his attraction to the world Bergmann inhabits, Georg cannot conceal the fact that he does not belong: "nur Georg schaute sauertöpfisch drein, was ihm selbst nicht behagte, was aber wohl seine Natur war: die emsländische Natur" (*T,* 123). Unlike Steven, the English Ph.D. student also in Bergmann's service, Georg is neither shrewd in business nor media-wise. Instead, he is humiliated by his lack of worldliness. Asked whether he likes New York, Georg responds: "'It's okay,'" in his predictably impoverished English. The suitably self-assured answer, he laments, would have been: "'It's just great' oder 'it's marvellous, it's wonderful'" (*T,* 121).

Bergmann's success derives from the fact that he has been able to shake off his own "emsländische Herkunft" (*T,* 23). He understands that the only way to achieve an international profile is to abandon the outmoded sentimentality associated with German artistic traditions and adopt the affectation of urban sophistication required of "high-brow" performers within the global culture industry. Georg, in contrast, is unable to set aside his provinciality in his own artistic endeavors. Consequently, he produces only unoriginal imitations of landmark German works. His model, he claims absurdly, is "Goethes junger Werther" who "[sich] dann als der größte Künstler fühlen konnte, wenn er sich in die freie Natur begab, auf einen Hügel setzte und die Sonne aufgehen ließ" (*T,* 29). Yet his efforts are pitiful. He has published a short volume of maudlin verse in the aptly-named *Edition Ausweg,* improvises (badly) Beethoven along with Hendrix, and, when asked by Bergmann to write a "Hymne" for a new piece of music, copies liberally from a Georg Heym poem (*T,* 215–16).

In Treichel's work, the province has no metaphysical significance. Yet nor has Germany developed a metropolitan self-confidence which can engage with the outside world in anything but an imitative, anxiously diffident fashion. *Tristanakkord* touches on issues of globalization, cultural homogenization, and the present-day relevance of the German literary and philosophical heritage, but, unlike in the writing of Strauß, Handke or Stadler, there is no sense that the banality of contemporary culture might be resisted by means of an appeal to the "spiritual superiority" of German traditions rooted in the "authenticity" of the province. Much as Georg is drawn to emulate the "German" sensibility embodied by Wagner, he is incapable even of recognizing the composer's famed Tristan chord. Georg desires to revive a tradition that is, with Wagner, "sehnsüchtig-traurig und unerlöst" (*T,* 79), and yet the connection to this heritage is too tenuous.

Andreas Maier, an author somewhat younger than Strauß, Handke, Stadler or Treichel (he was born in 1967), writes, as Wolfgang Emmerich notes in his review of Maier's *Klausen* (2002), "über ganz andere Dinge als die selbsternannten Sprecher seiner Generation. DressCodes, Popsongs, TV-Formate — die ganze Welt als mediale Simulation: nichts davon kommt bei Maier vor."[44] Yet this need not be taken to imply that his *Wäldchestag* (2000), a book, which as Dieter Stolz claims, speaks "im weitesten Sinne von Heimat," remains at a distance from current deliberations on the style, form, and substance of the Berlin Republic. In common with works by other younger writers, Stolz proposes, including Christoph Hamann's *Seegfrörne* (1998), Christoph Peters's *Stadt Land Fluß* (1999) and Karen Duve's *Regenroman* (1999), Maier's text reveals a "literarisch bearbeitete, zum Mikrokosmos verdichtete Provinz." These novels present what Stolz describes as an "entzaubernde Bestandsaufnahme in säkularisierten Zeiten."[45]

Narrated, as Stolz observes, "fast durchgehend im Konjunktiv I" and consisting of only two sentences "auf 315 Seiten,"[46] *Wäldchestag* tells the story of the death of Sebastian Adomeit, a seventy-year-old local man not much liked by his neighbors, and of the opening of his will on the Tuesday following Whitsun, on "Wälchestag," a day traditionally given over to drunken revelry in the woods around Florstadt in the Wetterau region of Hessen. Outraged by what they take to be his deliberate decision to organize his death, funeral, and testament in such a fashion as to interrupt their carousing, Adomeit's neighbors nonetheless turn up to the reading of the will and are joined there by "outsiders," including Sebastian's estranged sister, Jeanette Adomeit, Herr Halberstadt, a lawyer looking after her interests, her daughter Frau Mohr and son-in-law Herr Mohr, her granddaughter Katja, and an aged relative Frau Lenchen. Kaja's boyfriend, Benno, also arrives, without her knowledge, shortly before the festivities which take place the night before the will is made public. Benno, the "Südhesse," quickly becomes something of an obsession for local youth Anton Wiesner, who, despite his relationship with Ute (daughter of the Bertholds) and his unresolved flirtation with a Turkish girl, Günes, is drawn to Katja but barely able to speak to her. Wiesner, along with his friend Kurt Bucerius, plans to travel to China in a bus which they have reconditioned but never achieves more than a brief flight over the area in a light aircraft that he takes from the nearby airport. Indeed, they are lucky to escape detection during a police sweep on their improvised garage to check for stolen engines and are saved only by the incompetence of the officer in charge.

More minor figures feature throughout. These include Frau Weber, Wiesner's grandmother; Weihnöter, the solicitor originally hailing from the city who is entrusted with the opening of the will; Breitinger, an avid composer of *Leserbriefe;* Herr Munk, a man given to swift moral judgments; Mulat, about whom little detail is given; Becker, the priest who is always quick with a platitude; Rudolf, a local politician, and his wife. We are also introduced to Frau Strobel, Adomeit's maid, who becomes the subject of local gossip. The target of Breitinger's anti-Semitic slurs: "die Strobel rede auch immer jüdisch,"[47] Strobel suffers a heart attack on the day of the opening of the will and subsequently becomes the subject of much attention. Assuming that Strobel has inherited money from her brother, because of her "*eigenartiger* Beziehung zu dem Verstorbenen" (*W,* 244), Jeanette Adomeit arrives at the hospital in order to claim what is rightly hers. In fact, it turns out that Adomeit has simply rewarded years of service with the proceeds from the sale of land for the construction of the regional airport, money that he himself had always refused to touch.

The web of relationships between characters is as complex as the novel's narrative method. To this extent, *Wäldchestag* offers a west German counterpart to the depiction of the east German province in Ingo Schulze's deceptively named *Simple Storys* (1998). Unlike Schulze's text, however, the density of both social and narrative networks does not imply the possibility of local resistance to the hegemonic aspirations of globalized capitalism. Instead, the province is seen as entirely integrated into the modern consumer society. Just as was the case in Treichel's work, moreover, there is no suggestion that any transcendent gain might be extracted from disenchantment with the destruction of the sense of community associated with the province.

The opening lines of the novel read as follows: "Es ist, hat Schossau gesagt, als sei allem etwas entzogen worden, wie durch einen chemischen Vorgang, eine Substanz, die *nicht mehr* in den Dingen vorhanden sei, obgleich sie doch eigentlich in ihnen vorhanden sein müßte." The text begins, therefore, in a manner that might be expected of Walser, Handke or Stadler — that is, with a declaration of the *deprivation* of the province in modern times, drained of the substance that once inhered in its objects, landscape, and traditions. Yet the narrator continues: "es sei aber, genau betrachtet, nichts in den Dingen nachweisbar, was auf eine vormalige Anwesenheit hindeuten würde." The mythologization of the province is an empty distraction, a mere illusion of presence. The same can be said of the tale that he and his friend Schuster seem to have told the narrator: "Er könne gar nicht mehr sagen, was von dieser ganzen Geschichte tatsächlich passiert sei" (*W*, 7). In this story, there will be no make-believe, no metaphysical union of word and deed. In fact, the attempt to reconcile what he has seen and what he relates can only lead to a disorientating split: "Ein aggressiver innerer Dialog habe sich zwischen ihm und ihm selbst entsponnen" (*W*, 8). The content, as much as the form, will remain in the conditional tense.

Schossau and Schuster are the only people to have had an understanding of Adomeit. A third man, Wollitz, has left, presumably for the city. All three are described by Becker as "wirklich schätzenswerte Erben" of Adomeit's "Streitkultur" (*W*, 110). The tribute, of course, is ironic. Adomeit was a constant reminder to local people of their lack of autonomy and, more substantively, of their collusion in the annihilation of their local heritage. Thus it turns out that the rift between Adomeit and his sister had to do with the fact that she had been the one who sold their land, without his prior knowledge, to the developers of the site for the airport against which he had long protested on account of its environmental impact. Adomeit is a "Naturkundler" (*W*, 31) and, as such, cannot help but be aggrieved by the presence of an airport built to give the Wetterauer the feeling that they are "modern." In fact, as Weihnöter — the lawyer who originates in the city — reports, Adomeit was the only local whose manner of living embodied "schlicht und einfach sein Wetterauer Sein" (*W*, 62).

Towards the end of his life, we are told, Adomeit's daughter-in-law was well on the way to imposing upon him precisely the "Normalität" which, Schossau reports, local people always felt he lacked. Indeed, this unwanted attention may have been the cause for Adomeit's putative decision to die prematurely and deny his neighbors the satisfaction of seeing him forced into dependence upon their patronizing, even colonizing benevolence. In bringing the increasingly debilitated man soup, then, his daughter-in-law was finally able to turn him into a "ganz normalen Greis mit einer ganz normalen Bedürftigkeit" (*W*, 9–10). Normality, for the inhabitants of Florstadt, as elsewhere in the Republic, is a matter of ensuring the greatest possible individual affluence at the lowest possible cost. The *Krankenkasse* hence becomes the greatest social good, an instrument of public enlightenment, albeit enlightenment in the narrowest sense of the pursuit of maximum economic effectiveness: "je mehr die Leute selbst für ihre Gesundheit sorgten und auf diese achteten, desto billiger sei das, und dann könnten die Beiträge sinken, die ja im Augenblick sehr hoch seien" (*W,* 11). Indeed, the *Krankenkasse* is elevated to an almost metaphysical status. This is the paradox of the narrative. Schossau's disillusionment with the futility of efforts to invest the province with higher significance leads him to present his observations to the narrator, as the novel's somewhat unusual subtitle indicates, "zur Vorlage an die Kommission zur Bewilligung von Kuren auf Betragsbasis der hiesigen Kassenstelle." This, presumably, signals his ironic response to the advertisement with which the text comes to a close: "*AOK-Kuren: Existenzen neuen Sinn geben*" (*W,* 315). (*AOK* stands for *Allgemeine Ortskrankenkasse*).

By means of their insights on the day of the funeral, in the course of the *Wäldchestag* festivities, and during the reading of the will, Schossau and Schuster provide a revealing commentary on the social masks donned by the locals for the sake of sustaining the myth of a community at one with itself. More generally, however, as Helmut Karasek avers, Maier's narrative also portrays "das dicht gewebte Panorama einer kleinen Welt, die unsere große ist." Its complex testimonies are, Karasek goes on to say: "Nachrichten aus der Provinz, in der wir alle leben."[48] The new German "normality" represents a form of continuity: a sheltered, if dull, provinciality appears to be firmly entrenched.

The texts by Strauß, Stadler, Treichel considered in this chapter recall, each in its own way, the criticisms directed at the "old," pre-1990 Federal Republic, and indeed of post-unification Germany, by Karl Heinz Bohrer[49] and Frank Schirrmacher[50] discussed at the beginning of chapter one. For Strauß and Stadler, as indeed for Martin Walser, Germany's mediocrity is only to be overcome by drawing on the truly "authentic" traditions of the German province and the German cultural heritage. In Stadler's case, as we have seen, such an appropriation may only ever be ironic. In Treichel's work, conversely, the very notion of a "genuine" German sensibility is presented as an illusion from the outset. In *Der irdische Amor* (2002), the protagonist, a student of art history, travels to Italy in the footsteps of Herder, Winckelmann, and Goethe (although he refers directly only to Winckelmann's visits to Greece)[51] but is plagued by flashbacks to his boarding school in *Osthessen* and his childhood as the son of refugee parents who had fled the Russian advance.[52] This German can never leave behind the history that has spawned him. At the end of the book, Albert accepts that he will never be truly "international" and travels home on the advice of a German girl he has met: "'Vergiss die Heimat nicht'" (*DIA,* 242). Here, the return to *Heimat* is an admission of failure, that is, of an inadequate cosmopolitanism.

Maier's *Wäldchestag* too participates in the discussion on the appeal of the "province" in the epoch of globalized consumerism. Unlike the works by Strauß, Stadler, and Treichel examined above, however, it focuses for the most part upon its younger characters. These reject the complacent compliance of their parents who were socialized within the West German welfare state and desire only that their accustomed sense of security should be guaranteed. Yet such displays of alienation are themselves entirely non-productive. Wiesner and his friend Bucerius dream of adventures far from home, but continue to obsess about an everyday reality that consists of snatched kisses with the girls they meet in second-rate discos and, in Wiesner's case, adolescent quarrels with his parents and a short flight that never takes him out of sight of the Wetterau. Benno, the "Südhesse," cannot express himself, whether to Katja or to anybody else. The enigmatic statements which so fascinate Wiesner thus intimate teenage melancholia rather than true rebellion as does Benno's wild proposition, an unconscious allusion perhaps to Goethe's *Werther:* "Man hätte zum Beispiel eine Pistole nehmen und gegen den eigenen Kopf richten können, das wäre eine Form für den Beweis gewesen" (*W,* 184–85). Even Schossau and Schuster, for all their insight into the narrow-mindedness of provincial Germany, fail to leave.

If Maier's younger characters *were* to quit the province, where would they go? In our next section, we look at the attempt, at the end of the 1990s, to re-establish Germany's "new-old" capital city as a showcase for the values of openness, tolerance, experimentation, and cultural diversity espoused by the intellectual and political elites of the Berlin Republic. Would Berlin be transformed into a metropolitan center to compete with New York, London or Paris? Could this be the city in which the next generation might be able to define a German "normality" relieved of the burden of the Nazi past and weighed down neither by illusions of "German authenticity" nor by a melancholic parochialism?

Berlin

"Die Gründung durch Umzug hat Berlin wider alle Erwartungen zum exemplarischen Ort der Jetztzeit für die neue Bundesrepublik gemacht," noted Heinz Bude in 2001 in his commentary on contemporary social trends, *Generation Berlin.*[53] The relaunching of Berlin as a global hub of leisure and commerce entailed, on the one hand, an extensive program of architectural development ranging from the reconstruction of the Potsdamer Platz to the restoration of historic buildings such as the Hotel Adlon. This agenda was promoted by civic authorities and by private enterprises in a number of "open events," including, for example, the *Stadtforum Berlin,* a panel of town-planning specialists which presided over a series of public meetings, the *InfoBox,* an information box located on the Potsdamer Platz, and the *Schaustelle Berlin* of 1996, a project designed to promote new public spaces.[54] On the other hand, events such as the "wrapping" in silver fabric and subsequent "unwrapping" of the *Reichstag* by Bulgarian artist Christo appeared to signal a new mood of experimentation in the *cultural* life of the city as much as the political reinvigoration of the country as a whole. Berlin was the only place, insists the youthful protagonist of Benjamin Lebert's *Der Vogel ist ein Rabe* (2003), to be seen: "Das hat man zumindest zu einer bestimmten Zeit gehört [. . .] du musst unbedingt dahin."[55]

In light of the way Berlin came, in the late 1990s, to be so closely associated with the onset of a new phase in German history, summed up in the designation "Berlin Republic," it is not surprising that the fiction of the period should refer directly to the transformation of the city as a metaphor for the broader transformation of the country as a whole. Accordingly, as Susanne Ledanff asserts, a "schiere Masse neuer Berlin-literatur" has since emerged.[56] Uwe Timm's *Johannisnacht* (1996), for instance, portrays the misunderstandings plaguing the relationship between east and west Germans early in the decade and suggests that the "coincidence" of the unwrapping of the *Reichstag* with the summer solstice — another "Wende," this time the "Sonnenwende" — might herald change: "Danach wird etwas anders sein."[57] The obvious question is whether this will be for the better or the worse. F. C. Delius's *Die Flatterzunge* (1999) hints at a negative response to this question. Thus Hannes, the disgraced trombonist who signed a bar tab in Israel with the words Adolf Hitler, turns up at the Potsdamer Platz and feels overwhelmed by the urge to blast out a series of mockingly triumphant chords. Here, Jörg Magenau suggests, omitting any reference to its proximity both to Hitler's Bunker and the Gestapo headquarters from the rebuilding of the Potsdamer Platz functions as "eine Metapher für die unbewältigte deutsche Geschichte, auf der sich die neue Berliner Republik erhebt."[58] In Delius's *Königsmacher* (2001), similarly, the architectural debates of the 1990s point to a fundamental ambivalence in the psyche of the Berlin Republic. Berlin — and, by extension, the "new" Germany — is to be rebuilt, the narrator declares, "entweder mit nachgebauter Tradition oder mit einem gigantischen Triumph über die Tradition, den jedoch niemand überzeugend entwerfen konnte."[59]

Peter Schneider's *Eduards Heimkehr* (1999), Ulrike Zitzlsperger proposes, as much as *Café Komplott: Eine glückliche Begebenheit* (1998) by east German writer Peter Wawerzinek, demonstrate that images of Berlin are frequently shaped by individuals' perceptions of their "past, not by new beginnings."[60] In Schneider's novel, the protagonist struggles to unravel the possible complicity of a grandfather in the expropriation of Jewish property during the Nazi period whilst confronting the squatters occupying the house he has inherited. Wawerzinek's text, on the other hand, tells the story of four east Germans who rob a bank the day the *Reichstag*, renovated by Sir Norman Foster, is to be ceremonially reopened: when one of them commits suicide by jumping from the roof of the Hotel Adlon, the incident draws the attention of the world's media away from this day of national celebration. Thomas Hettche's *Nox* (1995), in which the now-dead narrator follows his murderer through Berlin on 9 November 1989 — the night the new Germany was conceived — and ends up observing her in a pathological institute being mounted by a border guard dog, might similarly allude to the manner in which Berlin's totalitarian pasts patrol the city's efforts to start afresh. In Volker Braun's *Der Wendehals* (1995), the character ICH, an author who has given up writing, accompanies ER, a member of the East German *Akademie der Künste* dismissed after unification, on a walk through Berlin and is prompted by the familiar sights of the city to ruminate on complicity, guilt, and opportunism. Much the same, of course, happens in Christa Wolf's *Leibhaftig* (2002), as discussed in chapter two.

Other recent literary texts, however, are less concerned with Berlin's national socialist or communist pasts and allude instead to the tradition of the "Berlin novel" associated with the late nineteenth and early twentieth century and particularly with the Weimar Republic in the 1920s. Indeed, the unification of Berlin in 1989 and the subsequent accessibility of spaces previously closed off as a consequence of division, means that the city is once more a place in which it is possible to enact what Walter Benjamin, in his *Passagenwerk*, famously referred to as the practice *des illustrativen Sehens*. Berlin in the 1990s is, as it was in the 1920s, once again a city full of railway stations, exhibition halls, and department stores where the *flâneur* may observe and directly experience the exhilarations of modern life and mass society.[61] Berlin's buildings, monuments, public spaces, and transport networks, therefore, may be more than mere triggers for a protagonist's musings on the cruel vagaries of German history. As is demonstrated by "In Berlin," a short story by the Greek-Swiss writer Perikles Monioudis, the city stages a mass of sensory and emotional impressions. For example, a dog is hit by a car — "So etwas habe ich noch nie gesehen" — a woman steps out of the *Friedrichspassagen* and drives away in her car, and a small girl watches on enviously as another child is kissed by her father. In the midst of these apparently banal experiences the story's narrator is afforded a moment of insight into the private worlds of other people inhabiting the city and, in the course of his observations, constantly assesses and reassesses the extent of the interpenetration of his own subjectivity with the world he inhabits: "Indem ich durch die Stadt streife und sie monogrammiere, gerate ich, als Betrachter, aus der Welt — 'Get lost!' ist die letzte Verwünschung englischer Sprache."[62]

Tanja Dückers's *Spielzone* (1999) similarly depicts Berlin as an anthropological event. In its two parts — the first set in the west, in Neuköln, the second in Prenzlauer Berg in the east — characters of various backgrounds and generations mingle and watch one another having sex, shopping or simply existing. This novel, accordingly, is grounded in the act of voyeurism and in the notion of the city as a carnevalesque space — a *Spielzone* — in which the individual can observe, appropriate, and try out a range of identities and forms of subjectivity: here, Benjamin and Bakhtin meet. All the while, the physical proximity created by their shared occupancy of a relatively small area of the city encourages the narrative's many characters to imagine stories for one another. More often than not, these relate back to the individual's own sense of the marginality of his or her everyday life, lived out in apparent anonymity, and yet the exchange of glances, acknowledgments, and even disconnected dialogues which provoke these stories can also, on occasion, make possible a sense of community. Laura, the fourteen-year old who dreams of a truly satisfactory first sexual experience, thus initially only gravitates towards the local cemetery because for her it is an "abgefahrene Party-Location."[63] Once she is there, however, she meets Rosemarie, the older woman who comes to visit her husband's grave. Later, these two very different characters are joined by a man who tells them of the regret he feels for not having placed flowers at his grandmother's tomb, and Laura gives the man a kiss (*SZ*, 67). A family of sorts is created, if only briefly, as Laura, who feels misunderstood by her "68er" parents with their affectedly indulgent yet detached responses to her adolescent anxieties, glimpses that these two people have both experienced the longing that she now feels and suffered its consequences.

"Auch ich verschönere die Welt" (*SZ*, 13), acknowledges the narrator. Indeed, the desire to achieve a union with another person so perfect as to inure the individual against the unpredictability of his or her environment routinely remains unfulfilled. Elida and Jason, the couple whose apparent harmony and display of telepathic understanding makes them the object of envy of all the other characters in the novel, are, accordingly, as artificial and illusory as the "Abgeschlossenheit von mathematischen Formeln." The "Kosmos für sich" (*SZ*, 12) they project does not truly exist. The reality of the city, and of modern life, is the alternation between the feeling that it is possible to redefine oneself endlessly and a terrifying awareness of one's own vulnerability. Thus Katharina, who emerges as a key figure in part two when she moves from west Berlin to Prenzlauer Berg, discovers a "wunderbare Grauzone," an area that is "nicht mehr Osten, noch nicht Westen," a place that is "genau richtig, um sich selber auszutesten" (*SZ*, 108). An arson attack which leaves behind a number of charred bodies heightens her awareness of the fragility of life, expands her sense of the elasticity of the boundaries of her self, and intensifies the orgasm she experiences with her boyfriend. At the same time, however, she is forced to endure the insult "Votze" (*SZ*, 99) thrown at her by a man on the street. Other characters explore their personal limits by means of self-mutilation, cross-dressing, and violent sex, thereby recreating the dynamic of experimentation and vulnerability within their own bodies.

Dückers's Berlin is the Berlin of the mid- to late 1990s. The eastern part of the city in particular is exoticized as a space in which a certain freedom to experiment can be experienced before the arrival of global capitalism. Already, towards the end of the text, it is rumored that a McDonald's is about to be built (*SZ*, 191), a development that will once and for all defeat the desire of many of the novel's characters, including Katharina, to discover a form of community untainted by the fake intimacy of consumerism. More broadly, however, this novel projects a vision of a *provincial* Berlin within the metropolis, a city of subcultures and alternative lifestyles, whether it be Neuköln in the west or Prenzlauer Berg in the east, which at least has the *potential* to undermine the efforts of the civic authorities and powerful multinationals to incorporate the city into the global consumer network. This is the kind of "Zentrum-Pheripherie" described by Kathrin Röggla, or the "plurality of Berlins" alluded to by Norbert Niemann: "Das ist ein sehr dezentraler Ort, ganz verschiedene Orte, unendlich viele Berlins, zwischen denen man hin- und herwechselt."[64]

Yet Dückers's efforts to paint a picture of the potential for resistance to cultural homogeneity to be discovered at the periphery, in the multiplicity of lifestyles and forms of subjectivity contained within the "vielen Berlins," may be the exception rather than the rule in contemporary Berlin fiction. Timm Menke, accordingly, argues that the majority of Berlin novels of the 1990s are concerned less with local color or the city's unique ambience than with the way life in this particular metropolis functions more generally as a "Metapher für Großstadt-Dasein."[65] Stephen Brockmann, similarly, posits that Berlin in post-unification fiction is a city "emptied of physical significance,"[66] and Hania Siebenpfeiffer concludes: "So erzählen fast alle Berlinromane Geschichten entwurzelter [. . .] Figuren, die die Stadt auf der Suche nach ihrer eigenen Vergangenheit, einer verlorenen Liebe oder einer erhofften Zukunft [. . .] durchstreifen."[67] Julia Franck's *Liebediener* (1999), which depicts a young woman's absolute isolation at the heart of the urban experience, or Judith Hermann's "Sommerhaus, später," the title story of her 1998 collection, would be more typical of recent writing set in Berlin. In Hermann's text the young narrator's relationship to the city is entirely contingent: her life is dominated by international pop culture including ecstasy, Bret Easton Ellis's *American Psycho,* and the band Massive Attack. She and her friends exist, as it were, in a twilight zone of indecision, between a Berlin landscape filled with historical markers with which they are unable to identify — the city is seen as "autark"[68] — and an entirely manufactured search for novelty and unfettered autonomy. Beth Linklater explores this sense of disconnection from Berlin, and from Germany as a whole, in relation to Hermann's second collection *Nichts als Gespenster* (2003) and short stories by Tanja Dückers (*café brazil,* 2001), Julia Franck (*Bauchlandung,* 2000), Jenny Erpenbeck (*Tand,* 2001), and Katrin Dorn (*Tangogeschichten,* 2002).[69]

In literary depictions of Berlin from the mid-1990s onwards, it is possible to glimpse a variation on the "provinciality debate" discussed throughout this chapter. Dückers's *Spielzone,* therefore, features areas at the margins in which an "authentic" sense of self may be discovered even as it concedes that these areas are about to be colonized: "Klingt nach Werbeslogan" (*SZ,* 108). Judith Hermann's short stories, alternatively, present this colonization as a *fait accompli.* They appear to sum up the doubts voiced by Joachim Bessing in a contribution to *Tristesse Royale* (1999), the deliberations on pop culture in the Berlin Republic produced by Bessing, Christian Kracht, Eckhart Nickel, Alexander von Schönburg, and Benjamin von Stuckrad-Barre: "Ich kann mir nicht vorstellen, daß sich dieses Berlin zur Metropole entwickelt."[70] Hermann's political stance is almost certainly quite different from the brash cultural conservatism "performed" by Bessing and his "pop quintet" colleagues, and yet her work displays a similar anxiety regarding a modern-day German culture that is seen as imitative, deferential, and lacking in self-confidence. Berlin, it seems, remains as "provincial" as the new Republic that has taken its name.

In our considerations of contemporary German literature in this and previous chapters we have returned time and again to the question of how a more "normal" German identity is to be defined. For some authors and critics, it is a matter of rediscovering authentic "German" traditions untainted by Nazism which might then be set against both the univeralist, anti-nationalist ideology of "political correctness" espoused by a left-liberal elite of former "68ers" and the growing hegemony of an Anglo-American culture. For other, mainly younger writers, the desire to shake off the shackles of an imposed political consciousness, whether this be the social engagement and moralizing anti-fascism ordained by the generation of '68 or the compulsory activism of the former GDR, frequently implies a partial acceptance, at least, of global consumerism even as this is inflected with markers of "local" specificity. In both cases, the response to the challenge of moving beyond an obsession with the Nazi past whilst insisting that the new German "normality" need not be subsumed into the cultural homogeneity of the global consumer culture can easily appear defensive. Certainly, it seems that many German writers of the present day feel compelled to resort to irony, or to enact rearguard actions in defense of biographies formed by distinctively German experiences and now threatened with incorporation, or to indulge in anxious deliberations on the nature of German provinciality.

In the final section of this chapter, we turn to Georg Klein's *Libidissi* (1998), a novel that alludes to the possibility of a more vigorous, less hesitant German culture. In the place of a retrograde fetishization of national traditions implied by the search for a "longitudinal normality" or the implicit acknowledgment of the hegemony of the global consumer culture contained within the endeavor to inflect a "latitudinal normality" with a German "sensibility," *Libidissi* essays a genuine hybridity, an appropriation of the tropes of the neo-colonialist ideology associated with global capitalism in the name of a more adaptable "local" identity. The province, in this novel, truly fights back.

The Berlin Republic — A Hybrid Identity?

Georg Klein's *Libidissi* is a spy-story, a staple of the Anglo-American tradition, with hints of John Le Carre and Graham Greene, and of John Grisham's crime thrillers. Indeed, the emphasis on story-telling, plot, and idiosyncratic characters, as well as its appeal to a sensuous appreciation of atmosphere, would certainly endear the novel to the proponents of *Neue Lesbarkeit,* as discussed in chapter one.[71] At the same time, however, the novel has been spoken of as the start "einer neuen Moderne."[72] Its labyrinthine social world, problematization of narrative stance, and inclusion of details that resist interpretation all remind of "high" Modernism.

Thematically, the text's exploration of the cultural clash between east and west is reminiscent of Conrad's *Heart of Darkness.* The protagonist, Spaik (recalling the English word "spy"), has "gone native" in an indeterminate but seemingly "oriental" country and must be eliminated by other spies sent out by the "Bundeszentralamt." The novel alternates between chapters in which Spaik narrates his story, referring to himself in a form between third and first person, "ich=Spaik," which is typical of the local argot, and chapters in which one of the spies describes the way he and his partner were sent by spy master Kuhl to hunt Spaik. This he does by recounting his colleague's action in the "du" form. Both Spaik and his trackers pass through the various establishments frequented only by foreigners, including Freddy's "Dampfbad," the Hotel Esperanza, and the Naked Truth Club. On their journey they run into a variety of exotic characters. These include: Freddy, who claims to be of mixed Maltese and local descent but is in fact German; his manifold "Houseboys" — provided for the delectation of his male guests;Lieschen, Spaik's adopted daughter/lover, who, he claims, was "mir von der Stadt aufgenötigt";[73] Doc Zinally, an American doctor of Jewish lineage and a fanatic for genetic purity; Der kleine Calvin, who is taken to be a girl by Spaik's trackers; and a Japanese tourist who turns out to be an American spy. In the background, the city is preparing for the ninth anniversary of the public suicide of Gahis, the religious fundamentalist who briefly seized power after the withdrawal of the colonial power. At the close of the novel, his followers stage a public relations stunt for the world's media by attacking UN forces at the airport, action that is relayed in parallel with a third person narrator's account of Spaik's liquidation of his pursuers.

The description of both location and locale is detailed and yet indeterminate. The immediate suggestion of "the orient" provoked by the elaborate rendering of the exotic sights, sounds, and smells of the city, its utter chaos and the lackadaisical and unhurried attitude of its inhabitants, is undoubtedly atmospheric. The reader may be reminded of E. M. Forster's *Passage to India:* the "east" is "other," the opposite of western rationality, order, and civilization.[74] Yet the novel is deliberately unspecific in pinning down location, purposely quick to dissolve any sense of a "real place" into cliché. *Libidissi* is set both nowhere and everywhere — the Middle East as much as the former GDR. Its reach is global and its subject is the mismatch between local identity and the momentum towards ever greater standardization. Even as it critiques globalization and its antecedents in colonialism, technology, and monopoly capitalism, however, the novel offers little succor to those attached to the nostalgic fiction of an uncorrupted national culture. Resistance to globalization is to be found in hybridity rather than in glorious isolation and mythic purity.

Klein's art in *Libidissi* is to intimate an archaeology of western expansionism. Hence evidence of colonialism endures in the buildings erected by the "Fremdmacht" alongside the remnants of western technological innovations, in particular the "Rohrpost" later adapted for the illegal distribution of "Suleika," a highly toxic alcoholic drink, and an unfinished "Stadtbahn." The mutation of western colonialism into a self-assigned mission to bring technology and "culture" to "less fortunate peoples" and finally into global capitalism is also documented in city's street names, including the "lichtflirrenden Boulevard Der Meinungsfreiheit" (*L,* 30). Yet "local" cultural practices feature too. The hotel Esperanza, the name an allusion to the Enlightenment aspiration towards unending progress, combines "alle nur vorstellbaren historischen Elemente hiesiger Baukunst" in order to give the building "eine Vielfalt und Tiefe vortäuschende Fassade" (*L,* 67). Fundamentalists, though otherwise atavistic, install cameras in burnt-out tanks to transmit their military operations to satellite TV (*L*, 191–92). Native rap poets, alternatively, excavate "untergangenes Liedgut und vergessene Erzählweisen" in a nightclub frequented by local youths (*L*, 101) and rapidly rhyme together the "Namen international bekannter Firmen" (*L*, 107) to generate an image of unbridled corporate copulation, a "Firmen-Fick-Nummer" (*L*, 110).

The novel's focus on cultural intermingling externalizes the concept of hybridity and disables the misappropriations of Darwinism that inform capitalism. A version of Darwin that glorifies the survival of the fittest in the battle to achieve a monopoly is confronted with a less intoxicating reality in which adaptation favors the bastard rather than the pedigree. The reality is that there can be no purity. The architecture, infrastructure, and life of the city are endlessly adapted and turned to uses that were never intended. Everything is recycled. No sooner is the man who collects parts for salvage dead than he too becomes part of the circulation of reusable goods (*L*, 54). Likewise, the antiquated "Rohrpost" is adjusted to transport illegal "Suleika" and then messages for Spaik, an "uralter Walkman" conceals a decoder "relativ neuer Mode" (*L*, 51), and the primitive "Militärnetz" established by the colonial power is now used to transmit mobile phone calls (*L*, 151). Technology is even converted into art. Spaik purchases "eine Art Collier" made "aus den Innereien elektronischer Geräte" (*L*, 28) whose labyrinthine structure mirrors the evolution towards an ever more complex hybridity: "Sein Netzwerk aus Drähten, Widerständen, Diödchen und Transistörlein schillerte in den Farben der polierten Edelmetalle und der vielfältigen Lakierungen" (*L*, 27–28). That technology may be made to serve purposes for which it was never intended undermines the colonizing impulses of capitalism.

People too are hybrid. The myth of a pure ethnicity and a national culture does not correspond to reality. Freddy passes as a mix of Maltese and local descent but is "really" German. A Japanese tourist turns out to be American, a "US-Schlitzauge," in Spaik's derogatory terms (*L*, 141). The houseboys hail from all parts, but cannot be definitively placed. Shoemaker and arms dealer Axom is presumed to be Greek but professes to derive from one of the region's "kriegerischen Bergstämme" (*L*, 58), and the "native" owner of the hotel Esperanza is struck down by Mau-Mau, a disease said to affect only foreigners. Spaik himself, of course, is no longer quite Spaik but has become, during his years abroad, "ich= Spaik," a form of address borrowed from the local pigeon vernacular. This is a hybrid language *par excellence* which in its use of personal pronouns denies its speakers any sense of an "authentic identity": "der Redende nennt sich stets mit dem Namen, mit dem ihn sein jeweiliges Gegenüber anspricht" (*L*, 16–17). It is perfectly suited to Spaik whose ego has been erased by its incorporation of outside influences which have, collectively, taken the place "meines verflossenen Ichs" (*L*, 73).

Piddi-Piddi, as the local patois is called, embodies the hybridity that emerges with the globalization of trade and culture, a process that began with colonialism. It initially appears to be a highly reductive mixture of languages, especially English, but is in fact "gerade in ihrem Stottern voll vorwärtsdrängender Lust" (*L*, 42). All languages, of course, mutate. Spaik's German is thus increasingly divergent from the form used by his superiors in the "Bundeszentralamt." Both sides perceive this process of modification as one of degeneration. Yet there can be no "pure" language. The German spoken by talk show host Heinz, a "deutschstämmiger Australier der dritten Generation" on the "German Fun" channel, is incomprehensible to those back "in der alten Heimat" but expatriates delight in his "schaurigen Knödeln" (*L*, 50). Lieschen's ethnicity, moreover, is no barrier to "foreign" language acquisition. The "native" girl's German is "glasklar" (*L*, 60).

This insistence on hybridity is important for any understanding of the closing chapters of the novel. Following an encounter with his pursuers in the Naked Truth Club, Spaik abandons the mixed narrative pronoun "ich=Spaik" and reasserts a conventional ego as "ich." Subsequently, he leaves behind his previous apathy. Determined to survive, he buys a weapon, and, in a final shoot-out, he eliminates his would-be killers and thereby also rescues Lieschen, with whom it appears he is now in love. In effect, then, "ich=Spaik" becomes "ich" at the point at which the hybrid acquires its own sense of identity and becomes resolved to assert itself against the forces that formed it but which it has now outlived. A different configuration has emerged, a new more dynamic mix.

The key to survival is constant adaptation to circumstances. Those who insist on glorious isolation will perish. This was the fate of the "Egichäer," a minority massacred after the withdrawal of the colonial power. Their insistence on their language and religion made them unable to adapt. Only in refuge in the United States — that great experiment in adaptation — did some endure and even become millionaires (*L*, 7). Spaik too survives not because he is a Nietzschean *Übermensch* or because he has adopted the purist fundamentalism of Gahis's supporters (he has cast aside the Gahist robe he had been wearing as a disguise) but because he has forged his own identity from a self-serving blending of a variety of influences. His strategy of subversive appropriation permits him to liberate himself from moribund traditions without being subsumed into the "ever-new" of consumerism.

Klein's *Libidissi* usefully responds to many of the issues at the heart of our discussions of contemporary German literature throughout this book. Its energetic incorporation of "German" and "American" forms and themes, and its subversion of both, undermines the desire for a "pure" tradition. At the same time, the novel implies that by *producing* culture from *within* the interaction of a variety of influences — rather than simply *inflecting* an apparently hegemonic discourse — the new Germany might also be able to avoid the risk of merely imitating globalized culture. In conclusion, then, it might be possible to imagine a future in which the Berlin Republic would no longer measure itself against the "normality" of others or seek to return to an "untainted" past but would make its own unique — if hybrid — contribution to the global exchange of ideas and culture.

Notes

[1] W. G. Sebald, *Unheimliche Heimat: Essays zur österreichischen Literatur* (Salzburg: Residenz Verlag, 1991), 12.

[2] W. G. Sebald, "Damals vor Graz: Randbemerkungen zum Thema Literatur und Heimat," *Neue Zürcher Zeitung,* 21 May 1991, 42.

[3] Norbert Mecklenburg, *Erzählte Provinz: Regionalismus und Moderne im Roman* (Königstein: Äthenäum, 1982), 16–17.

[4] Norbert Mecklenburg, *Erzählte Provinz,* 18.

[5] See Elizabeth Boa and Rachel Palfreyman, *Heimat — A German Dream: Regional Loyalties and National Identity in German Culture* (Oxford: Oxford UP, 2000).

[6] Martin Walser, *Dorle und Wolf,* in Martin Walser, *Deutsche Sorgen* (Frankfurt a.M.: Suhrkamp, 1997), 276–405, here 360.

[7] Norbert Mecklenburg, *Die Grünen Inseln* (Munich: iudicium, 1986), 50 and 51.

[8] Norbert Mecklenburg, *Die Grünen Inseln,* 247.

[9] Thomas Assheuer, "Was ist rechts? Botho Strauß bläßt ins Bockshorn," in Franz Josef Görtz, Volker Hage, and Uwe Wittstock, eds., *Deutsche Literatur 1993* (Stuttgart: Reclam, 1994), 269–72, here 272. See Eva Geulen, "Nationalisms: Old, New and German," *Telos* 105 (1995): 2–20.

[10] Stephen Brockmann, *Literature and German Unification* (Cambridge: Cambridge UP, 1999), 115.

[11] Botho Strauß, "Anschwellender Bocksgesang," originally in *Der Spiegel,* 8 February 1993, 2–7. Quotations here are from Botho Strauß, *Der Aufstand gegen die sekundäre Welt. Bemerkungen zu einer Ästhetik der Anwesenheit* (Munich: Carl Hanser Verlag, 1999), 55–79, here 64. Hereafter *AB.*

[12] Botho Strauß, *Die Fehler des Kopisten* (Munich: Deutscher Taschenbuch Verlag, 1999 [1997]), 16. Hereafter *FK.*

[13] Botho Strauß, "Der Aufstand gegen die sekundäre Welt: Bemerkungen zu einer Ästhetik der Anwesenheit," in Botho Strauß, *Der Aufstand gegen die sekundäre Welt* (Munich: Hanser, 1999), 37–53, here 50.

[14] Jan-Werner Müller, *Another Country: German Intellectuals, Unification and National Identity* (New Haven: Yale UP, 2000), 30.

[15] Botho Strauß, "Zeit ohne Vorboten," in *Der Aufstand gegen die sekundäre Welt*, 93–105, here 96. Hereafter *ZV*.

[16] Botho Strauß, *Das Partikular* (Munich: Hanser, 2000), 204 and 73.

[17] See Jay Julian Rosellini, *Literary Skinheads? Writing from the Right in Reunified Germany* (West Lafayette: Purdue UP, 2000), 96–103.

[18] This was followed by *Sommerlicher Nachtrag zu einer winterlichen Reise* (Frankfurt a.M.: Suhrkamp, 1996).

[19] Peter Handke, *Eine winterliche Reise zu den Flüssen Donau, Save, Morawa und Drina oder Gerechtigkeit für Serbien* (Frankfurt a.M.: Suhrkamp, 1996), 12–13. Hereafter *GS*.

[20] Handke published a further report with the telling title: *Unter Tränen fragend: nachträgliche Aufzeichnungen von zwei Jugoslawien-Durchqueren im Krieg, März und April 1999* (Frankfurt a.M.: Suhrkamp, 1999).

[21] Hans Hahn, "'Es geht nicht nur um Literatur': Some Observations on the 1990 'Literaturstreit' and its Recent Anti-Intellectual Implications," *German Life and Letters* 50:1 (1997): 65–81, here 68.

[22] Hans Hahn, "'Es geht nicht nur um Literatur,'" 68.

[23] Hermann Bauschinger, Manfred Bosch, and Martin Walser (participants in a discussion), "Heimat — aber woher nehmen?," *Allemende* 54/55 (1997): 22–53, here 29.

[24] Arnold Stadler, "Erbarmen mit dem Seziermesser," *Badische Zeitung*, 26 October 1999, 15.

[25] Arnold Stadler, "Heimat? Eine Grabschändung," *Badische Zeitung*, 9 October 1999, 14–5, 14.

[26] Arnold Stadler, "Heimat?," 14.

[27] Arnold Stadler, "Erbarmen mit dem Seziermesser," 15.

[28] Interview in *Der Spiegel* 29 (1999), 158–60, 159.

[29] Arnold Stadler, *Mein Hund, meine Sau, mein Leben* (Frankfurt a.M.: Suhrkamp, 1996 [1994]), 8. Hereafter *MH*.

[30] Arnold Stadler, *Der Tod und ich, wir zwei* (Frankfurt a.M.: Suhrkamp, 1998 [1996 with Residenz Verlag]), 210. Hereafter *DTI*.

[31] See my "The Novels of Arnold Stadler from *Ich war einmal* to *Ein hinreissender Schrotthändler*," *Neophilologus* 87 (2003): 119–32.

[32] Arnold Stadler, *Ein hinreissender Schrotthändler* (Cologne: Dumont, 1999), 9. Hereafter *HS*.

[33] Botho Strauß, "Anschwellender Bocksgesang," 65.

[34] Harald Klaus, "Appetit auf eine Seele," *Die Presse*, 2 October 1999, *Spektrum*, vii.

[35] Arnold Stadler, *Sehnsucht* (Cologne: Dumont, 2002), 264. Hereafter *S*.

[36] Hans-Ulrich Treichel, "Lektionen der Leere: Eine Kindheit auf dem Lande. Oder wie ich Schriftsteller wurde," *Neue Zürcher Zeitung,* 15/16 April 2000, 50.

[37] Hans-Ulrich Treichel, "Heimatkunde," in Hans-Ulrich Treichel, *Heimatkunde oder alles ist heiter und edel* (Frankfurt a.M.: Suhrkamp, 1996), 47–57.

[38] See David Basker, "'Schlüsselszenen der Erfahrung': (Dis)location in the Prose Work of Hans-Ulrich Treichel," in David Basker, ed., *Hans-Ulrich Treichel* (Cardiff: U of Wales P, 2004), 37–60.

[39] Hans-Ulrich Treichel, "Prägende Sätze," *Neue Zürcher Zeitung,* 10 October 1998, 50.

[40] Martin Ebel, "In der Komponistenumlaufbahn," *Stuttgarter Zeitung,* 21 March 2000, 4.

[41] See my "'Sehnsüchtig-traurig und unerlöst': Memory's Longing to Forget. Or Why *Tristanakkord* is Not Simply A Reprise of Martin Walser," in David Basker, ed., *Hans-Ulrich Treichel,* 79–93.

[42] Hans-Ulrich Treichel, *Tristanakkord* (Frankfurt a.M.: Suhrkamp, 2000), 17. Hereafter *T.*

[43] Bergmann's hostility to his rival Nerlinger no doubt draws on Treichel's experience of writing libretti for Hans Werner Henze, whose difficult relationship with fellow composer Karlheinz Stockhausen is well-known.

[44] Wolfgang Emmerich, "Andreas Maier, *Klausen,*" introduction to the CD version of *Klausen* (2002), 4–8, 4.

[45] Dieter Stolz, "Alles eine Frage der Perspektive: Prosa-Debüts der deutschsprachigen Gegenwartsliteratur," *Sprache im technischen Zeitalter* 162 (2002): 156–70, here 163 and 166.

[46] Dieter Stolz, "Alles eine Frage der Perspektive," 163.

[47] Andreas Maier, *Wäldchestag* (Frankfurt a.M.: Suhrkamp, 2002 [2000]), 126. Hereafter *W.*

[48] Helmuth Karasek, "Vorgelesen," *Der Tagesspiegel,* 31 December 2000, W4.

[49] Karl Heinz Bohrer, "Provinzialismus,' *Merkur* 44 (1990): 1096–1102; 45 (1991): 255–66, 358–65, 719–27; 46 (1992): 89–90.

[50] Frank Schirrmacher, "Idyllen in der Wüste oder Das Versagen vor der Metropole," in Andrea Köhler and Rainer Moritz, eds., *Maulhelden und Königskinder. Zur Debatte über die deutschsprachige Gegenwartsliteratur* (Reclam, Leipzig, 1998), 15–27, 15. Originally in the *Frankfurter Allgemeine Zeitung,* 10 October 1989.

[51] Hans-Ulrich Treichel, *Der irdische Amor* (Frankfurt a.M.: Suhrkamp, 2002), 247. Hereafter *DIA.*

[52] See Rhys Williams, "'Caravaggio in Preußen': Hans-Ulrich Treichel's *Der irdische Amor,*" in David Basker, ed., *Hans-Ulrich Treichel,* 94–110.

[53] Heinz Bude, *Generation Berlin* (Berlin: Merve Verlag, 2001), 28.

[54] See Ulrike Zitzlsperger, "Filling the Blanks: Berlin as Public Showcase," in Stuart Taberner and Frank Finlay, eds., *Recasting German Identity* (Rochester: Camden House, 2002), 37–51.

[55] Benjamin Lebert, *Der Vogel ist ein Rabe* (Cologne: Kiepenheuer & Witsch), 10.

[56] Susanne Ledanff, "'Metropolisierung' der deutschen Literatur? Welche Möglichkeiten eröffnet das vereinigte Berlin und die neue Berliner Urbanität?," in Gerhard Fischer and David Roberts, eds., *Schreiben nach der Wende. Ein Jahrzehnt deutscher Literatur 1989–1999* (Tübingen: Stauffenberg, 2001), 275–89, here 275.

[57] Uwe Timm, *Johannisnacht* (Munich: Deutscher Taschenbuch Verlag, 1999 [1996]), 193.

[58] Jörg Magenau, "Posaunen gegen Berlin," *Frankfurter Allgmeine Zeitung*, 28 August 1999, *Literatur* 42.

[59] F. C. Delius, *Der Königsmacher* (Berlin: Rowohlt, 2001), 198–99.

[60] Ulrike Zitzlsperger, "A Worm's Eye View and A Bird's Eye View: Culture and Politics in Berlin since 1989," in William Niven and James Jordan, eds., *Politics and Culture in Twentieth-Century Germany* (Rochester: Camden House, 2003), 185–99, here 191.

[61] See Walter Benjamin, *Das Passagenwerk*, volume 1, ed. by Rolf Tiedemann (Frankfurt a.M.: Suhrkamp, 1983), 525–69.

[62] Perikles Monioudis, "In Berlin," in Jürgen Jakob Becker and Ulrich Jenetzki, eds., *Die Stadt nach der Mauer* (Berlin: Ullstein, 1998), 13–23, here 13 and 15.

[63] Tanja Dückers, *Spielzone* (Berlin: Aufbau Verlag, 1999), 21. Hereafter *SZ*.

[64] Helmut Böttiger and Wolfram Schütte, "Metropole ist eine Fiktion," Interview with Kathrin Röggla, Norbert Niemann, Ingo Schulze, and Burkhard Spinnen, *Frankfurter Rundschau*, 28 November 1998, 22.

[65] Timm Menke, "Lebensgefühl(e) in Ost und West als Roman: Ingo Schulzes *Simple Storys* und Norbert Niemanns *Wie man's nimmt*. Mit einem Seitenblick auf Timm Staffels *Terrordrom*," in Gerhard Fischer and David Roberts, eds., *Schreiben nach der Wende*, 253–61, 261.

[66] Stephen Brockmann, "The Written Capital," *Monatshefte* 3 (1999): 376–95, here 391.

[67] Hania Siebenpfeiffer, "Topographien des Seelischen. Berlinromane der neunziger Jahre," in Matthias Harder, ed., *Bestandsaufnahmen … Deutschsprachige Literatur der neunziger Jahre aus interkultureller Sicht* (Würzburg: Königshausen & Neumann, 2001), 85–104.

[68] Judith Hermann, "Sommerhaus, später," in Judith Hermann, *Sommerhaus, später* (Frankfurt a.M.: Fischer, 1999 [1998]), 139–56, 141.

[69] Beth Linklater, "Germany and Background: Global Concerns in Recent Women's Writing in German," in Stuart Taberner, ed., *German Literature in the Age of Globalisation* (Birmingham: Birmingham UP, 2004), 67–88.

[70] Joachim Bessing, ed., *Tristesse Royale. Das popkulturelle Quintett mit Joachim Bessing, Christian Kracht, Eckhart Nickel, Alexander v. Schönburg and Benjamin von Stuckrad-Barre* (Berlin: Ullstein, 1999), 85.

[71] See my "A New Modernism or "Neue Lesbarkeit"? — Hybridity in Georg Klein's *Libidissi*," *German Life and Letters* 55:2 (2002): 137–48.

[72] Lothar Müller, *Frankfurter Allgemeine Zeitung*, 2 October 1998, 27.

[73] Georg Klein, *Libidissi* (Berlin: Alexander Fest Verlag, 1998), 52. Hereafter *L*.

[74] This process is described in Edward Said's seminal work, *Orientalism* (1978).

Concluding Remarks

> Alles ist normal. *Wir sind alle ganz normal.*
> — Norbert Niemann, *Wie man's nimmt*

THE OPENING CHAPTER OF THE present volume began by proclaiming the heterogeneity of post-unification German writing. In this first chapter and in the chapters that follow, I hope to have given something of the flavor of this contemporary diversity in a series of close readings of individual novels and allusions to further works by authors from east and west and of the older, middle, and younger generations.

The diversity of recent German fiction has to do, in part, with changed market conditions and changed audience expectations. Indeed, the publishing environment in which German authors operate, the kinds of books that are in demand and the way they are promoted, is itself a major theme of much recent writing. Some authors reject what they see as the increasing conformity of German literature with international trends and attempt to return to "German" forms; some attempt to inflect global trends with a "local" sensibility, whereas others, at first glance, at least, seem to accept a dominant international "pop" culture. In many cases, evidently, an engagement with what at first appear to be "merely" aesthetic questions implies an engagement with the broader question of the kind of "normality" that is being established in the new Berlin Republic as a whole. Whether to seek inspiration in "German" traditions cleansed of their association with the horrors of Nazism, or in international trends adapted to German circumstances, or in what superficially appears to be the liberating ahistoricity of the globalized consumer culture — these are the possibilities that define contemporary German society as much as contemporary German literature.

In chapter one, the focus was on the way the infiltration of a more "commercial" ethos into the German book business, its integration into an ever-more competitive global publishing industry, has created a tension between the tendency towards standardization and the efforts of the more interesting of contemporary authors to subvert this trend and to reinstate a sense of "distinctiveness," whether this be national, biographical, or aesthetic. This tension was further explored in chapters two and three in which we demonstrated that the engagement with the former GDR and the "old" Federal Republic, respectively, both reponds to specifically

"German" debates on the nation's totalitarian legacy, the problems of unification, and the enduring impact of key moments such as '68 and, again, to the desire to inflect globalized culture. In chapters four and five, the question of German "normalization" was examined from a different angle via an analysis of novels dealing with the Nazi past. Here, as in the subsequent chapter on the "German-Jewish symbiosis," the emphasis was once more on the extent to which it is possible to define "uncontaminated" traditions and a "viable" German heritage that might be deployed in the struggle to preserve — or reinvent — a new German "normality" capable of resisting appropriation.

At the close of the final chapter, in which the clash between the assertion of the "authenticity of the German province" and the charge of a "German *provinciality*" was assessed, Georg Klein's *Libidissi* (1998) was adduced as an example of an alternative model of "normality," one which might even dissolve the very concept. Out of a properly dynamic engagement with a variety of influences — as opposed to the vain excavation of past traditions or a seemingly defensive strategy of inflecting a hegemonic culture with markers of local difference — a true hybridity emerges which escapes the traps of nostalgia and imitation and which develops genuinely new forms. It is perhaps not too farfetched to imagine that this aspiration might one day come to motivate the politics and society of the Berlin Republic as much as its literature. Should this come to pass, students of German culture and society will need to develop new tools. Klein's novel, for instance, might usefully be subjected to the kind of post-colonial analysis that has become common in Anglo-American English and French studies and this, indeed, might offer a model for future investigations. What kind of literature might be expected to emerge from a country that has only recently left behind semi-sovereignty and deference to "colonial powers" (the visible supremacy of the Soviet Union in the GDR and, in the "old" FRG, the more subtle stewardship of the United States) and is threatened by re-colonization in the guise of globalization? Which concepts of identity and history will be generated within this literature as it attempts to negotiate the possibilities and pitfalls of what Homi Bhabha has termed mimicry[1] and of what Stuart Hall has described as the tension between the longing to "return" to a "pre-colonial 'true self'"[2] and the production of a genuinely dynamic culture?

For now, however, it must suffice to assert that contemporary German literature, and politics, history, and society in the Berlin Republic as a whole, remains, and will remain for the foreseeable future, a genuinely fascinating and worthwhile subject for our attention and study.

Bibliography

Primary Texts

This is a list of works of fiction, essays by authors, and interviews referred to in this volume and is by no means a comprehensive catalog of contemporary German literature.

Altenburg, Matthias. *Landschaft mit Wölfen*. Cologne: Kiepenheuer & Witsch, 1997.

———. "Sehr geehrter Herr Seligmann," *Zeitmagazin* 32, 1 August 1997, 7.

———. "Kampf den Flaneuren: Über Deutschlands junge, lahme Dichter." In Andrea Köhler and Rainer Moritz, eds., *Maulhelden und Königskinder: Zur Debatte über die deutschsprachige Gegenwartsliteratur*. Leipzig: Reclam Verlag, 1998. 72–85.

———. *Irgendwie alles Sex*. Cologne: Kiepenheuer & Witsch, 2001.

———. "Generation Nix." In Matthias Altenburg, *Irgendwie alles Sex*, 122–24.

———. *Partisanen der Schönheit*. Münster: Oktober Verlag, 2002.

———. "Flaubert und die toten Juden." In Matthias Altenburg, *Partisanen der Schönheit*, 78–81.

———. "Sehr geehrter Herr Seligmann." In Matthias Altenburg, *Partisanen der Schönheit*, 81–84.

Becker, Peter von. *Die andere Zeit*. Frankfurt a.M.: Suhrkamp, 1994.

Behrens, Katja. "Alles normal." In *"bin ich um den Schlaf gebracht." Literarische Texte von vierzehn Autorinnen und Autoren. Heinrich-Heine-Haus, Lüneburg 1993*. Lüneburg: Altstadt-Druck, 1993. 83–88.

———. *Salomo und die anderen*. Frankfurt a.M.: Fischer, 1993.

———. "Arthur Mayer oder das Schweigen." In Katja Behrens, *Salomo und die anderen*, 67–152.

Berg, Sibylle. *Ein paar Leute suchen das Glück und lachen sich tot*. Leipzig: Reclam, 1997.

———. *Gold*. Hamburg: Hoffmann und Campe, 2000.

———. *Sex II: Amerika*. Hamburg: Hoffmann und Campe, 2000.

———. *Das Unerfreuliche zuerst*. Cologne: Kiepenheuer & Witsch, 2001.

———. *Ende gut*. Cologne: Kiepenheuer & Witsch, 2004.

Berkéwicz, Ulla. *Engel sind schwarz und weiß*. Frankfurt a.m.: Suhrkamp, 1990.

Bernig, Jörg. *Niemandszeit*. Munich: Deutsche Verlags-Anstalt, 2002.

Bessing, Joachim. ed. *Tristesse Royale: Das popkulturelle Quintett mit Joachim Bessing, Christian Kracht, Eckhart Nickel, Alexander v. Schönburg and Benjamin von Stuckrad-Barre*. Berlin: Ullstein, 1999.

———. *Wir Maschine*. Stuttgart: Deutsche Verlagsanstalt, 2001.

Beyer, Marcel. *Flughunde*. Frankfurt a.m.: Suhrkamp, 1996 [1995].

———. *Spione*. Frankfurt a.m.: Fischer, 2002 [2000].

Biller, Maxim. *Wenn ich einmal reich und tot bin*. Cologne: Kiepenheuer & Witsch, 1990.

———. *Harlem Holocaust*. Cologne: Kiepenheuer & Witsch, [1990] 1998.

———. *Die Tempojahre*. Munich; Deutscher Taschenbuchverlag, 1991.

———. *Land der Väter und Verräter*. Cologne: Kiepenheuer & Witsch, 1994.

———. "Goodbye Columbus. Randlage oder: über die Voraussetzungen jüdischer Literatur." *Frankfurter Rundschau*, 2 March 1995, 9.

———. "Und wenn der Kater kommt." In Martin Hielscher, ed., *Wenn der Kater kommt. Neues Erzählen: 38 deutschsprachige Autorinnen und Autoren*. Cologne: Kiepenheuer & Witsch, 1996, 161–73.

———. "Soviel Sinnlichkeit wie der Stadtplan von Kiel." In Andrea Köhler and Rainer Moritz, eds., *Maulhelden und Königskinder: Zur Debatte über die deutschsprachige Gegenwartsliteratur*. Leipzig: Reclam Verlag, 1998), 62–71.

———. *Die Tochter*. Cologne: Kiepenheuer & Witsch, 2000.

———. "Feige das Land, schlapp die Literatur: Über die Schwierigkeiten beim Sagen der Wahrheit." *Die Zeit*, 13 April 2000, 47–49.

———. *Deutschbuch*. Munich: Deutscher Taschenbuch Verlag, 2001.

———. "Heiliger Holocaust." In Maxim Biller, *Deutschbuch*, 27–29.

———. *Esra*. Cologne: Kiepenheuer & Witsch, 2003.

Biskupek, Matthias. *Der Quotensachse*. Berlin: Ullstein, 1998 [1996].

———. *Schloß Zockendorf*. Leipzig: Gustav-Kiepenheuer-Verlag, 1998.

Bohrer, Karl Heinz. "Die permanente Theodizee." *Merkur* 41 (1987): 267–86.

———. "Kulturschutzgebiet DDR?" *Merkur* 44:500 (1990): 1015–18.

———. "Provinzialismus." *Merkur* 44 (1990): 1096–1102; 45 (1991): 255–66, 358–65, 719–27; 46 (1992): 89–90.

———. "Warum wir keine Nation sind. Warum wir eine werden wollen," *Frankfurter Allgemeine Zeitung,* 13 January 1990, *Bilder und Zeiten,* 1–4.

———. *Das absolute Präsens.* Frankfurt a.M.: Suhrkamp, 1994.

———. "Zeit und Imagination: Das absolute Präsens der Literatur." In Karl Heinz Bohrer, *Das absolute Präsens,* 143–83.

———. "Erinnerung an Kriterien: Vom Warten auf den deutschen Zeitroman." In Andrea Köhler and Rainer Moritz, eds., *Maulhelden und Königskinder: Zur Debatte über die deutschsprachige Gegenwartsliteratur.* Leipzig: Reclam Verlag, 1998, 137–50.

———. *Provinzialismus.* Munich: Carl Hanser, 2000.

———. "Nationale Nachgedanken zur Wehrmachtsausstellung." In Karl Heinz Bohrer, *Provinzialismus,* 142–49.

———. "Seit '45 ohne Metropole." In Karl Heinz Bohrer, *Provinzialismus,* 81–98.

———. "Verlust an historischem Gedächtnis." In Karl Heinz Bohrer, *Provinzialismus,* 150–63.

Braun, Volker. "Das Eigentum." In Carl Otto Konrady, ed., *Von einem Land und vom anderen: Gedichte zur deutschen Wende.* Frankfurt a.M.: Suhrkamp, 1993, 51.

———. *Das Nichtgelebte.* Leipzig: Faber und Faber, 1995.

———. *Der Wendehals.* Frankfurt a.M.: Suhrkamp, 1995.

Broder, Henryk. *Volk und Wahn.* Hamburg: SPIEGEL-Buchverlag, 1996.

———. "Auschwitz für alle!" In Henryk Broder, *Volk und Wahn,* 210–11.

———. "Die Germanisierung des Holocaust." In Henryk Broder, *Volk und Wahn,* 214–28.

———. *Jedem das Seine.* Augsburg: Öllbaum, 1999, 93–96.

———. "Jedem sein Adolf." In Henryk Broder, *Jedem das Seine,* 93–96.

Brumme, Christoph. *Nichts als das.* Frankfurt a.M.: Fischer, 1996 [1994].

Brussig, Thomas. *Helden wie wir.* Berlin: Volk & Welt, 1995.

———. *Am kürzeren Ende der Sonnenallee.* Berlin: Volk & Welt, 1999.

———. *Leben bis Männer.* Frankfurt a.M.: Fischer, 2003 [2001].

Buch, Hans Christoph. *Der Burgwart der Wartburg.* Frankfurt a.M.: Suhrkamp, 1994.

———. "Schönen Gruß von Charlie Chaplin." *Tagesspiegel,* 18 November 1999, 49.

Burmeister, Brigitte. *Unter dem Namen Norma.* Stuttgart: Klett-Cotta, 1994.

———. *Pollock und die Attentäterin.* Stuttgart: Klett-Cotta, 1999.

De Bruyn, Günter. *Zwischenbilanz: Eine Jugend in Berlin.* Frankfurt a.M.: Fischer, 1992.

———. *Vierzig Jahre.* Frankfurt a.M.: Fischer, 1996.

Delius, F. C. *Die Birnen von Ribbeck.* Reinbek bei Hamburg: Rowohlt, 1993 [1991].

———. *Der Sonntag, an dem ich Weltmeister wurde.* Reinbek bei Hamburg: Rowohlt, 1996 [1994].

———. *Der Spaziergang von Rostock nach Syrakuse.* Reinbek bei Hamburg: Rowohlt, 1999 [1995].

———. *Amerikahaus und der Tanz um die Frauen.* Reinbek bei Hamburg: Rowohlt, 1999 [1997].

———. *Die Flatterzunge.* Reinbek bei Hamburg: Rowohlt, 1999.

———. *Der Königsmacher.* Berlin: Rowohlt, 2001.

Deutschkron, Inge. "Mit den Jahren wuchsen die Zweifel." In Helmut Lotz and Kai Precht, eds., *Deutschland, mein Land?.* Munich: Deutscher Taschenbuch Verlag, 1999, 247–53.

Dieckmann, Dorothea. *Damen & Herren.* Stuttgart: Klett-Cotta, 2002.

Dische, Irene. *Ein fremdes Gefühl.* Berlin: Rowohlt, 1993.

Dischereit, Esther. *Joëmis Tisch.* Frankfurt a.M.: Suhrkamp, 1988.

———. *Merryn.* Frankfurt a.M.: Suhrkamp, 1992.

Dorn, Katrin. *Lügen und Schweigen.* Berlin: Aufbau, 2000.

———. *Tangogeschichten.* Munich: Deutscher Taschenbuch Verlag, 2002.

Drawert, Kurt. *Spiegelland.* Frankfurt a.M.: Suhrkamp, 1992.

Dückers, Tanja. *Spielzone.* Berlin: Aufbau Verlag, 1999.

———. *Café Brazil.* Berlin: Aufbau, 2001.

———. "Lakritz (Warzawa)." In Christine Eichel, ed., *Es liegt mir auf der Zunge.* Munich: Goldmann, 2002, 227–49.

———. *Himmelskörper.* Berlin: Aufbau, 2003.

Duve, Karen. *Keine Ahnung.* Frankfurt a.M.: Suhrkamp, 1999.

———. "Keine Ahnung." In Karen Duve, *Keine Ahnung,* 7.

———. *Regenroman.* Berlin: Eichborn, 1999.

———. *Dies ist kein Liebeslied.* Frankfurt a.M.: Eichborn, 2002.

Enzensberger, Hans Magnus. *Die große Wanderung*. Frankfurt a.M.: Suhrkamp, 1994 [1992].

———. *Zickzack*. Frankfurt a.M.: Suhrkamp, 1999 [1997].

———. "Bosnien, Uganda." In Hans Magnus Enzensberger, *Zickzack*, 89–94.

———. *Wo warst du, Robert?* Munich: Deutscher Taschenbuch Verlag, 2002 [1998].

Erpenbeck, Jenny. *Geschichte vom alten Kind*. Berlin: Eichborn, 1999.

———. *Tand*. Frankfurt a.M.: Eichborn Verlag, 2001.

———. "Im Halbschatten meines Schädels." In Jenny Erpenbeck, *Tand*, 7–13.

———. "Tand." In Jenny Erpenbeck, *Tand*, 31–45.

Forte, Dieter. *Das Muster*. Frankfurt a.M.: Fischer, 1992.

———. *Der Junge mit den blutigen Schuhen*. Frankfurt a.M.: Fischer, 1995.

———. *In der Erinnerung*. Frankfurt a.M.: Fischer, 1998.

———. *Schweigen oder sprechen*. Frankfurt a.M.: Fischer, 2002.

———. "Luftkrieg im Literaturseminar." In Dieter Forte, *Schweigen oder sprechen*, 31–36.

———. "Schweigen oder sprechen." In Dieter Forte, *Schweigen oder sprechen*, 69–70.

Franck, Julia. *Der neue Koch*. Zurich: Ammann, 1997.

———. *Liebediener*. Cologne: Dumont, 1999.

———. *Bauchlandung. Geschichten zum Anfassen*. Cologne: Dumont, 2000.

———. "Bäuchlings." In Julia Franck, *Bauchlandung. Geschichten zum Anfassen*, 7–16.

———. "Mir nichts, dir nichts." In Julia Franck, *Bauchlandung*, 95–111.

———. "Strandbad." In Julia Franck, *Bauchlandung*, 37–49.

Fries, Fritz Rudolf. *Die Nonnen von Bratislava*. Munich: Piper, 1995.

Goetz, Rainald. *Celebration. Texte und Bilder zur Nacht*. Frankfurt a.M.: Suhrkamp, 1998.

———. *Jeff Koons*. Frankfurt a.M.: Suhrkamp, 1998.

———. *Rave*. Frankfurt a.M.: Suhrkamp, 2001 [1998].

———. *Abfall für alle*. Frankfurt a.M.: Suhrkamp, 1999.

———. *Dekonspiratione*. Frankfurt a.M.: Suhrkamp, 2000.

———. *Katarakt*. Frankfurt a.M.: Suhrkamp, 2000.

———. *Jahrzehnt der schönen Frauen*. Frankfurt a.M.: Suhrkamp, 2001.

Goosen, Frank. *liegen lernen*. Frankfurt a.m.: Eichborn, 2000 [1999].

————. *Pokorny lacht*. Frankfurt a.m.: Eichborn, 2003.

Grass, Günter. *Deutscher Lastenausgleich. Wider das dumpfe Einheitsgebot: Reden und Gespräche*. Frankfurt a.M.: Luchterhand, 1990.

————. "Viel Gefühl, wenig Bewußtsein." In Günter Grass, *Deutscher Lastenausgleich. Wider das dumpfe Einheitsgebot: Reden und Gespräche*, 13–25. Also in Günter Grass, *Gegen die verstreichende Zeit: Reden, Aufsätze und Gespräche*, 13–27.

————. *Ein Schnäppchen namens DDR*. Frankfurt a.M.: Luchterhand, 1990.

————. "Ein Schnäppchen namens DDR." In Günter Grass, *Ein Schnäppchen namens DDR*, 39–60.

————. "Kurze Rede eines vaterlandslosen Gesellen." In Günter Grass, *Ein Schnäppchen namens DDR*, 7–14.

————. *Schreiben nach Auschwitz*. Munich: Deutscher Taschenbuch Verlag, 1990.

————. *Gegen die verstreichende Zeit: Reden, Aufsätze und Gespräche*. Hamburg: Luchterhand, 1991.

————. *Unkenrufe*. Göttingen: Steidl, 1992.

————. *Ein weites Feld*. Göttingen: Steidl, 1995.

————. *Für und Widerworte*. Göttingen: Seidl, 1999.

————. "Der lernende Lehrer." In Günter Grass, *Für und Widerworte*, 7–35.

————. *Mein Jahrhundert*. Göttingen: Steidl, 1999.

————. *Im Krebsgang*. Göttingen: Steidl, 2002.

Hahn, Ulla. *Unscharfe Bilder*. Munich: Deutsche Verlagsanstalt, 2003.

Hamann, Christoph. *Seegfrörne*. Göttingen: Seidl, 1998.

Handke, Peter. *Eine winterliche Reise zu den Flüssen Donau, Save, Morawa und Drina oder Gerechtigkeit für Serbien*. Frankfurt a.M.: Suhrkamp, 1996.

————. *Sommerlicher Nachtrag zu einer winterlichen Reise*. Frankfurt a.M.: Suhrkamp, 1996.

————. *Unter Tränen fragend: Nachträgliche Aufzeichnungen von zwei Jugoslawien-Durchqueren im Krieg, März und April 1999*. Frankfurt a.M.: Suhrkamp, 1999.

Härtling, Peter. *Große, kleine Schwester*. Cologne: Kiepenheuer & Witsch, 1998.

Hein, Christoph. *Von allem Anfang an*. Aufbau: Berlin, 1997.

————. *Willenbrock*. Frankfurt a.M.: Suhrkamp, 2001 [2000].

Hein, Jakob. *Mein erstes T-Shirt*. Munich: Piper, 2001.

———. *Formen menschlichen Zusammenlebens*. Munich: Piper Verlag, 2003.

Hennig von Lange, Alexa. *Relax*. Berlin: Rowohlt, 1997.

———. *Ich bin's*. Reinbek: Rogner und Bernhard Verlag, 1999.

———. *Ich habe einfach Glück*. Reinbek: Rogner und Bernhard Verlag, 2002.

———. *Lelle*. Reinbek: Rogner und Bernhard Verlag, 2002.

———. *Woher ich komme*. Reinbek: Rowohlt, 2003.

Hennig, Falko. *Alles nur geklaut*. Munich: Goldmann, 2001 [1999].

Hensel, Jana. *Zonenkinder*. Reinbek bei Hamburg: Rowohlt, 2002.

Hensel, Kerstin. *Auditorium Panoptikum*. Leipzig: Mitteldeutscher Verlag, 1991.

———. *Im Schlauch*. Frankfurt a.M.: Suhrkamp, 1993.

———. *Tanz am Kanal*. Frankfurt a.M.: Suhrkamp, 1994.

———. *Im Spinnhaus*. Munich: Luchterhand, 2003.

Hermann, Judith. *Sommerhaus, später*. Frankfurt a.M.: Fischer, 1999 [1998].

———. "Camera Obscura." In Judith Hermann, *Sommerhaus, später,* 157–65.

———. "Hurrikan (Something farewell)." In Judith Hermann, *Sommerhaus, später,* 31–54.

———. "Rote Korallen." In Judith Hermann, *Sommerhaus, später,* 11–29.

———. "On Carver: Ein Versuch." *Transatlantik* 3 (October 2001): 4–5.

———. *Nichts als Gespenster*. Frankfurt a.M.: Fischer, 2003.

———. "Nichts als Gespenster." In *Nichts als Gespenster*, 195–232.

———. "Ruth (Freundinnen)." In Judith Hermann, *Nichts als Gespenster,* 11–59.

Hettche, Thomas. *Nox*. Frankfurt a.M.: Suhrkamp, 1995.

Hielscher, Martin, ed. *Wenn der Kater kommt. Neues Erzählen. 38 deutschsprachige Autorinnen und Autoren*. Cologne: Kiepenheuer & Witsch, 1996.

Hilbig, Wolfgang. *Alte Abdeckerei*. Frankfurt a.M.: Fischer, 1991.

———. *<<Ich>>*. Frankfurt a.M.: Fischer, 1993.

———. *Die Kunde von den Bäumen*. Frankfurt a.M.: Fischer, 1996 [1994].

———. "Kamenzer Rede." In *Preis- und Dankreden*. Rheinsberg: Kurt Tucholsky Gedenkstätte, 1996, 13–16.

———. *Das Provisorium*. Frankfurt a.M.: Fischer, 2000.

Hilsenrath, Edgar. *Der Nazi & der Friseur*. Munich: Piper, 1977.

Honigmann, Barbara. *Roman von einem Kind.* Darmstadt: Luchterhand, 1986.

———. *Eine Liebe aus Nichts.* Berlin: Rowohlt, 1991.

———. *Soharas Liebe.* Berlin: Rowohlt, 1996.

———. *Am Sonntag spielt der Rabbi Fußball.* Heidelberg: Wunderhorn, 1998.

———. "Am Sonntag spielt der Rabbi Fußball." In Barbara Honigmann, *Am Sonntag spielt der Rabbi Fußball,* 36–37.

———. *Damals, dann und danach.* Munich: Hanser, 1999.

———. "Meine sefardischen Freundinnen." In Barbara Honigmann, *Damals, dann und danach,* 63–82.

———. "Selbstporträt als Jüdin". (1992). In Barbara Honigmann, *Damals, dann und danach,* 11–18.

———. "Von meinem Urgroßvater, meinem Großvater, meinem Vater und von mir." In Barbara Honigmann, *Damals, dann und danach,* 39–55.

———. *Alles, Alles Liebe.* Munich: Hanser, 2000.

Hoppe, Felicitas. *Picknick der Friseure.* Reinbek bei Hamburg: Rowohlt Verlag, 1998 [1996].

Jirgl, Reinhard. *Mutter Vater.* Berlin: Aufbau, 1990.

———. *Das obszöne Gebet. Totenbuch.* Frankfurt a.M.: Jassmann, 1992.

———. *Abschied von den Feinden.* Munich: Hanser, 1995.

———. *Hundsnächte.* Munich: Hanser, 1997.

———. *Die Atlantische Mauer.* Munich: Hanser, 2000.

———. *Die Unvollendeten.* Munich: Hanser, 2003.

Jochimsen, Jess. *Das Dosenmilch-Trauma: Bekenntnisse eines 68er-Kindes.* Munich: Deutscher Taschenbuch Verlag, 2000.

Kaminer, Wladimir. *Russendisko.* Munich: Goldmann, 2000.

———. ed. *Frische Goldjungs.* Munich: Goldmann, 2001.

———. *Militärmusik.* Munich: Goldmann, 2001.

———. "Vorwort." In Jakob Hein, *Mein erstes T-Shirt.* Munich: Piper, 2001, 6.

———. *Die Reise nach Trulala.* Munich: Goldmann, 2002.

———. *Mein deutsches Dschungelbuch.* Munich: Goldmann, 2003.

Kant, Hermann. *Abspann.* Berlin: Aufbau, 1991.

———. *Kormoran.* Berlin: Aufbau, 1994.

———. *Escape. Ein WORD-Spiel.* Berlin: Aufbau, 1995.

Kempowski, Walter. *Das Echolot: Fuga furiosa*. Munich: Albrecht Knaus Verlag, 1993–99.

———. *Der rote Hahn: Dresden im Februar 1945*. Munich: Goldmann, 2001.

Khan, Sarah. *Gogo Girl*. Berlin: Rowohlt, 1999.

———. *Dein Film*. Berlin: Rowohlt, 2001.

Kirchhoff, Bodo. "Das Schreiben: ein Sturz. In der Wüste des Banalen — zur Lage des Schriftstellers in glücklicher Zeit." In Franz Josef Görtz, Volker Hage, Uwe Wittstock, eds., *Deutsche Literatur 1992*. Stuttgart: Reclam, 1993, 295–306.

Klein, Georg. *Libidissi*. Berlin: Alexander Fest Verlag, 1998.

———. *Anrufung des blinden Fisches: Erzählungen*. Berlin: Alexander Fest, 1999.

———. *Barbar Rosa*. Berlin: Alexander Fest Verlag, 2001.

Klemperer, Victor. *Tagebücher 1933–1945,* edited by Walter Nowojski with Hadwig Klemperer. Berlin: Aufbau Verlag, 1995.

Klüger, Ruth. *weiter leben*. Munich: Deutscher Taschenbuch Verlag, 1995 [1992].

Koeppen, Wolfgang. *Jakob Littners Roman Aufzeichungen aus einem Erdloch*. Frankfurt a.M.: Jüdischer Verlag, 1992.

———. *Einer der schreibt: Gespräche und Interviews,* ed. by Hans-Ulrich Treichel. Frankfurt a.M.: Suhrkamp, 1995.

Kolb, Ulrike. *Frühstück mit Max*. Stuttgart: Klett-Cotta Verlag, 2000.

Königsdorf, Helga. *Gleich neben Afrika*. Berlin: Rowohlt, 1992.

———. *Im Schatten des Regenbogens*. Berlin: Aufbau, 1993.

———. *Die Entsorgung der Großmutter*. Berlin: Aufbau, 1997.

Kracht, Christian. *Faserland*. Munich: Deutscher Taschenbuch Verlag, 2002 [1995].

———. *1979*. Munich: Deutscher Taschenbuch Verlag, 2003 [2001].

Krauß, Angela. *Die Überfliegerin*. Frankfurt a.M.: Suhrkamp, 1995.

———. *Milliarden neuer Sterne*. Frankfurt a.M.: Suhrkamp, 1999.

Krausser, Helmut. *Tagebuch des Oktober 1997. Tagebuch des November 1998. Tagebuch des Dezember 1999*. Reinbek: rororo, 2000.

Kubiczek, André. *Junge Talente*. Berlin: Rowohlt, 2001.

———. *Die Guten und die Bösen*. Berlin: Rowohlt, 2003.

Kuckart, Judith. *Die schöne Frau*. Frankfurt a.M.: Fischer Verlag, 1999 [1997].

———. *Der Bibliothekar*. Frankfurt a.M.: Eichborn, 1998.

———. *Wahl der Waffen*. Frankfurt a.M.: Eichborn, 1999.

———. *Die Autorenwitwe*. Cologne: DuMont, 2003.

Kumpfmüller, Michael. *Hampels Fluchten*. Cologne: Kiepenheuer & Witsch, 2000.

Kunze, Reiner. *Deckname Lyrik*. Frankfurt a.M.: Fischer, 1990.

Lager, Sven, and Elke Naters. *The Buch. Leben am pool*. Cologne: Kiepenheuer & Witsch, 2001.

———. *Im Gras*. Cologne: Kiepenheuer & Witsch, 2002.

Lebert, Benjamin. *Crazy*. Cologne: Kiepenheuer & Witsch, 1999.

———. *Der Vogel ist ein Rabe*. Cologne: Kiepenheuer & Witsch, 2003.

Ledig, Gert. *Die Vergeltung*. Frankfurt a.M.: Suhrkamp Verlag, 1999 [1955].

Lehr, Thomas. *Nabokovs Katze*. Berlin: Aufbau, 1999.

Link, Heiner. *Trash-Piloten. Texte für die 90er*. Leipzig: Reclam, 1997.

Loest, Erich. *Der Zorn des Schafes*. Leipzig: Linden-Verlag, 1990.

Lottmann, Joachim. *Deutsche Einheit*. Zurich: Haffmans Verlag, 1999.

Maier, Andreas. *Wäldchestag*. Frankfurt a.M.: Suhrkamp, 2002 [2000].

———. *Klausen*. Frankfurt a.M.: Suhrkamp, 2002.

Manzel, Mattis. *Peinlich*. Zurich: Ammann, 1995.

Maron, Monika. *Die Überläuferin*. Frankfurt a.M.: Fischer, 1986.

———. *Stille Zeile Sechs*. Frankfurt a.M.: Fischer, 1991.

———. "Writers and The People." *New German Critique* 52 (1991): 36–41.

———. *Animal Triste*. Frankfurt a.M.: Fischer, 1996.

———. *Pawels Briefe*. Frankfurt a.M.: Fischer, 1999.

———. *Endmoränen*. Frankfurt a.M.: Fischer, 2002.

Meinecke, Thomas. *Church of John F. Kennedy*. Frankfurt a.M.: Suhrkamp, 1996.

———. *Mode und Verzweiflung*. Frankfurt a.M.: Suhrkamp, 1998.

———. *Tomboy*. Frankfurt a.M.: Suhrkamp, 1998.

———. *Hellblau*. Frankfurt a.M.: Suhrkamp, 2001.

Monioudis, Perikles. "In Berlin." In Jürgen Jakob Becker and Ulrich Jenetzki, eds., *Die Stadt nach der Mauer*. Berlin: Ullstein, 1998, 13–23.

Müller, Heiner. "SELBSTKRITIK." In Heiner Müller, *Werke,* edited by Frank Hörnigk. Vol. 1. *Gedichte*. Frankfurt a.M.: Suhrkamp, 1998.

Müller, Herta. *Heimat ist das was gesprochen wird*. Blieskastel: Gollenstein Verlag, 2001.

Nadolny, Sten. *Selim oder die Gabe der Rede*. Munich: Piper, 1990.

———. *ER oder ICH*. Munich: Piper, 1999.

Naters, Elke. *Königinnen*. Cologne: Kiepenheuer & Witsch, 1998.

———. *Lügen*. Cologne: Kiepenheuer & Witsch, 1999.

———. *G.L.A.M*. Cologne: Kiepenheuer & Witsch, 2001.

———. *Mau-Mau*. Munich: Deutscher Taschenbuch Verlag, 2004.

Naters, Elke, and Sven Lager, *The Buch. Leben am pool*. Cologne: Kiepenheuer & Witsch, 2001.

Neumeister, Andreas. *Ausdeutschen*. Frankfurt a.M.: Suhrkamp, 1994.

———. *Gut laut*. Frankfurt a.M.: Suhrkamp, 1998.

———. *Angela Davis löscht ihre Website*. Frankfurt a.M.: Suhrkamp, 2002.

Neumeister, Andreas, and Marcel Hartges, eds. *Poetry! Slam! Texte der Pop-Fraktion*. Reinbek bei Hambug: Rowohlt, 1996.

Niemann, Norbert. *Wie man's nimmt*. Munich: Hanser, 1998.

———. "Realismus der Verarmung." *Süddeutsche Zeitung,* 21 October 2000, *Feuilleton,* 17.

Noltensmeier, Jürgen. *Geburtenstarke Jahrgänge*. Cologne: Kiepenheuer & Witsch, 2002.

Ortheil, Hanns-Josef. *Abschied von den Kriegsteilnehmern*. Munich: Piper, 1999 [1992].

Özdamar, Emine Sevgi. *Mutterzunge*. Berlin: Rotbuch Verlag, 1993.

Peltzer, Ulrich. *"Alle oder keiner"*. Zurich: Ammann Verlag, 1999.

Peters, Christoph. *Stadt Land Fluß*. Frankfurt a.M.: Frankfurter Verlagsanstalt, 1999.

Pleschinski, Hans. *Bildnis eines Unsichtbaren*. Munich: Hanser, 2002.

Politycki, Matthias. *Weiberroman*. Hamburg: Luchterhand, 1997.

———. *Die Farbe der Vokale*. Munich: Luchterhand, 1998.

———. "Das Gequake von satten Fröschen. Die Generation der Vierzig-jährigen und ihre Angst vor Verantwortung." In Matthias Politycki, *Die Farbe der Vokale*, 13–18.

———. "Endlich aufgetaucht: Die 78er Generation." In Matthias Politycki, *Die Farbe der Vokale*, 19–22.

———. "Kalbfleisch mit Reis! Die literarische Ästhetik der 78er Generation." In Matthias Politycki, *Die Farbe der Vokale*, 23–44.

———. "Der amerikanische Holzweg." *Frankfurter Rundschau*, 18 March 2000, *Zeit und Bild*, 2.

———. "Das Medium ist die Massage." *die tageszeitung,* 25 May 2000, *Kultur,* 13–14.

———. *Ein Mann von vierzig Jahren.* Hamburg: Luchterhand, 2000.

———. "Simplifizierer und Schubladianer." *die tageszeitung* 27–28 October 2001, 13.

Röggla, Kathrin. *Abrauschen.* Frankfurt a.M.: Fischer, 2001 [1997].

———. *irres wetter.* Salzburg: Residenz, 2000.

———. "unsere gesamtgesundheit." *Akzente* 3 (2001): 59.

———. *really ground zero.* Frankfurt a.M.: Fischer, 2001.

Rosenlöcher, Thomas. *Die verkauften Pflastersteine.* Frankfurt a.M.: Suhrkamp, 1990.

———. *Die Wiederentdeckung des Gehens beim Wandern: Harzreise.* Frankfurt a.M.: Suhrkamp, 1991.

———. *Ostgezeter.* Frankfurt a.M.: Suhrkamp, 1997.

Rothmann, Ralf. *Milch und Kohle.* Frankfurt a.M.: Suhrkamp, 2000.

Saeger, Uwe. *Die Nacht danach und der Morgen.* Munich: Piper, 1991.

Schindel, Robert. *Gebürtig.* Frankfurt a.M.: Suhrkamp, 1992.

Schirmer, Bernd. *Schlehweins Giraffe.* Frankfurt a.M.: Eichborn, 1992.

Schlink, Bernhard. *Der Vorleser.* Zurich: Diogenes, 1997 [1995].

———. "Ich lebe in Geschichten." Interview in *Der Spiegel,* 24 January 2000, 180–84.

———. *Liebesfluchten.* Zurich: Diogenes, 2000.

———. "Die Beschneidung." In Bernhard Schlink, *Liebesfluchten,* 199–255.

———. *Vergangenheitsschuld und gegenwärtiges Recht.* Frankfurt a.M.: Suhrkamp, 2002).

———. "Die Gegenwart der Vergangenheit." In Bernhard Schlink, *Vergangenheitsschuld und gegenwärtiges Recht,* 145–56.

Schmidt, Jochen. *Triumphgemüse.* Munich: Beck'sche Verlagsbuchhandlung, 2000.

———. *Müller haut uns raus.* Munich: C. H. Beck, 2002.

———. "*New York is fun!.*" In Jochen Schmidt, *Müller haut uns raus,* 296–304.

Schmidt, Kathrin. *Gunnar-Lennefsen-Expedition.* Cologne: Kiepenheuer & Witsch, 1998.

Schneider, Peter, *Vati.* Darmstadt: Luchterhand, 1987.

———. *Extreme Mittellage: Eine Reise durch das deutsche Nationalgefühl.* Reinbek: Rowohlt, 1990.

———. "Man kann sogar ein Erdbeben verpassen." In Peter Schneider, *Extreme Mittellage: Eine Reise durch das deutsche Nationalgefühl,* 54–78.

———. *Paarungen.* Berlin: Rowohlt, 1992.

———. *Vom Ende der Gewißheit.* Berlin: Rowohlt, 1994.

———. "Die Intellektuellen als Grenzschützer." In Peter Schneider, *Vom Ende der Gewißheit,* 97–120.

———. *Eduards Heimkehr.* Berlin: Rowohlt, 1999.

———. *Die Diktatur der Geschwindigkeit.* Berlin: Transit, 2000.

———. "Rassismus und Erklärungssucht." In Peter Schneider, *Die Diktatur der Geschwindigkeit,* 123–26.

———. *"Und wenn wir nur eine Stunde gewinnen . . . ."* Berlin: Rowohlt, 2002 [2001].

———. *Das Fest der Missverständnisse.* Reinbek bei Hamburg: Rowohlt Verlag, 2003.

———. "Skizze eines Enthüllers." In Peter Schneider, *Das Fest der Missverständnisse,* 26–51.

Schoch, Julia. *Der Körper des Salamanders.* Munich: Piper, 2001.

Schöfer, Erasmus. *Ein Frühling irrer Hoffnung.* Cologne: Dittrich Verlag, 2001.

Scholz, Leander. *Das Rosenfest.* Munich: Hanser, 2001.

Schönburg, Alexander von. *Der fröhliche Nichtraucher.* Reinbek bei Hamburg: Rowohlt, 2003.

Schöne, Lothar. *Das jüdische Begräbnis.* Munich: Deutscher Taschenbuch Verlag, 1999 [1996].

Schwanitz, Dietrich. *Der Campus.* Frankfurt a.M.: Eichborn, 1995.

Schwerdtfeger, Malin. *Café Saratoga.* Cologne: Kiepenheuer & Witsch, 2001.

———. *Leichte Mädchen.* Cologne: Kiepenheuer & Witsch, 2001.

Sebald, W. G. "Damals vor Graz. Randbemerkungen zum Thema Literatur und Heimat," *Neue Zürcher Zeitung,* 21 May 1991.

———. *Unheimliche Heimat: Essays zur österreichischen Literatur.* Salzburg: Residenz Verlag, 1991.

———. *Die Ausgewanderten.* Frankfurt a.M.: Suhrkamp, 1997 [1994].

———. *Die Ringe des Saturn.* Frankfurt a.M.: Eichborn, 1995.

———. *Luftkrieg und Literatur.* Munich: Hanser, 1999.

———. *Austerlitz*. Munich: Hanser, 2001.

Seligmann, Rafael. *Rubensteins Versteigerung*. Munich: Deutscher Taschenbuch Verlag, 1991 [1989].

———. *Die Jiddische Mamme*. Frankfurt a.M.: Eichborn, 1990.

———. *Mit beschränkter Hoffnung*. Hamburg: Hoffmann and Campe, 1991.

———. *Der Musterjude*. Munich: Deutscher Taschenbuch Verlag, 1999 [1997].

———. "Deutsche Musterjuden. Oder: Schluß mit dem Totenkult." In Michael Gerwarth, *Innensichten Deutschland*. Berlin: Parthas Verlag, 1997, 76–78.

———. "So simpel ist Antisemitismus," *Zeitmagazin*, 1 August 1997, 6.

———. *Schalom meine Liebe*. Munich: Deutscher Taschenbuch Verlag, 1999 [1998].

———. *Der Milchmann*. Munich: Deutscher Taschenbuch Verlag, 2000 [1999].

———. "Hier geblieben! Warum tun deutsche Juden noch so, als seien sie Zionisten?." *Die Zeit*, 28 August 1999, 13.

Senger, Valentin. *Der Heimkehrer*. Munich: Luchterhand, 1995.

Şenocak, Zafer. *Atlas des tropischen Deutschlands*. Berlin: Babel, 1992.

———. *War Hitler Araber? IrreFührungen an den Rand Europas*. Berlin: Babel, 1994, 75–78.

———. "Feindbild Türkei." In Zafer Şenocak, *War Hitler Araber? IrreFührungen an den Rand Europas*, 75–78.

———. *Gefährliche Verwandtschaft*. Munich: Babel, 1998.

———. *Der Erottomane*. Munich: Babel, 1999.

———. *Zungenentfernung*. Munich: Babel, 2001.

Sloterdijk, Peter. *Die Verachtung der Masse*. Frankfurt a.M.: Suhrkamp, 1999.

———. *Regeln für den Menschenpark*. Frankfurt a.M.: Suhrkamp, 1999.

Sparschuh, Jens. *Der Zimmerspringbrunnen*. Munich: Goldmann Verlag, 1997 [1995].

———. *Lavaters Maske*. Cologne: Kiepenheuer & Witsch, 1999.

———. *Eins zu Eins*. Cologne: Kiepenheuer & Witsch, 2003.

Stadler, Arnold. *Kein Herz und keine Seele*. St. Gallen: Erker-Verlag, 1986.

———. *Feuerland*. Salzburg: Residenz, 1992.

———. *Mein Hund, meine Sau, mein Leben*. Frankfurt a.M.: Suhrkamp, 1996 [1994].

————. *Der Tod und ich, wir zwei.* Salzburg: Residenz, 1996.

————. *Gedichte aufs Land.* Düsseldorf: Eremiten-Presse, 1998.

————. *Ausflug nach Afrika.* Eggingen: Edition Isele, 1999.

————. *Ein hinreissender Schrotthändler.* Cologne: Dumont, 1999.

————. "Erbarmen mit dem Seziermesser," *Badische Zeitung,* 26 October 1999, 15.

————. "Heimat? Eine Grabschändung," *Badische Zeitung,* 9 October 1999, 14–15.

————. *Volubilis. Oder Meine Reise ans Ende der Welt.* Eggingen: Edition Isele, 1999.

————. *Sehnsucht.* Cologne: Dumont, 2002.

Staffel, Tim. *Terrordrom.* Berlin: Ullstein, 1999 [1998].

————. *Heimweh.* Berlin: Volk & Welt, 2000.

Stahl, Enno. *Trash Me!.* Cologne: KRASH, 1992.

————. ed. *German Trash.* Berlin: Galrev, 1996.

————. *Pewee Rocks.* Cologne: KRASH, 1997.

Strauß, Botho. *Beginnlosigkeit.* Munich: Hanser, 1992.

————. "Anschwellender Bocksgesang." *Der Spiegel,* 8 February 1993, 202–7.

————. *Wohnen, Dämmern, Lügen.* Munich: Hanser, 1994.

————. *Die Fehler des Kopisten.* Munich: Deutscher Taschenbuch Verlag, 1999 [1997].

————. *Der Aufstand gegen die sekundäre Welt.* Munich: Hanser, 1999.

————. "Anschwellender Bocksgesang." In Botho Strauß, *Der Aufstand gegen die sekundäre Welt,* 55–79.

————. "Der Aufstand gegen die sekundäre Welt: Bemerkungen zu einer Ästhetik der Anwesenheit." In Botho Strauß, *Der Aufstand gegen die sekundäre Welt,* 37–53.

————. "Zeit ohne Vorboten." In Botho Strauß, *Der Aufstand gegen die sekundäre Welt,* 93–105.

————. *Das Partikular.* Munich: Hanser, 2000.

Stuckrad-Barre, Benjamin von. *Soloalbum.* Cologne: Kiepenheuer & Witsch, 1998.

————. *Livealbum.* Cologne: Kiepenheuer & Witsch, 1999.

————. *Remix.* Cologne: Kiepenheuer & Witsch, 1999.

————. *Blackbox.* Berlin: Goldmann, 2002 [2000].

———. *Remix 2.* Cologne: Kiepenheuer & Witsch, 2004.

Szymanski, Silvia. *Chemische Reinigung.* Leipzig: Reclam, 1998.

———. *Kein Sex mit Mike.* Hamburg: Hoffmann und Campe, 1999.

———. *Agnes Sobierajski.* Hamburg: Hoffmann und Campe, 2000.

———. *652 Kilometer nach Berlin.* Hamburg: Hoffmann und Campe, 2002.

Timm, Uwe. *Die Entdeckung der Currywurst.* Cologne: Kiepenheuer & Witsch, 1998 [1993].

———. *Johannisnacht.* Munich: Deutscher Taschenbuch Verlag, 1999 [1996].

———. *Rot.* Cologne: Kiepenheuer & Witsch, 2001.

———. *Am Beispiel meines Bruders.* Cologne: Kiepenheuer & Witsch, 2003.

Treichel, Hans-Ulrich. *Heimatkunde oder alles ist heiter und edel.* Frankfurt a.M.: Suhrkamp, 1996.

———. "Heimatkunde." In Hans-Ulrich Treichel, *Heimatkunde oder alles ist heiter und edel,* 47–57.

———. *Der Verlorene.* Frankfurt a.M.: Suhrkamp, 1999 [1998].

———. "Prägende Sätze." *Neue Zürcher Zeitung,* 10 October 1998, 50

———. *Der Entwurf des Autors: Frankfurter Poetikvorlesungen.* Frankfurt a.M.: Suhrkamp, 2000.

———. "Lektionen der Leere. Eine Kindheit auf dem Lande. Oder wie ich Schriftsteller wurde." *Neue Zürcher Zeitung,* 15/16 April 2000, 50.

———. *Tristanakkord.* Frankfurt a.M.: Suhrkamp, 2000.

———. *Der irdische Amor.* Frankfurt a.M.: Suhrkamp, 2002.

Tuschick, Jamal. *Morgen Land: Neueste deutsche Literatur.* Frankfurt a.M.: Fischer, 2000.

Vanderbeke, Birgit. *Abgehängt.* Frankfurt a.M.: Fischer Verlag, 2001.

Wagner, David. *Meine nachtblaue Hose.* Berlin: Fest, 2000.

———. *Was alles fehlt.* Munich: Piper, 2002.

Walser, Martin. "Über die Neueste Stimmung im Westen." *Kursbuch* 20 (1970): 19–42.

———. *Die Gallistl'sche Krankheit.* Frankfurt a.M.: Suhrkamp 1972.

———. *Die Verteidigung der Kindheit.* Frankfurt a.M.: Suhrkamp, 1991.

———. *ohne einander.* Frankfurt a.M.: Suhrkamp, 1993.

———. "Reise ins Innere. Oder wie man erfährt, was man erlebt hat." In Martin Walser, *Stimmung 94.* Eggingen: Edition Isele, 1994, 37–57.

———. *Das Prinzip Genauigkeit. Laudatio auf Victor Klemperer.* Frankfurt a.M.: Suhrkamp, 1995.

———. "Das Trotzdemschöne." "Nachwort" to Arnold Stadler, *Mein Hund, meine Sau, mein Leben.* Frankfurt a.M.: Suhrkamp, 1996.

———. *Deutsche Sorgen.* Frankfurt a.M.: Suhrkamp, 1997.

———. "Deutsche Sorgen 1." In Martin Walser, *Deutsche Sorgen,* 430–38.

———. *Dorle und Wolf.* In Martin Walser, *Deutsche Sorgen,* 276–405.

———. "Händedruck mit Gespenstern." In Martin Walser, *Deutsche Sorgen,* 213–27.

———. "Über Deutschland reden. Ein Bericht." In Martin Walser, *Deutsche Sorgen,* 406–27.

———. "Über freie und unfreie Rede." In Martin Walser, *Deutsche Sorgen,* 468–85.

———. With Hermann Bauschinger and Manfred Bosch. "Heimat — aber woher nehmen?," *Allemende* 54/55 (1997): 22–53.

———. "Die Utopie in der Sprache." In Martin Walser, *"Ich habe so ein Wunschpotential." Gespräche mit Martin Walser.* Frankfurt a.M.: Suhrkamp, 1998, 121–29.

———. *Ein springender Brunnen.* Frankfurt a.M.: Suhrkamp, 1998.

———. "Erfahrungen beim Verfassen einer Sonntagsrede." In Frank Schirrmacher, ed., *Die Walser-Bubis-Debatte.* Frankfurt a.M.: Suhrkamp, 1999, 7–17.

———. "Über das Verbergen der Verzweiflung." *Der Spiegel* 29 1999, 161–62.

———. *Der Lebenslauf der Liebe.* Frankfurt a.M.: Suhrkamp, 2002.

———. *Tod eines Kritikers.* Frankfurt a.M.: Suhrkamp, 2002.

Wawerzinek, Peter. *Café Komplott: Eine glückliche Begebenheit.* Berlin: Transit-Verlag, 1998.

Wildenhain, Michael. *Erste Liebe — Deutscher Herbst.* Frankfurt a.M.: Fischer, 1997.

Woelk, Ulrich. *Rückspiel.* Frankfurt a.M.: Fischer, 1993.

Wolf, Christa. *Was bleibt.* Frankfurt a.M.: Luchterhand, 1990.

———. *Medea. Stimmen.* Frankfurt a.M.: Luchterhand, 1996.

———. *Leibhaftig.* Munich: Luchterhand, 2002.

Zaimoğlu, Feridun. *Kanak Sprak: 24 Mißtöne vom Rande der Gesellschaft.* Hamburg: Rotbuch, 1995.

———. *German Amok.* Cologne: Kiepenheuer & Witsch, 2002.

Zelter, Joachim. *Das Gesicht.* Tübingen: Klöpfer und Meyer Verlag, 2003.

Zschokke, Matthias. *Der dicke Dichter.* Cologne: Bruckner & Thünker Verlag, 1995.

Works Consulted

Adelson, Leslie A. "Touching Tales of Turks, Germans and Jews: Cultural Alterity, Historical Narrative and Literary Riddles of the 1990s." *New German Critique* 80 (2000): 93–124.

———. "The Turkish Turn in Contemporary German Literature and Memory Work." *Germanic Review* 77:4 (2002): 326–38.

Angier, Carole. "In the Killing Fields," *Guardian,* 23 May 1998, 9.

Anz, Thomas, ed. *"Es geht nicht nur um Christa Wolf." Der Literaturstreit im vereinten Deutschland.* Munich: Spangenberg, 1991.

———. "Westwärts," *Die Zeit* 41, 2 October 1992, 11.

Arnold, Heinz Ludwig. ed. *Blech getrommelt: Günter Grass in der Kritik.* Göttingen: Steidl, 1997.

———. ed. *DDR-Literatur der neunziger Jahre, Text + Kritik.* Munich: Richard Boorberg Verlag, 2000.

———. ed. *Pop-Literatur, Text + Kritik.* Munich: Richard Boorberg Verlag, 2003.

Assheuer, Thomas. "Was ist rechts? Botho Strauß bläßt ins Bockshorn". In Franz Josef Görtz, Volker Hage, and Uwe Wittstock, eds., *Deutsche Literatur 1993.* Stuttgart: Reclam, 1994, 269–72.

Assmann, Aleida, and Ute Frevert, *Geschichtsvergessenheit, Geschichtsversessenheit: Vom Umgang mit deutschen Vergangenheiten nach 1945.* Stuttgart: Deutsche Verlags-Anstalt, 1999.

Bartmer, Rose. "Die Debütanten und der Markt." *Sprache im technischen Zeitalter* 162 (2002): 193–205.

Bartov, Omer. "Germany as Victim." *New German Critique* 80 (2000): 29–40.

Basker, David. "The Author as Victim: Wolfgang Koeppen, *Jakob Littners Aufzeichnungen aus einem Erdloch.*" *Modern Language Review* 92:4 (1997): 903–11.

———. ed., *Hans-Ulrich Treichel.* Cardiff: U of Wales P, 2004.

———. "'Schlüsselszenen der Erfahrung': (Dis)location in the Prose Work of Hans-Ulrich Treichel." In David Basker, ed., *Hans-Ulrich Treichel.* Cardiff: U of Wales P, 2004, 37–60.

Baßler, Moritz. *Der deutsche Pop-Roman.* Munich: Beck, 2002.

Bathrick, David. *The Powers of Speech: The Politics of Culture in the GDR.* Lincoln and London: U of Nebraska P, 1995.

Baumann, Rainer, and Gunther Hellmann. "Germany and the Use of Military Force: 'Total War,' the 'Culture of Restraint,' and the Quest for Normality," *German Politics* 10:1 (2001): 61–82.

Baumgart, Reinhard. "Deutsch-deutsche Sprechblasen: Friedrich Christian Delius' Beitrag zur deutschen Einheit." *Die Zeit,* 22 March 1991, 13.

———. "Das Luftkriegstrauma der Literatur." *Die Zeit,* 20 April 1999, 55.

Bauschinger, Hermann, Manfred Bosch, and Martin Walser. "Heimat — aber woher nehmen?." *Allemende* 54/55 (1997): 22–53.

Becker, Jürgen Jakob, and Ulrich Jenetzki, eds. *Die Stadt nach der Mauer.* Berlin: Ullstein, 1998.

Benjamin, Jessica, and Anson Rabinbach. "Germans, Leftists, Jews." *New German Critique* 31 (Winter/Summer, 1984): 188–95.

Benjamin, Walter. *Das Passagenwerk.* Vol. 1, ed. by Rolf Tiedemann. Frankfurt a.M.: Suhrkamp, 1983, 525–69.

Berger, Stefan. *The Search for Normality.* Oxford: Berghahn, 1997.

Berghahn, Klaus, ed. *The German-Jewish Dialogue Reconsidered.* Bern: Peter Lang, 1996.

Bergmann, Werner. "Sind die Deutschen antisemitisch? Meinungsumfragen von 1946–1987 in der Bundesrepublik Deutschland." In Werner Bergmann and Rainer Erb, eds., *Antisemitismus in der politischen Kultur nach 1945.* Opladen: Westdeutscher Verlag, 1990, 108–30.

Bhabha, Homi. "Of Mimicry and Man: The Ambivalence of Colonial Discourse." *October* 28 (1984): 15–33.

Biendarra, Anke S. "Der Erzähler als 'Popmoderner Flaneuer' in Christian Krachts Roman *Faserland.*" *German Life and Letters* 55:2 (2002): 164–79.

Blumenthal, Michael. *Daniel Libeskind and the Jewish Museum of Berlin. Leo-Baeck Memorial Lecture 44.* New York: Leo Baeck Institute, 2000.

Boa, Elizabeth, and Rachel Palfreyman. *Heimat — A German Dream: Regional Loyalties and National Identity in German Culture.* Oxford: Oxford UP, 2000.

Böttiger, Helmut, and Wolfram Schütte. "Metropole ist eine Fiktion," Interview with Kathrin Röggla, Norbert Niemann, Ingo Schulze, and Burkhard Spinnen. *Frankfurter Rundschau,* 28 November 1998, 22.

Brockmann, Stephen. "The Politics of German Literature." *Monatshefte* 84:1 (1992): 46–58.

———. *Literature and German Unification.* Cambridge: Cambridge UP, 1999.

————. "The Written Capital." *Monatshefte* 3 (1999): 376–95.

Browning, Christopher R. *Ordinary Men: Reserve Police Battalion 101 and the Final Solution in Poland*. New York: HarperPerennial, 1998 [1992].

Bude, Heinz. *Generation Berlin*. Berlin: Merve Verlag, 2001.

Büsser, Martin. "'Ich stehe auf Zerfall.' Die Punk- und New-Wave-Rezeption in der deutschen Literatur." In Heinz Ludwig Arnold, ed., *Pop-Literatur, Text + Kritik*. Munich: Richard Boorberg Verlag, 2003, 149–57.

Cheesman, Tom. "Akçam — Zaimoğlu — 'Kanak Attak': Turkish Lives and Letters in German." *German Life and Letters* 55:2 (2002): 180–95.

————. "Ş/ß: Zafer Şenocak and the Civilization of Clashes." In Tom Cheesman and Karin Yeşilada, eds., *Zafer Şenocak*. Cardiff: U of Wales P, 2003, 144–59.

Cheesman, Tom, and Karin Yeşilada, eds. *Zafer Şenocak*. Cardiff: U of Wales P, 2003.

Clarke, David. "Guilt and Shame in Hans-Ulrich Treichel's *Der Verlorene*." In David Basker, ed., *Hans-Ulrich Treichel*. Cardiff: U of Wales P, 2004, 61–78.

Cooke, Paul. "From *Opfer* to *Täter*? Identity and the *Stasi* in Post-*Wende* East German Literature." In Martin Kane, ed., *Legacies and Identity: East and West German Literary Responses to Unification*. Bern, Peter Lang, 2002, 51–66.

————. "Beyond a *Trotzidentität*? Storytelling and the Postcolonial Voice in Ingo Schulze's *Simple Storys*." *Forum for Modern Language Studies* 39:3 (2003): 290–305.

————. "Performing *Ostalgie*: Leander Haußmann's *Sonnenallee*." *German Life and Letters* 56:2 (2003): 156–67.

————. "The Stasi as Panopticon: Wolfgang Hilbig's *»Ich«*." In Paul Cooke and Andrew Plowman, eds., *German Writers and the Politics of Culture: Dealing with the Stasi*. Basingstoke: Palgrave, 2003, 139–53.

————. "East German Writing in the Age of Globalisation." In Stuart Taberner, ed., *German Literature in the Age of Globalisation*. Birmingham: Birmingham UP, 2004), 25–46.

————. "Escaping the Burden of the Past: Questions of East German Identity in the Work of Ingo Schramm." *Seminar* 40:1 (2004): 35–49.

————. *Representing East Germany since Unification: From Colonization to Nostalgia*. Oxford: Berg, forthcoming, 2005.

Cooke, Paul, and Andrew Plowman, eds. *German Writers and the Politics of Culture: Dealing with the Stasi*. Basingstoke: Palgrave, 2003.

Cornils, Ingo. "Successful Failure? The Impact of the German Student Movement on the Federal Republic of Germany." In Stuart Taberner and Frank Finlay, eds., *Recasting German Identity*. Rochester: Camden House, 2002, 109–26.

———. "Long Memories: The German Student Movement in Recent Fiction." *German Life and Letters* 56:1 (2003): 89–101.

Costabile-Heming, Carol Anne, Rachel J. Halverson, and Kristie A. Foell, eds. *Textual Responses to German Unification*. Berlin: Walter de Gruyter, 2001.

Cowley, Jason. 'Forgotten Victims', *Guardian,* 27 March 2002, 27.

Cullen, Michael S., ed. *Das Holocaust-Mahnmal: Dokumentation einer Debatte*. Zurich: Pendo Verlag, 1999.

Dahlke, Birgit, and Beth Linklater, eds. *Kerstin Hensel*. Cardiff: U of Wales P, 2002.

Dahn, Daniela. *Westwärts und nicht vergessen: Vom Unbehagen in der Einheit*. Berlin: Rowohlt, 1997.

Deiritz, Karl, and Hannes Krauss, eds. *Der deutsch-deutsche Literaturstreit oder "Freunde, es spricht sich schlecht mit gebundener Zunge"*. Hamburg: Luchterhand, 1991.

Diner, Dan. "Negative Symbiose: Deutsche und Juden nach Auschwitz." *Babylon* 1 (1986): 9–20.

Donahue, William Collins. "Illusions of Subtlety: Bernhard Schlink's *Der Vorleser* and the Moral Limits of Holocaust Fiction." *German Life and Letters* 54:1 (2001): 60–81.

Doomernik, Jeroen. *Going West: Soviet Jewish Immigrants in Berlin since 1990*. Aldershot: Avebury, 1997.

Dreike, Beate M. "Was wäre denn Gerechtigkeit? Zur Rechtsskepsis in Bernhard Schlinks *Der Vorleser*." *German Life and Letters* 55:1 (2002): 117–29.

Ebel, Martin. "In der Komponistenumlaufbahn." *Stuttgarter Zeitung,* 21 March 2000, 4.

Eckhardt, Ulrich, and Andreas Nachama, eds. *Jüdische Orte in Berlin*. Berlin: Nicolai Verlag, 1996.

Eichel, Christine, ed. *Es liegt mir auf der Zunge*. Munich: Goldmann, 2002.

Emmerich, Wolfgang. "Für eine andere Wahrnehmung der DDR-Literatur." In Wolfgang Emmerich, *Die andere deutsche Literatur*. Opladen: Westdeutscher Verlag, 1994, 190–207.

———. *Kleine Literaturgeschichte der DDR. Erweiterte Ausgabe*. Leipzig: Aufbau Verlag, 2000.

———. "Andreas Maier, *Klausen*," introduction to the CD version of *Klausen* (2002), 4–8.

Ernst, Thomas. *Popliteratur*. Hamburg: Rotbuch Verlag, 2001.

———. "German Pop Literature and Cultural Globalization." In Stuart Taberner, ed., *German Literature in the Age of Globalisation*. Birmingham: Birmingham UP, 2004, 169–88.

Evans, Richard J. *In Hitler's Shadow: West German Historians and the Atempt to Escape from the Nazi Past*. New York: Pantheon, 1989.

Fachinger, Petra. *Rewriting Germany From the Margins: "Other" German Literature of the 1980s and 1990s*. Montreal: McGill-Queen's UP, 2001.

Fiedler, Leslie. "Das Neue Zeitalter der neuen Literatur." *Christ und Welt*, 13 and 20 September 1968.

———. "cross the border, close the gap," *Playboy*, December 1969.

Fiedler, Theodor. "'eine sehr komplizierte Rechtslage wegen der Urheberrechte.'" *Colloquia Germanica* 32:2 (1999): 103–4.

Finkelstein, Norman. *The Holocaust Industry*. London: Verso, 2000.

Finlay, Frank. "'Dann wäre Deutschland wie das Wort Neckarrauen': Surface, Superficiality and Globalisation in Christian Kracht's *Faserland*." In Stuart Taberner, ed., *German Literature in the Age of Globalisation*. Birmingham: Birmingham UP, 2004, 189–208.

Finlay, Frank, and Sally Johnson. "(Il)literacy and (Im)morality in Bernhard Schlink's *The Reader*." *Written Language and Literacy* 4:2 (2001): 195–214.

Finlay, Frank, and Stuart Taberner, eds. *Recasting German Identity*. Rochester: Camden House, 2002.

Finnan, Carmel. "Autobiography, Memory and the Shoah: German-Jewish Identity in Autobiographical Writings by Ruth Klüger, Cordelia Edvardson and Laura Waco." In Pól O'Dochartaigh, ed., *Jews in German Literature Since 1945. German-Jewish Literature, German Monitor*. Amsterdam: Rodopi, 2000, 447–61.

Fischer, Gerhard, and David Roberts, eds. *Schreiben nach der Wende: Ein Jahrzehnt deutscher Literatur 1989–1999*. Tübingen: Stauffenberg, 2001.

Fischer, Joschka. "Deutschland, deine Juden." In Michael Naumann, ed., *"Es muß doch in diesem Land wieder möglich sein . . . ," Der neue Antisemitismus-Streit*. Frankfurt a.M.: Ullstein, 2002, 43.

Flanagan, Clare, and Stuart Taberner, eds. *1949/1989: Cultural Perspectives on Division and Unity in East and West, German Monitor* 50. Amsterdam: Rodopi, 2000.

Florin, Christian. "Die Toten morsen SOS." *Rheinischer Merkur*, 22 February 2002, 21.

Foell, Kristie A., Carol Anne Costabile-Heming, and Rachel J. Halverson, eds. *Textual Responses to German Unification*. Berlin: Walter de Gruyter, 2001.

Foell, Kristie, and Jill Twark. "'Bekenntnisse des Hochstaplers Klaus Uhltzscht': Thomas Brussig's Comical and Controversial *Helden wie Wir*." In Paul Cooke and Andrew Plowman, eds., *German Writers and the Politics of Culture: Dealing with the Stasi*. Basingstoke: Palgrave, 2003, 173–94.

Frevert, Ute, and Aleida Assmann. *Geschichtsvergessenheit, Geschichtsversessenheit: Vom Umgang mit deutschen Vergangenheiten nach 1945*. Stuttgart: Deutsche Verlags-Anstalt, 1999.

Friedrich, Jörg. *Der Brand: Deutschland im Bombenkrieg*. Munich: Propyläen, 2002.

———. *Brandstätten*. Munich: Propyläen Verlag, 2003.

Fuchs, Anne. "'Phantomspuren': Zu W. G. Sebalds Poetik der Erinnerung in *Austerlitz*." *German Life and Letters* 56:3 (2003): 281–98.

Fulbrook, Mary. *German National Identity after the Holocaust*. Cambridge: Polity Press, 1999.

Gabler, Wolfgang. "Der Wenderoman als neues literarisches Genre." In Wolfgang Gabler and Nikolaus Werz, eds., *Zeiten-Wende — Wendeliteratur*. Weimar: Edition I, 2000, 70–93.

Gabler, Wolfgang, and Nikolaus Werz, eds. *Zeiten-Wende — Wendeliteratur*. Weimar: Edition I, 2000.

Gay, Caroline. "Remembering For the Future, Engaging with the Present: National Memory Management and the Dialectic of Normality in the Berlin Republic." In William Niven and James Jordan, eds., *Politics and Culture in Twentieth-Century Germany*. Rochester: Camden House, 2003, 201–26.

Gerstenberger, Katharina. "Difficult Stories: Generation, Genealogy, Gender in Zafer Şenocak's *Gefährliche Verwandtschaft* and Monika Maron's *Pawels Briefe*." In Stuart Taberner and Frank Finlay, eds., *Recasting German Identity*. Rochester: Camden House, 2002, 242–55.

———. "Writing by Ethnic Minorities in the Age of Globalisation," in Stuart Taberner, *German Literature in the Age of Globalisation*. Birmingham: Birmingham UP, 2004, 209–28.

Geulen, Eva. "Nationalisms: Old, New and German." *Telos* 105 (1995): 2–20.

Gilman, Sander. "German Unification and the Jews." *New German Critique* 52 (1991): 173–91.

————. "Negative Symbiosis: The Reemergence of Jewish Culture in Germany after the Fall of the Wall." In Klaus L. Berghahn, ed., *The German-Jewish Dialogue Reconsidered*. Bern: Peter Lang, 1996, 207–32.

Gilman, Sander, and Hartmut Steinecke, eds. *Deutsch-jüdische Literatur der neunziger Jahre. Die Generation nach der Shoah. Beiheft zur Zeitschrift für Deutsche Philologie* 11 (2002).

Gilman, Sander, and Jack Zipes, eds. *The Yale Companion to Jewish Writing and Thought in German Culture, 1096–1996*. New Haven: Yale UP, 796–804,

Gilman, Sander, and Karen Remmler, eds. *Reemerging Jewish Culture in Germany: Life and Literature since 1989*. New York and London: New York UP, 1994.

Goer, Charis. "Cross the Border — Face the Gap: Ästhetik der Grenzerfahrung bei Thomas Meinecke und Andreas Neumeister." In Heinz Ludwig Arnold, ed., *Pop-Literatur, Text + Kritik*. Munich: Richard Boorberg Verlag, 2003, 172–82.

Goldhagen, Daniel Jonah. *Hitler's Willing Executioners: Ordinary Germans and the Holocaust*. New York: Knopf, 1996.

Graves, Peter. "Karen Duve, Kathrin Schmidt, Judith Hermann: 'Ein literarisches Fräuleinwunder.'" *German Life and Letters* 55:2 (2002): 196–207.

Greiner, Ulrich. "Die deutsche Gesinnungsästhetik." In Thomas Anz, ed., *"Es geht nicht nur um Christa Wolf." Der Literaturstreit im vereinten Deutschland*. Munich: Spangenberg, 1991, 208–16.

————. "Mangel an Feingefühl." In Thomas Anz, ed., *"Es geht nicht nur um Christa Wolf." Der Literaturstreit im vereinten Deutschland*. Munich: Spangenberg, 1991.

————. "Der Betrieb tanzt. Über Literatur und Öffentlichkeit," *neue deutsche literatur* 520:4 (1998): 159–69.

Günter, Joachim. "Opfer und Tabu: Günter Grass und das Denken im Trend." *Neue Zürcher Zeitung*, 23 March 2002, 33

Habermas, Jürgen. "Die Moderne — Ein unvollendetes Projekt." In Jürgen Habermas, *Kleine politische Schriften I-IV*. Leipzig: Reclam, 1991, 444–64.

Hage, Volker. "Auf der Suche nach Arnold." *Der Spiegel*, 23 March 1998, 244–49.

————. "Zeitalter der Bruchstücke." In Andrea Köhler und Rainer Moritz, eds., *Maulhelden und Königskinder: Zur Debatte über die deutschsprachige Gegenwartsliteratur*. Leipzig: Reclam Verlag, 1998, 28–41.

————. "Literarisches Fräuleinwunder." *Der Spiegel*, 22 March 1999, 7.

————. "Gewicht der Wahrheit." *Der Spiegel*, 29 March 1999, 242–43.

———. "Die neuen deutschen Dichter." *Der Spiegel,* 11 October 1999, 244–58.

———. *Hamburg 1943: Literarische Zeugnisse des Feuersturms.* Frankfurt a.M.: Fischer, 2003.

Hahn, Hans. "'Es geht nicht um Literatur': Some Observations on the 1990 "Literaturstreit" and its Recent Anti-Intellectual Implications." *German Life and Letters* 50:1 (1997): 65–81.

Hall, Katharina. "Jewish Memory in Exile: The Relation of W. G. Sebald's *Die Ausgewanderten* to the Tradition of the *Yizkor* Books." In Pól O'Dochartaigh, ed., *Jews in German Literature Since 1945. German-Jewish Literature, German Monitor.* Amsterdam: Rodopi, 2000, 153–64.

———. "'Bekanntlich sind Dreiecksbeziehungen am kompliziertesten': Turkish, Jewish and German Identity in Zafer Şenocak's *Gefährliche Verwandtschaft.*" *German Life and Letters* 56:1 (2003): 72–88.

Hall, Stuart. "Cultural Identity and Diaspora." In Padmini Mongia, ed., *Contemporary Postcolonial Theory: A Reader.* London: Arnold, 1996, 110–21.

Halverson, Rachel J., Carol Anne Costabile-Heming, and Kristie A. Foell, eds. *Textual Responses to German Unification.* Berlin: Walter de Gruyter, 2001.

Harder, Matthias, ed. *Bestandsaufnahmen . . . Deutschsprachige Literatur der neunziger Jahre aus interkultureller Sicht.* Würzburg: Königshausen & Neumann, 2001.

Harig, Ludwig. *Weh dem, der aus der Reihe tanzt.* Munich: Hanser, 1990.

———. *Wer mit den Wölfen heult, wird Wolf.* Munich: Hanser, 1996.

Heckner, Elke. "Berlin Remake: Building Memory and the Politics of Capital Identity.'" *Germanic Review* 77:4 (2002): 304–25.

Heidelberger-Leonard, Irene. "Ruth Klügers *weiter leben* — ein Grundstein zu einem neuen Auschwitz-'Kanon'?" In Stephan Braese, Holger Gehle, Doron Kiesel, Hanno Loewy, eds., *Deutsche Nachkriegsliteratur und der Holocaust.* Frankfurt a.M.: Campus, 1998, 157–69.

Heimler, Gabriel, Britta Jürgs, Michael Frajman, eds., *DAVKA: Jüdische Visionen in Berlin.* Berlin: AvivA, 1999.

Heimrod, Ute, Günter Schlusche, and Horst Seferens, eds. *Denkmalstreit — das Denkmal? Die Debatte um das "Denkmal für die ermordeten Juden Europas."* Berlin: Philo, 1999.

Hellmann, Gunther, and Baumann, Rainer. "Germany and the Use of Military Force: 'Total War,' the 'Culture of Restraint,' and the Quest for Normality." *German Politics* 10:1 (2001): 61–82.

Hessing, Jakob. "Im Exil: Zur deutsch-jüdischen Literatur." *Merkur* 567 (1996): 491–501.

Hielscher, Martin. "Literatur in Deutschland — Avantgarde und pädagog-ischer Purismus." In Andrea Köhler and Rainer Moritz, eds., *Maulhelden und Königskinder: Zur Debatte über die deutschsprachige Gegenwarts-literatur.* Leipzig: Reclam Verlag, 1998, 151–55.

Hillgruber, Andreas. *Zweierlei Untergang: Die Zerschlagung des Deutschen Reiches und das Ende des europäischen Judentums.* Berlin: Seidler, 1986.

Hogwood, Patricia. "After the GDR: Reconstructing Identity in Post-Communist Germany." *Journal of Communist Studies and Transition Poli-tics* 16:4 (2000): 45–68.

Hörisch, Jochen. "Verdienst und Vergehen der Gegenwartsliteratur." In Christian Döring, ed., *Deutsche Gegenwartsliteratur: Wider ihre Verächter.* Frankfurt a.M.: Suhrkamp, 1995, 30–48.

Hosek, Jennifer Ruth. "Dancing the (Un)Stated: Narrative Ambiguity in Kerstin Hensel's *Tanz am Kanal.*" In Beth Linklater and Birgit Dahlke, eds., *Kerstin Hensel.* Cardiff: U of Wales P, 2002, 107–19.

Huyssen, Andreas. "After the Wall: The Failure of German Intellectuals." *New German Critique* 52 (1991): 109–43.

Hyde-Price, Adrian. "Germany and the Kosovo War: Still a Civilian Power?" *German Politics* 10:1 (2001): 19–34.

Illies, Florian, *Generation Golf.* Frankfurt a.M.: Fischer, 2002 [2000].

———. *Generation Golf zwei.* Munich: Karl Blessing Verlag, 2003.

James-Chakraborty, Kathleen. "Memory and the Cityscape: The German Ar-chitectural Debate about Postmodernism." *German Politics and Society* 17:3 (1999): 71–83.

Jasper, Willi, Julius Schoeps, and Bernhard Vogt, eds. *Russen und Juden in Deutschland. Integration und Selbstbehauptung in einem fremden Land.* Weinheim: Athenäum, 1996.

Jeismann, Michael, ed. *Mahnmal Mitte: Eine Kontroverse.* Cologne: Dumont, 1999.

———. *Auf Wiedersehen Gestern.* Stuttgart: Deutsche Verlags-Anstalt: 2001.

Jenetzki, Ulrich, and Jürgen Jakob Becker, eds. *Die Stadt nach der Mauer.* Berlin: Ullstein, 1998.

Jeutter, Ralf. "'Am Rand der Finsternis.' The Jewish Experience in the Con-text of W. G. Sebald's Poetics." In Pól O'Dochartaigh, ed., *Jews in German Literature Since 1945. German-Jewish Literature, German Monitor.* Am-sterdam: Rodopi, 2000, 165–79.

Johnson, Sally, and Frank Finlay, "(Il)literacy and (Im)morality in Bernhard Schlink's *The Reader.*" *Written Language and Literacy* 4:2 (2001): 195–214.

Johnson, Sally, and Stephanie Suhr. "From 'Political Correctness' to 'Politische Korrektheit': Discourses of 'PC' in the German Newspaper Die Welt." Discourse and Society 14:1 (2002): 49–68.

Jordan, James, and William Niven, eds. Politics and Culture in Twentieth-Century Germany. Rochester: Camden House, 2003.

Jucker, Rolf. "SchriftstellerInnen der DDR als Verräter und Aufklärer zugleich: Zu Christa Wolf, Sascha Anderson, Rainer Schedlinski und Heiner Müller." In Osman Durrani, Colin Good, and Kevin Hilliard, eds., The New Germany: Literature and Society After Unification. Sheffield: Sheffield Academic Press, 1995, 1–13.

Kane, Martin. "'Zuweilen verliere ich mich in fantastischen Zusammenhängen.': Fritz Rudolf Fries' Extravaganza Die Nonnen von Bratislava." In Clare Flanagan and Stuart Taberner, eds., 1949/1989: Cultural Perspectives On Division and Unity in East and West, German Monitor 50. Amsterdam: Rodopi, 2000, 161–75.

———. ed. Legacies and Identity: East and West German Literary Responses to Unification. Bern, Peter Lang, 2002.

Karasek, Helmut. "Vorgelesen." Der Tagesspiegel, 31 December 2000, W4.

Kiderlen, Elisabeth. "'Wie die Gänse auf dem Kapitol.' Der Schriftsteller Rafael Seligmann über Antisemitismus heute." Badische Zeitung, 3 May 2002, 3.

Klaus, Harald. "Appetit auf eine Seele." Die Presse, 2 October 1999, Spektrum, vii.

Knopp, Guido. Der Untergang der "Gustloff." Munich: Econ Taschenbuch, 2002.

Köhler, Andrea, and Rainer Moritz, eds. Maulhelden und Königskinder: Zur Debatte über die deutschsprachige Gegenwartsliteratur. Leipzig: Reclam Verlag, 1998.

Koneffke, Jan. "Der Traum von der Nationalliteratur." Wespennest 115 (1999): 61–65.

Kraft, Thomas, ed. aufgerissen: Zur Literatur der 90er. Munich: Piper, 2000.

———. "Einleitung." In Thomas Kraft, ed., aufgerissen: Zur Literatur der 90er. Munich: Piper, 2000, 11–22.

Kramer, Jane. "The Politics of Memory." New Yorker, 14 August 1995, 48–65.

Krauss, Hannes, and Karl Deiritz, eds. Der deutsch-deutsche Literaturstreit oder "Freunde, es spricht sich schlecht mit gebundener Zunge". Hamburg: Luchterhand, 1991.

Kübler, Gunhild. "Dem Freund erzählen, was nicht zum Aushalten ist." Die Weltwoche 15 February 2001, 41.

————. "Stille Helden, von Mitgefühl getrieben." *Die Weltwoche,* 5 April 2001, 41.

Kühner, Claudia. "Ein Buch geht um die Welt." *Rheinischer Merkur,* 16 April 1999, 18.

Ladd, Brian. *The Ghosts of Berlin.* Chicago: U of Chicago P, 1997.

Langner, Beatrix. "Gleichnis vom ewigen Juden." *Süddeutsche Zeitung,* 20 June 1996, 14.

Ledanff, Susanne. "'Metropolisierung' der deutschen Literatur? Welche Möglichkeiten eröffnet das vereinigte Berlin und die neue Berliner Urbanität?" In Gerhard Fischer and David Roberts, eds., *Schreiben nach der Wende: Ein Jahrzehnt deutscher Literatur 1989–1999.* Tübingen: Stauffenberg, 2001, 275–89.

Lehmann, Albrecht. "Die Kriegsgefangenen," *aus politik und zeitgeschichte,* 10 February 1995, 13–14.

Lewis, Alison. "The 'Phantom-Pain' of Germany: Mourning and Fetishism in Martin Walser's *Die Verteidigung der Kindheit.*" In Peter Monteath and Reinhard Alter, eds., *German Monitor, Kulturstreit – Streitkultur.* Amsterdam: Rodopi, 1996, 125–44.

————. 'The Stasi, the Confession and Performing Difference: Brigitte Burmeister's *Unter dem Namen Norma.*" In Paul Cooke and Andrew Plowman, eds., *German Writers and the Politics of Culture: Dealing with the Stasi.* Basingstoke: Palgrave, 2003, 155–72.

Libeskind, Daniel. "Between the Lines: Das Jüdische Museum." In *Jüdisches Museum Berlin.* Berlin: Jüdisches Museum Berlin, 1999, 6–11.

Lichtenstein, Heiner, ed. *Die Fassbinder-Kontroverse, oder das Ende der Schonzeit.* Königstein: Athenäum, 1986.

Linklater, Beth. "'Philomela's Revenge': Challenges to Rape in Recent Writing in German." *German Life and Letters* 54:3 (2001): 253–71.

————. "Germany and Background: Global Concerns in Recent Women's Writing in German." In Stuart Taberner, ed., *German Literature in the Age of Globalisation.* Birmingham: Birmingham UP, 2004, 67–88.

Linklater, Beth, and Birgit Dahlke, eds. *Kerstin Hensel.* Cardiff: U of Wales P, 2002.

Littler, Margaret. "Diasporic Identity in Emine Sevgi Özdamar's *Mutterzunge.*" In Stuart Taberner and Frank Finlay, eds., *Recasting German Identity.* Rochester: Camden House, 2002, 225–40.

Long, Jonathan. "History, Narrative, and Photography in W. G. Sebald's *Die Ausgewanderten.*" *Modern Language Review* 98:1 (2003): 117–37.

Lüdke, Martin. "Die Frau weint, der Mann schläft." *Frankfurter Allgemeine Zeitung,* 19 July 2000, 20.

Lutz, Felix Philipp. "Historical Consciousness and the Changing of German Political Culture." *German Politics* 11:3 (2002): 19–34.

Magenau, Jörg. "Posaunen gegen Berlin." *Frankfurter Allgemeine Zeitung, Literatur,* 28 August 1999, 42.

Maier, Charles. *The Unmasterable Past.* Cambridge, MA: Harvard UP, 1988.

Mecklenburg, Norbert. *Erzählte Provinz: Regionalismus und Moderne im Roman.* Königstein: Äthenäum, 1982.

———. *Die Grünen Inseln.* Munich: iudicium, 1986.

Menke, Timm. "Lebensgefühl(e) in Ost und West als Roman: Ingo Schulzes *Simple Storys* und Norbert Niemanns *Wie man's nimmt.* Mit einem Seitenblick auf Timm Staffels *Terrordrom.*" In Gerhard Fischer and David Roberts, eds., *Schreiben nach der Wende: Ein Jahrzehnt deutscher Literatur 1989–1999.* Tübingen: Stauffenberg, 2001, 253–61.

Mertens, Matthias. "Robbery, assault, and battery." In Heinz Ludwig Arnold, ed., *Pop-Literatur, Text + Kritik.* Munich: Richard Boorberg Verlag, 2003, 201–17.

Michalzik, Peter. "Wie komme ich zur Nordsee? Ingo Schulze erzählt einfach Geschichten, die ziemlich vertrackt sind und die alle lieben." In Thomas Kraft, ed. *aufgerissen: Zur Literatur der 90er.* Munich: Piper, 2000, 25–38.

Michel, Andreas. "Convergences? Peter Schneider's Critique of the Left-Liberal Consensus and the Emergence of the German New Right." *Colloquia Germanica* 31:3 (1998): 237–58.

Mittenzwei, Werner. *Die Intellektuellen: Literatur und Politik in Ostdeutschland 1945–2000.* Leipzig: Faber & Faber, 2001.

Mohr, Reinhard. *Zaungäste: Die Generation, die nach der Revolte kam.* Frankfurt a.M.: Fischer, 1992.

Moritz, Rainer, and Andrea Köhler, eds. *Maulhelden und Königskinder: Zur Debatte über die deutschsprachige Gegenwartsliteratur.* Leipzig: Reclam Verlag, 1998.

Müller, Jan-Werner. *Another Country: German Intellectuals, Unification and National Identity.* New Haven: Yale UP, 2000.

———. "Karl Heinz Bohrer on German National Identity: Recovering Romanticism and Aestheticizing the State." *German Studies Review* 23:2 (2000): 297–316.

Nachama, Andreas, and Ulrich Eckhardt, eds. *Jüdische Orte in Berlin.* Berlin: Nicolai Verlag, 1996.

Naumann, Michael, ed. *"Es muß doch in diesem Land wieder möglich sein . . ." Der neue Antisemitismus-Streit.* Frankfurt a.M.: Ullstein, 2002.

Negt, Oskar. *Der Fall Fonty: Ein weites Feld von Günter Grass im Spiegel der Kritik.* Göttingen: Steidl, 1996.

Neuhaus, Stefan. *Literatur und nationale Einheit.* Tübingen: A. Francke Verlag, 2002.

Niven, Bill. "The Reception of Steven Spielberg's 'Schindler's List' in the German Media." *Journal of European Studies* 25 (1995): 165–89.

———. *Facing the Nazi Past.* London: Routledge, 2002.

———. "Bernhard Schlink's *Der Vorleser* and the Problem of Shame." *Modern Language Review* 98:2 (2003): 381–96.

———. "Martin Walser's *Tod eines Kritikers* and the Issue of Anti-Semitism." *German Life and Letters* 56:3 (2003): 299–311.

———. "The Globalisation of Memory and the Rediscovery of German Suffering." In Stuart Taberner, ed., *German Literature in the Age of Globalisation.* Birmingham: Birmingham UP, 2004, 229–46.

Niven, William, and James Jordan, eds. *Politics and Culture in Twentieth-Century Germany.* Rochester: Camden House, 2003.

Nolden, Thomas. *Junge jüdische Literatur.* Würzburg: Königshausen & Neumann, 1995.

Nolte, Ernst. "Die Vergangenheit, die nicht vergehen will." In *"Historikerstreit": Die Dokumentation der Kontroverse um die Einzigartigkeit der nationalsozialistischen Judenvernichtung.* Munich and Zurich: Piper, 1987, 39–47.

O'Dochartaigh, Pól, ed. *Jews in German Literature Since 1945: German-Jewish Literature, German Monitor.* Amsterdam: Rodopi, 2000.

Otto Eke, Norbert. "'Was wollen Sie? Die Absolution?.'" In Sander L. Gilman and Hartmut Steinecke, eds., *Deutsch-jüdische Literatur der neunziger Jahre: Die Generation nach der Shoah, Beiheft zur Zeitschrift für Deutsche Philologie* 11 (2002): 89–107.

Owen, Ruth. *The Poet's Role: Lyric Responses to German Unification by Poets from The GDR.* Amsterdam: Rodopi, 2001.

Palfreyman, Rachel, and Elizabeth Boa. *Heimat — A German Dream: Regional Loyalties and National Identity in German Culture.* Oxford: Oxford UP, 2000.

Parkes, Stuart. "Looking forward to the Past: Identity and Identification in Martin Walser's *Die Verteidigung der Kindheit.*" In Arthur Williams and Stuart Parkes, eds., *The Individual, Identity and Innovation: Signals from Contemporary Literature and the New Germany.* Bern: Peter Lang, 1994, 57–74.

Parkes, Stuart, and Arthur Williams, eds. *The Individual, Identity and Innovation: Signals from Contemporary Literature and the New Germany.* Bern: Peter Lang, 1994.

Parkes, Stuart, and Fritz Wefelmeyer, eds. *Martin Walser, German Monitor.* Amsterdam: Rodopi, 2004.

Paul, Georgina. "Schwierigkeiten mit der Dialektik: Zu Chista Wolfs *Medea. Stimmen.*" *German Life and Letters* 50:2 (1997).

Peitsch, Helmut. "'Vereinigung': Literarische Debatten über die Funktionen der Intellektuellen." In Hans Hahn, ed., *Germany in the 1990s, German Monitor.* Amsterdam: Rodopi, 1995, 39–65.

———. "Vom Preis nationaler Identität: *Dorle und Wolf.*" In Heike Doane and Gertrud Pickar Bauer, eds., *Leseerfahrungen mit Martin Walser, Houston German Studies* 9. Munich: Fink, 1995, 171–88.

Plowman, Andrew. "Escaping the Autobiographical Trap." In Paul Cooke and Andrew Plowman, eds., *German Writers and the Politics of Culture: Dealing with the Stasi.* Basingstoke: Palgrave, 2003, 227–42.

———. "'Was will ich denn als Westdeutscher erzählen?': The 'old' West and Globalisation in Recent German Prose." In Stuart Taberner, ed., *German Literature in the Age of Globalisation.* Birmingham: Birmingham UP, 2004, 47–66.

———. "'Westalgie'? Nostalgia for the 'old' Federal Republic in Recent German Prose." *Seminar* 40:3 (2004): 249–61.

Plowman, Andrew, and Paul Cooke, eds. *German Writers and the Politics of Culture: Dealing with the Stasi.* Basingstoke: Palgrave, 2003.

Preckwitz, Boris. "ready — steady — slam: Notizen zum *Poetry Slam.*" *Weimarer Beiträge* 49:1 (2003): 70–79.

Preece, Julian. "Seven Theses on 'Der Fall Monty.'" In Clare Flanagan and Stuart Taberner, eds., *1949/1989: Cultural Perspectives on Division and Unity in East and West, German Monitor* 50. Amsterdam: Rodopi, 2000, 215–30.

———. *The Life and Work of Günter Grass.* New York: Palgrave, 2001.

———. "The Stasi as Literary Conceit." In Paul Cooke and Andrew Plowman, eds., *German Writers and the Politics of Culture: Dealing with the Stasi.* Basingstoke: Palgrave, 2003, 195–212.

Pulzer, Peter. "Unified Germany: A Normal State?." *German Politics* 3:1 (1994): 1–17.

Rabinbach, Anson. "Beyond Bitburg: The Place of the 'Jewish Question' in German History after 1945." In Kathy Harms, ed., *Coping with The Past: Germany and Austria after 1945.* Madison: U of Wisconsin P, 1990, 187–218.

———. "The Jewish Question in the German Question." *New German Critique* 44 (1988): 159–92.

Rabinbach, Anson, and Jessica Benjamin. "Germans, Leftists, Jews," *New German Critique* 31 (Winter/Summer, 1984): 188–95.

Rabinbach, Anson, and Jack Zipes, eds. *Germans and Jews Since the Holocaust: The Changing Situation in West Germany.* New York: Holmes and Meier, 1986.

Radisch, Iris. "Die Bitterfelder Sackgasse." *Die Zeit,* 25 August 1995, 111.

———. "Der Herbst des Quatschocento: Immer noch, jetzt erst recht, gibt es zwei deutsche Literaturen: selbstverliebter Realismus im Westen, tragischer Expressionismus im Osten." In Andrea Köhler and Rainer Moritz, eds., *Maulhelden und Königskinder: Zur Debatte über die deutschsprachige Gegenwartsliteratur.* Leipzig: Reclam Verlag, 1998, 180–88.

———. "Zwei getrennte Literaturgebiete: Deutsche Literatur der neunziger Jahre in Ost und West." In Heinz Ludwig Arnold, ed., *DDR-Literatur der neunziger Jahre, Text + Kritik.* Munich: Richard Boorberg Verlag, 2000, 13–26.

———. "Der Waschbär der falschen Welt." *Die Zeit,* 5 April 2001, 55.

Reiss, Hans. "Victor Klemperer (1881–1960): Reflections on his 'Third Reich' Diaries." *German Life and Letters* 51:1 (1998): 65–92.

Remmler, Karen. "The 'Third Generation' of Jewish-German Writers After the Shoah Emerges in Germany and Austria." In Sander L. Gilman and Jack Zipes, eds., *The Yale Companion to Jewish Writing and Thought in German Culture, 1096–1996.* New Haven: Yale UP, 796–804.

Remmler, Karen, and Sander Gilman, eds. *Reemerging Jewish Culture in Germany: Life and Literature since 1989.* New York and London: New York UP, 1994.

Richter, Gerhard. "Verschüttete Kultur — Ein Gespräch mit Monika Maron." *GDR Bulletin* 18:1 (1992): 2–7.

Riordan, Colin. "German-Jewish Relations in Peter Schneider's Works." In Pól O'Dochartaigh, ed., *Jews in German Literature Since 1945: German-Jewish Literature, German Monitor.* Amsterdam: Rodopi, 2000, 625–36.

Roberts, David, and Gerhard Fischer, eds. *Schreiben nach der Wende. Ein Jahrzehnt deutscher Literatur 1989–1999.* Tübingen: Stauffenberg, 2001.

Robertson, Ritchie. *The "Jewish Question" in German Literature, 1749–1939.* Oxford: Oxford UP, 2001 [1999].

———. "Rafael Seligmann's *Rubensteins Versteigerung:* The German-Jewish Family Novel before and after the Holocaust." *Germanic Review* 75:3 (2000): 175–93.

Robertson, Roland. *Globalization: Social Theory and Global Culture*. London: Sage, 1992.

———. "Globalisation or Glocalisation?." *Journal of International Communication* 1:1 (1994): 33–52.

Rosellini, Jay Julian. *Literary Skinheads? Writing from the Right in Reunified Germany*. West Lafayette: Purdue UP, 2000.

Rosenhaft, Eve. "Facing up to the Past — Again? Crimes of the Wehrmacht." *Debatte* 5:1 (1997): 105–18.

Ross, Corey. *The East German Dictatorship*. London: Arnold, 2002.

Rossbacher, Brigitte. "(Re)visions of the Past: Memory and Historiography in Monika Maron's *Stille Zeile Sechs*." *Colloquia Germanica* 27:1 (1994): 13–24.

Schacht, Ulrich. "Stigma und Sorge: Über deutsche Identität nach Auschwitz." In Heimo Schwilk and Ulrich Schacht, eds., *Die selbstbewußte Nation*. Frankfurt a.M.: Ullstein, 1994, 57–68.

Schacht, Ulrich, and Heimo Schwilk, eds. *Die selbstbewußte Nation*. Frankfurt a.M.: Ullstein, 1994.

Schirrmacher, Frank, ed. "Abschied von der Literatur der Bundesrepublik." *Frankfurter Allgemeine Zeitung*, 2 October 1990, L1, 2.

———. "Dem Druck des härteren, strengeren Lebens standhalten." In Thomas Anz, ed., *"Es geht nicht nur um Christa Wolf." Der Literaturstreit im vereinten Deutschland*. Munich: Spangenberg, 1991, 77–89.

———. "Idyllen in der Wüste oder Das Versagen vor der Metropole." In Andrea Köhler and Rainer Moritz, eds., *Maulhelden und Königskinder: Zur Debatte über die deutschsprachige Gegenwartsliteratur*. Leipzig: Reclam Verlag, 1998, 62–71.

———. *Die Walser-Bubis-Debatte*. Frankfurt a.M.: Suhrkamp, 1999.

Schlant, Ernestine. *The Language of Silence: West German Literature and the Holocaust*. New York: Routledge, 1999.

Schmid, Thomas. "Ein wüstes Feld." *Wochenpost*, 24 August 1995, *Literatur*, 40–41.

Schmitz, Helmut. *Der Landvermesser auf der Suche nach der poetischen Heimat: Hanns-Josef Ortheils Romanzyklus*. Stuttgart: Verlag Hans-Dieter Heinz, 1997.

———. "The Return of the Past: Post-Unification Representations of National Socialism: Bernhard Schlink's *Der Vorleser* and Ulla Berkéwitz's *Engel sind schwarz und weiß*." In Clare Flanagan and Stuart Taberner, eds. *1949/1989: Cultural Perspectives on Division and Unity in East and West, German Monitor* 50. Amsterdam: Rodopi, 2000, 259–76.

————. ed. *The Future of Vergangenheitsbewältigung*. Aldershot: Ashgate, 2001.

————. "Malen nach Zahlen? Bernhard Schlinks *Der Vorleser* und die Unfähigkeit zu trauern." *German Life and Letters* 55:3 (2002).

————. "Denouncing Globalisation: Ingo Schramm's *Fitchers Blau*." In Stuart Taberner, ed., *German Literature in the Age of Globalisation*. Birmingham: Birmingham UP, 2004, 145–67.

————. *On their Own Terms: German Literature and the Legacy of National Socialism after Unification*. Birmingham: Birmingham UP, 2004.

Schödel, Kathrin. "Normalising Cultural Memory? The 'Walser-Bubis-Debate' and Martin Walser's Novel *Ein springender Brunnen*." In Stuart Taberner and Frank Finlay, eds., *Recasting German Identity*. Rochester: Camden House, 2002, 69–87.

————. "Jenseits der *political correctness*— NS-Vergangenheit in Bernhard Schlinks *Der Vorleser* und Martin Walsers *Ein springender Brunnen*." In Stuart Parkes and Fritz Wefelmeyer, eds., *Martin Walser, German Monitor*. Amsterdam: Rodopi, 2004, 307–23.

Scholem, Gerschom. *". . . und alles ist Kabbala." Gerschom Scholem im Gespräch mit Jörg Drews*. Munich: edition text + kritik, 1980.

Schönherr, Ulrich. "Topophony of Fascism: On Marcel Beyer's *The Karnau Tapes*." *Germanic Review* 73:4 (1998): 329–48.

Schramm, Ingo. *Fitchers Blau*. Berlin: Verlag Volk und Welt, 1996.

Schröder, Gerhard. "'Weil wir Deutschlands Kraft vertrauen . . .': Regierungserklärung des Bundeskanzlers vor dem Deutschen Bundestag vom 10 November 1998." *Bulletin der Bundesregierung* 74, 11 November 1998, 902.

Schröder, Julia. "Was noch kommen kann." *Stuttgarter Zeitung,* 8 October 2002, iii.

Schulze, Ingo. *Simple Storys*. Berlin: Berlin Verlag, 1998.

Schütte, Wolfram. "Leservergnügen: Den Sorgen lektorierender Hausväter entsprungen." In Franz Josef Görtz, Volker Hage, Uwe Wittstock, eds., *Deutsche Literatur 1993*. Stuttgart: Reclam, 1994, 325–28.

Schütte, Wolfram, and Helmut Böttiger. "Metropole ist eine Fiktion." Interview with Kathrin Röggla, Norbert Niemann, Ingo Schulze, and Burkhard Spinnen. *Frankfurter Rundschau,* 28 November 1998, 22.

Schwilk, Heimo, and Ulrich Schacht, eds. *Die selbstbewußte Nation*. Frankfurt a.M.: Ullstein, 1994.

Sewing, Werner. "Herz, Kunstherz oder Themenpark? Deutungsversuche des Phänomens Potsdamer Platz." In Yamin von Rauch und Jochen Visscher, eds., *Der Potsdamer Platz*. Berlin: Jovis, 2000, 47–58.

Seyhan, Azade. *Writing Outside the Nation*. Princeton: Princeton UP, 2001.

Sharp, Ingrid. "Male Privilege and Female Virtue: Gendered Representations of the Two Germanies." *New German Studies* 18:2 (1994/5): 87–106.

Shaw, Gisela. "'Keine Macht aber Spielraum' oder 'Das Ende einer Sprachlosigkeit': Brigitte Burmeisters Roman *Unter dem Namen Norma*." In Clare Flanagan and Stuart Taberner, eds., *1949/1989: Cultural Perspectives On Division and Unity in East and West, German Monitor* 50. Amsterdam: Rodopi, 2000, 199–213.

Siebenpfeiffer, Hania. "Topographien des Seelischen. Berlinromane der neunziger Jahre." In Matthias Harder, ed., *Bestandsaufnahmen ... Deutschsprachige Literatur der neunziger Jahre aus interkultureller Sicht*. Würzburg: Königshausen & Neumann, 2001, 85–104.

Slessor, Catherine. "Gehry's Geode," *Architectural Review* 210.1254 (2001): 48–54.

Smith, Dinitia. "Seeking guilt, finding fame." *New York Times* 30 March 1999, E-1.

Solomon, Robert C. "Introduction: Reading Nietzsche." In Robert C. Solomon and Kathleen M. Higgens, eds., *Reading Nietzsche*. New York and Oxford: Oxford UP, 1988, 3–12.

Spittler, Horst. "Die Dichter der 'Generation Golf.'" *literatur für leser* 25:3 (2002): 189–96.

Stahl, Enno. "Trash, Social Beat und Slam Poetry." In Heinz Ludwig Arnold, ed., *Pop-Literatur, Text + Kritik*. Munich: Richard Boorberg Verlag, 2003, 258–78.

Steinecke, Hartmut. "Einleitung." In Sander L. Gilman and Hartmut Steinecke, *Deutsch-jüdische Literatur der neunziger Jahre: Die Generation nach der Shoah, Beiheft zur Zeitschrift für Deutsche Philologie* 11 (2002): 9–16.

Steinecke, Hartmut, and Sander Gilman, eds., *Deutsch-jüdische Literatur der neunziger Jahre: Die Generation nach der Shoah, Beiheft zur Zeitschrift für Deutsche Philologie* 11. (2002).

Steingröver, Reinhild. "'Not Fate Just History': Stories and Histories in *Tanz am Kanal* and *Gipshut*." In Beth Linklater and Birgit Dahlke, eds., *Kerstin Hensel*. Cardiff: U of Wales P, 2002.

Sterling, Eleonore. "Judenfreunde — Judenfeinde: Fragwürdiger Philosemitismus in der Bundesrepublik." *Die Zeit*, 10 December 1965, 30.

Stern, Frank. *Im Anfang war Auschwitz. Antisemitismus und Philosemitismus im deutschen Nachkrieg*. Gerlingen: Beicher Verlag, 1991.

Stewart, Janet. "*Das Kunsthaus Tacheles:* The Berlin Architecture Debate of the 1990s in Micro-Historical Context." In Stuart Taberner and Frank Finlay, eds., *Recasting German Identity.* Rochester: Camden House, 2002, 53–68.

Stolz, Dieter. "Alles eine Frage der Perspektive: Prosa-Debüts der deutschsprachigen Gegenwartsliteratur." *Sprache im technischen Zeitalter* 162 (2002): 156–70.

Strzelczyk, Florentine. *Un-Heimliche Heimat: Reibungsflächen zwischen Kultur und Nation.* Munich: iudicium, 1999.

Stürmer, Michael. "Geschichte in geschichtslosem Land." In *"Historikerstreit": Die Dokumentation der Kontroverse um die Einzigartigkeit der nationalsozialistischen Judenvernichtung* Munich and Zurich: Piper Verlag, 1987, 36–38.

Suhr, Stephanie, and Sally Johnson. "From 'Political Correctness' to '*Politische Korrektheit*': Discourses of 'PC' in the German Newspaper *Die Welt.*" *Discourse and Society* 14:1 (2002): 49–68.

Süskind, Patrick. "Deutschland, eine Midlife-crisis." *Der Spiegel,* 17 September 1990, 118–25.

Taberner, Stuart. "Feigning the Anaethestisation of Literary Inventiveness: Günter Grass's *örtlich betäubt* and the Public Responsibility of the Politically Engaged Author." *Forum for Modern Language Studies* 34:1 (1998): 71–81.

———. "'Wie schön wäre Deutschland, wenn man sich noch als Deutscher fühlen und mit Stolz als Deutscher fühlen könnte': Martin Walser's Reception of Victor Klemperer's *Tagebücher 1933–1945* in *Das Prinzip Genauigkeit* and *Die Verteidigung der Kindheit.*" *Deutsche Vierteljahrsschrift* 73 (1999): 710–32.

———. "A Manifesto For Germany's 'New Right'? — Martin Walser, the Past, Transcendence, Aesthetics, and *Ein Springender Brunnen.*" *German Life and Letters* 53:1 (2000): 126–41.

———. "'Deutsche Geschichte darf auch einmal gutgehen': Martin Walser and the 'German Question' from *Ehen in Philippsburg* to *Ein springender Brunnen.*" In Helmut Schmitz, ed., *The Future of Vergangenheitsbewältigung.* Aldershot: Ashgate, 2001, 45–64.

———. "'ob es sich bei diesem Experiment um eine gescheiterte Utopie oder um ein Verbrechen gehandelt hat': Enlightenment, Utopia, the GDR and National Socialism in Monika Maron's Work from *Flugasche* to *Pawels Briefe.*" In Carol Anne Costabile-Heming, Rachel J. Halverson, and Kristie A. Foell, eds., *Textual Responses to German Unification.* Berlin: Walter de Gruyter, 2001, 35–57.

———. "The Final Taboo?: Philosemitism, the *Meinungsindustrie,* and the New Right in Martin Walser's *Ohne Einander.*" *Seminar* 37:2 (2001): 154–66.

———. "A New Modernism or "Neue Lesbarkeit"? — Hybridity in Georg Klein's *Libidissi.*" *German Life and Letters* 55:2 (2002): 137–48.

———. "A Matter of Perspective?: Martin Walser's Fiction in the 1990s." In Martin Kane, ed., *German Literature after Unification.* Bern: Peter Lang, 2002, 145–69.

———. ed. *Der Vorleser* by Bernhard Schlink. London: Duckworth, 2002.

———. "Hans-Ulrich Treichel's *Der Verlorene* and the 'Problem' of German Wartime Suffering," *Modern Language Review* 97 (2002): 123–34.

———. "'Normalization' and the New Consensus on the Nazi Past: Günter Grass's *Im Krebsgang* and the Problem of German Wartime Suffering." *Oxford German Studies* 31 (2002): 161–86.

———. "'Nichts läßt man uns, nicht einmal den Schmerz, und eines Tages wird alles vergessen sein': The Novels of Arnold Stadler from *Ich war einmal* to *Ein hinreissender Schrotthändler.*" *Neophilologus* 87 (2003): 119–32.

———. "'Wie kannst du mich lieben?': 'Normalising' the Relationship between Germans and Jews in the 1990s' Films *Aimée und Jaguar* and *Meschugge.*" In William Niven and James Jordan, eds., *Politics and Culture in Twentieth-Century Germany.* Rochester: Camden House, 2003, 227–43.

———. ed. *German Literature in the Age of Globalisation.* Birmingham: Birmingham UP, 2004.

———. "German Nostalgia? Remembering German-Jewish Life in W. G. Sebald's *Die Ausgewanderten* and *Austerlitz.*" *Germanic Review* 79:3 (2004): 181–202.

———. "'Sehnsüchtig-traurig und unerlöst': Memory's Longing to Forget. Or Why *Tristanakkord* is Not Simply A Reprise of Martin Walser." In David Basker, ed., *Hans-Ulrich Treichel.* Cardiff: U of Wales P, 2004, 79–93.

———. "The Triumph of Subjectivity: Martin Walser's Novels of the 1990s and his *Der Lebenslauf der Liebe* (2001)." In Stuart Parkes and Fritz Wefelmeyer, eds., *Martin Walser, German Monitor.* Amsterdam: Rodopi, 2004, 429–46.

Taberner, Stuart, and Clare Flanagan, eds. *1949/1989: Cultural Perspectives on Division and Unity in East and West, German Monitor* 50. Amsterdam: Rodopi, 2000.

Taberner, Stuart, and Frank Finlay, eds. *Recasting German Identity.* Rochester: Camden House, 2002.

Tate, Denis. "Günter de Bruyn: The 'Gesamtdeutsche Konsensfigur' of Postunification Literature?." *German Life and Letters* 50:2 (1997): 201–13.

Teetz, Kristian. "Helden, still und tapfer." *Die Welt,* 28 July 2001, 5.

Theisen, Alfred. "Die Vertreibung der Deutschen — ein unbewältigtes Kapitel europäischer Geschichte." *aus politik und zeitgeschichte,* 10 February 1995, 20–33.

Turner, Henry Ashby. "Victor Klemperer's Holocaust." *German Studies Review* 22:3 (1999): 385–96.

Ullmaier, Johannes. *Von Acid nach Adlon und zurück.* Mainz: Ventil, 2001.

Ullrich, Volker. "Daniel J. Goldhagen in Deutschland: Die Buchtournee wurde zum Triumphzug." *Die Zeit,* 13 September 1996.

Ulrich, Roland. "Vom Report zum Roman: Zur Textwelt von Wolfgang Koeppens Roman *Jakob Littners Roman Aufzeichungen aus einem Erdloch.*" *Colloquia Germanica* 32:2 (1999): 135–50.

Vogt, Jochen. "Langer Abschied von der Nachkriegsliteratur." In Karl Deiritz and Hannes Krauss, eds., *Der deutsch-deutsche Literaturstreit oder "Freunde, es spricht sich schlecht mit gebundener Zunge".* Hamburg: Luchterhand, 1991, 53–68.

Von Dohnanyi, Klaus. "Eine Friedensrede: Walser notwendige Klage." In Frank Schirrmacher, ed., *Die Walser-Bubis-Debatte.* Frankfurt a.M.: Suhrkamp, 1999, 146–50.

Von Oppen, Karoline. "'Wer jetzt schwarzweiss malt, hat keine Ahnung': Friedrich Christian Delius's *Die Birnen von Ribbeck* and the Predicament of 'Wendeliteratur.'" *German Life and Letters* 54:4 (2001): 352–65.

Ward, Simon. "Koeppen's *Jakob Littners Roman Aufzeichungen aus einem Erdloch.*" In Pól O'Dochartaigh, ed., *Jews in German Literature Since 1945: German-Jewish Literature, German Monitor.* Amsterdam: Rodopi, 2000, 651–63.

———. "'Zugzwang' or 'Stillstand'? — Trains in the Post-1989 Fiction of Brigitte Struzyk, Reinhard Jirgl, and Wolfgang Hilbig." In Stuart Taberner and Frank Finlay, eds., *Recasting German Identity.* Rochester: Camden House, 2002, 172–89.

Wefelmeyer, Fritz, and Stuart Parkes, eds. *Martin Walser, German Monitor.* Amsterdam: Rodopi, 2004.

Wehdeking, Volker. "Die literarische Auseinandersetzung mit dem Themenkomplex Staatssicherheit, Zensur und Schriftstellerkontrolle." In Volker Wehdeking, ed., *Mentalitätswandel in der deutschen Literatur zur Einheit (1990–2000).* Berlin: Erich Schmidt Verlag, 2000, 43–55.

Weißmann, Karlheinz. *Rückruf in die Geschichte.* Berlin: Ullstein, 1993.

Wilds, Karl. "Identity Creation and the Culture of Contrition: Recasting 'Normality' in the Berlin Republic." *German Politics* 9:1 (2000): 83–102.

Williams, Arthur. "'Das korsakowsche Symptom': Remembrance and Responsibility in W. G. Sebald." In Helmut Schmitz, ed., *German Culture and the Uncomfortable Past*. Aldershot: Ashgate, 2001, 65–86.

Williams, Arthur, and Stuart Parkes, eds. *The Individual, Identity and Innovation: Signals from Contemporary Literature and the New Germany*. Bern: Peter Lang, 1994.

Williams, Rhys. "'Mein Unbewußtes kannte . . . den Fall der Mauer und die deutsche Wiedervereinigung nicht': The Writer Hans-Ulrich Treichel." *German Life and Letters* 55:2 (2002): 208–18.

———. "'Caravaggio in Preußen': Hans-Ulrich Treichel's *Der irdische Amor*." In David Basker, ed., *Hans-Ulrich Treichel*. Cardiff: U of Wales P, 2004, 94–110.

Winkels, Hubert. "Grenzgänger. Neue deutsche Pop-Literatur." *Sinn und Form* 51:4 (1999): 581–610.

Winkler, Willi. "Die Sprache verwaltet das Nichts." *Süddeutsche Zeitung,* 19/20 September 1998, 15.

Wittstock, Uwe. *Leselust: Wie unterhaltsam ist die neue deutsche Literatur? Ein Essay*. Munich: Luchterhand, 1995.

———. "Das Gebot mit dem Freund der Freundin zu schlafen." *Die Welt,* 26 November 2001, 29.

Wolffsohn, Michael. *Keine Angst vor Deutschland!* Erlangen: Straube, 1990.

———. *Meine Juden — Eure Juden*. Munich: Piper Verlag, 1997.

Yeşilada Karin and Tom Cheesman, eds. *Zafer Şenocak*. Cardiff: U of Wales P, 2003.

Young, James. "Berlin's Holocaust Memorial: A Report to the Bundestag Committee on Media and Culture." *German Politics and Society* 17:3 (1999): 54–70.

———. *At Memory's Edge*. New Haven: Yale UP, 2000.

Zachau, Reinhard. "Das Originalmanuskript zu Wolfgang Koeppens *Jakob Littners Roman Aufzeichnungen aus einem Erdloch*." *Colloquia Germanica* 32:2 (1999): 115–33.

Zipes, Jack. "The Vicissitudes of Being Jewish in West Germany." In Jack Zipes and Anson Rabinbach, eds., *Germans and Jews since the Holocaust: The Changing Situation in West Germany*. New York: Holmes and Meier, 1986.

————. "The Contemporary German Fascination for Things Jewish: Toward a Jewish Minority Culture." In Sander Gilman and Karen Remmler, eds., *Reemerging Jewish Culture in Germany: Life and Literature since 1989.* New York and London: New York UP, 1994, 15–46.

Zipes, Jack, and Anson Rabinbach, eds. *Germans and Jews since the Holocaust: The Changing Situation in West Germany.* New York: Holmes and Meier, 1986.

Zipes, Jack, and Sander Gilman, eds. *The Yale Companion to Jewish Writing and Thought in German Culture, 1096–1996.* New Haven: Yale UP, 796–804.

Zitelmann, Rainer. *Wohin treibt unsere Republik?.* Frankfurt a.M.: Ullstein, 1995.

Zitzlsperger, Ulrike. "Filling the Blanks: Berlin as Public Showcase." In Stuart Taberner and Frank Finlay, eds., *Recasting German Identity.* Rochester: Camden House, 2002, 37–51.

————. "A Worm's Eye View and A Bird's Eye View: Culture and Politics in Berlin since 1989." In William Niven and James Jordan, eds., *Politics and Culture in Twentieth-Century Germany.* Rochester: Camden House, 2003, 185–99.

Index

A number of terms have been omitted from this index; the frequency with which they appear in the text would render any listing here of limited value. These include, for example: America; Berlin Republic; GDR; FRG; Hitler; Holocaust; normality; normalization; Nazi; unification; *Vergangenheitsbewältigung;* '68; '78; '89, etc.